"NO ORDINARY MAN"

An oil portrait by S. W. Shaw, posthumously
painted from a photograph. Original in
Scott Hall, San Francisco Theological Seminary.

"The commodious church of Dr. Scott contained a large and
genteel congregation, deeply absorbed in the contemplation of
the subject presented to their consideration by the talent of
no ordinary man. The mantle of the Apostles did not descend
on shoulders unable to bear it gracefully and with dignity,
when Dr. Scott wrapped himself in its sacred folds."

New Orleans Evening Mercury, April 17, 1846

WILLIAM ANDERSON SCOTT

"No Ordinary Man"

by

CLIFFORD MERRILL DRURY

THE ARTHUR H. CLARK COMPANY

Glendale, California

1 9 6 7

to the memory of
ANN NICHOLSON SCOTT
beloved wife of William Anderson Scott

Contents

Illustrations

An Introduction

Dr. William Anderson Scott, whose life spanned seventy-two years of the nineteenth century, 1813-1885, walked into my life in the pages of this book. Dr. Drury has made him live again, a century later.

This biography of Dr. Scott is more than the story of a colorful, dynamic leader. Here is a commentary on the stirring events of those times; here we see mirrored the frontier community life of Tennessee and Illinois, the Black Hawk War in which Scott served as an eighteen year old chaplain, the dramatic years leading up to the Civil War, the vigilante days in frontier San Francisco, together with many, many other fascinating sidelights.

Dr. Scott was the outstanding Presbyterian preacher of his generation on the West Coast. Although of an irenic nature, he was constantly being involved in controversy and the inside story of these controversies adds much to the interest of this book. He was far in advance of his generation in his opposition to the compulsory reading of the Bible in public schools and in his condemnation of the vigilante do-it-yourself law enforcement as practiced in California. Twice was he hanged in effigy in San Francisco, a dubious distinction given to no other California clergyman. He founded two churches, a college, a religious magazine, and a theological seminary in San Francisco.

The coming centennial of that San Francisco Theological Seminary in October 1971 makes this volume especially timely, and of interest to those of us who know and love that graduate school. As a member of the Board of Trustees of the Seminary, I commend the book to you.

Also, I wish to introduce to the readers of this book Dr. Clifford M. Drury, who for twenty-five years occupied the California Chair of Church History in San Francisco Theological Seminary. He has made the collection of rare and hitherto unpublished material a matter of special interest for over twenty-five years and has had access to a wealth of source material. The appendix of this book gives Dr. Drury's personal account of how and where he found his sources.

In order to permit the narrative to flow without interruption, all footnotes have happily been eliminated but the reader can be assured that the author has been scrupulously accurate in the use of his sources. His is not fiction but history in the best tradition.

I invite you to read a story then which might be subtitled, "One Way the West Was Won!"

FREDERICK W. CROPP

His Early Years

The Scott boy was lame. His left leg was slightly shorter than his right. When asked the reason, his mother would sadly explain how William had suffered a "violent attack of inflamatory rheumatism," when the family lived in Sangamon County, Illinois. The attack must have come, therefore, when the little boy was between five and nine years of age. It is possible that he had had a mild attack of poliomyelitis. Whatever the cause, this we know: William Anderson Scott was lame. He walked with a halting gait that became even more noticeable when he reached his full height of six feet and one inch.

A physical handicap usually leaves an indelible stamp upon the unfortunate person thus afflicted. William was no exception to this general rule. In his later life he once looked back upon the days when he attended school in a frontier community near Memphis, Tennessee, to which the Scott family moved after leaving Illinois, and wrote:

> I was not happy at this school as I was late going to it, the other scholars almost all had the start of me. I was considered poor and my lameness prevented me from running and jumping as fast and as far as others. I was ambitious to excel at play but could not often do so on account of my lameness. I was reproached for it; called awkward; called names. . . I used to go away out into the woods alone and cry over these things and beat the ground and stamp, and then lie on my back and gaze away up into the skies and pray and wish to die. Even then I found praying the only thing that could soothe me.

Notice the words: "I was ambitious to excel." If it had not been for that lameness; if it had not been for that attendant feeling of frustration, William Anderson Scott might have been able to excel in physical prowess. As just another stalwart son of the Tennessee frontier with two muscular legs and two mighty arms swinging from his broad shoulders, he might have become a local celebrity through his skill in splitting logs, digging out tree stumps, and carving farms out of the forest. William Anderson Scott, if he had only had two good legs of the same length, might have been all of this but unknown even to his own generation outside of a limited circle of frontier folk in western Tennessee.

The feelings of frustration which came when he realized that he could not compete with other boys of his age in physical activities inspired him to excel in other fields. He would be a scholar. He would master foreign languages and learn the thoughts of the world's greatest philosophers. He would write books and travel in foreign lands. He would be a great orator and hold vast audiences in the hollow of his hand by his magic spell. Day dreams of great achievements to be realized in some distant future burned their images upon the impressionable mind of the boy, William Anderson Scott, of Big Creek, Tennessee.

As the boy moved through adolescence into adulthood, the crippled foot seemed to have played a decreasing role in any feeling of frustration. Scott finally accepted his handicap with equanimity. The affliction had already determined the road he would follow. Only once in the intimacy of his diaries or journals is there any word of complaint or regret. This came in his thirtieth year when he was in the early part of his ministry in New Orleans. On August 15, 1843, after some depressing experiences, he commented: "I never suffered so much in my life from languor and debility . . . my lame leg, my crooked foot." When he was seventy years old, some uninformed reporter for the *San Francisco Call*, describing Scott's appearance in the pulpit, wrote: ". . . barring his lameness, occasioned by a fall some months ago . . . he appears hale and vigorous." So much was his lameness taken for granted that the memory of it largely faded when those who knew him personally passed away. Most of the second and third generations of his descendants knew nothing of it.

Scott came out of Scotch-Irish ancestry. Impelled by religious persecutions and economic factors, a flow of immigrants from Scotland and North Ireland to the New World, which had begun as early as 1680, became a mighty stream by 1730. No nationalistic group coming to the New World was so united in its support of the Revolutionary War or so uniform in its religious beliefs as were these Scots and Scotch-Irish. Practically all were Presbyterians even though most of them failed to join Presbyterian churches after settling in the New World.

Joining this trans-Atlantic migration shortly before the Revolutionary War were Scott's progenitors on both his father's and his mother's side. His paternal grandfather, James Scott, is reported to have migrated from Derry, North Ireland, to Carlisle, Pennsylvania. He reached the colonies in time to serve as a soldier in the war. James married Lydia Nichols to which union were born six sons, including Eli, possibly an abbreviation of Elisha, who became the father of William, the subject of this study. Two of Eli's brothers, John and Joshua, will be mentioned in connection with William's youth. Sometime after the birth of Eli at Carlisle on December 14, 1774, the family moved to Salisbury, Rowan County, North Carolina, where Eli grew to manhood.

On Scott's maternal side, his grandfather, William Anderson, came from Belfast and settled at Carlisle, Pennsylvania. He married Elizabeth Holmes, who was also from North Ireland. During the Revolutionary War, Anderson served under General Greene in the Carolina campaign. Their daughter, Martha, who was the mother of our William, was born at Carlisle on October 2, 1772.

FROM ROCK CREEK TO BIG CREEK, TENNESSEE

Sometime before 1810 William and Elizabeth Anderson moved across the Appalachian Mountains and settled on or near Rock Creek in what was then Bedford County in the southern part of the great central basin of Tennessee. Settlements on the rich red soil spotted with wooded hills had been spurred by land grants to Revolutionary soldiers. By 1810 Bedford County reported a population of 8,242. Later two new counties were carved out of Bedford, including Marshall on the west in 1837. Meandering through what is now Marshall County is Rock Creek, a tributary of Duck River, and its branches, West Rock Creek and East Rock Creek.

Into this frontier community consisting largely of Scottish and Scotch-Irish settlers came a pioneer Presbyterian minister from Kentucky by the name of the Rev. Samuel Finley. He organized the Bethbirei (from the Hebrew meaning "house of my creation") Church on June 1, 1810, with twenty-four charter members. A log building was erected shortly afterwards which served the community for many years. This was located about one-half mile from the banks of West Rock Creek, five and one-half miles north of present day Lewisburg, and two and a half miles west of Farmington. In May 1814 the Rev. Thomas J. Hall began a thirty-five year ministry as pastor of this church. He retired in 1849. He was affectionately known as "Father Hall" and left an imprint upon the church and community which was long remembered. Under his leadership, the church reached its maximum membership of 183 in 1818. Today this church is a part of the Presbyterian Church in the United States.

Among the charter members of the Bethbirei Church were William and Elizabeth Anderson. Finding the Rock Creek community agreeable, they induced their daughter Martha and her husband to join them. Eli Scott and Martha Anderson were married in Iredell County, North Carolina, on May 10, 1809. Their first son, James, born in November 1810, died in infancy. Eli served in the War of 1812 and it may be that he qualified for a land grant in Tennessee from the government. Since Eli and Martha Scott are not listed as charter members of the Bethbirei Church, it seems evident that they did not settle on Rock Creek until after 1812.

On January 30, 1813, at "Rock Creek, Bedford County, Tennessee," Martha Scott gave birth to her second child, a boy, who was named after her father, William Anderson Scott. The baby was baptized soon after birth, undoubtedly in the Bethbirei log church, by the Rev. Thomas J. Hall. In later life Scott made several references to the fact that he was baptized by Father Hall. Such references linked his parents to the Bethbirei Church and pin-pointed William's birthplace as being within a radius of five miles or so from the present building.

The Rock Creek Bible Society, which is still in existence, was organized in 1815. Its first president and most active member was Thomas J.

Hall who was zealous in persuading all of the families of his parish to own a family Bible. Indeed his activities in promoting the sale and distribution of the Bible extended far beyond the limits of his immediate community. During those days, the nation's best known Bible publisher was Matthew Carey of Philadelphia. During his publishing career, Carey brought out over sixty editions of the King James version. Today the most prized item to come from his press is considered to be the first American printing of the Roman Catholic Rheims-Douay Bible which appeared in 1790. The King James family Bible, which was available when Hall was inducing the pioneer families of his parish to buy, was of folio size and weighed nine pounds. An order of one hundred such Bibles would have presented a serious transportation problem. Any overland shipment from Philadelphia into the Ohio Valley was both difficult and expensive. So the Bibles were sent by sea to New Orleans and from there by river boat up the Mississippi, the Ohio, and the Cumberland rivers to Nashville. The Bibles were then carried by wagon to the Rock Creek community.

One of the cherished possessions of one of Dr. Scott's granddaughters, the late Mrs. Mary F. Kuechler of Ross, California, was an illustrated 1815 Carey family Bible with a concordance and psalter. Under the cover in Scott's handwriting is the following notation: "This Bible was bought by my father, Eli Scott, in 1816 for $12.50. It was in this book I first learned my letters & was taught to read by my mother. W.A. Scott." No doubt William was given this treasured volume when his father, Eli, died in August 1844. On the pages inserted for such purposes, the Bible contains the record of births, deaths, and marriages of two generations of the Scott family, that of Eli and of William. Herein we read of the birth of a second son to Eli and Martha on July 6, 1816. His full name was Eli Davis but to avoid being confused with his father, he was called Davis.

Eli and Martha found life hard and sometimes rather grim. Money was scarce and creature comforts few. They lived in log cabins, made most of the clothes they wore, and raised their own food. As they made their way farther west, finally settling in western Tennessee, they were a part of the cutting edge of the frontier movement which was gradually claiming all of the Ohio Valley for white civilization. The Scott family shared the privations and dangers common to all pioneers caught up in this westward movement. Their manner of living which today would be called intolerable was simply taken for granted.

Information about William's early years is scanty and fragmentary. From scattered bits of information we learn that two of Eli's brothers, John and Joshua, had moved to the rich prairie lands of Illinois while Eli was still at Rock Creek. John settled on a farm at Edwardsville in Madison County to the northeast of St. Louis. Joshua owned property at Golconda on the Ohio River. Sometime in 1817 or 1818, perhaps at the suggestion of his brothers, Eli moved his family to Edwardsville where for a time they lived on John's farm. John and Eli had married sisters. Their parents, the Andersons, also moved to Illinois. William was four or five years old at this time.

About a year after Eli and his family had moved to Edwardsville, John Scott sold his farm and moved to the vicinity of what is now Springfield in Sangamon County. The Eli Scott family and the Andersons went along. William was now old enough to gather lifelong memories. Years later he recalled how his family squatted on land on a beautiful prairie near some woods between the Sangamon River and a small settlement which grew into the city of Springfield. The country was still full of Indians and the land was not surveyed. Eli was employed for a time in helping to survey the site of Springfield.

In his later years William recalled the recurring sickness that visited the family every summer. They called it ague. Today we call it malaria. There at Springfield, both Grandfather and Grandmother Anderson died. And it was there in Sangamon County that William, not more than nine years old at the most, suffered "a violent attack of inflamatory rheumatism" which left its permanent mark in a crippled left foot. Another son came to Eli and Martha on June 20, 1820, who was named James Nichols. Thus William grew up with two younger brothers, separated by three and seven years.

Sometime in 1822, Uncle John Scott sold his farm at Springfield and purchased another on Big Creek near what came to be Raleigh, Tennessee, now a suburb of Memphis. This part of western Tennessee had been purchased from the Indians in 1819, in which year Memphis was founded on the east bank of the Mississippi below the mouth of Wolf Creek. Again Eli and Martha decided to follow the John Scott family and they too moved to the Big Creek community which was just emerging from the raw wilderness. The Scotts left Sangamon County about nine years before Abraham Lincoln made Springfield his home. Years later the tall shadow of that Illinois lawyer-politician cast its influence upon William Scott, but this story belongs to a later chapter.

William was nine years old in 1822 and was able to remember the events taking place around him. He later told how his father and mother moved their few belongings by wagon to Golconda where his Uncle Joshua lived. There the Eli Scott family spent the winter of 1822-23. William remembered that his Uncle Joshua "was comfortably situated, being Clerk of the Court and having landed property." Both Joshua and John Scott seem to have had more of this world's goods than Eli. Since Joshua had small children and Eli had two boys of school age, a "Miss Ruth" was hired to teach them. This was William's first experience under the tutelage of some one besides his parents. Here also at Golconda was a Presbyterian church in which Uncle Joshua served as an elder. And here William's religious education had opportunity to broaden.

In the spring of 1823, after the ice had broken up in the Ohio River,

William saw his first steamboat ascending the river at Golconda. The little boy never forgot the thrill of that sight—the churning paddle wheel, the belching smoke, and the miracle of a boat going upstream against the current! Years later he wrote: "It was terrific to me." This was his introduction to one of the most inexpensive and convenient methods of travel in the Ohio and Mississippi valleys before the coming of the railroads. The rivers were the liquid highways of that generation. Scott was to take many trips on the river steamers.

As soon as the Ohio River was free of ice that spring, a number of men at Golconda made preparations to ship their farm produce by flat-boats down the river to the city markets. Eli decided to take his family and travel with the party as far as Memphis. He got a flatboat on which he loaded his belongings including, as William later recalled, "horses, dogs, children, & all." As the small flotilla began its voyage down the river, ten-year-old William was deeply impressed with the concern of his mother who was fearful that one of her boys might fall overboard.

On the way down the Mississippi, the party met with a violent storm which "drove a number of flatboats on shore on Willow Island near Mills Point [above Hickman, Kentucky] and several were totally wrecked." Drawing upon the vivid memory left by the storm, William later wrote:

> The wind blew, the rain fell in torrents, the waves surged over the sand and washed all over the bank. The banks kept caving in. The boats were tied by ropes and chains but nothing could hold them. The strongest chains were broken. We rocked so that we had to get out and were thoroughly drenched and cold all night on the sand beach. One of the boats loaded with corn, sheep, and turkeys sank.

Poor frightened Martha, utterly disconsolate, did her best to comfort and protect her three little boys. After the storm subsided, the party had to remain at the island several days in order to repair damages and rearrange their battered cargoes. Dr. Scott's account continues:

> My father having a small family & not much goods, sold his boat to one of the owners of one of the wrecked boats, & took passage for us in one of the boats of the company. As a passenger on a flatboat, I first saw Memphis. We were crowded. The boat was exceedingly filthy, which was a very great annoyance to my dear Mother. My Mother was remarkable for neatness both in her food & dress. She was in bad health. I remember that it distressed me very much to see how she was troubled with the dirt & disagreeable companions we had on the boat. I remember even now with pain scenes of danger & hardship through which she passed in settling in new places & travelling . . . that makes my heart ache. She was one of the purest minded & most conscientious persons I ever saw.

The Scott family disembarked near Memphis at the mouth of Wolf Creek where it emptied into the Mississippi. Memphis was still nothing more than a trading post for Indians with two or three buildings surrounded by a peach orchard. During that first night at Wolf Creek, William set out a baited line for fish. To his excited joy he found the next morning that he had hooked a large catfish which weighed ninety pounds! Here was a fish story about which the lad long boasted.

Eli secured another flatboat, loaded his belongings and family on it, and started the toilsome journey of some twenty miles up Wolf Creek into Loosahatchie River, and finally up Big Creek. The Loosahatchie, having changed its course during the years, now flows directly into the Mississippi. Big Creek was a wide swath of bottom land which drained a large part of northern Shelby County. Many years later, Scott, looking back upon those days, wrote:

> We had to ascend Wolf River and then Big Creek about twenty miles. This was done by poling and hooking and pulling by spikes and bushes. . . At last we had gotten as far as the boat could go, the whole face of the earth was still covered with water. My mother was sick and father carried her and she sometimes walked wading through the water until at last we got to a little house in the woods.

Nearly thirty years later, on December 18, 1850, in a letter to his wife written from Rome, William commented: "The Tiber is a muddy little creek, not so large as Wolf River at Raleigh."

The exact site of Eli Scott's cabin is unknown. There are several references to its being about twelve miles from Memphis and about two miles northwest of Raleigh. The community was known as Big Creek, and it was of some importance when both Memphis and Raleigh were very small. Eli built a cabin on a corner of his Brother John's farm and "set up a foot lathe and made chairs." A few acres were cleared for a garden and the family raised "melons, chickens, etc." Here the parents remained the rest of their lives. Martha died in 1834 and Eli in 1844.

William Anderson Scott spent six and a half years at Big Creek, that is from the spring of 1823 to the fall of 1829. Big Creek was home to him and when he went to college in Kentucky and to Princeton Theological Seminary, he gave Big Creek, Tennessee, as his address. This part of the state was still very primitive when the Scott family settled there. The Indians were still in the country. In 1854 when Dr. Scott was asked to contribute a biographical sketch of himself for the *New Orleans Directory*, he summarized these years of his early youth by writing: "His boyhood and youth were passed on the frontier, exposed to all the hardships of that life; and he was accustomed to the axe, the plough, and to the rifle from the time he was able to lift them."

All evidence points to a normal happy home. After receiving a letter from his father in October 1835, Scott noted in his diary: "My father is a calm, calculating, plain, simple country gentleman. He is pious and his judgment is remarkably clear." At the time of his father's death in August 1844, Scott commented in a letter to a friend that his father had been a member of the Presbyterian Church for forty years and had served for a long time as an elder. It was his mother, though, who seemed to have made the deepest impression upon the son. Scott was a student at Princeton, New Jersey, when he learned of her death in August 1834. Pouring out his grief in his diary, he wrote: "My dear Mother was a timid, humble Christian. She was remarkable for humility, and a love for Watts hymns, which she had been taught in her child-hood. . . Often have I heard her pour out her soul in sweetening prayer for her family. She died full of faith."

William's mother was his first teacher. Looking back upon his child-hood, he made the following entry in his 1846 diary: "I knew no book but the Bible. Knew nothing of society. Was an honest, sincere, active boy in homespun with a wool hat—quick temper—bold, daring, warm hearted." Soon after the Eli Scott family settled at Big Creek, William, his brother Davis, and his cousins, the children of John Scott, began attending a school taught "by an Irishman by the name of Jones," whom William remembered as being "a good scholar who wrote a good hand, and made us read and spell." He also recalled on another occasion that the school was several miles distant from his home and that it was held in a log cabin with a dirt floor. Of course, the children walked both ways.

It was in this school that William was taunted by the other children because of his crippled foot. And he remembered how some reproached him because his father was "a poor chair maker." Such taunts and reproaches burned indelible memories in the mind of the sensitive lad.

Unable to compete with other boys of his age along physical lines, William concentrated on his studies. He developed an insatiable desire for knowledge. An incident from those adolescent years is related by the Rev. James Woods in his *Recollections of Pioneer Work in California,* which was published in San Francisco in 1878 during Dr. Scott's life-time. Undoubtedly Woods got the story direct from Scott himself. After commenting on the scarcity of books in the community in which he was reared, Woods wrote: "A neighbor had one of rare merit, which the lad greatly desired to possess. But he had not the money to purchase it, so he negotiated for the book by agreeing to give three days' work in plow-ing." According to a family tradition, this was a Greek book and it may have been the first volume Scott ever owned.

College and Seminary Years

Before one can appreciate Dr. Scott's struggle for an education and his early religious experience, it is necessary to have some understanding of the intellectual and spiritual destitution of the western frontier during the first decades of the nineteenth century. This background cannot be ignored. Scott was born in it. He lived through it. He rose with it and above it. Somehow because of his ravenous appetite for books, his deep religious convictions, his indomitable will, and his burning zeal to excel, this backwoods boy emerged from this unpromising background to become both an erudite scholar and one of America's greatest preachers.

The public school system in Tennessee was not established until 1830. Before that date primary education was conducted in the home or in a privately sponsored school. The larger communities had academies, usually church sponsored, sometimes with separate boarding departments for boys and girls. William Scott's education began at his mother's knee with the family Bible as the text book from which he learned his letters. The first schools he attended were those at Golconda and Big Creek which had been sponsored by his uncles for the benefit of their children and those of Eli Scott. Since there was no academy in the vicinity of Big Creek, William had to seek out a private tutor in order to get the basic training required for entrance into even a backwoods college.

The westward flow of people following the Revolutionary War presented a situation to the churches of the young nation for which they were totally unprepared. The churches had neither the men nor the money to satisfy even the minimum demands of the frontier. The demoralizing effects of the Revolutionary War, the rise of deism and atheism, and the almost complete secularization of such colleges as Yale, Harvard, and Princeton, originally founded for the purpose of training a ministry, added to the problems presented by the frontier to produce the worst spiritual depression this country has ever seen. Leonard Woolsey Bacon in his *History of American Christianity* declared: "The closing years of the eighteenth century show the lowest low-water mark of the lowest ebb-tide of spiritual life in the history of the American church." The leading authorities in American church history estimate that not more than seven per cent of the total population of 5,308,483 in the United States in 1800 were members of a church. Since most of those who were so listed lived in the older and more settled communities in the original thirteen colonies, the spiritual decline was therefore even more apparent throughout the frontier areas west of the Appalachian Mountains.

Since the Scots and Scotch-Irish are reputed to have composed one-third of the total population of the nation at this time, and since their original immigration was motivated largely by religious persecution and by their rigid adherence to Presbyterian doctrines and policy, the question naturally arises why so few of them were members of any Protestant church in 1800. There is no satisfactory answer to this query. However, it can be pointed out that the Scottish and Scotch-Irish immigration came late. Other national groups were well represented in the colonies before they arrived. The seaboard was settled. The latest arrivals were obliged to press on to the western frontiers. The sparse settlements in the wilderness and the poverty of the people were not conducive to the establishment of churches. Out of their dire poverty these people had little which they could give to support a ministry among them.

Even though the percentage of actual church membership among the Scots and Scotch-Irish in 1800 was pitifully small, this does not mean that religion ceased among these people. Family worship remained a common practice. Children were taught the catachism by their parents. Undoubtedly there was, however, a dilution of religious indoctrination with the passing of the years and the lack of pastoral oversight.

Then came what is known in American church history as the Second Great Awakening, to distinguish it from an earlier movement that visited the colonies about 1734-1745. The revival began in Logan County, Kentucky, about 1797. Camp meetings were held which became increasingly popular. James McGready, a Presbyterian minister of Scotch-Irish parentage, was the main leader. Most of the ministers who took part in the revival were Scotch-Irish Presbyterians but some Methodists and Baptists were also active. The movement was especially strong in the Cumberland area of both Kentucky and Tennessee. The Rev. Barton W. Stone, a Presbyterian, introduced the camp meeting idea into his parish in Bourbon County, Kentucky, with astonishing results. A great gathering of frontier folk was held at Cane Ridge in August 1801 when the attendance was variously estimated at from 10,000 to 25,000. The eagerness with which the people flocked to such camp meetings speaks eloquently of their deep hunger for spiritual things.

The highly emotional nature of many of these gatherings gave rise to certain physical phenomena such as the jerks, trances, rolling, and dancing. The "falling exercise" was common when a person under conviction would fall helpless to the ground. A sort of mass hysteria would grip the people and affect even those who were trying to resist the impulse to take part in the physical manifestations. These excesses gave rise to criticism, especially in the more staid religious circles of the East. The Presbyterian General Assembly of 1805, after giving some faint praise to the revival movement, declared that "God is a God of order and not of confusion; and whatever tends to destroy the comely order of his worship, is not from him, for he is consistent with himself."

Out of this Second Great Awakening came the Cumberland Presbyterian Church in which William Anderson Scott was to become at first a member and then a minister. The original Cumberland Presbytery was a constituent part of the Synod of Kentucky and included within its jurisdiction those parts of Kentucky and Tennessee where the camp meeting movement was the strongest. At that time the presbytery had only ten minister-members among whom were two of the most prominent leaders of the revival party, James McGready and William McGee. The presbytery became divided almost equally between the Revival and the Anti-Revival parties. The Revivalists, in an effort to meet the crying need of the frontier for more ministers, insisted on ordaining men who did not meet the educational standards of the Presbyterian Church. As a result of certain irregularities, the Synod of Kentucky dissolved the presbytery in 1806. When the General Assembly upheld the action of the synod, the Revivalists, now reduced to three, organized an independent presbytery on February 4, 1810, and called it Cumberland Presbytery after that which had been dissolved.

For several years the members of the new Presbytery fervently hoped that a reconciliation could be effected with the Mother Church. Finally, abandoning hope of such a reconciliation and noting the success of their evangelistic labors, the members of the presbytery constituted themselves into a synod on October 3, 1813. That event marks the beginning of the Cumberland Presbyterian Church. This was also the year of the birth of William Anderson Scott. The new church grew so rapidly that a General Assembly was erected in 1828.

The Cumberland Church made an admirable adaptation to frontier conditions. Like the Methodists and the Baptists, the church sent out circuit riders. Some of these men had but little education. They did have what was called experimental religion and made up in zeal what was lacking in education. Sometimes licentiates were appointed to a circuit before they were ordained. Each itinerant was expected to hold a service in a different community each night of the week if possible, over a four or five week period. The meetings were held in private homes, schoolhouses or courthouses as available, or in the open. During the nineteenth century the Cumberland Church expanded at the average rate of a presbytery a year. In 1906 the Cumberlands, with the exception of two synods in Tennessee, were reunited with the Mother Church. The continuing body beginning in Tennessee and spreading beyond the borders of that state, carries on the traditions and work of the Cumberland Presbyterian Church to this day.

Among the early Cumberland presbyteries erected was that of Hopewell, authorized in 1824 to include all of Tennessee west of the Tennessee River. One of the four charter members was Richard Beard who was destined to play an important role in Scott's early ministry.

STUDIES FOR THE MINISTRY

Sometime in 1827, perhaps earlier, an itinerant Cumberland minister began holding services in or near Raleigh, Tennessee. In January 1828, at the age of fifteen, William Anderson Scott joined the Cumberland Presbyterian Church of Raleigh. Years later in an autobiographical note, he explained that there was at that time "no other Presbyterian Church in that place or in the whole of the country." There is no indication in any of Dr. Scott's extant writings which would suggest that he passed through some great emotional experience before making his public confession of faith in Jesus Christ. Rather it seems reasonable to assume that the religious training of his home was such that he was never conscious of a time when he was not a Christian. When an opportunity presented itself to become a church member, he did so as the natural and right thing to do.

In October 1860, while serving as pastor of Calvary Presbyterian Church, San Francisco, Dr. Scott addressed an anniversary celebration of a mission Sunday School. The *San Francisco Bulletin* of October 15th reported: "He began by saying that the first Sabbath School he ever attended was when he was sixteen years old, and then he had to walk four miles through a wilderness, beset by wild Indians." Since the reference here is to his sixteenth year, it may be that the Sunday School was not started until a year or so after the church itself had been organized. The whole Sunday School movement in the United States was then in its infancy.

All evidence points to the fact that William decided to be a minister at the time he joined the church or shortly thereafter. Certainly his parents would have given their hearty approval to this decision. Possibly the minister who welcomed William into the church had suggested the idea. This we know from the original records of Hopewell Presbytery that on October 15, 1828, William Anderson Scott was received as a candidate for the ministry when the presbytery met at the "Bethel meeting house, Carroll County." William was then in his sixteenth year. The Rev. Richard Beard, fourteen years older than Scott and already a veteran in the service of the Cumberland Church, was moderator. A warm friendship united the two which continued throughout their lives. The minutes of the presbytery also indicate that Scott was present at the meeting held April 14-17, 1829, at "Mount Comfort meeting house, Hardeman County" when he was "examined on Divinity and Geography" and assigned a discourse on certain verses from 1st Peter. He also attended the meeting of the presbytery at Trenton, Gibson County, on October 6th, when it continued the examination of his preparation for licensure.

In line with the custom of the Cumberland Church of that day, Scott began his ministerial studies under a tutor. In the Scott Collection in Bancroft Library is a letter from Mrs. W. A. Scott to General W. W. Wright which gives considerable biographical information about her husband. The letter is undated but was written after the death of

Dr. Scott in January 1885. Regarding his education, she wrote: "He prepared for college by private study with various teachers and the aid of ministers and graduates of colleges living in the counties near, and by studying on a missionary circuit."

Dr. Scott had a deeply ingrained hesitancy about drawing upon his own experiences to illustrate his sermons or addresses. But there are a few exceptions. Among his manuscripts in the San Francisco Theological Seminary is a lecture on "The Teacher's Work and Encouragement" which he delivered at the opening of the Female Academy at Winchester, Tennessee, on December 4, 1837. In this lecture is the following:

> It was my misfortune to be born and brought up pretty much in the back woods, deprived of schools, and indeed at the age of sixteen when I began my [high school] education, there were no Latin scholars within the whole region of the country in which my father lived devoted to the instruction of youth. I left home some 50 miles, lived in a kind and excellent family, and studied all day alone, and at dark mounted a little old grey horse (who would often fall down & throw me over his head) . . . every evening rain or shine, cold or hot, I bolted off four miles to the residence of Mr. A. Shelby, (son of old Governor Shelby of Ky.,) who was once wealthy and educated, but now very poor and blessed with a large family.

The reference to "Mr. A. Shelby" is undoubtedly to the Rev. Aaron Shelby, a minister who is mentioned in McDonnold's *History of the Cumberland Presbyterial Church* as being wealthy and also much interested in the struggling college founded by that denomination at Princeton, Kentucky, in 1825. How Shelby happened to lose his wealth and become reduced to the straits described by Scott is not known. The meager evidence at hand suggests that William spent the fall of 1829 and spring of 1830 studying under Shelby's direction. His account continues:

> He lived in a poor barren place, in a log house, where winter's winds kept holyday [sic]. And as he had not time in the day, he devoted his nights to my instruction. He would grub or chop all day long, and then spend every evening till "the witching time of midnight" and even later with me. Yes, methinks I see him now —his dingy hat, brown coat that had seen better days, his piercing black eyes, and the welcoming smile with which he always saluted me. There is his log fire—there his bed, filled with his wife and children—and here the table and miserable lamp, the only light. This however was always agreeable to me, as it reminded me of Demosthenes' study. Thus he would spend the night with me, pouring over Latin and philosophy and astronomy—from the pure love of imparting instruction, for it was entirely gratuitous. During this winter I learned much I never shall forget, till the ice of death

has frozen around my heart, and things the most indelible have faded from my memory.

The next documented event in Scott's life came on April 8, 1830, when he was licensed to preach the Gospel by Hopewell Presbytery over which Richard Beard was still presiding as moderator. Scott was then seventeen years old. According to the minutes, Scott and two other young men satisfied the presbytery as to their "moral character . . . aptness to teach . . . their experimental acquaintance with religion . . . their internal call and motives to the ministry, and as to their proficiency in divinity" whereupon the three were duly licensed. The minutes then state: "Ordered that William A. Scott ride and preach the whole of his time on the Carroll and Obion Circuit." The fall meeting of the presbytery was held at the Shiloh meeting house in Carroll County, October 7-11. Scott was present and was again assigned to the circuit in the two northwest counties of Tennessee.

Sometime during the spring of 1830, or possibly a year later, Scott had an experience which echoed some fourteen or fifteen years later. For the first time in his life, he had occasion at Memphis to take passage up the Mississippi River on a steamboat. The novelty of the experience was heightened by the fact that the great American statesman, Henry Clay of Kentucky, was on board. In a letter to Messrs. Roselius and Peters of New Orleans dated November 4, 1844, Scott explained: "When told of the arrival of the steamboat and that Mr. Clay was on board, I was so delighted with the idea of seeing him that with others, I ran down the bluff waving my hat and shouting hurrah for Henry Clay."

On the Saturday night after embarking, William, naive and uninformed in the ways of the world, saw some men playing cards. This, according to his later statements, was the first time he had ever seen a card game. There were piles of money on the table. William assumed that this indicated the men were gambling. And one thing more which the young man never forgot, the great Henry Clay was seated at the table playing cards and presumably gambling. When William went to bed that night, the men were still at the table. On Sunday morning the central saloon was prepared for divine service. Of course William attended and noted that Henry Clay remained in his stateroom during the entire service. In 1844 when Clay was running for the presidency of the United States, Scott happened to make some passing remark about this incident to a friend. The remark, embellished and published in the daily press, became the cause of a bitter controversy involving Scott in an ecclesiastical trial which finally reached the Presbyterian General Assembly in 1847. Regarding this, more will be said later.

GOSLING PREACHER ON A TENNESSEE CIRCUIT

In their effort to reach the scattered communities on the frontier, the Cumberland Presbyterians departed from the traditional emphasis of their ancestors by licensing and ordaining men who did not have full college and seminary training. But after taking this into consideration, the licensing of William A. Scott when he was only seventeen years old and sending him out on a circuit for a year was unusual even for the Cumberland Presbyterians. The very fact that it was done is evidence that his abilities were recognized. Scott later wrote:

> Some of the old Elders looked at me doubtingly at first & said I was a gosling preacher for I had never begun to shave. Everywhere I was treated, and without exception, by the greatest kindness. And on my last round of the circuit they gave me money at every place and loaded me down with homespun clothes and socks. It was a happy year's work for me. I am always profoundly thankful for it.

The circuit to which the presbytery assigned Scott contained about thirty preaching points in the five counties of Carroll, Henry, Weakley, Obion, and Gibson in the northwestern part of Tennessee. There were also "short excursions into the adjoining parts of Kentucky." Scott rode horseback carrying a few belongings and some books in saddlebags. Nothing is known about compensation but it may be assumed that he got very little money beyond free accommodations in the homes of the people and some homespun clothing. He was able to cover the circuit about once a month and would then start over again.

Looking back on those months spent as a circuit rider, Scott wrote:

> I preached as a rule once or twice every day, losing but seven days out of the year, generally the preaching was in a rude school house, court house, or log dwelling of the people. The roads were of a most primitive style, often only a blazed path conducted me from one house or country town to another.

His unquenchable zeal for knowledge created opportunities for study even in those primitive surroundings. He wrote:

> I arranged to carry with me some volumes, and to leave them at different stations—such as Brown's Dictionary of the Bible, Erskine Sermons, Davis Sermons, and Thos. Scott's notes on the New Testament. I had sufficient knowledge of Greek to read the New Testament and was quite able to read fluently Horace and Cicero. I read riding along the road and when I had time to spare before reaching my appointment, wrote out briefs of my sermons sitting on a log or the root of a tree while my horse picked about for refreshment and also by the log fires and pine knot lights of the people who entertained me, obtaining permission to sit up after the family retired.

On April 10, 1830, two days after he was licensed, Scott began a record book of "texts preached on and places." His first sermon was delivered in the Bethel Church of McLemoresville in Carroll County. Today Bethel remains as the oldest Cumberland church in west Tennessee. His text was from Psalm 58:11: "So that a man shall say, Verily there is a reward for the righteous." Scott followed the practice of noting in his record book his personal judgment as to the effectiveness of his preaching. Here in his first entry are the illuminating words: "Tongue liberty." Evidently he felt pleased with himself after his first sermon. A review of some thirty-eight of these self-appraisals shows that on seven occasions he noted "Bad" or "Very Bad;" eight times he wrote "Tolerable" or "Tolerable Liberty;" and twenty-two times he commended himself by writing "Good" or "Very Good." The attendance usually numbered from fifteen to twenty but sometimes, when preaching in one of the few organized churches on the circuit, it rose to fifty or more. Once, on February 20, 1831, which was a Saturday, preaching at Mt. Pleasant, Henry County, he reported an attendance of one hundred. Occasionally he noted: "No persons at all" or "No person except one."

Shortly before Dr. Scott closed his pastorate in New York City in 1869, he granted an interview to a writer who was compiling biographical sketches for a book which was published in 1874 under the title *Lives of the Clergy of New York and Brooklyn.* Drawing upon his memory of experiences as a circuit rider, he related the following incident: "On one occasion he had an appointment at a log building, but a storm kept away all save one man, to whom the sermon was preached, as a large fire crackled on the dirt in the center of the apartment." This may have been the same incident mentioned in his diary for January 9, 1831, when he wrote: "Snowed all day. No person except one man, Mr. Hawkins, who argued freely."

The places listed in his record include the present county seats of Huntingdon, Paris, and Dresden. Also mentioned are some country churches which continue as Cumberland Presbyterian churches to this day. Among them is Shiloh a few miles distant from McKenzie. At Huntingdon, William met Dr. Robert Nicholson, a widower, and his lovely daughter, Ann, who five years later was to become his wife. Mr. and Mrs. Nicholson and their daughter, who was born at Kilkeel, County Down, North Ireland, on November 11, 1811, migrated in 1817 to Simpson County, Kentucky. Ann was, therefore, about fourteen months older than William. Mrs. Nicholson died in 1820.

Kilkeel lies about forty miles south of Belfast on the tip of the southeast coast of Ulster, in the center of a coastal plain ringed in the back by the Mourne Mountains and washed on its eastern side by the waters of the Irish Sea. The plain measures about twelve miles along the coast and in the center reaches inland about five miles to the mountains. It is known as the Kingdom of Mourne since in ancient times the land was ruled by an Irish king. Here is some of the best potato-growing land in all of Ireland. Here, too, as elsewhere throughout Ireland, one sees the endless stone walls dividing the acreage and lining the roads. Bordering Kilkeel, about one mile from the village church, is a locality known as Derryogue, meaning "flat place." Here was located the Robert Nicholson farm of about nine acres sloping gently down to the sea.

BIRTHPLACE OF ANN NICHOLSON
At Kilkeel, County Down, North Ireland.

During the summer of 1966, my wife and I visited Kilkeel and Derryogue. We found the old stone cottage still standing in which Ann Nicholson lived as a little girl. The cottage has two chimneys and the walls are high enough to provide sleeping rooms under the thatched roof. Thus it was a better home than some of its neighbors. Since the house has been unoccupied for the past ten years, the thatched roof has caved in and the interior is cluttered with debris.

We called on the Rev. Alan Flavelle, minister of the Mourne Presbyterian Church in Kilkeel and learned from him that the church has no records going back to the period when the Nicholson family lived there. The present church building in Kilkeel postdates their residence. A number of Nicholson tombstones in the church's cemetery bear testimony to the continued presence of the Nicholson name in the community. The beach below the old Nicholson home at Derryogue is known as Nicholson Beach.

About three miles to the southeast of Kilkeel is Greencastle which stands at the north entrance of Carlingford Lough. Across this body of water is the Republic of Ireland. This lough was a favorite place for emigrants to board ships bound for America 150 or more years ago. It was convenient for the sailing vessels en route from Liverpool to drop anchor there and take on additional passengers who would be rowed out in small boats. Undoubtedly, it was there that Robert Nicholson, his wife, and their six-year-old daughter, Ann, took ship for the New World in 1817. Robert left his farm in the care of a brother who never made proper settlement. More about this will be told later.

Robert Nicholson was still a young man when he settled with his family in Kentucky. Deciding to study medicine, he enrolled at Transylvania University at Lexington, Kentucky, where he earned his doctor's degree. In 1826, several years after the death of his wife, he and his daughter moved to Huntingdon, Tennessee. The Carroll County tax list shows that Dr. Nicholson was the owner of five hundred acres of land in 1826. Since land was then very cheap, this does not in itself indicate that he was wealthy. The records also carry a notation on June 14, 1830 of a gift from the father to the daughter of a Negro girl called Mila.

Scott's records for these months when he was itinerating through northwestern Tennessee contain nothing more than the usual prosaic references to his services, with no mention of any incipient romance. In October 1832, while serving as a chaplain in the Black Hawk War, he confided in his diary that he dearly loved Ann Nicholson, and then added: ". . . but she does now know it."

Scott's friend, Richard Beard, had preached for about twelve years before going to college, but such a course did not commend itself to Scott. "I was so dissatisfied with my education," he wrote, "that at the end of the year I resigned my missionary work and repaired to Cumberland College, Princeton, Kentucky.

In 1878, one of Dr. Scott's contemporaries in California, the Rev. James Woods, published his *Recollections of Pioneer Work* in which he devoted a chapter to his reminiscences of Dr. Scott. Woods wrote: "In my earliest ministerial life, I traveled and preached in the region of Tennessee where he had exercised his ministry a very few years before. The country was full of his fame. A men said to me that it was wonderful how so young a man could have acquired such a fund of knowledge, and possess such powers of preaching."

AT CUMBERLAND COLLEGE

In 1825 the twelve-year-old Cumberland Synod founded its first college at the little town of Princeton, Kentucky. Out of their poverty the Cumberland Presbyterians did what they could to provide a college education for their aspiring young men and especially for their ministerial candidates. About $28,000 was raised in subscriptions of which only one-fourth was ever collected. A farm, variously reported as being five hundred or seven hundred acres in size, was purchased on credit. Tools and livestock were bought with borrowed money and several log building were erected, also on credit. Thus the infant institution was born under the dark shadow of a heavy debt.

The original two-story log farm house was enlarged and converted into a boarding house. Another building described as being "of hewed logs, two stories high, with stone chimneys and wide, country-like fireplaces, was erected for college purposes." This measured forty by seventy feet. A row of log cabins was built "a convenient distance from both the college building and the refectory" to provide sleeping accommodations. These were described as having "puncheon floors, clapboard roofs, and chimneys constructed of wood and mortar, the fire-places having backs of stone."

The Rev. Franceway R. Cossitt, D.D., a graduate of Middlebury College, Vermont, and a former Episcopal minister who had joined the Cumberland Church, accepted the presidency of the infant college and began his duties on March 1, 1826. All contemporary references to Dr. Cossitt speak highly of his ability, his zeal for education, and his love for his students. The institution was patterned after the manual labor schools which were common in that generation in certain sections of the northern states. Each student was expected to work two hours each day at whatever kind of labor the farm manager might prescribe. When the college was first opened, the full charge for a term of ten and a half months for both board and tuition was only $60. In later life, Scott made frequent mention of Dr. Cossitt and always in terms of respect and appreciation.

A good description of life at the log college shortly before Scott enrolled is found in the reminiscences of Richard Beard who began his studies there in May 1830. At that time the school had 125 students and a faculty of five, including Dr. Cossitt and two tutors for the preparatory students. Beard wrote:

> It was literally a log college, as rough in its exterior as an ordinary barn. Its interior fitness was by no means superior to its outward appearance. The dormitories of the students were coarse cabins, furnished with straw beds, and other conveniences of a similar character. . . The college seemed a good deal like a bee-hive. Each teacher was ringing a bell every hour for his class; and every two hours the horn was blowing for the laboring divisions. All seemed to be interest and animation. . . In addition to all, the faculty, dressed in their long black [academic] gowns, presented rather an imposing appearance to a frontier circuit-rider and common school teacher.

As Beard recalled, the faculty gave up the custom of wearing gowns at the end of that year.

To this struggling frontier institution dignified by the title of college, came the eighteen-year-old William A. Scott in the spring of 1831. One of the first books that he purchased was Charles Buck's *A Theological Dictionary* and on the flyleaf he wrote his name, the price, $1.75 and the date, April 28, 1831. Few students ever turned to books with such an eager absorbent mind as did he. A college which could boast of less than five hundred volumes in the library would be pitifully inadequate by modern standards, but this was considered a veritable treasure-trove of learning in the almost barren wilderness.

A CHAPLAIN IN THE BLACK HAWK WAR

After a busy, happy year at Cumberland College, Scott found it necessary to interrupt his studies in order to make some money. The college had increased the cost of board and tuition to $80 a year. Scott's father was never able to render any financial assistance and according to a statement made by Mrs. W. A. Scott years later, her husband never received any scholarship aid for either his college or his seminary education. He was thrown in both cases entirely upon his own resources. At times he was obliged to borrow money, all of which he repaid. Just at the time when Scott felt the necessity of interrupting his studies, a call came from the United States Army post at Fort Crawford, Prairie du Chien, Wisconsin, for a chaplain who would also serve as teacher of the grade school. Scott applied for the position and was accepted. Since he had not seen his parents for over two years, he felt that he should pay them a visit before reporting for duty at the fort. He left the college on Thursday, March 22, 1832, and traveled overland to Eddyville where for three dollars he engaged deck passage on a steamer bound for Memphis. Passengers who could not afford the luxury of a cabin paid a minimum fare for the right to sleep on the deck and they provided their own food.

While at Eddyville, Scott began a diary which remains as the oldest of the several he wrote which are extant. The record book kept on the circuit is not a diary as it contains only memoranda regarding his services. The first entry in the diary, dated March 22nd, is the following:

> Preface. The author being very desirous to improve his time & talents, and while travelling wishing to obtain every laudable part of knowledge by observation; and thinking that a good way by which to accomplish this desirable object was to make a short though imperfect memorandum by which he may be able to call to mind past events and thereby always make the future still wiser than the past from the reflection & experience of those [years] passed by.
>
> His grand object is improvement; and the end of improvement ought to be usefulness; so from these considerations this diary is commenced. May it be productive of much good. Author.

The voyage down the rivers took most of three days and three nights. Scott disembarked at Memphis early Sunday morning, March 25th. Since he shared the opinion then common among the members of his church about the sinfulness of traveling on Sunday, Scott found a room and spent the rest of the day in the town before starting out for his home on Big Creek. He attended church and was invited by the pioneer Cumberland minister of the community, Father Whitsit, to preach at the evening service. Scott accepted. In his diary entry for the day, he mentioned the text he used, I John 4:16: "God is love; and he that dwelleth in love dwelleth in God, and God in him." After the service he wrote: "I tried to preach . . . to a small, but attentive & weeping congregation. My own poor soul was refreshed." A complimentary description of an effective preacher in the early years of our country's history was to call him a "painful preacher." This meant that the minister had the ability to prick the consciences of his hearers. Here as a nineteen-year-old youth, we see evidence of a speaking ability which within fifteen years was to make William Anderson Scott one of the leading preachers of the nation. Even in these youthful years, Scott was a "painful preacher;" he could make the members of his congregation weep.

On Monday, March 26, 1832, Scott recorded: "Rode in the U.S. Mail Stage to Raleigh. Thence to my Father." Even though the first United States general issue of postage stamps did not appear until 1847, here is evidence that the government was engaged in regular mail delivery. The usual charge then was twenty-five cents for a foolscap one-page letter which was so folded as to permit part of the back to carry the address.

Scott spent a month at his old home during which time he suffered an attack of measles. He renewed acquaintance with neighbors and old friends. With his father, he made a shopping trip to Memphis and bought cloth for "a great coat." On Friday, April 27th, he wrote: "After various miscellaneous duties, which I deem unworthy of notice . . . I engaged a passage on the steamer "Conroy" for the mouth of Ohio River for $6.00. At 9 o'clock a.m., she left Memphis." He was on his way to Fort Crawford and the neighboring Indian Agency located at Prairie du Chien on the east bank of the Mississippi River about fifty miles below the Illinois-Wisconsin line.

Scott landed in St. Louis on Wednesday, May 2nd, and took a room "at the Union Hotel on Main Street." According to his diary, he spent the day "walking about and viewing the scenes in the city. I visited the churches and the markets,&c. I saw all kinds of people and heard various languages spoken. I was in wonder & amazement all the time." He was a country boy in a big city. St. Louis was then the headquarters of the booming fur trade which reached out its tentacles to the upper waters of the Missouri River, over into the Oregon country, and across the plains to Santa Fe in Mexico. The streets of the city were crowded with mountain men, trappers, explorers, traders, emigrants, and Indians. This was the great center of trade for the whole upper Missouri Valley and scores of river steamers were constantly being loaded or unloaded at the city's docks.

"I am now in a large & populous city without friends or acquant-ances," wrote Scott. "How great are its inhabitants. How little & low am I. . . O Lord, thou art my God." Thus was Scott introduced to life in a great city. Little did he then dream that he would spend over forty years of his life as a pastor in such metropolitan centers as New Orleans, San Francisco, and New York.

By this time Scott was aware of the fact that trouble was brewing with the Sac (sometimes spelled Sauk) and Fox Indians under the leader-ship of Chief Black Hawk. White settlers were moving in on Indians lands. Friction had also developed between certain Indian tribes. On April 8, 1832, General Henry Atkinson with a force of 220 men had embarked at St. Louis for Rock Island with the hope of keeping Black Hawk and his band of about 500 warriors and their families from crossing the Mississippi to return to their old homes in Illinois. But Atkinson arrived at Rock Island too late. The Indians had already crossed the river and were moving up Rock River into northern Illinois. Fort Crawford at Prairie du Chien was in the very center of this troubled area.

> Monday, May 3rd . . . I purchased a pair of lasting pantaloons for $4.00. About 11 o'clock a.m., I embarked on board the S. Boat "Dove" for Galena. . . I thought earnestly of taking a deck passage but on the whole from the very disagreeable condition of the deck, fearing lest a passage thus exposed would relapse me again into bad health, I finally concluded to pay the $18.00 and take a cabin passage. . . Purchased a seal skin trunk for $4.00 to put my cloth in.

The steamboat reached Galena, Illinois, on May 9th. Since the boat did not go any farther up the river, Scott found it necessary to go ashore. After waiting for several days in the vain hope that he could get water transportation for the remaining fifty miles to Prairie du Chien, he rented a horse for eight dollars and started overland on Monday, May 14th. In the meantime, learning that there was a dearth of religious services in Galena, Scott held two services as the following entry in his diary for Sunday, May 13th, indicates: "On Friday night, I endeavored to preach to a small congregation in the Town School House. . . On Sabbath at 4 o'c p.m., I tried again to preach to a large and attentive congregation."

On Monday Scott rode twenty miles and spent the night in a home on Platt River. That evening he wrote: "Here I was considerably alarmed for fear of being attacked by the Indians." During the so-called Black Hawk War, about seventy white settlers and soldiers were killed. The Indian losses were much heavier being estimated at from five to six hundred. Rumors of the possibility of attack by marauding Indians were no doubt rife all through the thinly inhabited area through which Scott was riding. On Tuesday he rode to Cassville, a small town on the east bank of the Mississippi, and the next day rode into Prairie du Chien. "This evening," he wrote, "I became acquainted with Genl. J. M. Street, who introduced me to his family, with whom I tarried all night." General Street was then the Indian agent at Fort Crawford.

His notation for Friday, the 18th, reads: "Today I engaged with the School Committee of Prairie du Chien to teach school five months & 8 days; to commence on 21st May 1832. For the small sum of $125 and my boarding, washing, & all found. I know this is a very small sum, but to do good is my object." He made no mention of any compensation for his religious services. A search has been made of United States Army records in Washington, D.C. without finding any record of an official appointment of Scott as a chaplain in the Black Hawk War. However, it was learned that during these years some army posts had locally selected chaplains who were paid by voluntary contributions. These chaplains had no federal status and left virtually no records.

On Sunday, May 20th, Scott began his religious services at Fort Crawford. His diary entry for that day reads: "At 11 o'clock I endeavoured to preach in the Garrison to Capt. Loomis' Company and sundry citizens on Luke 2:10, 'The good tidings.' The congregation was attentive. I only had tolerably good liberty. Half past 3 o'clock p.m., I tried again to preach to a small, attentive congregation in Genl. Street's dwelling house." Captain Gustavus Loomis, mentioned by Scott in this entry, was attracted by the earnest young minister and later, as will be told, helped to make it possible for Scott to attend Princeton Theological Seminary.

Scott's next entry touches on the excitement and strain of those days when rumors of an impending attack by the Indians reached the Fort. "Monday 21. Today I feel very unwell having been deprived of sleep on the succeeding evening by alarms of being attacked by the Indians. This night I was under arms; and prepared for shedding blood." As far as available records indicate, this is the nearest that Chaplain Scott came to actual combat.

After a one day delay, Scott opened his school on Tuesday, May 22nd. He quickly found himself immersed in a situation so fraught with difficulties that he was greatly tempted to resign and go home. On June 3rd, he wrote:

> During the week I was much dissatisfied and wished to leave all and go to my Father's. I was much discouraged and have very serious views of forsaking all civil society & making my abode in the forest, living a savage life in order that I might get out of the confusion & sin of this world. . . O Lord what shall I do? I labor and toil with no apparent success. I feel almost despairing. My school was very troublesome. The students were refractory & rebellious. My perplexity was very great. O how I long for the peace & innocence of my boyhood.

Evidently the problem of maintaining discipline in a schoolroom filled with untamed frontier children was almost too much for the nineteen-year-old youth. But he did not give up and at the end of the term wrote in his diary: "I however think in teaching I have done a little good. The pupils advanced very fast & when examined at the exhibition on Friday, 20th Oct., they acquitted themselves respectably."

The notebook containing the first part of Scott's diary at Fort Crawford closes with an entry for June 24th. The next book begins with September 24th. The diary for the intervening three months, if such were kept, seems to have disappeared. During these summer months, United States troops defeated Black Hawk's band at the Battle of Bad Axe. Black Hawk evaded capture at that time but was taken prisoner a few days later. On August 28, 1832, General Joseph Street wrote from Prairie du Chien to the Bureau of Indian Affairs in Washington saying in part: "The celebrated Sac Chief Black Hawk, and the Prophet were delivered to me yesterday by a party of Winnebagoes of my agency sent out by me some time past in pursuit of them. The same day I turned them over to Colo. Z. Taylor commdg. Fort Crawford."

A number of great American figures were involved in this brief Black Hawk War. The Z. Taylor referred to in Street's letter was Zachary Taylor who won fame in the Mexican War of 1846 and who in 1849 became the twelfth president of the United States. Abraham Lincoln, as captain of a company of Illinois volunteers, saw service during this campaign, and Lieutenant Jefferson Davis was one of the officers responsible for escorting the captured chief from Fort Crawford to Jefferson Barracks. Although Chaplain Scott may not have met Abraham Lincoln during this summer, he certainly would have seen both Colonel Taylor and Lieutenant Davis.

The Rev. James Woods, in a memorial tribute to Scott printed in the San Francisco *Occident* following the latter's death in January 1885, claimed that Scott "wrote out the treaty of capitulation signed by Blackhawk." It is probable that in writing the treaty Scott was merely serving as a clerk for General Street or for any other officials responsible for the final negotiations. One stipulation of the treaty called for the complete removal of all Sac Indians from Illinois across the Mississippi into Iowa.

Scott's diary reveals the fact that he was often deeply depressed during the fall of 1832. His entry for September 24th is typical of some others:

> This day is most gloomy and sad to me. I am very much displeased with the treatment I have generally received at this place. I feel much hurt with Genl. Street in particular. His very name is an abominable thing to me. The Lord forgive me. I feel determined if the Lord will to go home this fall—and then I think, I will simply try & live with my Father as an obscure & unknown person, laboring with my hands to support myself & aid my old Mother.

Scott's displeasure with General Street stemmed from the general's failure to make any statement regarding compensation for Scott's religious services. The diary shows that Scott was on each Sunday conducting a Sabbath School in the morning, a worship service at 11:00 o'clock, a Bible class and prayer-meeting at 2:00 p.m., and an evening service. Nothing had been said about money except the guarantee of $125 above expenses for his work in the school. Scott was worried about finances. On September 28th he wrote that he needed at least $200 in order to return to college. Evidently this need was finally communicated to General Street for the full $200 above all expenses was paid before Scott left Prairie du Chien on October 29th. He then wrote in his diary: "I am much attached to many friends at P. du C. & leave them with a great deal of reluctance, among these are Genl. S. and family, but especially Mrs. Street. . . She has been very kind to me. . .

And as to Genl. S., whatever may have been my previous feelings, I must regard him as my warm friend."

Another reason for these periods of depression arose out of loneliness and bad health. His diary for Friday, October 12th, carries the following entry: "William Anderson Scott, School House, Prairie du Chien, Michigan Territory, near Fort Crawford . . . about one of the Clock—rather watch." The latter remark seems to indicate that he possessed a watch. "I feel unusually melancholy. I am in very bad health. I do not read much. I am entirely sunk under discouragements. I feel as if I was surely a fool and one of the vilest sinners on earth . . . I feel very anxious to go home so that I can raise a faithful dog as a friend to me if all other earthly friends forsake me. I am very anxious to leave this place." Some of his loneliness was due to pining for a sweetheart. He wrote:

> I feel like, in spite of my cold logic and theory, that I must take myself a rib—a rib—yes, I think this would be a great thing for me. It looks like if I had but some gentle bed on which to rest, with a smiling wife, and her kind hands to bear me up; it would be a *Paradise.* But the misery is this—those in all probability that I want, do not want me—and those that want me, I hate. This is a tremendous evil! May Minerva give me wisdom to escape. I am as poor as Job's turkey; and if I marry a poor girl, we would all be poor, and die loving one another for want of some mush and potatoes. There is one dear Angel, I love—Yes, I must say I love her but she does not know it, and I do not know that she loves me. Her name is A-- N--.

Ann Nicholson was the charming daughter of Dr. Robert Nicholson of Huntingdon whom Scott had met while riding the circuit in northwestern Tennessee two years previous.

Still another reason for these periods of despondency was the feeling that perhaps he was not fitted for the ministry.

> If Cupid will leave off darting me & I can elude the grasp of Mother Venus, I will after graduating turn my attention to the study of law. . . This seems to me much better than any other profession; and I must do something to make a living. . . I now feel like it would be base wickedness to pursue the ministry, arising from my unprepared condition, as to talents & piety, and I am in serious doubts as to my own poor soul. It seems to me, and oh! how awful too, that I have no religion.

This was written on October 13th, shortly before he was to leave Prairie du Chien. He spent most of the day in deep soul-searching. He read some sermons by Dr. Timothy Dwight of Yale on the ministry. He sought divine guidance through prayer. Finally, at the end of the day, he wrote:

I feel as though I might try & pursue the ministry and pray God to direct me. O! if I should preach Jesus & the Resurrection to poor sinners, may I do it in preference to any and everything else. Lord may I do thy will. . . If I should pursue the theological studies of a minister, I determine to sacrifice everything else to it and make it my whole business. I will, the Lord willing, take a Theological Course.

The decision here made to give his whole heart and soul to the Gospel ministry was never questioned again. This was the Lord's will for him.

It is evident that Scott had talked over his problem with his friend Captain Loomis, who, having been deeply impressed with the latent possibilities of the young man, had strongly urged him to go to Princeton Theological Seminary after graduation from Cumberland College. On the basis of later developments, we can imagine the captain saying: "William, you can not afford to be content with anything but the best. The education you can get at Cumberland College is not enough. You must go to a good well-established seminary. Go to Princeton in New Jersey." And William no doubt replied: "But captain, that takes money and I am without funds." "Don't let that stop you," replied the captain, "I'll lend you what you need."

RETURN TO COLLEGE

Since there were no regular steamboats plying between Prairie du Chien and lower ports on the Mississippi River at that time, Scott was faced with the necessity of descending the river in a canoe. This meant a hazardous trip of over three hundred miles to Keokuk where a steamer could be boarded for St. Louis. The west bank of the Mississippi through most of this territory was inhabited by the Sac and Fox Indians who, owing to their recent defeat by United States troops, were not in a friendly mood toward white men passing through their land or along their borders.

Under the circumstances Scott found it advisable to get a companion. For several weeks before his departure from Fort Crawford, Scott had shown interest in a teen-age half-breed Sioux boy by the name of Lackapelle. On October 7, 1832, Scott wrote in his diary: "This evening I spoke to Lackapelle about going to College with me. He has no funds. . . I told him if he could get the consent of his friends to go, that I would try by some means to aid him. . . I believe he is a good boy and it might be productive of great good to give him an education." Consent of the lad's mother was obtained and plans were made for the two to start on their long perilous journey on Monday, October 29th.

Scott preached his farewell sermon on the Sunday afternoon preceding, taking for his text II Timothy 4:6-8 which includes the words: ". . . the time of my departure is at hand. I have fought a good fight, I have finished my course, I have kept the faith." That night he commented in his diary: "Many tears fell profusely. My own feelings

were indescribable. I could hardly speak for shedding tears myself. . .
After sermon, in which I had good liberty, I went round the congregation while they were singing 'Alas and did my Saviour' and gave them
my hand—all appeared melted down into tears. An early candle-
lighting prayer-meeting at Gen. Street's." Scott was overcome with the
thought that in all probability he would never again see those people
with whom he had been so closely associated for five months till "the
judgment day." "How solemn! Awful!" he wrote, "What an account
must ministers & people give at that tremendous day!!!"

Monday morning was spent getting ready to leave. It was not until
1:00 o'clock that the two were ready to depart. General and Mrs. Street
and a number of other friends were at the boat landing to bid the two
farewell. Captain Loomis was not there as he had been ordered east on
official business. As Scott moved among the group shaking hands and
saying his goodbyes, he came to the Sioux Indian woman, the mother of
Lackapelle. The tears were rolling down her cheeks and impulsively
"she gave me a most sweet & impressive kiss." Scott was both taken by
surprise and deeply moved. "It glowed warm on my cheek for many
hours," he wrote, "& will not be forgotten by me. This is the first kiss
ever received from a female since my baby days. It was a pure & warm
kiss from her very heart."

It took twelve days for the two to reach Keokuk. Scott's entries in
his diary show that they were on constant alert against hostile Indians.
They camped in secluded places, sometimes on islands, sometimes not
daring to build a fire. They also encountered stormy weather. The following quotations are from the diary:

Oct. 30. We rose early. . . We run about 25 miles below
Cassville. Very much fatigued. Slept all night on an island without any fire. . .
Thurs. Nov. 1, 1832. . . We proceeded on our journey. . .
At night we were very much afraid of Indians as all of the west
bank of the Mississippi is the Sac country. . .
Saturday Nov. 3rd. At about 11 o'clock we landed at Rock
Island. We heard that the cholera is raging at St. Louis—that
about 30 persons die daily in that city of the plague. Here we
find that there is no prospects for a steam boat and no stage—so
we have to make our journey still in our canoe. We run on, & the
wind rose; have had a considerable storm . . . run on several
rocks & passed through many dangers—still the Lord blessed us &
was very merciful to us—about 8 or 9 o'c p.m., we crossed to the
east side of the River, or at least to an Island near this side . . .
hid our canoe, lay down to sleep under some little willows on a
sandy point near the edge of the water. . . We had no fire, and
thus concealed ourselves to keep from being discovered by the
Indians.
Sabbath Nov. 5. This morning we awoke in peace & safe-

ty. . . We had not designed to travel on Sabbath; but as we
were situated & it threatened to rain, we supposing there was a
house within 15 or 20 miles, concluded we would endeavor to
arrive at it. . . Accordingly we again set out . . . as we
were running on, we spied two canoes of Indians—Sacks. The
first one had an old man & two women in it. He hailed us with
the usual salutation & we passed on. The second contained two
young men & one squaw. We hailed them with a salutation, held
a little conversation in the Chippeway language, as that is said to
be their mother tongue. They asked us for some bread—we gave
them one loaf. They examined our canoe & looked suspiciously;
but made no hostile attack. So we bade them goodby & passed
on. . . This day I felt that the Lord was very merciful to us.
It will surely be a great mercy if we reach Cumberland College in
safety.

The reference here to the Chippewa language suggests the possibility
of Scott having had some knowledge of it. On Monday the two ran into
a severe storm. They found an uninhabited house on the east bank in
which they took refuge. In his diary for that night, he referred to his
concern for his "dear old Mother" and wished he could do something to
ease her toil "in her old, frail days." His mother was then fifty years
old which, in the normal life expectancy of that generation, was old
indeed.

The storm continued through Tuesday, November 7th, and the two
were obliged to remain in their shelter. "Much difficulty," wrote Scott,
"with Mr. Lackapelle. He is very headstrong." On Wednesday they
continued their travels and descended the river another fifty miles.
They reached Keokuk on Thursday. Here Scott said goodby to his Indian
companion, for by this time he had given up the idea of taking the
Indian lad with him to college. Scott had to wait until Saturday before
he was able to get passage on a steamboat to St. Louis, and his diary
contains a vivid description of Keokuk which he called a "modern
Sodom." He was alarmed over his personal safety and was in constant
fear of being robbed. There was also the added danger of getting cholera, then present in the city, which could strike with sudden lethal
effect.

Although greatly desiring to visit his parents near Memphis, Scott
found it necessary at St. Louis to take a steamer headed for the Ohio
River in order to get back to his college studies in time to be graduated
with the class of 1833. He spent Sunday, November 19th, at Smithland
at the mouth of the Cumberland River waiting for another steamer to
take him to Eddysville. Here he confided in his diary some of his concerns regarding the policies of the Cumberland Presbyterian Church,
reflecting, no doubt, some of the opinions of his friend, Captain Loomis:
"I fear and tremble for the Cumberland Presbyterian Church. I think in

my humble opinion that there are many errors in the management of it, especially in educating ministers."

Scott was happy to be back in the peaceful surroundings of the college. He learned, however, that the dread cholera had made its appearance in the little village of Princeton, Kentucky, that fall. In some undated notes made to be used in a letter to his friend, Captain Loomis, Scott wrote: "I begin to feel at home in my little room and I wish you were here to see my home, as I sit by my blazing fire in the cold evenings. College certainly has charms, though I have a few things rankling in my heart which will not let me be quite happy. Ora, ora, pro me."

The oldest letters in the Scott Collection in Bancroft Library are from Captain Loomis, one of which was written when Scott was still at Prairie du Chien. The captain was then in the East and had taken time to investigate the possibility of Scott's getting aid from the American Education Society which was founded for the purpose of helping "pious youths" get a theological education. Loomis wrote: "Does your purpose still hold to go to Princeton, New Jersey? If so I do not think you need be under any apprehension as to the funds requisite, as by an application to the Edn. Society I am confident no difficulty will be found. But to do that perhaps pride must be brot low." Only indigent students were aided and it is possible that Scott was loath to sign such a statement. There is no evidence that he ever received scholarship aid from this source. Loomis' letter continues with a warning: "There is great danger of a young man of elevated standards of piety upon going to college that, without great watchfulness and humility, he come out having exchanged his religion for learning."

Scott found the little college still struggling under financial limitations. The Cumberland General Assembly at its June 1832 meeting turned its attention to this distressing situation and in order "the more effectually to preserve economy among the students" passed the following: "Resolved, That in future the students and faculty of said college be, and they are hereby advised to wear as their weekly apparel during winter, good strong woolen jeans, or cassinette; and for summer, flax, linen, or hemp linen, of some other article of domestic manufacture . . . also that each student be requested to furnish himself with a large and strong linen apron, which may be used when at work, so as to preserve his other clothes. . ." Even the faculty was to wear homespun.

During the spring of 1833 the college erected a two story brick building, sixty-five by thirty-nine feet, containing dormitory rooms, some classrooms, and a chapel. Since Scott was then classified as a senior, it is probable that during the last months of his residence at the college, he enjoyed the luxury of a room in a brick building.

There is no diary extant for these months. However, one of his memorandum books contains the following short note under date of June 5, 1833: "Oh! that I could always think and store up a rich supply of ideas in my mind, to so occupy my soul that I would have no time to sin. . . O! thou God of intellect, give me power of Soul, give me strength of mind. . . My soul is bent on the acquisition of ideas. Oh! that every day & hour I could acquire new ideas, or recall to mind those that once I knew, but are now fled."

During the summer of 1833, Scott wrote to Princeton Theological Seminary regarding the possibility of taking work there. Dr. Archibald Alexander replied on September 17th saying: "If you bring with you a certificate of church membership, a certificate of having been graduated [from college] or the diploma itself, and a letter of recommendation from your principal instructor or from some respectable minister of the Gospel, you will need nothing more to gain admission." A simple process then as compared with modern day requirements for all prospective Presbyterian seminarians.

Among the prized items in the Scott Collection of papers is the original parchment diploma neatly inscribed in Latin which Scott received when he was graduated from Cumberland College on December 4, 1833. He received the Bachelor of Arts degree, his only earned scholastic degree. He was the valedictorian in his class of seven, described as being "a large and respectable class."

A YEAR AT PRINCETON THEOLOGICAL SEMINARY

Scott spent over a month with his parents and younger brothers at his old home on Big Creek before leaving for Princeton, New Jersey. He found his mother in frail health. She passed away during the following August, so this was the last time he was to see her. On Monday, January 13, 1834, Scott celebrated his twenty-first birthday. He had now reached man's estate by the calendar but actually he had attained that status long before. On the 28th he bade his loved ones a tearful farewell and left for another adventure in higher learning.

He traveled by water up the Mississippi and Ohio Rivers to Wheeling in what is now West Virginia, visiting Louisville, Kentucky, on February 4th. A couple of days later he was in Cincinnati. Of this visit, Scott commented briefly: "Did not stay long. It is a most splendid city. . . It is the 'Queen of the West'. It has 22 churches. In theology Dr. Beecher is the orator." Dr. Lyman Beecher was then president of Lane Theological Seminary, a Presbyterian institution which had been established at Walnut Hills, a suburb of the city, as a college of arts in 1829. The first theological class began in November 1833 with an enrollment of forty-two. Henry H. Spalding, who later became a famous missionary to Oregon, was a member of this class which he described as being the "largest Junior Theological Class in America." It was even larger than the one at Princeton.

Here at Cincinnati, perhaps for the first time in his life, Scott was confronted with the growing abolition sentiment. On February 4th, just two days before he landed in Cincinnati, the students at Lane, during the temporary absence of Dr. Beecher, began a series of eighteen evening debates on the slavery issue. Opinion was sharply divided over the relative merits of colonization, which called for the return to Africa of liberated Negroes, or complete abolition. Some of the theological students who strongly favored abolition decided to treat the Negro as their social equal. They invited the colored people into their homes and boarding places. They walked with them arm in arm on the streets. Since many of the residents of Cincinnati were from the South, they were deeply shocked. Before the debates were ordered stopped, the city was in a turmoil. Of course Scott did not see all of this, but he was there when the debates began and he could not have been unaware of the issues being discussed. Scott never dreamed in the wildest fancy of some terrible nightmare how deeply this ugly question of slavery was to affect his own life. For him the whole idea of abolition was then somewhat academic. The Civil War was still twenty-seven years away.

At Wheeling, Scott took the stage over the mountains to Frederick, Maryland, a ride of nearly three hundred miles. There he boarded "a car for Baltimore on the Rail Road," his first train ride. He noted its speed: it took seven hours to go eighty miles, but this was much faster and much more comfortable than riding on a stagecoach. At Baltimore he took passage on a steamboat which left at 6:00 a.m. for Frenchtown, on the eastern shore of Maryland, the terminus of a railroad which connected with New Castle. Frenchtown is near what is now Elkton, Maryland. The railroad which crossed the peninsula was sixteen and a half miles long, and had been completed in 1831. At first, the coaches, each of which carried fifteen passengers inside and out, were drawn by horses, but in September 1832 a steam locomotive was used. The claim is made that this was the first regular steam railroad passenger service in the United States. The train took an hour to make trip and Scott commented on the speed: "16 miles an hour!" It was an amazing achievement to him. At New Castle he boarded another steamer which carried him to Philadelphia. The whole journey from Baltimore took nine hours and the fare was "$4.00 exclusive of meals."

Scott did not indicate in his diary just how he traveled the last forty miles from Philadelphia to Princeton. Since he matriculated on Tuesday, February 18, 1834, we find that it took him about three weeks to go from his home in Tennessee to the seminary. By modern standards such slowness of travel would be considered a tedious waste of time. But a new era was dawning, and the railroads were beginning to weave a network of steel across the land.

Princeton Theological Seminary, founded by the Presbyterian Church in 1812, was in its twenty-second year when Scott enrolled. The seminary's campus was adjacent to that of the College of New Jersey which in 1896 was renamed Princeton University. In 1834 the seminary had two buildings, a faculty of four, and about 135 students. One of the buildings, Alexander Hall, contained classrooms, refectory, library, and student apartments. This building is now being used as a men's dormitory. The second building, also still standing, was Miller Chapel which had been erected the year before Scott's arrival. These structures were named after the seminary's first two professors, Archibald Alexander and Samuel Miller, both of whom were still active on the faculty when Scott was a student. In addition there was Dr. Charles Hodge who was to serve as a professor at the seminary for fifty-eight years, 1820-78. Because of his great learning, his long service, and the indelible stamp he left upon the theological thinking of the Presbyterian Church throughout the nineteenth century, he has been called the Thomas Aquinas of Princeton. The fourth member of the faculty when Scott enrolled was Joseph Addison Alexander, a son of Archibald, who was an instructor in the field of Oriental and Biblical literature.

Several of Scott's schoolmates were to become closely associated with him in later years. Among them were George Burrowes of the class of 1835, and Sylvester Woodbridge, Jr., of the class of 1834, both of whom became pioneer missionaries to California and were colleagues of Dr. Scott's when he lived in San Francisco. A third was James Adair Lyon, of the class of 1836, with whom Scott formed a warm friendship. Lyon unwittingly became a key figure in the Clay controversy of which fuller mention will be made later. The best description of Scott as a theological student is found in a book review written by Lyon of Scott's *Daniel* published in 1854. Lyon wrote:

> He is remembered as a great, big, fat, serious, sober, ruddy, smooth-faced, awkward boy, (yes, boy), with now and then a gleaming from his eyes! And for his ambitious diligence in study, and for a voracious appetite for books. Every dollar that came into his hands was laid out in books, until he had not, any longer the wherewith to meet his current expenses for board and clothing.

Scott was homesick and lonely during the first weeks at Princeton. Everything was on a much bigger scale than he had ever before experienced. He longed for the friendly atmosphere of Cumberland College. On February 21st he wrote to his friend Richard Beard back in Princeton, Kentucky: "This whole Seminary seems to me to act under the auspices of Self. All the operations of a grand machine savor of solitary self. It has no social bone in it. . . My operations are solitary . . . I wish I had such a telescope as would enable me to take a view of old C. College—and for a few moments enjoy the society of those whom I love."

But such feelings quickly passed as new friendships were formed. Soon Scott was deeply engrossed in his studies. He began the study of Hebrew. Joseph A. Alexander took a special interest in the young man from the backwoods of Tennessee and introduced him to Syriac and Arabic. Thus five of the eleven languages of which Scott attained some mastery were connected with the writings of the Sacred Scriptures, namely, Hebrew, Greek, Latin, Syriac, and Arabic. A warm friendship grew between J. A. Alexander and his student and it continued throughout their lives.

Captain Loomis, who used the title of "major" in his 1834 letters, was true to his promise regarding the lending of money. In his letter to Scott of October 21, 1833, he wrote: "Your wardrobe will no doubt want replenishing to appear like 'one of us'." Homespun was not in style at Princeton. Writing from Fort Snelling on August 29, 1834, the major repeated his promise "to send you as much as you need." By this time, however, Scott was becoming concerned over the amount of the indebtedness. This was the chief factor which caused him to leave Princeton that fall.

Among the items found in one of the chests containing Scott's manuscripts, mentioned in the appendix of this volume, was a diary which opened with an entry for August 16, 1834. This becomes another window through which we can look into the life of the young theological student at Princeton. Most of the entries deal with his spiritual meditations. On August 19th, he received a letter from his father telling of the death of his mother on July 29th. The diary shows not only the depth of his grief but also his great concern for his father and younger brothers. On August 31st he wrote: "Oh, that I could comfort them in some way —all I can do is to give my prayer—sometimes I have thoughts of going home, & comforting my Dear Father & trying to educate my Beloved Brothers."

Another disturbing factor was a call from the Presbyterian Church at Dutch Neck, located about five miles south and east of Princeton, to be its pastor. On August 31st, Scott stated his problem in his diary:

> I am now in great anxiety of mind. Instead of becoming stated preacher to P. church at Dutch Neck, I have received an unanimous & pressing call from the whole session to take charge of their congregation. I feel my own sinfulness, my own weakness, the great & awful & fearful responsibility of the office, so much that I fear & tremble exceedingly under it. Souls, immortal, precious, never-dying souls will be doubtless concerned in this matter. . . I tremble to take charge of it.

He pleaded his youth and inexperience but the elders continued to urge him to accept. Yielding to their persuasion, he consented to remain for a short time as stated supply. Already, even as a theological student, he was demonstrating those qualities which are essential in a successful minister, sincerity of personal faith, speaking ability, keenness of mind, and an unusual skill in expouding the Scriptures. Added to these assets were a pleasing personality, a love for people, and a genius for making friends. No wonder the church at Dutch Neck did all that was possible to induce this promising young man to be its minister.

On September 3rd, Scott noted in his diary: "Feel in great anxiety and distress in my mind on subject of taking charge of Congregation at Dutch Neck. I am afraid of going backward, or forward, or to the right or to the left. Lord teach me what to do . . . O that I may be useful." On September 6th, he wrote: "Yesterday received a letter from my dear friend, Rev. Prof. R. Beard of Cumberland College which makes me feel a good deal like leaving here; and going out into the world to preach Jesus and him crucified to perishing sinners." We are not told just what Beard wrote but judging by later developments it appears he urged Scott to terminate his studies at Princeton and take a church. It is probable that Beard reported the need for a pastor for a new church that had been organized about two years before at Opelousas, Louisiana. At the time Beard wrote there were only three Cumberland Presbyterian ministers at work in Louisiana. More were needed as the erection of a Cumberland Presbytery was being considered. No doubt Beard appealed to his denominational loyalty: Scott was a member of the Cumberland Church; he had been licensed by Hopewell Presbytery; he had been educated in Cumberland College; and now the church, his church, needed him. Would he go?

The letter arrived at a critical time. Scott was concerned over finances. His mother's death was an emotional shock which had left him restless. The church at Dutch Neck was urging him to accept its call. Moreover, there was a longing to return to his home for a visit. Scott sought out Dr. Archibald Alexander, who, after listening to his story, advised him to go but urged him to return later for his remaining two years of theological education. On September 21st, Scott wrote: "I have concluded it is my duty to leave here and go to the Southern States so that by some means I may be able to do something for my Dear Father & Bros. If God permit, I shall leave this Seminary soon and cast myself into the world pennyless, without experience, homeless!!! . . . O for a closer walk with God. . . O for eminent usefulness in the work of the Gospel Ministry!"

On Wednesday, October 1, 1834, Scott left Princeton for New York, where he planned to take passage on a ship bound for New Orleans. The Scott Collection in Bancroft Library contains the following statement of his work at Princeton:

> I do hereby certify, to all whom it may concern, that Mr. William Anderson Scott, entered the Theological Seminary at Princeton on the 18th day of February, A.D. 1834, that he continued to be a regular student in the Institution until the close of the ensuing summer session, when he withdrew from the Seminary for a time intending to return but that having been providentially prevented from fulfilling that intention, he is now regularly dismissed from the Institution in good standing. Given at Princeton this 29th day of April, A.D. 1836. Saml. Miller, Clerk pro tem of the Faculty.

This ended Scott's formal education which included two years at Cumberland College and seven and a half months at Princeton Theological Seminary. Since he was able to accomplish in his life so much on the basis of this limited formal education, we wonder what he might have done had he been able to take a full college and a complete seminary course in some well-established institutions.

Four Pastorates

The critical years in the lives of most ministers are those which follow graduation from seminary. This is the time when the young minister establishes a pattern of pastoral activities. He is still young and vigorous, eager to achieve. These are the years when the early hesitancy born out of inexperience grows into confidence and even boldness as he begins to use his training and discovers his abilities. These are often the years of short pastorates. There are always churches looking for young ministers of promise. Success in one parish leads to a call, usually with a larger stipend, in a larger field of usefulness.

During the seven years following his one year at Princeton Theological Seminary, Scott served in four different parishes with an average residence of about two years in each. These were years of rapid maturation as he moved upward in his profession from one field to another. When Scott left Princeton he was not ordained. He was still a licensed preacher in the Cumberland Presbyterian Church. Within seven years he had shown such promise of future greatness and had demonstrated such ability that he was called to the pulpit of the First Presbyterian Church of New Orleans, one of the leading churches of the entire South.

AT OPELOUSAS, LOUISIANA

Scott reached New York, Wednesday afternoon, October 1, 1834, and secured passage abroad a vessel bound for New Orleans for $50, "to pay on my arrival at the city." He noted in his diary that he was then "almost pennyless, a stranger among strangers." He had to wait several days before the ship was ready to sail during which time he had opportunity to see the sights of the city. Thirty years later he was to be pastor of one of the largest Presbyterian churches of New York, but in 1834 he had no crystal ball to forecast such an improbable future.

On Sunday, October 5th, he resumed writing in his diary: "Ship hauled off, sails unfurled, gentle breezes blow and about 12 a.m. we are under way just after having all New York echo with the sound of the church bells. It was a solemn sight on a calm Sunday to view the City with the Battery & Islands adjacent & fortifications & bid it a long farewell, perhaps an everlasting adieu!!"

Scott was seasick most of the first week of the voyage. He wrote: "Passed my time heavily. . . Felt a good deal concerned in my mind about my success if God should please to permit me to arrive in La., the present anticipated field of labor. I feel very anxious to be trying to preach and bring sinners to a knowledge of Jesus Christ. O that I may be an humble, useful, & holy instrument in converting souls to God." Then followed a prayer which is typical of many others which appear throughout his diaries. "Come Holy Spirit, come, come dwell in this cold heart of mine. . . May I be willing to do anything, live anywhere, or die anywhere, when & where it is your will. . . Most Gracious God, in solemn covenant I anew devote myself to Thee, & be forever thine, now, henceforth, and for ever. Even so Lord Jesus, Come quickly, reign in my heart. William A. Scott."

The voyage from New York to New Orleans lasted about twenty-three days. He spent much time reading. His comments on Goldsmith's *Vicar of Wakefield* give a flash of insight on his life's philosophy:

> Remember the Vicar of Wakefield says: "You see me, young man, I have no talents and I don't find that I have ever missed it. I have a full bottomed [i.e., lined] wig, and silk gown without talent; I have a thousand a year without talent; . . . and in short as I have no talent, I do not believe there is any good in it."—So I will try to get along with some name [i.e., reputation] for talents, and if I fail, then try without talents. There is a hole in the world for every frog; and if I can find my hole, I will squawk there till my light goes out.

An entry in Scott's diary for October 21st states that his ship was moving up the Mississippi towards New Orleans. We are not told how he secured the money after his arrival to pay for his passage. No doubt he was met in New Orleans by some representative of the Cumberland Presbyterian Church who relieved his financial needs and gave him directions as to his future parish at Opelousas. This was about sixty-five miles west of Baton Rouge in the heart of the Acadian country later to be made famous by Longfellow's *Evangeline*. The present word Cajun is a corruption of Acadian. The Cumberland Church began work in Louisiana in 1831 and the Rev. John W. Ogden organized the church at Opelousas with forty members in March 1832. A building was erected shortly thereafter.

Scott's diary shows that he began his work at Opelousas the first week of January, 1835. The interval between his arrival in New Orleans and his settlement at Opelousas would have given him time to proceed the 475 miles up the Mississippi River to Memphis and visit his father and brothers. We have reason to believe that while in New Orleans, Scott went to Lafayette Square where the First Presbyterian Church was erecting its new building. Construction began in the late fall of 1834. The pastor of the church was the Rev. Joel Parker who in 1840 became the second president of Union Theological Seminary in New York City. By no soaring flight of the imagination could the young Scott then have dreamed of the possibility of being pastor of that important church about seven years later.

A new diary-notebook was started on January 2, 1835, with the following entry: "Bayou Chicos, Lou. One more year is gone. A new one is commenced. It may be my last on earth. O that I may be humble and faithful in the service of my Blessed Saviour. I am now settling at Opelousas & with much fear and trembling. I am about to try to take charge of this congregation. Oh, how great is the responsibility." A note of humility is revealed in his frequent use of the expressions "to try to take charge" or "to try to preach." On January 5th he noted the rental of a house. A certain awareness of death is found in this diary, possibly caused by the memory of the passing of his mother. In this first entry he also wrote: "I do solemnly resolve to try to be ready to die, and yet willing and anxious to live, if God be pleased to spare me. But from my beginning of this new year and of my new residence, I will renewedly try to be ready, by grace, for a new habitation in Heaven, whenever God shall send for me. Amen."

The diary contains only a few entries for January and nothing more until April 3rd when under the heading "Pastor's Resolution" the following appears:

I will spend some extraordinary time in private devotions every Lord's Day, morning or evening, as opportunity may offer, and will then endeavor *to preach over to my own soul* that doctrine which I preach to others. At the close of each week and month, I will carefully review, that I may see what improvements or want of improvement I have made. To see what good has been done or what opportunities of doing good I have neglected.

In all my duties I will strive to be patient, to seek and humbly rely upon divine aid and to be serious, tender and affectionate to all, especially to the young.

The oldest extant manuscript sermon of Dr. Scott's, now on deposit in the San Francisco Theological Seminary, is one written for Sunday, April 19, 1835. It is titled, "The Way to be Saved." In this early sermon we see the pattern of his sermonizing methods which he followed throughout his life. He had no time-saving typewriter. Everything was laboriously written out by hand, and for years with a quill pen. By modern standards, his early sermons would be judged to be too long, too doctrinal, and lacking in good illustrations. Scott was a confirmed Calvinist and his sermons were deeply imbued with the teachings of the Westminster Confession of Faith.

An entry in Scott's diary for September 26, 1835, reveals his preaching methods: "Have just finished a sermon," he wrote, "and feel much disposed to read it. I doubt the propriety. This congregation are prejudiced against reading sermons." In the early years of his ministry, Scott often read his discourses. Even when he did not do so, he liked to have his manuscript on the pulpit before him. All evidence points to the conclusion that when preaching, he often broke through the manuscript barrier and spoke extemporaneously with great effectiveness. These dry and literally musty old sermons that have been exhumed from the once water-soaked chests fail to reveal the flash of his personality, the contagious enthusiasm of his voice, and the deep sincerity of his faith. These were the indescribable qualities which flowed together into that attractive personality which drew people to him.

Scott had the custom during the early years of his ministry of saving most of his sermon manuscripts. Sometimes they would be used again after revision and notations made on the back as to when and where they were delivered. This sermon dated April 19, 1835, also bears the notation, "San Francisco, 14 March 1858."

Louisiana Presbytery of the Cumberland Presbyterian Church was organized on March 13, 1835, with three charter minister members. The first meeting, subsequent to its organization, was held in the Cumberland Church of Alexandria on May 17th at which time William Anderson Scott was ordained. Kneeling with him when the hands of the presbyters were laid on his head in the ordination service was another young man, Sumner Bacon, who was to win acclaim as a self-appointed and self-supporting missionary to Texas, then a foreign land.

With Opelousas as his headquarters, Scott made itinerating trips on horseback through the surrounding country and even across the border into southern Arkansas. He later wrote of visiting "Red River, Bayou Boeuf, and Alexandria," and of his experiences "fording creeks, and swimming bayous infested with alligators, often in peril of life." Although the country through which he rode was more developed than that which he had covered four years ealier as a circuit rider in northwestern Tennessee, yet much of it was still raw frontier.

Scott opened a school at Opelousas. An entry in his diary for October 23, 1835, reads: "I began teaching on Monday the 12 inst. Have 22 scholars." He found this a heavy load to carry in addition to his other duties, but justified it by writing: "I hope to do good to some poor children. I had rather be in my grave then to be idle." On the first page of his Opelousas diary, he scheduled his studies. "I find I must have system to save time," he wrote. "Monday, Hebrew; Tuesday, Greek; Wednesday, Hebrew; Thursday, Greek; Friday, Miscellany; Saturday, Latin and Church History. Sabbath try to preach." The expression "try to preach" which occurs so frequently in Scott's earlier writings reflects his humble realization that he was not measuring up to his ideal as a preacher.

Opelousas is located in the heart of Louisiana's French community. It was bilingual in Scott's day and still is, although the French spoken there today is a distinct dialect, quite different from that used in France. Since Scott became eloquent in the French language, we may assume that he acquired some fluency in its use during his residence at Opelousas. His diary records frequent periods of illness during these days. On January 21, 1835, he noted: "To-day am quite ill. My bones ache exceedingly. I am in a great deal of misery." And on September 18th: "I have been ill for a week, a relapse of billious fever which first came on me about 25 of August." In later years Scott suffered much from ill health of which further mention will be made later.

Now in his twenty-third year, it was natural that Scott should think of getting married. We know from references in his diary written while at Prairie du Chien that he was in love with Ann Nicholson. It may be assumed that some correspondence had passed between them and possibly Scott had had some opportunity to visit her, but of this we have no record. On September 22, 1835, we find him writing:

> For several days, indeed for months, I have felt much at a loss to know what course to take for the next year. . . It is now my conviction that but for one circumstance, I should return to the Theo. Seminary and spend another year. The forbidding circumstance is a tender of my hand and heart to Miss————, whether she will reciprocate or not I do not know. Time will reveal. O Lord direct me. If she gives me a capote, [i.e., here's your hat], it is my deliberate determination to return to the Seminary.

Included in the Scott Collection in the Bancroft Library are a few letters to Ann Nicholson from her father or from friends for the years 1832-35. The first of this series from Dr. Nicholson is dated September 13, 1832, from Huntingdon and is addressed to his daughter at the "Female Academy, Nashville." Evidently Ann had then been at the academy long enough to have become well established for her father wrote: "You now have the good fortune to be a favorite in the Institution and to be highly esteemed by many of the good citizens of Nashville, and have attracted the attention of almost all your old acquaintances from this place. This is to me a great satisfaction." The letter also carried the following reference to Ann's childhood. "Your early life," the father wrote, "was one of difficulty and trouble, the clouds of adversity lowered long and dark on your infant head." Again on November 16th of the same year Dr. Nicholson wrote: "We have not had a ball here since you went away which by the bye I don't care for, but it will give you some idea of the falling off. We have had little preaching either & when we have one he is a jackleg. I mention this lest you should think the cessation of dancing was owing to religious zeal, but no such thing for we are almost here in a state of nonentity."

Another letter from the father, dated December 5th, indicates his difficulty in raising enough money to cover her expenses. "I shall be able to collect something between fifty & one hundred dollars," he wrote, "I know this will come far short of paying up." Dr. Nicholson wrote again on January 23, 1833, saying that he had sold his house for $360 and was closing his practice preparatory to moving but he did not indicate where. "The state of affairs here at present," he wrote, "is disheartening beyond any thing I have experienced." He mentioned

Mila, Ann's Negro slave, and added that "I shall take her with me." The last letter of the series from the father to his daughter is dated May 22, 1835, and was written from Canton in Madison County, Mississippi, where he had settled and was practicing medicine.

We do not know just when Ann was graduated from the academy. There is evidence that she was a teacher at the academy beginning with the fall term of 1834. A letter from a friend dated March 4, 1835, includes the request: "Will you be so good as to see that Miss Wilson drinks freely of the surip [i.e., cough syrup]." No doubt Ann was then serving not only as a teacher but also as one of the supervisors in the boarding department.

Uncertain as to whether Ann would accept his proposal, William felt it wise to consider alternate plans. If she rejected his offer of marriage, he would return to Princeton, New Jersey. His diary continues:

> [I would] send my trunk in a box to New York via New Orleans, travel through myself on horse back and so see a great portion of the country . . . so as to begin at the commencement of a new year. Ho! what an airy castle! But how knows but that I may yet realize it. Lord have mercy upon me and lead me. Education —my thirst is so great for knowledge that were it not for my proposal to Miss ---, I would humbly relying on Divine Providence make the attempt [i.e., to return to Princeton].

Ann accepted. Scott promptly gave up all thoughts of re-entering the seminary, as theological seminaries in those days rarely accepted married students. Plans were hastily made for the marriage to take place in January. A brief news item in the *Nashville Republican* for January 21, 1836, recorded the big event: "Married. In this place, Jan. 19th by the Rev. Mr. Lapsley, Rev. W. A. Scott of Louisiana to Miss Ann Nicholson of this city." Lapsley, a Presbyterian, U.S.A., minister, was then principal of the Nashville Female Academy.

William A. Scott was doubly blessed in finding such a helpmate as Ann Nicholson. Few professions are so demanding upon the wife as the ministry. A minister can be made or unmade by his wife. Although not a church member at the time of her marriage, Ann soon afterwards joined and gave her husband full and sympathetic support in his ministerial labors. Much of William's later success in the ministry may be credited to this loyal and effective cooperation rendered by Ann.

Ann was a vivacious brunette, tall and slender. Well-educated for her day, she loved music and played the piano. Her letters show her to have been a sensible and capable person. Throughout her married life, she was an affectionate wife, a loving mother to their nine children, and was most efficient in the management of her household.

Scott failed to make any entries in his diary during the first four months of 1836. Then on May 8th, he made a brief reference to his marriage and indicated that he and his bride had stopped over at Mem-

ANN NICHOLSON SCOTT, ABOUT 1853
Possibly by the artist who painted Dr. Scott in New Orleans.
Original owned by Mrs. Anna Draper of San Francisco.

phis to see his father and brothers. William's father, Eli Scott, remarried on November 23, 1835. His second wife, Sarah Irwin, was a widow, twenty-five or thirty years younger than he. Eli was then sixty-one. Since only occasional references to Sarah have been found in any of the extant source material, we know little about her. William probably met her for the first time when he and Ann visited them in February 1836.

While in Memphis William purchased a four-volume set of Oliver Goldsmith's A *History of the Earth and Animated Nature* and gave the books to his bride. Not knowing Ann's interest in such a scientific work, we may safely surmise that her husband found them fascinating. Volume I bears an inscription in William's handwriting: "A. N. Scott's book, Memphis, 1836, $8.00." Volumes II and IV carried the notation: "A. N. Scott's, Opelousas, La." Volume III contains a longer inscription: "A. N. Scott's, Opelousas, La. Presented by her affectionate husband, Feb. 6, 1836." This set was donated to the library of San Francisco Theological Seminary by Paul Eli Scott, a grandson.

On their way down the Mississippi, William and Ann stopped at Vicksburg and went inland to Canton to visit Ann's father, Dr. Nicholson. "Finally arrived at home in Opelousas the 18th day of February," he wrote in his diary, "and resumed my school labors as usual."

Judging by later developments, Scott, while at Nashville, applied for a position which was opening up at Winchester, Tennessee, about eighty-five miles southeast of Nashville. There the Cumberland Presbyterian Church needed a minister who would serve in the double capacity as pastor of the local congregation and principal of a female academy. According to an entry in Scott's diary for May 8, 1836, he received word on the previous March 8th of the call having been extended "inviting me to become their Pastor and also from the Trustees of the Female Institute at Winchester to take the presidency of it and Mrs. Scott in the head department." Although Scott had served in Opelousas for only fourteen months when he received the news of the call, yet both he and Ann felt that they should move. Of this Scott wrote in his diary: "After much prayer . . . I at length determined to remove to Winchester —simply because my health was bad & would probably become worse, and my field of labor was very much confined. But the field presented there is large & the prospect of health & usefulness much greater."

On April 25th, William and Ann said goodby to their friends in Opelousas and left for New Orleans where they secured passage on a river boat for Nashville. By May 8th, they were back in Memphis. They arrived in Nashville in time for William to take part in the sessions of the Cumberland General Assembly which opened on May 17th. William was enrolled as a commissioner from the Presbytery of Louisiana.

The author of this book and his wife visited Opelousas in the spring of 1962 and found that all memory of Scott's sixteen-month ministry in that community had passed. There is no longer a Cumberland Presbyterian church in the locality. The First Presbyterian Church, U.S., of Opelousas was founded in 1871, nearly forty years after the Cumberland Presbyterians had started their work but there seems to be no connection between the two bodies. Opelousas today retains its Spanish colonial atmosphere with a strong French flavor, and it is still bilingual. Standing amidst moss draped oaks are a number of old southern mansions which were there when the Scotts were residents.

TWO YEARS AT WINCHESTER

Scott took an active part in the deliberations of the Cumberland General Assembly which met that year in Nashville. Although he was only twenty-three years old and had been ordained for only a little more than one year, he was given some important assignments. He was made a member of the board of directors of the Foreign Missionary Society. He served as clerk of the committee to report on the "State of Religion" and wrote the narrative printed in the Assembly's minutes. The following extract from this article is typical of the flamboyant style found in some of his writings when he strove to be eloquent: "Let her [i.e., the church] not think of laying aside the armor of truth, until the song of redeemed souls from the valley of the Mississippi be echoed by the kindred spirits of the Rhine, the Danube, and the Nile, and the incense of a grateful heart and the song of glory to God for redeeming grace, shall ascent simultaneously from the banks of the Euphrates and the far western Islands." This report is no doubt the first time that any of his writings were published.

Shortly after the close of the General Assembly, the Scotts moved to Winchester. This, the county seat of Franklin County, was located in a farming community. Scott began his work at once in the church and some time in June both he and his wife began teaching in the newly established female academy. The Cumberland Presbyterian Church of Winchester was organized in July 1825 and in 1827 erected a log church on North Jefferson Street. It is interesting to note how much of Scott's early life was connected with the raw frontier of which the log cabin was a vivid symbol. He was born in a log cabin and his early homes in Sangamon County, Illinois, and at Raleigh, Tennessee, were log cabins. His first schools were held in log cabins and he attended a log cabin college in Kentucky. Now at Winchester he was preaching in a log cabin church.

The original minutes of the session of this church have not been located but we are able to obtain a good idea of his activities from the diary which William kept with fair regularity through the summer months of 1836.

> June 25. Tonight I was wearied having been confined all day writing a sermon on Acts 16:30. I have been wofully negligent in two respects, not keeping up my Diary and in not rising early. Do I not know that no man will come to any considerable usefulness

who does not rise early? Resolved, by the help of the Lord, that I will try to reform. I do resolve that I will rise at 5 o'c.   .   .

June 26. This was sabbath. Preached at $\frac{1}{2}$ past 10 a.m. to a large congregation.   .   . Heard a Mr. Green preach at 3 o'c p.m. in the Methodist Church. Preached again at candle lighting. Attended sabbath school this morning. I am now very much fatigued from the labors of the day.   .   . But I rejoice that I am counted worthy to labor for Him who has done so much to redeem my soul from hell.   .   . Lord Jesus I would earnestly and sincerely devote and dedicate my time, my talents, my heart, & all, that thou hast given me to thy service.   .   . O Lord bless my dear wife, Thou in thy providence hast given her to me. O that I may be an affectionate, tender & faithful husband.

June 27. Today quite well. All day in the Academy.   .   . To night attended a meeting of the citizens of Winchester to form A. Bible Society auxiliary to the American Bible Society. Was elected President of the Society. My dear wife accompanied me to church. O how thankful to heaven for such a companion, one so well suited to me. One so lovely & interesting.

The organization of a branch of the American Bible Society in Winchester reminds us that another auxiliary had been formed in the Rock Creek community in 1815 in which Scott's parents were members.

Scott made occasional references in his diary to periods of ill health. He was thus afflicted for at least twenty years. At the very beginning of his ministry in Winchester, he found the task of teaching five days a week in the academy and then preaching twice on Sunday a heavy burden. In a short review of her husband's life written after his death in 1885, Mrs. Scott remembered that he often worked until one or two o'clock in the morning "to effect the careful preparation without which he never entered the pulpit." His diary continues with this entry for Wednesday, June 19th:

To day in tolerable good health—somewhat melancholy—discouraged—am settling in a new place, my character is to form— and my labors are so numerous, and I feel so ignorant and so poor a servant, that I am almost ready to yield under the burden. To teach all week & preach two or three sermons too. This evening my dear wife accompanied me to Benjamin Deckerd's Esq. We spent a pleasant evening—took tea. Read the 25th chapter of Isaiah & prayer. Lord bless us.

July 5th 1836. Rose this morning late, owing to my feeble state of health, and the extreme fatigue of last evening—preached last night, being monthly concert for prayer.   .   . Large and attentive congregation.   .   . I find my wife to be truly an helpmate—a solace to me in all my troubles—her smiles lighten up the hours of gloom. Her warm heart shares and soothes my griefs.   .   . She studies my happiness, and all my wishes find a feeling echo in her bosom.

July 6th (Wednesday) Rose early this morning—tolerable health. Rode out several miles and returned to breakfast. Feel calm and composed as to myself. Devoting the scraps of time that I can command from the Academy to thinking on a sermon for the next Lord's day. My time is so occupied and my health so feeble, that I have to preach without the preparation which I desire, & which I think very necessary for the pulpit.

This entry has the following brief reference to his courtship. "How true is it that a good wife is a gift from the Lord! What a gracious providence preserved us during a separation of near six years, & brought us together then to be all the world to each other." Six years earlier, or in the spring of 1830, Scott was riding the circuit in northwestern Tennessee.

Again we find a complaint about ill health in an entry for July 12th. "Seems to me I am declining," he wrote, "pain in breast, and oh! my labors are so asiduous and numerous—but it is better to wear out than to rust out as Bishop Cumberland said." This well-known quotation of Bishop Richard Cumberland (1632-1718) was one of Scott's favorites and serves as a good index to his life's philosophy.

Scott's diary shows that Ann was sharing his pastoral duties with him as well as his school work. She accompanied him on his calls and took part in their private devotions. In July she joined the church on confession of faith. Scott tells of his joy in his diary. "July 15 . . . What a gift has thou confered on me, in giving me an *affectionate, mild, good tempered* and *exceedingly kind,* and now I can add *pious* wife. Truly a good wife is from the Lord." The word "pious" was double underlined. "My dear wife conversed with the Session of elders and minister [i.e., himself] as to the work of grace in her heart and they received her into the full fellowship and communion of this church. . . This was an event long and fervently desired by me. Sabbath July 17 . . . The congregation was very large and attentive. . . At the close of the sermon, we had the sacrament of Lord's Supper. . . I saw my dear wife for the first time communing with the Lord's people." We are not told why Ann delayed so long before joining a church. Although it is possible that there was no organized church in Huntingdon where she spent her girlhood, she surely would have had an opportunity to become a member when she was teaching in Nashville shortly before her marriage.

Scott was imbued with the old Puritanical objections to undue levity and any sinful waste of time. There was something incompatible in the mind of the Puritan between being pious and having fun. From his earliest infancy William Scott had been imbued in his home, his schools, and his church with such ideas. Life was serious business. It was permissible for children to play but not adults. This commonly accepted standard of conduct, so widely held in that generation by those reared in the Puritan tradition, should be remembered when we come to the following entry in Scott's diary for Monday, July 18th, after he and Ann had spent an evening with some neighbors. "To-day," he wrote, "suffering from a headache in school. Evening accompanied by ever beloved Ann to Mr. Campbell's. There contrary to our expectations, we found preparations for a party. That vexed me, remained in a sort of purgatory until tea—which was late." As soon as they could politely do so, the Scott's left. He concluded the entry for that day with the following:

> Whereas family and tea parties are evils—a waste of opportunities to improve my own mind and to do good to others—a murderer of time, the most precious of heaven's gifts—and calculated to lead the soul away from God, & to increase a desire for the world & its vanities. Therefore, by me, Resolved, never to go to such parties by whomsoever given;—unless, I am induced to believe they will be religious and ended by prayer. O that I were more humble as a Christian, and more holy and faithful as a minister.

Little is known about the Winchester Female Academy since the original records are believed to be lost. Winchester had a school for boys known as Carrick Academy which antedated the founding of the school for girls. In the original record book of this school, under date of March 3, 1835, is the notation of a loan for $800 made to the trustees of the Female Academy which was then in the process of getting established. A two-story building, for day students only, was erected in the center of a large vacant block dotted with beautiful oak trees. The building faced on what is now North Cedar Street. Sometime in the middle 1850s the academy became a part of the public school system. The building burned in 1894. Some idea of the tuition charges in the Female Academy may be secured from the records of Carrick Academy where the following notation for June 26, 1837, reads: "Small boy, beginning reading & spelling, $10.00. Higher branches . . . $12.50; Mathematics and Classics $16.00. The above prices per session."

Among the extant Scott manuscripts are two sermons written for his Winchester congregation for Sundays, October 9 and 23, 1836, and an address given on December 4, 1837, before an audience of parents, trustees, teachers, and friends of the academy. This is the address which contained the personal reference to his studying under the Rev. Aaron Shelby to which mention has already been made. The following quotation from the lecture shows how Scott was magnifying the work of the teacher: "When a man loses all anxiety for the good opinion of his fellowmen, he has lost all self-respect, and deserves neither the confidence nor the esteem of the community. . . An education that does not regard the heart as well as the head; the religious as well as the intellectual faculties, is defective. While knowledge is power, it is not necessarily virtuous." Scott rose to the climax of his lecture with the words:

There is no profession that requires so much diligence and punctuality, such habits of order and attention, as that of the teacher. His life is a continued climbing up hill, a continual rowing against the current. He has his pupils to govern and instruct —a hundred tempers to manage and a thousand little passions to curb—the parents and public to please and gratify—and what is more, he must conquer his own love of ease and overcome a deep rooted, long innate & perverse ignorance. Then, who needs so much stimulus, so much encouragement as the humble and devoted teacher? How else can he be prevailed upon to continue a calling so responsible, so laborious and oftentimes so perplexing?

Wise words from a young man only twenty-three years old!

Several entries in Scott's diary for the last of July and the first part of August tell of recurring periods of depression. On July 27th, he wrote: "To day very feeble and melancholy. All morning thought I surely would die soon. Old as I am, to be so gloomy and melancholy is a sin. Lord forgive me." And on August 1st: "This is the first day of a new month. I may not live to the end of it and am now nearer to my journey's end than ever before. My time to labor grows shorter and shorter."

There were in the vicinity of Winchester a number of mineral springs which were highly valued by the local residents for their medicinal qualities. Resorts had been established at several of these springs at the time the Scott's were living in the county. This explains the following entry in the diary for August 30, 1836: "To day in company with Hon. Judge [Nathan] Green & family came to the Caliliah Spring, 10 miles from Winchester. I have obtained release from my labors for two weeks on account of ill health. . . But one circumstance & this would be a palace—that is the dear partner of my life is not with me. . ." A few days later Ann joined her husband at Chalybeati Springs. William was overjoyed. "She came out on Friday," he noted in his diary, "to stay with me in this solitary place till Monday. To day I am quite well."

William and Ann had missed the romance and thrill that lovers often find in months and sometimes years of a happy courtship. Now in the early part of their married life they were tasting for the first time the bliss of a consuming passion which bound them together. On September 8th, Scott noted the receipt of a letter from Ann and then broke forth in his diary in a paean of praise for love. "O that I could comprehend the anatomy of love; that I could analyse this mysterious yet divine passion—an affection always strong, but constantly growing stronger and stronger—taking root deeper and deeper." He added that nothing except death itself could be worse than absence from his beloved. Several days passed without a letter from Ann and then another arrived. "A letter, a letter—a precious letter," he exulted. "It has been read—read— read numberless times & kissed again and again, and oh, it is signed 'Ever, Ever, Ever your own Anna'."

On January 21, 1837, two days after they had celebrated the first anniversary of their marriage, Ann gave birth to a baby boy. Even as William had been named after his maternal grandfather, William Anderson, so the new arrival was given the name of Ann's father, Robert Nicholson. The proud father told his friends that January was his lucky month. He was born and married in January and now his first-born had arrived in the same month. When the subject of baptism was raised, William suggested that they ask the Rev. Thomas J. Hall, who was still serving as pastor of the Bethbirei Church near Lewisburg, Tennessee, about forty miles from Winchester, to officiate. Father Hall had baptised William when he was a baby. The Scott family Bible contains the record of Robert's birth with the additional notation: ". . . and was solemnly dedicated to Almighty God in ordinance of Baptism by Rev. Mr. Hall on Sab. the 13th of August 1837. In Winchester."

Little is known of the activities of the Scott's during the remaining months of their residence in Winchester as William seems to have been too busy to have kept up his diary. On July 8, 1837, he wrote: "It is now almost one year since any notice of my life has been penned in this book. . . When I look over the past year! How great has been the goodness and longsuffering and forbearance of my Heavenly Father. My health has been delicate, but he has lengthened out my life. My cup runneth over. He has spared my dearest wife—a companion of my labors and sorrows and joys and hopes. And he has given us a son & spared him with us." Another entry appears two days later: "To day have been writing all day. I am very anxious to do something in this world that I may be an humble, holy and useful pastor."

In the Scott Collection in Bancroft Library is a letter from Joseph A. Alexander, one of Scott's instructors at Princeton Theological Seminary, dated August 22, 1837. Evidently Scott had written to Alexander asking for information about books on Arabic and Syriac. Alexander replied that such works were difficult to obtain. He also wrote: "The interruption of your studies here was a matter of regret to myself as well as you. I am glad to find that I was not mistaken as to your capacity & taste for philological pursuits. At present I can only say that if you design to be a thorough philologist, you should study German." Later Scott acted on this advice.

TWO YEARS AT NASHVILLE

In the spring of 1838, following the resignation of the Rev. Robert A. Lapsley as principal of the Nashville Female Academy, the trustees of that institution extended a call to Scott to fill the vacancy. He accepted with pleasure as he had found the combined work of being the head of a school and the pastor of a church, where two sermons were expected each Sunday in addition to the usual parish duties, too much for him. Although he was probably aware that he would be expected to conduct Sunday services in two country churches near Nashville on alternate Sundays, still preaching one sermon in the same church every other week

THE FEMALE ACADEMY, NASHVILLE, TENNESSEE

As it appeared about the time Scott served as its principal. Courtesy of the City Library, Nashville.

was much easier than preparing two new sermons for each Sunday. Moreover, by this time Scott had a supply of sermons on hand which could be used over again and this he often did as notations of time and place on the back of the manuscripts indicate. Undoubtedly since the academy in Nashville was older and much larger than the newly established school in Winchester, it could provide a larger stipend. The Scott's moved to Nashville in the late summer or early fall of 1838.

The Nashville Female Academy was founded by a Scotch Presbyterian clergyman, the Rev. John Hume, in 1816. By 1838 it had the reputation of being the best girls' academy in the state with both boarding and day school departments. The buildings were located on a five-acre campus on Church Street east of the later Chattanooga railroad depot and were described in the *Nashville City Directory* of 1860 as being "large, commodious and convenient, containing 125 rooms for personal use, including the chapel, seventy four by fifty feet, and the exercise hall, 120 by 40 feet." The central part of the main building is pictured in an old print as having three stories, with a two-story wing on each end. The grounds were well shaded with native oaks and cedars.

According to the *History of Nashville,* the academy had 173 pupils in 1838 when Scott began his duties. The next year the attendance rose to 258 but dropped to 198 in 1840. Scott had about ten teachers on his staff. On the eve of the outbreak of the Civil War, the Nashville Female Academy had over five hundred students and claimed to be the largest girls' school in the country. When news of the capture of Fort Donelson on the Cumberland River by federal troops reached Nashville on February 16, 1862, the wildest excitement prevailed. All who could, fled the city. Of course it was unthinkable that a dormitory full of girls should remain when an army of soldiers was approaching. So within a few hours after the receipt of the terrifying news, most of the boarding students of the academy were sent away on one of the crowded trains leaving the city. This marked the end of a flourishing institution for all efforts failed to revive it after the war.

During his two years residence in Nashville, Scott served two small country Presbyterian churches on alternate Sundays. One was the Little Harpeth Church located near the Little Harpeth River on the Hillsboro road about ten miles southwest of Nashville. This church was organized, perhaps by Gideon Blackburn, the famous pioneer missionary to Tennessee, in 1811. The congregation worshipped in a log building until 1836 when a brick church measuring forty by sixty feet was erected. It was in this building that Scott conducted his services. In 1954 a bell tower and narthex were added to the front of the building and in 1958 an educational unit was built. The present sanctuary is the original building. The old pews and the pulpit, probably there in Scott's day, are still in use. The church in 1840 reported forty members.

On April 14, 1962, the author visited Harpeth and was shown the original sessional minutes of the church by its pastor, the Rev. Priestley

PRESBYTERIAN CHURCH AT HARPETH, NEAR NASHVILLE
Here Scott served as stated supply, 1838-40. The central section of the building is the
original structure used by Scott's congregation. Photo by the author.

Miller. The following two items which mentioned Scott were noted:
"Oct. 1838. The Reverend Wm. A. Scott appointed by Presbytery to
preach at the Little Harpeth Church until the next meeting of Presbytery" and for April 13, 1839: "The Reverend Wm. A. Scott appointed
by Presbytery as a supply at the Harpeth Church." No doubt Scott
followed the custom of riding horseback to the Harpeth community on
Saturday, spending the night in the home of one of the members, and
returning to Nashville on Sunday afternoon.

The second country church served by Scott during the years he lived
at Nashville was located on the estate of General Andrew Jackson eleven
or twelve miles east of Nashville. The history of the Hermitage Church
goes back to 1817 when religious services were conducted in a small
schoolhouse in the vicinity. When this building burned in 1819, Rachel,
the wife of General Jackson, told her husband that she felt lost without
a place in which she could meet with others to worship. Partly as a
result of her intercession, General Jackson donated a site of three acres
for a church less than a mile from his southern colonial mansion, the
Hermitage. A brick building, thirty by fifty feet, was erected in 1823
which was dedicated as the Ephesus Church the following year. About
1832 this church was received into the Nashville Presbytery of the
Presbyterian Church, U.S.A. The building is still in use.

General Jackson served two terms, 1829-37, as the seventh president of the United States. Although a deeply religious man, he was not a member of any church when elected to the presidency. He refrained from joining the church of his preference, the Presbyterian, during his occupancy of the White House for fear that some would say that he did so for political reasons. After his retirement to the Hermitage, in September 1837, Jackson was received into the membership of Ephesus Church on confession of faith. Dr. J. T. Edgar, then pastor of the First Presbyterian Church of Nashville, acted as moderator at the time the general was received. The church was crowded for the occasion with many black faces peering through the windows. Dr. Edgar, being fully aware of the strong likes and dislikes of the doughty old warrior asked him as he stood before the congregation to make his confession of faith: "Do you have any malice toward any one?" The general hesitated a moment and then in blunt frankness answered: "I have." "Then we can not receive you into this church," replied the minister. Again there was silence, a breathless silence shared by the congregation. Tears began to roll down the general's cheeks. Finally he said, "I forgive them all." With that, according to the story still being told by old-timers in Nashville, those staid Presbyterians broke out in shouts of joy. Jackson really made a double confession that day. His first was in Jesus Christ as his Savior; the second was in forgiving love.

After he had joined the church, the members wanted to make the general an elder. This office, however, he declined to accept saying that he was then seventy-two years old and the church should have younger men as elders. He remained as the most liberal supporter of the church and no one was more faithful in attendance than he.

The Ephesus Church had only eighteen members when Scott began his service as stated supply. During his two year ministry, two new members were received and Scott reported nine baptisms. At the September 1839 meeting of Nashville Presbytery, the name of the church was changed to the Hermitage Church by which it is still known. Perhaps Scott had something to do with this change of name. Both the Hermitage and the Harpeth churches are now part of the Presbyterian Church, U.S., often referred to as the Southern Presbyterian Church.

General Jackson's beloved Rachel died on December 22, 1828. They had no children but in 1809 he adopted a nephew of Mrs. Jackson's, of the Donelson family, who took the name Andrew Jackson, Jr. He married Sarah York who was greatly loved by the general, ranking next to his deceased wife in his affections. Fire destroyed much of the interior of the Hermitage in 1834 but the mansion had been repaired and redecorated by 1838. Today the Hermitage is the only great national shrine having the original furnishings throughout. The rooms as the tourists see them today are very much the same as they were when William and Ann were guests in the home.

The great hall is decorated with pictorial wall paper imported from

THE HERMITAGE CHURCH AT ANDREW JACKSON'S HOME
Here Scott served as stated supply, 1838-40. Photo by the author.

HERMITAGE, THE HOME OF GENERAL ANDREW JACKSON
Scott, while in Nashville, was a frequent visitor here.
Here also, Scott's daughter, Martha, was born. Photo by the author.

Paris. The graceful winding stairway, half-hanging in the air, is an architectural gem. The front and back parlors are tastefully furnished with mahogany pieces, lace curtains, and with a number of European and Oriental art objects. The dining room has not only the original sideboard, table and chairs, but also the general's silver service and glass. It was Scott's custom to ride out to the Hermitage on Saturday afternoon and spend the night there in order to be ready for the Sunday morning service. Writing of this after her husband's death in 1885, Ann commented on how greatly he had enjoyed those Saturday evenings "under that hospitable roof." It is easy to imagine the old general and the young minister retiring to the library after dinner for their cigars and coffee. Here are the bookcases, the desks, and the general's chair made from wood from the U.S. frigate *Constitution*, and many other items of historical interest.

Jackson's library has been described as being for thirty years the political center of the United States when he ruled as the most influential man in his party. Here no doubt was cemented that deep friendship between Scott and Jackson which lasted as long as the general lived. Here the young man at the beginning of his career sat as a disciple before a master teacher. The general could speak out of the depths of long years of experience in dealing with people. Scott's admiration for the general almost amounted to hero worship.

Sometimes Ann accompanied her husband on these week-end excursions to the Hermitage. The general with slave help and plenty of rooms, including a nursery, could have sent a carriage to bring out the minister and his family. This involved a two-hour trip each way. Among the letters in the Scott Collection in Bancroft Library is a brief note from Sarah Jackson to Ann dated "August 3," without reference to a year, in which she referred to a stray collar Ann had left in the church. This was found by "a little negro boy. . . I am pleased to have it in my power to restore it to you." There is a family tradition that when the time of Ann's second confinement approached, General Jackson insisted that she move to the Hermitage where she would receive good care. On October 16, 1838, a baby girl was born who was named Martha, after her paternal grandmother, and Ann, after her mother.

Unfortunately we do not have an extant Scott diary to mirror for us the experiences of these years. It is easy to believe that these contacts with the general and his family and the impressions of the tastefully furnished Hermitage left lifelong influences on both William and Ann. Both had come from a frontier background where advantages for education and culture had been strictly limited. Only four years earlier, Scott was at the log college in Kentucky wearing homespun and now he was pastor of an ex-president of the United States! Life at the Hermitage was like a school to William and Ann. Here their eager receptive minds learned the secrets of good taste and here they came to appreciate those finer indescribable qualities which make up refinement and culture.

MARTHA AND ROBERT SCOTT, ABOUT 1843
From the Foster family Bible.

On Saturday, April 14, 1962, the author visited the Hermitage and the Hermitage Church. Mr. C. Lawrence Winn, a grandson of Andrew Jackson, Jr., now an elder in the church brought out the original church records covering the period that Scott served as stated supply. On Sunday following the author attended the morning services in the church. The original pews and pulpit placed in the building in 1838 under General Jackson's supervision are still in use. Also there is the original communion table copied after a table in the Hermitage. During the service on that April Sunday, a fire crackled in the fireplace for the church can still be heated in part by this means. Being surrounded by such a wealth of authentic material reminders of the past, it was not hard to imagine services being held in the same sanctuary over one hundred and twenty years before with young William A. Scott in the pulpit and the aged general seated in his pew.

Scott carried on a correspondence with General Jackson during the three years following Scott's departure from Nashville. Fifteen letters from Scott to Jackson are in the Jackson Collection in the Library of Congress. This series begins November 18, 1838, and ends April 19, 1844. Twelve of Jackson's letters to Scott are extant, most of which are in the Bancroft Library in Berkeley, and two are in the Library of Congress including Jackson's last letter to Scott dated February 3, 1845. As a token of his affection for his young pastor, the general gave Scott a picture of himself which bears the following inscription on the back: "Genl. A. Jackson with kind regards, presents to his friend, the Reverend Mr. Scott, the enclosed picture of himself as a memento of his personal esteem and kind recollection of his friend Mr. Scott. Hermitage, Novbr. 29th, 1841. Andrew Jackson." This picture is now owned by one of Dr. Scott's descendants.

Following the death of General Jackson on June 8, 1845, Scott, who was then pastor of the First Presbyterian Church of New Orleans, preached a memorial sermon in honor of his old friend. Drawing upon his memory of the years when he conducted services at the Hermitage Church, he said:

> From my own knowledge, I know that for years after his retirement from the Presidency he was the most regular & punctual attendant upon this service in the whole congregation. In the winter when the weather was so inclement that no other members of the family could go out, when the ground was covered with ice & snow, I have repeatedly gone to the chapel to officiate as Pastor when he & his servant would be the only persons assembled. Upon entering I have repeatedly observed him with the Psalm Book & Bible that his wife so long used & so much prized open before him, engaged in devotional exercises. . . He acknowledged God at his table by imploring the Divine blessing upon his food, & maintained prayers in the family."

In 1862 Scott published his *The Church in the Army; or The Four Centurions* in which he made special mention of General Jackson in the chapter on "Christian Soldiers." Herein he wrote:

We had the best possible opportunities to look into his character and we know his inmost heart . . . and it is our deliberate judgment, that he was a truly wonderful man. It was his habit to keep the Lord's day as a day of rest and for religious service. If he had company, as he almost always had, still he would attend public worship as long as he was able to go. Sabbath morning, he informed his guests, that it was his custom to go to church, and that he would be happy to have their company, and that carriages and horses would be at their service. But ladies and gentlemen, you will please do as you like in my house. The parlor and library are at your disposal, if you do not wish to go to church, but you must excuse me.

When Scott was pastor of the 42nd Street Presbyterian Church in New York, he was asked for some information about the Hermitage Church. He replied on February 28, 1869, and after answering the inquiries made, wrote: "I have very distinct & affectionate remembrances of the Hermitage and of Mrs. Sarah Jackson . . . and of the Old Hero. I have perfect confidence in his piety and believe he was one of the best, greatest & most incorruptible men that has ever lived in this country or in the world. I had opportunity of knowing him well & thoroughly." This letter of Dr. Scott's is with the records of the Hermitage Church.

Scott's move from Winchester to Nashville was more than just a change of address. Also involved was a change of ecclesiastical affiliation. For ten years Scott had been a member of the Cumberland Presbyterian Church. Before accepting the call to be principal of the Nashville Female Academy and to be stated supply of the Harpeth and Hermitage churches, he had indicated his desire to join Nashville Presbytery, a part of the Old School Presbyterian Church. Scott saw two good reasons for making this ecclesiastical change. The first was financial. Opportunities for advancement in the Cumberland Church were strictly limited as the denomination was small and composed largely of country or frontier churches. The stipends in such churches were pitifully low. The second reason was doctrinal. In later years Mrs. Scott commented: "He decided to change . . . saying that he could find no middle ground or resting place between Augustine and Arminius."

Mrs. Scott's comment may need some explanation. John Calvin, who more than any other molded Presbyterian (called Reformed on the Continent) doctrine, based his theology on the writings of Augustine. After Calvin died in 1564, his followers out-Calvined Calvin and formulated a hard uncompromising theology which brought a reaction, especially in Holland. There a professor of theology in the University of Leydon by the name of Jacobus Arminius became the leader of a party known as the Remonstrants who toned down the strict Calvinism of the day by placing more emphasis upon man's part in salvation and less upon predestination. Arminius died in 1609, but his teachings continued to be popular. In November 1618 a synod of reformed theologians from several counties began its meetings at Dort in Holland. This synod continued until May 1619 and after examining all aspects of Arminianism condemned its five principal points. The two schools of theology, the Calvinist and the Arminian, continue with some modifications to the present day. John Wesley, chief founder of the Methodist Church, accepted the Arminian point of view. The Cumberland Presbyterians, who in their early years depended largely upon poorly trained preachers, found that the Arminian theology as preached by their Methodist contemporaries was more acceptable to the people on the frontier than the Calvinistic doctrines as set forth in the Westminister Confession of Faith.

Scott was troubled about the lack of emphasis on the need for a theological education among his Cumberland brethren. His year at Princeton Theological Seminary was a profoundly broadening experience. His three major professors, Archibald Alexander, Charles Hodge, and Samuel Miller, were Calvinists. Gradually as Scott sat in their classes he found himself being introduced to new depths of philosophy and theology that challenged not only his best thinking but also his deepest devotion. At Opelousas and again at Winchester, he found himself departing from the usual theological patterns of his Cumberland brethren. When the call came to take work under the auspices of the Old School Presbyterian Church, he accepted with alactrity. This is what Mrs. Scott meant when she wrote that her husband could find no "middle ground or resting place between Augustine and Arminius."

An explanation is also needed to clarify the reference to the Old School Presbyterian Church. In 1837 the main body of Presbyterians in the United States divided into the Old School and New School branches. The former had about five-ninths of the membership of the undivided church. Three issues were involved, doctrine, polity, and slavery. The Old School looked with suspicion upon the New School brethren who were fraternizing with the Congregationalists and who were sympathetic to the liberal New England theology. The practical issues of polity arose out of inter-denominational practices. In 1801 the Presbyterian and Congregational Churches entered into a Plan of Union which called for cooperation on the frontier. The plan gave rise to a number of inter-denominational agencies which were independent of any denominational control. This in time generated a sharp difference of opinion between the Old School men and those of the New School. The former advocated denominational boards while the latter supported the inter-denominational societies. The operation of the Plan of Union in western

New York and Ohio in particular also raised grave questions in the minds of many Old School men regarding the adherence of New School churches to the official standards of Presbyterian polity. This was the crucial question raised by the Old School majority in the Assembly of 1837 which resulted in the exscinding of about four-ninths of the membership of the Church. A discussion of the third issue, slavery, which was in the background of the 1837 division, will come later in this study when Scott's attitude to slavery will be reviewed.

Following the division of 1837, the Synod of West Tennessee, which included the Presbytery of Nashville, went Old School. Since the two country churches near Nashville which Scott wished to serve as stated supply were within the bounds of this Presbytery, it was logical that he should seek membership within that body. He was received on October 5, 1838. Breaking his ties with the Cumberland Presbyterian Church brought many regrets. "He often said," wrote Mrs. Scott after his death, "that since the days of the Apostles there had not arisen a sect of religious teachers more pure minded, devoted and self denying." Scott felt very much at home in the Old School Presbyterian Church. This was the denomination to which the professors at Princeton Seminary, whom he so much admired, belonged. And Scott was in hearty accord with the conviction held by many Old School leaders that the church should not mix religion and politics.

A letter from Major Loomis to Scott dated March 8, 1839, indicates that Scott was making payments on the loan received from him. The major wrote: "I was a little astonished to find you had left off the Cumberland part of your religious profession. I have no doubt that you have acted conscientiously upon the subject. . . I rejoice in your prosperity in a worldly point of view and I am glad to hear you express yourself so favorably of Genl. Jackson. . . Your station is now so high you are a mark for envy to shoot at. I exhort you therefore to be watchful." Loomis had the satisfaction of seeing that his faith in Scott's potentialities was abundantly justified.

All evidence points to the fact that Scott was so busy at Nashville that he did not take time to make regular entries in his diary. Only one entry, that for September 8, 1838, was made: "Been engaged all day in teaching," he wrote, "intervals in preparing an address for Literary Inst. & Coll. of Teachers." On March 17, 1839, he began a "Bibliotheca or Literary Journal" which he kept for several years. In this he listed the books read, number of pages, and often added a critique. The titles indicate a wide variety of subject matter as biography, travel, naval history, theology, poetry, together with contemporary periodicals including some from abroad, as the *London Quarterly Review*. His critiques often included notes about the author. Beginning about this time, Scott began a correspondence with his friend of seminary days, the Rev. James A. Lyon. It appears that both were reading many of the same titles and comparing notes. Thus one mind sharpened the other.

TWO YEARS AT TUSCALOOSA

Sometime during 1839, Scott found himself standing at a fork in his life's highway. One road led to an academic career, the other to the pastorate. At the age of twenty-six he was invited to become president of Jackson College, a frontier institution located at Columbia, Tennessee. (The college did not survive the Civil War.) He had to decide whether to be a teacher or a preacher. In three different parishes, Opelousas, Winchester, and Nashville, he had combined teaching with his pastoral duties. The same was true of his chaplaincy experience at Prairie du Chien. Scott chose the pulpit.

Sometime in the late summer or early fall of 1839, the Rev. Daniel Baker of Tuscaloosa, Alabama, visited Nashville and called on Scott. Baker had resigned his pastorate of a little more than two years with the First Presbyterian Church of Tuscaloosa on July 10th of that year and was planning to go to Texas. He wanted a letter of introduction from General Jackson to Sam Houston. Upon Scott's suggestion, General Jackson wrote such a letter. Undoubtedly at the time of this visit to Nashville, Baker told Scott of the vacant pulpit in Tuscaloosa.

Baker was widely known in his day as a successful although somewhat eccentric evangelist. Many stories were told of his unconventional practices. Among these is the account of how he increased the attendance at one of his weekly prayer meetings. Noting that attendance was languishing, Baker told his Sunday congregation that if they "would all meet him on Thursday evening at the appointed place of prayer, he would show them a strange sight." Their curiosity aroused, the people turned out in record numbers. When pressed to see the "strange sight," Baker explained: "Is this not a strange sight—to see so many people at a prayer meeting in Tuscaloosa?"

Perhaps on Baker's suggestion and recommendation, the Presbyterian Church in Tuscaloosa investigated the possibility of calling Scott to its pulpit. There was some correspondence in the latter part of 1839 regarding salary. Baker had warned Scott that the church was delinquent in its salary payments to him. In a letter to the church dated December 25, 1839, Scott inquired as to whether he could receive his salary in monthly installments rather than semiannually. The church invited Scott to visit Tuscaloosa and this he did during the first part of February 1840. After having had the opportunity to meet and hear him, the members held a congregational meeting on February 5th at which they extended an unanimous call. A salary of $1,500 per annum was offered and Scott was told that "it shall be the duty of the Treasurer to pay over to the Pastor any amt. of money that shall be collected for that purpose as fast as it may be obtained, irrespective of the engagement set forth in the call to pay semiannually."

Scott accepted the call. He was greatly attracted by the new opportunity which had come to him. He had found the combination of being principal of a female academy and pastor of two country churches very

demanding. Since he would have no teaching responsibilities at Tuscaloosa outside of those connected with his church work, he felt that he
would have more time for study. Moreover, his wife would also be
freed from her teaching responsibilities. The Tuscaloosa church with
between 130 and 140 members was the largest in the Presbytery of
Tuscaloosa. Having been organized on May 6, 1820, it was the fifth
Presbyterian church to have been established in the state of Alabama.

Tuscaloosa, a small city of about 5,000 people, offered many advantages to a young minister. Located at the head of navigation on the
Black Warrior River with steamboats making regular trips to Mobile, it
was then the seat of the state capital. (In 1846 this was moved to Montgomery.) The University of Alabama, founded in 1831, was located in
Tuscaloosa but its total enrollment in 1840 was only about two hundred.
In addition to the president, Dr. Basil Manly, the university had a faculty
of five professors and two tutors. Scott was delighted to learn that the
library had some four thousand volumes.

Scott returned to Nashville eager to pass on the good news to Ann.
For a time they kept their decision to move a secret. They could not
think of leaving until the academy closed in June. On May 28th Scott
wrote a long letter to General Jackson telling him of their decision to
move to Tuscaloosa. He listed three main reasons for going. The first
was financial. "The Trustees of the Academy," he wrote, "have not
allowed me a salary sufficient   .   .   .   I have a growing family to support. It is but justice, however, to the Trustees to say that since my
engagement at Tuskaloosa, they have offered to make my salary sufficient. But it is too late. *The Rubicon is past. I am not of those who put
their hands to the plough and then turn back."* His second reason was
his desire to be relieved of the heavy teaching responsibilities required
of both himself and his wife at the school. "We are compelled to deny
ourselves many of the duties and privileges which we owe to the little
ones God has given us," he wrote. And the third reason involved his
decision to major on the pulpit rather than the classroom. "As a minister," he added, "I believe it to be my duty to be wholly given to the
work.   .   .   To be wholly given to the duties and studies of a man of
God. This I cannot do while I remain in the Academy."

Scott confessed that the prospect of moving from Tennessee gave him
many "painful thoughts." And he expressed his deep admiration for the
general by writing: "Born in Tennessee in 1813 A.D., your name and
glorious deeds were mingled with my cradle dreams, with my mother's
milk I quaffed your praise, and with my father's first lessons, I was made
acquainted with your history. And with my growth and years, those feelings and principles have grown and strengthened." After expressing his
deep appreciation for the many kindnesses received from the general, he
concluded: "I shall cherish the memory of the Hermitage as one of the
dearest spots on earth." General Jackson replied on June 9th saying in
part:

Enclosed you will receive Twenty five dollars, being one half of my & my family subscription for your services in our church here, sincerely regret it is out of our power to send you the whole amount but so it is—out of upwards of $3,000 due us, we have not been able to collect one Dollar. . . We all sincerely regret to part with you. You carry with you not only our, but the prayers & good wishes of all your little flock here. We all see the propriety of your course. You owe it to yourself & your wife.

If General Jackson and his family gave but $50 a year to the support of the Hermitage church, then the full amount Scott received from that source could not have been over $100 per annum. Perhaps a like amount was received from the Harpeth congregation. Information is lacking as to how much the academy paid but the total amount from all three sources could not have been more than $1,000 a year, if that much. General Jackson was not able to pay the balance of his pledge until December 16th of that year when he sent the money to Scott at Tuscaloosa.

Among the extra responsibilities that Scott was carrying at Nashville was that of teaching a midweek adult Bible class which met in the First Presbyterian Church. Although by this time he had chosen the career of a parish minister instead of the academic life of a college professor, at heart he was always a teacher. The extant manuscripts of his sermons and lectures reveal a consistent emphasis on instruction. He liked to marshal his arguments in logical sequence. He drew heavily on history, the Westminster Confession of Faith, and the Bible for his material. By modern standards his type of presentation seems heavy and uninteresting. His manuscripts fail to convey the magic of his personality. The fact that people flocked to hear him speaks eloquently of some hidden appeal that radiated through his voice, his infectious smile, and his whole being. Some indication of the impact Scott made upon his Bible class in Nashville is to be found in a letter sent to him under date of June 11, 1840, by a member of the group. "When we speak of the amount of instruction received from you," the letter read, "our hearts rise in grateful adoration to God."

Scott closed his work at the academy on Saturday June 13th. After a few days spent in taking care of the necessary duties attendant upon moving, he loaded his few material possessions on a wagon and with his wife, their two little children, and Mila, the slave girl, started on the 240-mile overland journey to Tuscaloosa. No account has been discovered of their travel experiences. In a summary of the year's events written in his journal on December 31st, he merely reported: "Arrived [in Tuscaloosa] on Saturday 27 of June in the evening about 5 o'c. Was welcomed by the Chh."

In 1830 the Presbyterians of Tuscaloosa erected a New England style brick church on the southwest corner of Ninth Street and Greensboro Avenue. The building measured about forty by sixty feet and had a

FIRST PRESBYTERIAN
CHURCH, TUSCALOOSA
As it appeared when Dr. Scott
was pastor, 1840-42. The building
is no longer standing. From a
photo owned by the church.

steeple over the main entrance. The present church plant stands on the same site. In March 1839 the church erected a modest Sunday School building, at a cost of $700, adjacent to the main building. The church had no manse and it is assumed that Scott had to pay rent out of his salary. Action was taken on November 1, 1841, retroactive to January 1st, to increase Scott's salary by $250. This may have been granted in lieu of rent.

Scott entered with enthusiasm upon his new duties. He resolved to take full advantage of his release from teaching by spending more time in his study. He burned several hundred manuscripts of his old sermons, keeping only a few. He took no vacation that summer but continued to preach twice each Sunday and to give a lecture before the midweek meeting. Summing up his activities at the end of the year, he stated that he had missed only two Sundays since his arrival in Tuscaloosa, once because of illness and again because of a Presbytery meeting in a distant place.

At Tuscaloosa Scott began to realize his powers as a pulpit orator. Within a few weeks his reputation spread throughout the city and there was general agreement that an outstanding preacher was in their midst. The audiences doubled and then tripled in size. Soon there were more non-members than members attending. During the summer of 1841 the church found it necessary to build an extension in the form of a left transept to accommodate the enlarged congregations. By 1842 Scott estimated that about one thousand people were attending his services with more or less regularity.

The Presbytery of Tuscaloosa met on October 1st when Scott was formally examined as to his orthodoxy and ministerial ability, and received into its membership. The minutes of the presbytery show that the Presbyterians of that area used the old traditional Scottish term of "bishop" for an installed pastor. Each minister was a bishop. Scott was formally installed as bishop of the Tuscaloosa Church on Sunday, October 18, 1840. The main reason for the use of this title is the Presbyterian insistence that the two Greek words *presbuteros* and *episcopos* are used as synonyms in the New Testament.

An examination of the original sessional records of the First Presbyterian Church of Tuscaloosa during the time of Scott's ministry reveal the fact that much of the attention of the pastor and elders was taken up with disciplinary problems. The church kept a watchful eye over all of its members. Today the average church has far more members on its roll than the size of an average Sunday morning congregation, but the situation was reversed in Scott's generation. Then the non-members often outnumbered the members in church attendance. Perhaps one reason for this was the strict discipline exercised by the church. Many did not wish to submit to a rigid Puritanical code of ethics.

Among the first records in the minutes of the Tuscaloosa Church is the following: "Resolved, that in the view of this Session, the attendance of Church members at Balls, Dancing parties, theatres, Circus and other like places of worldly amusement is inconsistent with the Christian profession and demands the discipline of the Church." The circus came under the ban of the church because in that day it attracted a rough element and often sponsored what the church considered to be unholy amusements. In 1836 the University of Alabama found it necessary to suspend forty-six students out of a total student body of 158 because they had attended a circus in Tuscaloosa! The Presbytery of Tuscaloosa at its April 1841 meeting adopted the following resolution: "That parents who are in communion with the Presbyterian Church are not at liberty to countenance the Theater and Dancing Schools, or other places of amusement by permitting their children or wards to attend at such places." There is evidence to indicate that Scott was more broad-minded on such practices than the official stand of his church.

A typical example of a disciplinary case which came before the session June 19, 1841, when Scott was pastor, involved a young woman, wife of Mr. William M——, who gave "birth to a child a little more than 5 mo, after their lawful marriage and said child in good health &

full maturity." Since the report implied "the heinous sin of fornication," an elder was appointed to investigate. In his report at the following meeting of the session, he stated that "she confessed her crime and confessed deep and unfeigned penitence for the same, and that she desired to remain in communion & Christian fellowship with the church." The session then adopted the following resolution: "That upon the ground of her confession, repentence, & contrition, she be restored to full communion & fellowship of the church, and that the whole history of her case be read before the congregation. . ." Since nothing was said in the record about the husband of the young woman, it may be assumed that he was not a member of the church and therefore not subject to its discipline.

On February 27, 1842, the trustees of the church took the following action: "Resolved that W. A. Scott be and is hereby employed to allow his servant boy to act as sexton of the Presbyterian Church for the year 1842 for which he is to be paid a salary of $50 for the services of said Boy." Here is evidence that Scott owned a slave, in addition to the girl Mila who belonged to his wife. During slavery days, it was customary for masters to take all of the cash earnings of their slaves.

Sometime in the spring of 1841 Scott wrote to Dr. Archibald Alexander, one of his professors at Princeton, regarding the advisability of taking out life insurance with the Presbyterian Widow's Fund, now known as the Presbyterian Minister's Fund. Alexander replied on June 14th strongly recommending that he do so. The cost would be $24 per annum which, in case Scott died, would pay his widow $120 a year with certain specified benefits for minor children. This fund grew out of the Pious Fund established by the Presbyterian Church in 1717, which was incorporated in 1759 and claims the distinction of being the first life insurance company in the nation to be so recognized. Scott with admirable business foresight signed for a policy. This was the beginning of what was for that day a strong insurance program for he later supplemented it with policies in other companies. It should be remembered that in those days the Presbyterian Church made no provision for disability or retirement of its ministers.

Scott also inquired of Dr. Alexander regarding the possibility of buying a second hand set of Walton's *Polyglot* which was published in London 1755-57 with portions of the Scriptures appearing in nine different languages. This work remains as one of the greatest polyglots ever to appear. There were six large folio volumes with an accompanying lexicon. In reply Alexander stated that a set could be obtained for $200. It is doubtful that Scott could afford to pay such a price at that time but the very fact of his making inquiry about such an erudite work speaks highly of his scholarly interests.

After settling at Tuscaloosa, Scott found that he had more time for private study than ever before. At the end of 1840, he summarized his reading for the year in his Bibliotheca: "Have read, not including any periodicals . . . forty-five volumes—almost all octavoes—a few very large—& some half dozen duodecimo, making . . . 15,350 pages. In this I have not included what I have read . . . in theology & in the preparation of my Sabbath discourses." And yet after listing such an extensive amount of reading, he added: "And it seems to me that I have done nothing at all. O Lord give me proper & deep convictions of the value of time, of the shortness of human life, & the responsibility that rests upon me as a husband, a father, a member of Society, a professed disciple of Jesus Christ & a minister of the everlasting & glorious Gospel of the Grace of God."

The summary of reading done in 1841 mentions ninety-nine volumes, "mostly octavo," with a total of 28,422 pages. Here we see the result of a full year's residence in Tuscaloosa. Again this did not include periodicals, his devotional reading, or the necessary preparation for sermons and lectures. "Upon an average," he wrote, "including funerals & sacramental occasions & Thursday evening lectures, I have delivered three discourses a week for the whole year, two of which were written." Of course he had no typewriter. All manuscripts were hand written. He closed his record for 1841 with the following self-appraisal: "But oh how little I seem to have done!" Scott continued to keep a log of his reading through 1842. His notations, methodically summarized month by month, indicate a total of 27,889 pages read for the year. After leaving Tuscaloosa, the pressure of parish duties combined with long periods of ill health cut drastically into his studies, but by this time the foundation of his extensive knowledge of history and literature had been well laid.

In April 1842, less than a year after the Scotts had moved to Tuscaloosa, the University of Alabama conferred upon him the honorary degree of Master of Arts. This was a distinct honor as records indicate that down to 1842 the university had honored only fourteen with this degree. His original M.A. diploma, now in the Bancroft Library, is a most imposing-looking document with a two-inch blue ribbon eighteen inches long attached to one corner and bearing the seal of the university at the end. In the fall of 1841 Scott was offered a position on the faculty at the university but he declined.

Scott's keen interest in literary pursuits was again apparent when he took the initiative in organizing a lyceum in Tuscaloosa. The National American Lyceum was founded in 1826 in Massachusetts for the purpose of disseminating information on the arts, sciences, history, and public affairs. For some forty years it was a powerful force in adult education in this country. The lyceums waned after the Civil War and were succeeded by the Chautauqua movement. The story of the Tuscaloosa lyceum is found in the columns of the *Flag of the Union*, one of the city's newspapers. The issue of August 18, 1841, referred to the fact that "a number of gentlemen in this city have associated themselves together for the purpose of improvement in literature, science, morals, and general knowledge," and were holding their first meeting that evening in the Presbyterian church. "The Rev. Mr. Scott, a mature and accomplished scholar, from whom much is expected" was to be the speaker. All interested were invited to attend. A report of the meeting was published on August 25th. According to the newspaper, the audience was rather small "but highly respectable" consisting of both "gentlemen and ladies". As to Scott's presentation: "It was entertaining and instructive throughout, and in some parts rose to eloquence." The lyceum continued to hold its meetings in the Presbyterian church for a number of months, and Scott served as the first president of the organization.

During his two years' residence in Tuscaloosa, Scott joined the Masonic Lodge. The records of Rising Virtue Lodge, No. 4, of Tuscaloosa show that he was initiated on December 3, 1841, and raised to the third degree on February 4, 1842. In making this move, he followed the example of his father-in-law, Dr. Nicholson, and that of his hero, Andrew Jackson, both of whom were Masons. Before leaving Alabama, Scott also joined the higher Masonic bodies of the Royal Arch and the Council. Evidence is lacking as to how much interest he took in Masonry after leaving Tuscaloosa.

William and Ann became the parents of their third child, a son, on January 21, 1841. He was named Calvin Knox, after the two great founders of the Presbyterian faith. Now with a family of five, including himself, plus at least two servants, Scott began to feel the need for a larger income. He also wanted money for books and for travel. This was one of the reasons why in the fall of 1842 he listened with a receptive ear to overtures from the First Presbyterian Church of New Orleans to consider serving that congregation as pastor.

New Orleans as it Appeared from the Tower of St. Patrick's Church, 1852

The First Presbyterian Church, lower left, is at the southwest corner of Lafayette Square.

Courtesy of Tulane University Library, New Orleans.

Twelve Years in New Orleans

New Orleans, sprawling along the west bank of the Mississippi River with a population of over 102,000 in 1842, was the great commercial metropolis of the South. It was the terminus of an extensive river trade that moved up and down the Mississippi and its many tributaries. Here ships docked from all over the world making the waterfront a veritable modern Babel. The large French population made the city bilingual. Although largely Roman Catholic, still there was a strong Protestant element present among whom the Presbyterians and the Episcopalians were the most active.

Historic Canal Street cut the city into two parts. To the north was the old French Quarter with its picturesque architecture, reminiscent of the Old World, and to the south was the Second Municipal District dotted with commercial and public buildings. Several blocks south of Canal Street and three or four blocks from the waterfront was Lafayette Square with well landscaped walks, flower beds, trees and shrubs. A handsome iron railing surrounded the square and a statue of Benjamin Franklin stood in a prominent place. Lafayette Square was proudly described at that time as the "handsomest in the city."

Gracing the southwest corner of the square was the First Presbyterian Church of New Orleans, a stately brick structure in the Grecian Doric style with a tall steeple surmounted by a weathervane. The interior was described as "large and commodious." It was the most imposing Protestant church in the city and, although the official name was the First Presbyterian Church of New Orleans, it was commonly called "the church on Lafayette Square."

The church traced its beginnings back to 1818 when the brilliant young minister, the Rev. Sylvester Larned, arrived in the city. Larned died on August 21, 1820, his twenty-fourth birthday. Even though his ministry was short, he left an impression upon the church which lasted for generations. The church was blessed with several outstanding ministers including the Rev. Joel Parker, 1833-38, and the Rev. John Breckinridge, 1838-41. Under Parker's ministry, the building on Lafayette Square was erected. No doubt Scott visited the site in the fall of 1834 on his way from Princeton Theological Seminary to Opelousas.

CALLED TO NEW ORLEANS

The minutes of the session of the First Presbyterian Church of New Orleans show that at its first meeting following the death of Dr. Breckinridge, a resolution addressed to the professors of Princeton Theological

Seminary was passed in which the elders asked for a recommendation for their pulpit. The church was ready to pay an annual salary of $2,000 plus moving expenses. In reply the professors recommended William A. Scott of Tuscaloosa, then only twenty-eight years old but having greater promise of future usefulness than any other Princeton alumnus in the South.

Sometime in October 1841 Scott received a letter from the New Orleans church asking if he would like to be considered as a candidate for its pulpit. He was both surprised and somewhat flattered. The proposal came just about the time the University of Alabama had offered him a position on its faculty. Here was another minor crossroad in Scott's life and the old question of choosing between being a preacher or a teacher was raised again. Having previously decided on the pulpit, there was no hesitancy now. The prospect of being pastor of the First Presbyterian Church of New Orleans was most appealing, and he indicated his interest to the committee.

An invitation to visit New Orleans quickly followed and Scott made arrangements to be away from his pulpit in Tuscaloosa for some six weeks in December and January. Travel was slow as he had to go by river boat to Mobile and then by ocean steamer to New Orleans. Passage was booked on the "Hercules" scheduled to leave Tuscaloosa on Monday morning at 2 a.m., December 6th. On that day Scott began another journal which he titled *Ephemerae Vitae Meae*, or journal of my life. He began by summarizing the events of Sunday. He had preached in the morning "to a large & interesting audience" and again at three o'clock p.m. This was the first time since their marriage that he would be away from his family for any extended period and Ann was unhappy. "My dear wife has been more distressed than she ever was before," Scott wrote. "Our married life has been a most happy one. Indeed I never knew what it was to have or enjoy pure worldly happiness until I was married." Scott boarded the "Hercules" at nine p.m. Sunday evening and went to bed but, as he wrote:

> . . . not to sleep. Burning thoughts still rolled in waves of fire through my mind. Now I stood upon the mountain top of reflection, and looked back over my life, its beginnings, its wanderings, its mercies . . . then far in the distance I could see myself settled in New Orleans, preaching to large congregations, spending a summer in Princeton, N.J., a summer in Paris & some years hence when I shall have accomplished my mission in N. Orleans, retired to some respectable chh. or residenceship in a more healthful region of our country—my family around . . .

He was up early enough the next morning to see the sun rise. From the upper deck he watched the rolling of the great paddle wheel at the stern and noted "the rainbow formed by the spray of water." He marvelled at the power of the steam engine and later that morning wrote

FIRST PRESBYTERIAN CHURCH, NEW ORLEANS, LOUISIANA
Built in 1835 and used by Dr. Scott, 1842-54. The building burned in 1854.
From an engraving in Gibson's *Guide and Directory*, 1838.

in his journal: "What a wonder is the use of steam engines. Here it goes, groaning, roaring, pitching, belching, hissing, staggering . . ." He added that he did not feel well that day, in fact he was "very Mondayish." This term was often used by ministers of that generation to describe the lethargic feeling experienced after a very busy Sunday.

The Black Warrior River empties into the Tombigbee which in turn pours its waters into Mobile Bay. By air it is only about 180 miles between Tuscaloosa and Mobile but, by the tortuous windings of the two rivers, the distance is probably doubled. The "Hercules" docked at Mobile at 2:30 p.m. on Wednesday having taken more than sixty hours to make the journey. Such were travel conditions back in the 1840s. Scott was able to book passage for New Orleans on the "Creole" which was scheduled to sail at one p.m. the next day. The voyage was rough and he was seasick even before the vessel was out of Mobile Bay. He spent a restless night. The ship docked at New Orleans at 6 a.m. on Friday. He was welcomed by a committee of elders from the church including Alfred Hennen, one of the city's leading lawyers, who took Scott to his home. In his letter to his wife of December 13th, Scott reported: "Mr. Hennen . . . has been here for 32 years. He is one of the first lawyers of the city—a man of great wealth & fine accomplishments. He has one of the best libraries I have ever seen. It is valued at $50,000. . . He has the Antwerp Polyglott & many old and rare books—many that I never saw before. He has ten children. . . Has many old paintings, pictures, engravings, &c. . . His library is complete in Latin, Greek, Spanish & French, some Italian, Hebrew, Syriac &c—well all this is pleasant." Scott felt that his trip to New Orleans was worth while just to see that library. He remained as a guest in the Hennen home throughout this visit to New Orleans.

When Scott went to the church, he found the pulpit and lectern still draped in mourning because of the death of Dr. Breckinridge. He preached twice on Sunday to morning and evening congregations of white people and once in the afternoon to the "blacks." The church building had a seating capacity of about two thousand, although the membership then was only 160. In the letter to his wife dated Monday, December 13th, Scott reported that some of the members were expecting him to spend the entire winter with them. "As to the future," he wrote, "I cannot now say any thing for as yet I know nothing. Yes, I do know that I do not want to come here & nothing but the clearest sense of unavoidable duty can ever induce me to settle here." He felt overwhelmed with the "awful responsibility of this city." In the intimacy of this letter to his wife, he said that he did not feel worthy to follow such distinguished predecessors in that pulpit as Larned, Parker, and Breckinridge. But the main reason why he hesitated was the unhealthful environment. "It is too sickly," he wrote. "There were seven deaths last week from yellow fever. There is no danger as to myself now, but to be crowded into a city like this, seems to be absolutely intolerable. There is no free, pure air—nor any to be had anywhere near—a horrible dampness pervades everything & every place. . ."

Scott's letters to his wife during these weeks contain many expressions of tender affection. In one letter he wrote: "I always feel the poverty of language so much that I am dissatisfied with any epithets of endearment that I can command." And again: "Ah, dear wife, you cannot conceive how much I love you, & how much happiness I enjoy in your society & with the dear little children God has given us." At the Christmas season, he was especially disconsolate in his yearning to be back home with Ann and the children.

Writing to Ann on December 17th, Scott told of spending the previous evening as a guest in the home of Mr. and Mrs. Stephen Franklin. Franklin, an elder in the New Orleans church, was one of the promising young lawyers of the city, and was about two years older than Scott. A friendship began that evening between the two men which lasted until Scott's death in 1885.

In this same letter Scott mentioned taking a walk along the water-front where he was amazed at the "immense sea of masts and sails. There are about five hundred vessels here," he wrote, "from all parts of the world. . . The trade & commerce of this city are beyond calculation." He found New Orleans much larger than he had antici-pated and wrote: "It is second only to New York in my opinion." But there was a dark side of the picture which appalled him. He learned that there were "833 grog shops & coffee houses" in the city. Scott was no teetotaler or blue-stocking Puritan; he enjoyed a good cup of coffee and an after-dinner cigar; he liked an occasional glass of wine and sometimes imbibed a stronger drink. But the hundreds of grog shops and coffee houses in New Orleans which were pouring out what he called "streams of liquid damnation" were something different. Here was drunkness on a vast scale with its attendant evils of prostitution and gambling. New Orleans was just another great world seaport, perhaps no better or no worse than any other city of like importance, but seeing this was a new experience to him.

Within two weeks after his arrival in New Orleans the officers and members of the First Presbyterian Church were ready to give Scott a unanimous call. They were quick to see in him a rare combination of unusual qualifications which set him above and apart from all other known candidates for their pulpit. Having come out of a Cumberland Presbyterian background, Scott's faith was characterized by a warm piety, but without excessive emotion. He was orthodox and sound in the faith. On this point the New Orleans church was somewhat sensitive as one of its former pastors, the Rev. Theodore Clapp, had been deposed in 1833 for heresy. Scott was learned, even erudite, and the results of years of intensive reading were clearly evident. He was cultured and refined in his manners enabling him to move at ease in elite society. The fact that he had been Andrew Jackson's pastor for two years and a frequent visitor at the Hermitage was a further recommendation, especially in New Orleans where January 8th was celebrated each year in honor of Jackson's vistory over the British in 1815. In that engage-ment Alfred Hennen, then a young man, had been one of the general's picked bodyguard.

Scott was eloquent in the pulpit. His great success in building up the congregation in the Tuscaloosa church was known. The New Orleans church needed a preacher of that kind to fill its spacious sanctuary. Moreover, and this was a most important qualification, Scott was a Southerner by birth, training, and outlook. He had had a two years' ministry in Opelousas not far from New Orleans. He could speak French, another admirable accomplishment for a citizen of the bilingual city. And finally he was young. On January 30, 1842, he would be twenty-nine. There was no doubt about it; here was a brilliant young preacher standing at the threshold of a distinguished ministry. Fortunate indeed would be the church which could then secure the services of William A. Scott.

In the letters Scott wrote to his wife from New Orleans, he debated the pros and the cons of the possible move to New Orleans. He was tremendousy impressed with the need and the opportunities of the field. He referred to the city as being more important "than Calcutta or any other missionary past," and, he added, "the dangers & trials &c are just as great." On the other hand, there was the health hazard. Two of the former pastors of the New Orleans church, Larned and Breckinridge, had died within a period of twenty years while serving the church. The terrible scourge of yellow fever took an annual toll of thousands of lives. Other diseases, like malaria, then little understood, also claimed their victims by the hundreds. Scott debated the wisdom of taking his family into such a sickly situation, and yet thousands were making New Orleans their home. Scott was no coward. He wrote to his wife that if he were convinced it was God's will for him to accept the call, he would not hesitate to do so. "I have suffered great agonies on this subject," he said, "I wish to do nothing but what is clearly my duty to the great head of the Chh." He prayed for divine guidance.

After preaching for the New Orleans congregation for four Sundays, Scott started back to Tuscaloosa on Monday, January 3rd, and was home by the following Saturday. A congregational meeting was held in the New Orleans church on the evening of the 3rd at which an unanimous call was extended to Scott with a salary stipulation of $3,500 per annum. Records do not indicate if this included house rent or whether a manse was provided. There was evidently some correspondence over the matter of the salary, for the New Orleans church held another congregational meeting on March 27th at which time a stipend of $4,000 per annum was voted and also the following provision: "It was unanimously resolved that if in the Providence of God the Rev. Mr. Scott should die while in the service of the church as their pastor, the sum of one thousand dollars per annum for the space of five years from the date of his said decease be paid by the church and congregation to the widow and children of Mr. Scott." At still another congregational meeting, held on April 7th, this latter provision was changed to read $500 per annum for ten years. The very fact that the church agreed to such an action shows that Scott was deeply concerned about the possibility of dying, if he moved to New Orleans, and leaving his family almost penniless. In a day when the purchasing power of the dollar was four or five times what it is now, the $4,000 stipend was indeed a handsome amount. Only two years before in Nashville Scott was struggling along on about

$1,000 per annum, which sum had come from three different sources. His advancement in so short a time was indeed amazing.

After Scott returned to Tuscaloosa in the first part of January 1842, he found it difficult to carry on his work. That sensitive nerve which united pastor and people had been severed. Although he had great affection for his people in Tuscaloosa, and there was no doubt about their love for him, still his heart was already in New Orleans. Scott wrote to the faculty at Princeton for advice. All three of his major professors, Drs. Alexander, Hodge, and Miller, strongly urged him to accept the New Orleans call. "In my opinion," wrote Alexander, "a more important post for usefulness & influence could not be found in the world." On the other hand, the members of the Tuscaloosa church were insistent that their pastor remain with them.

Finally Scott decided to return to New Orleans with his wife and together come to a final decision. After making arrangements for a friend to care for their two older children, Scott, his wife, their baby Calvin Knox, and faithful Mila left Tuscaloosa on March 7th. They did not return until about May 8th. The fact that the New Orleans church held congregational meetings on March 27th and April 7th at which some aspects of the annual stipend were voted shows that these were some of the issues Scott wanted settled before he gave his final consent. According to Presbyterian polity, three parties are involved in the pastoral relationship of a minister and a church. They are the minister, the church, and the presbytery. All three must be in accord before a pastor can be released from his present church or be installed in another. In Scott's case two presbyteries were involved, the Presbytery of Tuscaloosa and the Presbytery of Louisiana.

The records of the Presbytery of Tuscaloosa for its April 1842 meeting report: "A letter from Rev. W. A. Scott was read containing his reasons for absence from the present sessions of this Presbytery, which reasons were not sustained." The mood of the Presbytery was clearly opposed to Scott's removal from their bounds. When the official call from the New Orleans church was presented, Prof. R. T. Brumby, an elder from the Tuscaloosa church and a member of the faculty of the University of Alabama, presented resolutions from his church showing why their pastor should not be permitted to leave. The New Orleans church sent one of its members, Mr. W. Bartell, to prosecute the call. He was heard after which a vote was taken not to dissolve the pastoral relation between Scott and the Tuscaloosa church. Bartell was back in New Orleans by April 21st and reported the failure of his mission. "This decision is very unexpected," wrote Scott in his journal, "and has perplexed my mind not a little."

The Scotts left New Orleans for their return trip to their home in Tuscaloosa on May 2nd. On May 20th, he addressed a long letter to his session in which he detailed the reasons why he felt it necessary to resign. "No motive or purpose under heaven has influenced me to the course I have taken," he wrote, "but the solemn conviction that the great Head of the Chh . . . has called me to labour in New Orleans." He asked for immediate acceptance of his resignation but promised to remain until that fall. Regretfully the members of the Tuscaloosa Presbyterian Church on June 2nd voted to concur in their pastor's request. Scott was relieved. He wrote in his journal a few days later: "I cannot now detail the harrowing events of the last 4 or 5 months. It is a great act of self denial for a minister to leave a tried, happy & affectionate people for an unknown surrounded with so many difficulties." The Presbytery of Tuscaloosa held a special meeting in July at which time all ecclesiastical barriers to his removal from Tuscaloosa were cleared, and he was dismissed to the Louisiana Presbytery. A new chapter in his life was about to open.

FIRST YEARS IN NEW ORLEANS

Summarizing the events of 1842 in his Bibliotheca, Scott compressed the account of the removal of himself and his family from Tuscaloosa to New Orleans into one paragraph:

Closed my labours at Tuskaloosa with a heavy heart & many fears, took my departure for New Orleans—7th Sept. Spent one week—preaching & for my dear brother Lyon at Columbus, & with him spent a few days in Aberdeen, Miss. Reached home of my father about 20 Sept. Filled with many troubled thoughts— was sick a few days, preached sixteen sermons in Memphis, & one in Raleigh—removed the body of my dear mother to Raleigh. Had been dead eight years.

From this brief statement we see that the Scotts went overland to Memphis, Tennessee, about 250 miles distant from Tuscaloosa, and then by river steamer to New Orleans. No doubt they sent their belongings by water to New Orleans and then took the stage to Memphis. Their first stop-over was at Columbus, Mississippi, about fifty miles distant, where one of Scott's closest friends, the Rev. James A. Lyon, was pastor of the Presbyterian Church. The friendship between the two men began when they were classmates in Princeton Theological Seminary. "After leaving the seminary," Scott once wrote, "a very warm and constant correspondence was carried on for the sake of mutual improvement." For years they thus shared the results of their reading with each other and often discussed questions of mutual interest. As will be noted later, Lyon played an important role in the unfortunate controversy which involved Scott and Senator Henry Clay at the time the latter was a candidate for president of the United States.

William had visited his father, Eli, and his stepmother in the spring of 1836, six years earlier. Now, perhaps for the first time, Eli met Ann and saw his three grandchildren. In turn Eli could present his three little children, a boy, Henry, and two girls, Sarah Ann and Martha Jane.

They were about the same ages as the three children of William and Ann. Thus at the age of sixty-one, Eli Scott was rearing a second family.

William and Ann spent five weeks at Raleigh. This was the first extended vacation they had enjoyed since their marriage. As noted above, Scott was called upon several times to preach in both Memphis and Raleigh. Here was another local boy who had made good and had returned to visit the scenes of his childhood. When he spoke at Raleigh, it would have been natural for him to have made some reference to the events of nineteen years earlier when as a lad ten years old he first came to that community with his parents and younger brothers. And it was there in Raleigh that he became a member of the Cumberland Presbyterian Church in January 1828. So much had happened in those fourteen intervening years! Although handicapped by the lack of educational opportunities, poverty, and a crippled foot, William by virtue of his insatiable longing for knowledge and his persistent application to his work had moved step by step upward until now he was going to the most important Presbyterian pulpit in the entire South.

At the time William's mother died, her body was laid in a grave on the farm where Eli was then living. This was quite customary in that day as not even Memphis had a public burying ground prior to 1827. During William's visit with his father, he had the remains of his mother moved to the Raleigh cemetery. One of the few letters extant written by Eli Scott is dated December 6, 1842, from "Shelby, Tennessee" to his son William in New Orleans. In this letter he referred to the fact that he was having "your Mother's grave walled in." William ordered a tombstone placed over the grave with the inscription: "Martha Scott, wife of Eli, mother of William, Davis, and James. b. Oct. 6, 1782; died July 29, 1834." In the summer of 1962, Mrs. H. W. Cooper, a local resident, located the grave at the request of the author. The inscription was still legible.

The letter of Eli dated December 6th also contained the following: "I have paid over the money that I got from you and have got a deed to the land, the ballance of the money is not yet paid, the sheriff is not pushing me now. I do not think he will untill after February." Evidently Eli was in arrears in payment of his taxes and his son had to come to his assistance. Throughout his life Eli was beset with money problems.

William and his family left Memphis on a river boat on October 31st and arrived in New Orleans on November 10th. They commenced housekeeping at once in their new home on Magazine Street about eight blacks from the church on Lafayette Square. Within five days after their arrival, Ann, then pregnant, was stricken with the dreaded yellow fever. The Scotts had deliberately delayed reaching New Orleans until after the worst of the yellow fever period was passed but to no avail. Their worst fears were now realized. Fortunately Ann recovered. "God had great mercy on us," her husband wrote. The illness gave her immunity. Never again was she to be afflicted.

Scott threw himself into the work of his church with enthusiasm. His preaching attracted crowds which overflowed the church. Scores of new members applied to join. The session met four times in December to receive them and to care for other important items of business.

The ingathering continued month after month. In March 1844 a total membership of 439 was reported to the Presbyterian General Assembly. This represented a threefold increase in about fifteen months. The growth in membership undoubtedly reflected a corresponding increase in church attendance.

Scott had the custom of writing soliloquies, prayers, or reflections on life in his journal from time to time. The following is a good example of this type of entry:

> Now it is ½ past 11 o'c p.m. at night but as this 30 Jany. is my birthday, I must leave this note of time & warning of my rapid approach to death & eternity. This day thirty years ago, a man child was born—the heir of suffering & sorrow, sensibility, labour & death. . . How short & hasty is my life. And now I am 30 years of age. It cannot, must not be—but look. Born 1813. This is 1843—30 years are the number of my days all told & sealed up for the day of final judgment. I have always supposed by the time I should be 30, I would be ready to stop reading & give myself wholly to labour for the Chh.; that by 30 I would have the foundations laid, & the stones polished & the timbers ready & could now build. But alas 30 is told & I feel so illy furnished. O that I could have had five years more of study & writing & experience as a Pastor before I was called to go in & out before a great people like this. Who is sufficient for this?

On March 3, 1843, the Scotts' fourth child, a son, was born. He was named William Wicliffe but years later, after expressing a dislike for the middle name, he became William Anderson Scott, Junior.

The Presbytery of Louisiana installed Scott as "Bishop of the First Presbyterian Church of New Orleans" on March 19, 1843. In his morning sermon of the following Sunday, Scott plainly stated some of the principles which were to guide him in his ministry there.

> It is my solemn intention, to preach as candidly, as plainly, and as effactually as God shall enable me, the great doctrines of Grace taught in the Catechism & Confesson of Faith of the Presbyterian Church. Not because they are taught in the standards of the Presbyterian Church but because I believe them to be the doctrines of the Bible. . . I hold myself responsible to God and not to man for the system of doctrines which I have embraced and which I intend to preach. I will always listen to advice—always be glad to have Christian counsel from the elders & members of the Chh. but must always feel myself accountable to God for what I preach rather than to man. No one has a right to dictate to the Pastor what subjects he may preach on.

He stated his desire to become acquainted with all members of the church and congregation and announced office hours for interviews for every Monday morning. He also invited them to call at his home "in Magazine street, white house, second door, right hand going up just above Melicerte." Regarding calling, he said: "It is obvious that much visiting in so large a congregation cannot be expected. . . . Persons sick or distressed or in actual need of the Pastor's presence, will always be attended to." He expressed a willingness to administer the sacraments of baptism and of the Lord's Supper in private "when there are good and sufficient reasons for so doing."

Regarding his illustrations drawn from life, Scott issued a word of warning: "Beware then of making personal the portraits which the minister draws from human nature in general," he said, "without the least design of particularizing any one. He will never gratify malice under the cloak of piety. Whatever strikes you, apply to yourselves. Leave your neighbor to his God and his conscience."

He made a plea for books. "It is your duty to furnish him [i.e., their pastor] with books, and allow him time to prepare for the pulpit. There are many peculiar reasons why the Pastor of this Chh should be eminently a man of reading & have at command a large library & standard volumes—the taste & intelligence of the congregation; the prominent position of this chh. in the Southwest; the growth and influence of this city; the fact that there are here no public libraries of rare theological works which can be consulted by the pastor." Scott emphasized the latter point and frankly asked his people to help him enlarge his library. "The more books you put into your pastor's hands," he said, "the more learned and able he will become."

Scott's appeal for books must have been successful for in 1854 his friend James A. Lyon said that his library contained between nine and ten thousand volumes. The manse must have been overflowing with books. Perhaps some were kept at the church. Summarizing his reading at the end of 1843, Scott noted that he had read 16,729 pages, compared to about 28,000 pages read each year while in Tuscaloosa. Thus it is evident that the pressure of parish duties in New Orleans had cut deeply into the time once reserved for study.

The Scotts took no vacation during the summer of 1843. Week after week he preached his two sermons on Sunday to large audiences and delivered a midweek lecture. Summarizing his work at the end of the year, he wrote that he had preached 134 times and had written fifty-seven new sermons. This meant that he was using notes of sermons delivered in Tuscaloosa. On May 21, 1843, he preached on "The Duty of Praying for our Rulers" which was subsequently published in pamphlet form in New Orleans. In this sermon Scott outlined his philosophy of the relationship of church and state. Principles were enunciated which were to guide him throughout his ministry especially during the critical days in San Francisco when he was involved in the vigilante affair of 1856 and again when he was accused of praying for Jefferson

Davis in 1861. Scott insisted on complete separation of church and state. He urged the necessity of Christian men accepting public office. "Pious men must seek offices of power and trust for the public good," he wrote, "or our government will fall into the hands of the ungodly." And above all Christians should pray for their rulers.

The summer grew hot and humid. Scott was not well and now began to comment in his journal on his continued ill health. The following is the entry for August 15th when a moment of depression he made one of the rare references to his crippled foot to be found anywhere in his writings:

> I never suffered so much in my life from languor and debility. When I am seated my limbs ache & I feel as though I could not rise. I lose all the morning sometimes from absolute debility. I seem to complain a great deal, but my own dear wife knows not half my suffering. It is very much against my nature to give up and be an old woman in the corner . . . yet sometimes I feel like I should be obliged to do so. My lame leg, my crooked foot, my general weakness.
>
> Naturally sensitive, extremely nervous & excitable, I have always had great difficulty in preserving equanimity of temper. I have always striven after earnestness—impassioned manner of speaking in public, which insensibly to me often affects my manner in private, and I seem to have passion when I have not. I do daily and almost hourly try to restrain my feelings.

Scott was not only afflicted with some real physical ailment, he was also under a nervous strain which gave rise to periods of despondency.

A further entry for August 15th provides a clue for this concern. "Have had great anxiety," he wrote, "about the Newspaper. It has cost me many an anxious thought & prayer. The church will never do her duty here without a journal. But the apathy, the unbelief . . ." Scott was not long in New Orleans before he recognized the need for a paper which would serve Presbyterian interests for the whole Southwest. He introduced a resolution calling for the establishment of such a periodical at the spring meeting of the Louisiana Presbytery but, to his surprise and disappointment, he found some of his brethren shaking their heads in objection. Questions were raised. Where were they to get the money? Who would have time to edit such a paper? And, after all, was there a need? The only action the presbytery would take was to appoint a committee of three, of which Scott was chairman, to make further investigation.

Scott then wrote to a number of influential Presbyterians in the North asking for financial help to buy a press and type. Among these was the well-known elder, the Hon. Walter Lowrie, of New York. A series of letters passed between Scott and Lowrie which throws much light upon the final launching of the *New Orleans Protestant*. In his letter of September 11, 1843, Scott said to Lowrie: "I am pained almost beyond measure that good brethren should misunderstand each other." There is evidence that some members of presbytery were somewhat suspicious of the ambitious plans of this new young pastor who had been called to the most important pulpit in the South. Scott was troubled. He decided to proceed without the official endorsement of his presbytery.

Having secured financial help from Lowrie, and with the local assistance of the Rev. John B. Warren, a home missionary serving in the New Orleans area, the first number of the *New Orleans Protestant* appeared on or about October 1, 1844. Warren's name appeared as editor. The library of Princeton Theological Seminary contains a partial file of this periodical, the only copies known to be extant. Warren died in August 1845, after which Scott had to assume the responsibilities of editorship.

Lowrie sent Scott a press with type which arrived in New Orleans sometime during October. Thus with the assistance of a part-time printer, Scott's journalistic venture was independent of commercial shops. On October 23rd, he drew up a formal agreement which he sent to Lowrie in which the conditions for the operation of the press were clearly stated. One article read: "The Presbytery of Louisiana, or the Presbytery of New Orleans when one is formed, shall at all times have such direction and control of said paper as they may see proper to exercise." In default of any of the stated conditions, the press and type would become "the property of said Walter Lowrie."

Sometime in 1845 or 1846 the name of the paper was changed to the *New Orleans Presbyterian*. The last copy in the Princeton file, dated January 12, 1850, carried the announcement that the paper was to be merged with another Presbyterian periodical not then identified. Years later, Scott supplied biographical material about himself to the compiler of *Lives of the Clergy in New York and Brooklyn*, in which he stated that he had served as editor of the *New Orleans Presbyterian* for three years. The apathy and even hostility of a few of his brethren to a denominational paper in both the presbytery and the synod was a source of great disappointment to Scott.

In a letter to Lowrie dated October 12, 1843, which dealt largely with business regarding the paper, Scott made the following reference to his illness with yellow fever: "The epidemic rages fatally—still on the increase. Strangers are arriving and departing for another world daily. On the 26th ult. I was attacked myself very violently, 36 hours are left as an entire blank in my history. God has had mercy upon me. . . I am now convalescent but exceedingly feeble." In another letter to Lowrie, dated October 23rd, he wrote: "The epidemic still continues. Last week there were some 75 deaths from the fever. Yesterday I preached to a large and solemn audience for the first time since my attack."

Scott felt that there was need for a new presbytery to be organized to be called the Presbytery of New Orleans. In his letter of October 23rd to Lowrie, he reported that a petition for such a presbytery had been submitted to the Synod of Mississippi. The request was granted. If Scott felt that he would have greater freedom in a smaller ecclesiastical body and at the same time be rid of some critics, he was badly mistaken, but more of this in a later section.

During Scott's ministry at the First Church of New Orleans, three new Presbyterian churches were established in the city with colonies from First Church. The first of this number was the Lafayette Church which was planted in a suburb of New Orleans on September 20, 1843, with a group of twenty former members of First Church. The Rev. James Twitchell was the pastor. During the winter of 1843-44, Scott led in the movement to establish another church known as the Second Presbyterian Church of New Orleans. In a letter to Lowrie dated February 27, 1844, he said: "We have purchased a lot 58 by 120 deep, corner Prytania and Calliope . . . it is one of the very best locations in the city. We pay $3,400 for the lot, cash. We have raised $2,880 and the balance we must have this week. This money is all a clear donation. . . I have had to go out personally to collect the money to pay for the lot—a thing I never did in my life before."

The need for more Presbyterian churches in New Orleans arose partly out of the overflow crowds trying to worship in First Church. The following is taken from a letter written by Scott to Lowrie in December 1843: "My own church is filled continually to overflowing. Every time some go away from the door because there is no room. There have been more than 100 additions in the last 12 mos." Writing again to Lowrie on February 24, 1844, he reported having received fifty-four new members into the church during January and that the Sunday School had an enrollment of between seven and nine hundred children. The church had also established a reading room and employed a chaplain for the thousands of seamen thronging the port city. Again he referred to the overflow crowds and the need for another Presbyterian church. "It is painful," he wrote, "to see crowds going away from our door every Sabbath for want of seats."

SOME HIGHLIGHTS OF 1844 AND 1845

Scott suffered increasingly from ill health during the winter of 1844-45. He complained about his throat and pains in his chest. He was afraid he had "consumption," a term commonly used then to indicate tuberculosis. The elders of the church at a meeting held on April 9, 1844, noted the poor health of their pastor "enfeebled by his constant and arduous labours" and "earnestly recommend that he should take a journey of three months, at the very least, for the restoration of his health and the invigorating of his physical constitution." Since Scott knew that his wife could manage very well with the help of Mila and the other servants, he agreed to leave.

Having decided to travel through the northern and eastern states, Scott began his journey by going up the Mississippi to Memphis. He made only irregular entries in his journal for these three months but enough is given to outline his trip for us. He reached Memphis on May 18th and paid a short visit on his father. A brief entry tells the story: "Hack to father's $5.00" His friend, James A. Lyon, who also took a vacation about this same time and for similar reasons, probably met Scott at Memphis and the two traveled together for several weeks.

During the summer of 1844 a spirited presidential election was engaging public attention. Senator Henry Clay was one of the chief contenders for the high office which was won by James K. Polk. During the time that Scott and Lyon were together, Scott happened to make some passing comment about Clay which contributed, according to Clay's friends, to his defeat at the polls in November of that year. If we may permit our imaginations to interpret several autobiographical references which appear in Scott's defense of himself, we may assume that as he and Lyon stood on the deck of the river steamer as he left Memphis to go up the river, Scott indulged in some reminiscences. He might have said:

> I had my first steamboat ride out of Memphis back in the spring of 1830 when I was on my way to Cumberland College in Kentucky. As the steamer tied up at the wharf in Memphis, word was spread abroad that the great Henry Clay was aboard. I remember running down the bluff with others, waving my hat and shouting hurrah for Henry Clay. But, James, my ideal of that man was shattered on Saturday night when I saw him playing cards and gambling. It was the first time I had ever seen men gambling. And on the Sunday morning following, Clay stayed in his cabin and did not attend divine service.

This was the innocent statement, or one very much like it, which became the genesis of the Clay controversy regarding which more will be said later.

The steamer reached Louisville, Kentucky, on or before May 16th. The Presbyterian General Assembly began its sessions at Louisville on the 16th and no doubt both Scott and Lyon attended some of the meetings as visitors. Fourteen years later, or in 1858, Scott was to be elected moderator of the Assembly when it met in the First Presbyterian Church of New Orleans. But surely such a possibility never occurred to him as he and his friend observed the highest legislative body of their church in action.

The two were in Washington, D.C., during the first week of June. There they made the usual tourist rounds including a visit to the White House. Evidently the two men had some occasion to discuss second marriages for Scott made the following entry in his journal:

> It does not seem to me to be absolutely and per se contrary to Scripture, nor do I suppose it is a sin. But it does seem to me very cruel & unnatural. Nevertheless I am perfectly willing on two

conditions for my wife to marry again after I am dead. 1st: That her second marriage shall really conduce to her happiness. There is a bitterness, a burning pang in the thought of lying down in the dust myself to rot & be forgotten & resigning her to another. This worse than death itself. But I am willing to submit to this, if it will only make her happy, if it will ease her of cares & tears and smooth her way to Heaven. 2nd: That if I am permitted by grace to go to Heaven, & if a man may there know any one as his wife, although the peculiar relation & feelings of husband & wife may not exist, still I believe in the recognition of acquaintances in Heaven, therefore I wish to recognize my wife as *my* wife even in Heaven and not to recognize her as one who was my wife on earth but now is anothers. If she marries again, it must be null & void at death—for she must be mine again in the world to come as far as the nature of the world to come will admit of such an appropriation. This may be weakness—God pity me—I can't help it.

The two men were in New York City on June 25th. They took a steamboat up the Hudson River, where they found the scenery grand and beautiful, on the way to Niagara Falls where they arrived on the 30th. Along the way, Scott sent travel letters back to his church which were read to the congregation. Writing to Scott on June 15th, Elder Hennen said: "The letters you have written have done great good. . . I could wish that you might continue to travel until fall but you must be guided by your own judgment."

Just when and where the two men separated is not known. By July 1st, Scott was eager to return home. On his way down the Mississippi, he stopped over at Memphis in order to visit his father again. William found him gravely ill and remained at Raleigh for about two weeks. Even though he knew that his father could not live long, William felt it imperative that he get back to his work, so he continued his journey and reached his home on July 30th. A few days later he learned that his father had died on August 2nd. Eli Scott was in his 68th year. Writing to his friend, Walter Lowrie, on August 17th, Scott said: "He was 40 years a member of the church & for many years an elder. He has left a second wife, my stepmother, & three small children that will greatly add to my responsibilities and expenses." Information is lacking as to how much or for how long Scott had to contribute to the support of the family. A few weeks after hearing of the death of his father, word came of the death of his younger brother, James Nichols, on August 22nd at Nashville. Sometime in 1845, the exact date unknown, Ann learned of the death of her father, Dr. Nicholson, at Livingstone, Mississippi.

Upon his return, Scott gave himself with renewed vigor to the multiplicity of duties connected with his ministry. His own church was being renovated at a cost of about $17,000. This involved the replacement of the roof and the addition of some sixty pews, making it the largest

Protestant church in the city. At the same time a new building was being erected at the corner of Prytania and Calliope for the proposed Second Presbyterian Church of New Orleans. This was being paid for by the beneficence of a wealthy Presbyterian elder of New York, James Lenox. First Church was paying the salary of the missionary, the Rev. Robert L. Stanton, who had been selected to be the pastor of the new congregation. The new building was completed on October 10th and the church was formally organized in April 1845 with a nucleus of twenty-two members from First Church. For some reason Stanton became hostile to Scott. Mrs. Scott once described him as "a violent partisan against husband." This may have been a case of professional jealousy.

A movement to launch a third colony to form the Third Presbyterian Church of New Orleans was started in the fall of 1844, but such a congregation was not officially organized until March 7, 1847. Again Scott took the lead in the new endeavor.

Following the custom of that day, the newspapers of New Orleans often published the sermons of the leading ministers of the city. Judging by the number of clippings in the Scott papers in Bancroft Library, Dr. Scott was considered to be unusually newsworthy. The printed copy of his sermons often extended over six or seven full-length columns of closely-set type in newspapers the size of the *New York Times*. What metropolitan paper of today would devote so much space to a sermon? And who today would have the patience to read such doctrinal dissertations? But that was a different generation.

Beginning with his New Orleans pastorate, Scott was keenly aware of the importance of the press. In addition to his editorial duties connected with the *New Orleans Presbyterian*, he was able to publish twelve pamphlets during his twelve-year residence in the city and the first of a series of eight books. One of the pamphlets was without a title-page, two had a New York imprint, and the other nine appeared in New Orleans. The titles of the pamphlets in their chronological sequence are:

Address on the Life and Character of George Washington. [New Orleans?, 1842?]

The Duty of Praying for our Rulers. New Orleans, 1843.

The House of God. New Orleans, 1845.

A Discourse at the Dedication of the Franklin School House. New Orleans, 1845.

Progress of Civil Liberty. New Orleans, 1848.

Hope of Republics. New York, 1849. This also appeared in the March 1849 issue of the *National Preacher.*

Faith, the Element of Missions. New York, 1852.

Emigration of Free and Emancipated Negroes to Africa. New Orleans, 1853.

The Bible, God's Crystal Palace. New Orleans, 1854.

Installation Charges in the Third Presbyterian Church. New Orleans, 1854.

Lecture on the Chinese Empire. New Orleans, 1854.
The Gospel Ministers' Character and Platform. New Orleans, 1854.

In his sermon on the *Hope of Republics,* Scott emphasized the great potentialities of the press. He said:

> The press is more mighty than armies, kings, and senates—as rapid and intelligent as thought. None are too low for it to reach. None can be above its influence. It fascinates, inspires, and forms the masses of society for every effort. The strugglings of the press for liberty, and of the conscience for freedom, have filled all Europe with convulsions. It was the press aided by the living teacher that produced the great revolutions of the sixteenth century. It was the press that made England a Protestant country.

Herein lies the key to Scott's absorbing interest in the publication and distribution of religious literature and in a church-controlled periodical.

The Synod of Mississippi, of which the Presbytery of Louisiana was a part, at its October 1844 meeting authorized the erection of the Presbytery of New Orleans, thus setting the stage for one of the major scenes in the drama of the Clay controversy. The original minutes of this new presbytery, now on deposit in the Historical Foundation, Montreat, North Carolina, show that the first meeting was held on December 13, 1844, with four ministerial charter members, namely, John B. Warren, William A. Scott, Robert L. Stanton, and Jerome Twitchell. A fifth minister, James Beattie, joined the presbytery by ordination in the following April. Beattie served as chaplain of the Seamen's Bethel, another First Church project, and together with Warren was a loyal supporter of Scott. The new presbytery began with three churches, First of New Orleans, First of Lafayette, and Pine Grove in St. Tammany parish. Second Church of New Orleans was organized soon after the presbytery was erected, and while Warren was elected the first moderator, Scott succeeded him in this office on April 7, 1845.

On December 22, 1844, Mr. Scott became Dr. Scott when the University of Alabama conferred upon him *in absentia* its honorary degree of Doctor of Divinity. In a letter informing him of the new honor, Dr. Basil Manly, president of the university at Tuscaloosa, said that the action taken was "to the great gratification of your numerous friends."

A number of letters passed between Scott and General Jackson during the first years of Scott's residence in New Orleans. The general wrote on June 16, 1842, saying: "I am happy to find that you have been received in New Orleans so kindly. There is an awful field there for your usefulness. . . I am sure if we had had the means here we would never have separated from you or let you have gone. All your little flock here still loves you. . ." Several of Jackson's letters carry reference to the "little flock" at the Hermitage which continued to hold Scott in "real love and affection." On February 6, 1844, the general wrote again: "My hand is still steady, but my affliction & debility are great and with pains in my head & declining vision, I seldom am in a condition to write." His last extant letter to Scott was dated February 3, 1845, to which reference will later be made.

When word reached New Orleans of the death of General Jackson on June 8, 1845, at the age of seventy-eight, the city set aside the 26th of that month as a day of remembrance. The session of the First Presbyterian Church asked Scott to conduct a memorial service. The original manuscript of Dr. Scott's sermon is now in the archives of the Library of Tulane University in New Orleans. He took for his text, II Samuel 1:27: "How are the mighty fallen, and the weapons of war perished!" Said Scott, "Next to the accomplishment of great events, the most useful work is to perpetuate their remembrance. It is a patriotic duty, i.e., a pious work, to dispute with time for the memory of those whom we revere, like that puritan of the olden time, whose indefatigable hand restored on the monumental stones the half defaced inscriptions of his people." Today the main square in the French Quarter of New Orleans is called Jackson Square. There a replica of the equestrian statue of Jackson in Washington, D.C., has been placed.

THE CLAY CONTROVERSY

Scott waited for over a year before submitting his sermon on Jackson to the editor of the *New Orleans Delta* for publication. Being aware that another anniversary of Jackson's victory at New Orleans was approaching, Scott submitted a copy of his memorial sermon to the paper in December 1846. In an accompanying letter to the editor, Scott explained one of the reasons for the delay. "It was not published then," he wrote referring to the time the sermon was delivered, "because I was passing through the furnace of the Clay Club." Here in a few words Scott revealed the intensity of the mental anguish he suffered through many months because of a casual remark made to a friend about Henry Clay during the presidential campaign of 1844. The remark was seized upon by political zealots who after embellishing it gave it wide publicity through the press. As a result Scott was sharply criticized by the friends of Senator Clay who claimed that the report was both false and malicious and that its wide dissemination contributed to his defeat at the polls in the November election for the United States presidency.

In a letter to Scott dated December 12, 1845, Lyon referred to the trip the two had taken in the summer of 1844 and then summarized what had happened:

> On my return home, which was in the middle of the hottest of the political contest, the subject of politics and the pending election was frequently introduced, and my opinion asked as a matter of course. On one or more occasions Mr. Clay's moral character being alluded to, I repeated what I understood you to say relative to Mr. Clay's conduct on a certain occasion in your presence—viz—that he had played cards on board of a steamboat—on Sab-

bath morning and at other times and when preparations were made for public worship, Mr. Clay retired to his state-room and there remained until worship was over. Such conversations, however, were always had with none except those whom I regarded as my particular friends, and in the most private manner. Nothing was further from my intention or expectation than to make "public" charges against Mr. Clay. Such an insinuation is as untrue as it is unkind and injurious. No one was ever authorized to use my name or statements for electioneering purposes.

Scott's first intimation of being involved in a political campaign came when he received a letter dated August 12, 1844, from Jonas Decherd, a friend in Columbus, Mississippi, who wrote asking for confirmation of the report that was there being circulated about Scott seeing Clay playing cards and gambling on Sunday. For some reason Scott delayed until September 2nd before replying. He then wrote:

I am sorry that my name has been used in any way with politics. I take no part whatever in the party politics of the day; but I have my own views, as every independent man should have. I go in for principles and good men, and not for party rage or purposes. In answer to your inquiry, I am sorry to say that I have seen Mr. Clay frequently at the card table. Whether he bet or not, I cannot say, for I was and am so profoundly ignorant of the whole subject, that I do not understand the technicalities of the profession; but I do know that there were piles of money on the table. The place was on a steamboat between Memphis and Smithland. It was the first time I ever saw Mr. Clay. . . It was I think in the spring of 1830.

Since Scott was writing to a friend, he added: "I am sorry to say that with all my respect for Mr. Clay's talents and public services, and they are very considerable, I am constrained to regard him as a very immoral and dangerous man." Although Scott later denied that he intended to be evasive in his letter to Decherd, it was pointed out that he did not categorically deny the allegation that he had seen Clay play cards and gamble on Sunday.

Decherd showed Scott's letter to members of the Clay Club of Columbus who, according to Lyon, "hideously distorted and misrepresented" the facts involved and published their report in the *Columbia Whig* on September 26th. Lyon was therein charged with being "an ecclesiastical politician" and as having publicly thrown himself into "the political arena" and also as having "circulated all over Mississippi these charges against Mr. Clay." "It is peculiarly painful and disturbing," wrote Lyon to Scott, "for a clergyman who is not accustomed to the asperities of life, and the tug of worldly conflict and enterprise, to be unceremoniously dragged before the public, through the columns of a secular paper, and mocked and denounced and abused and hated."

In order to defend himself and correct the accusations made regarding his alleged political activities, Lyons published a statement in the October 3rd issue of the *Whig* in which he explained: "On my return home nothing was more natural than that friends should ask my opinion with reference to the success of the two distinguished candidates for the Presidency. . . If my friends have been indiscreet in using my name and statements, all I have to say is that it was done without my will or pleasure and I am sorry for it."

The editor of the *Whig* sent this issue to Scott who then became aware of the heat being generated over the statement so innocently made. Scott and Lyon were both present at the meeting of the Synod of Mississippi held that year during the latter part of October in Natchez. Lyon was elected moderator that year, an indication of the high respect with which he was held by his brethren. In his letter of December 12, 1845, Lyon reminded Scott:

> There we met and had some conversation in relation to this matter. . . We had little opportunity to converse together on any subject; still less on an unpleasant one. I did not ask you whether this or that part of the statement was correct as I had no serious doubt on the subject. This explains why I did not inquire of you specifically whether I had correctly understood you in saying that Mr. Clay played cards "on Sabbath morning."

Clay's friends made capital of the fact that although Scott and Lyon had met at Natchez after publicity had been given to the allegation that Clay played cards and gambled on Sunday, yet the two made no effort to correct what critics considered to be a misquotation or a falsehood. In the meantime two young men of Columbus, one of whom was still a minor, wrote to Clay and gave him the embellished version of the report that was being circulated. They claimed:

> Lyon . . . publicly and repeatedly asserted on the authority of the Reverend Mr. Scott of same Church in New Orleans, that he (Mr. Scott) was travelling in company with yourself about eighteen months or two years ago, on a steamboat on the Mississippi river; that you played cards the whole of one Saturday night until Sabbath morning; at which time divine service was proposed, it being Sunday, whereupon you threw your cards upon the table, and retired to your stateroom and closed the door until service was over, when you resumed your cards.

Clay replied on October 9th saying of the report:

> . . . a base and vile calumny, destitute of all foundation. I never in my life played cards on the Sabbath on board of any steamboat whatever; and I never failed on any occasion whatever to attend divine service, wherever any was performed on board of any steamboat of which I was a passenger. I pronounce the tale

an atrocious calumny; and you may so inform the Reverend gentl-
men. . . . Although I am not a member of any church, I defy any
man to establish that I ever failed to treat religion with the profoundest respect on any occasion whatever.

Clay's letter added to the confusion as he claimed he always attended
church services on steamboats when such were held and Scott had a
clear memory that on the occasion of which he spoke, Clay had remained
in his stateroom. The fact that Scott was referring to something that had
happened fourteen years previously rather than eighteen months or two
years was an important point. Clay had been known as a habitual
gambler, but, when running for the presidency, he had publicly stated
that he had given up gambling. Then came the report attributed to
Scott that he had been seen gambling on a river steamer within the last
two years. It touched a sensitive nerve.

The two young men who received Clay's letter quickly showed it to
leaders of the Clay Club of Columbus who then called a special meeting
of the club for October 19th. The club voted to send a copy of the
letter to the Clay Club of New Orleans with the request that it be shown
to Dr. Scott. The Columbus group also appointed a committee to wait
on Lyon as soon as he returned from the meeting of the synod.

On Saturday, November 2nd, "at half-past two o'clock p.m.," Messrs.
C. Roselius and Samuel J. Peters of the New Orleans Clay Club called
on Dr. Scott at his home. The men presented the copy of Clay's letter.
Scott at once corrected the mistake in time and explained that the incident took place when he was a young man some fourteen years earlier.
He denied ever saying that Clay played cards and gambled on Sunday
but only on Saturday night. Scott hesitated to say much until he was
able to write to Lyon and learn more about what Lyon had said. In
their written account of the interview, the two men stated: "We left
Dr. Scott as we had met him, favorably impressed towards him: but
thinking he had acted with great indiscretion in speaking of circumstances which occurred so many years ago, and which from his account,
were of so trivial a nature but we thought he had done it without any
intention to injure our distinguished friend."

Scott hastened to write to Lyon. He made it very plain that he had
never said that he had seen Clay playing Cards and gambling on Sunday.
Lyon received the letter on November 13th and the next day inserted a
statement in the *Columbus Democrat* in which he stated that he had
misunderstood Scott's remark about Clay. But the election was over and
Polk had won over Clay. The following quotation from the *Kentucky
Observer and Reporter* for February 26, 1845, is typical of other newspaper comments about the correction: "It is a pretty business for
Ministers of the Gospel to engage in propagating falsehoods for political
purposes, which, after they have accomplished the object of their invention, are publicly retracted by them!"

On Monday, November 4th, following the visit of Roselius and Peters,

Scott wrote to them giving his recollections of the Clay incident. Not wishing to involve his friend Lyon more than was necessary, Scott failed to be specific regarding the key issue as to whether or not he had actually told Lyon that Clay had played cards and gambled on Sunday. Roselius and Peters were dissatisfied with the statement and felt that Scott was guilty of duplicity. If Clay had won the election on Tuesday, November 5th, perhaps this whole incident would have passed without further comment. But since Clay had lost, his friends angrily cast about for scapegoats and Dr. Scott was one on whom they vented their wrath. The *New Orleans Bee* of January 10, 1845, commented: "That Mr. Clay's defeat has been caused by the unceasing efforts of unscrupulous calumniators is a fact that cannot be disputed."

A number of letters passed between Roselius and Peters on the one hand and Scott on the other. "Your letter is silent on the main question," wrote the two men after receiving Scott's letter of November 4th, "what did you say to Mr. Lyon?" Scott replied on the 11th somewhat tartly: "What Mr. Lyon has said, it is not my business to know, or to defend. He is of age, and fully able to take care of himself. I have nothing to do with rumors or reports of second and third persons." On December 9th, Roselius and Peters notified the Clay Club of Columbus that Dr. Scott had "acted with duplicity" and with utter disregard of the truth. All of this correspondence was subsequently published. The review of events to this point is but a prelude to later developments.

SCOTT ON TRIAL IN CHURCH COURTS

Scott's involvement in the Clay controversy passed through two main phases. The first was political and lasted for only about four months. The second was ecclesiastical and spread over nearly three years. This latter phase began at Scott's request for an investigation into the facts and circumstances of the controversy by the Session of the First Presbyterian Church of New Orleans. After spending several days going over the evidence, the elders found that "the charges of duplicity of character and entire disregard of truth" to be unfounded. On January 15, 1845, Scott sent the findings of the session, signed by nine elders including such highly respected New Orleans business and professional men as Alfred Hennen, Stephen Franklin, and Joseph A. Maybin, to the *New Orleans Commerical Bulletin,* which published it.

News of the controversy reached General Jackson who, on February 3, 1845, wrote to Scott, saying in part:

> The outrageous political attack made upon [you] by such scamps as the Clay Club should give you no uneasiness. There are but few who do not know that Clay has been guilty of all card playing with which he is charged, and profligacy of immoral conduct, and altho many of the clergy have supported him, by which they have done great injury to true & vital religion, still a wise providence has counteracted all their exertions and saved our country from the

rule of as great a profligate as ever lived. Our republic & glorious
honor is safe. *The Lord reigneth. Let the people rejoice.*

In this, Jackson's last letter to Scott, we see his deep antipathy to Clay.
Jackson's sympathy and moral support must have been comforting to the
harassed minister.

The scene then shifted from the session of the First Presbyterian
Church to the Presbytery of New Orleans. Largely through Scott's
influence, the presbytery had been carved out of the larger Presbytery of
Louisiana in order to provide what he thought would be greater efficiency in the promotion of Presbyterian work in New Orleans. But the
contrary proved to be the case. Scott soon became aware of the un-
friendly attitude of R. L. Stanton of Second Church which later
developed into open antagonism. With the ordination and reception of
James Beattie into the presbytery in April 1845, Scott found he had two
friends, Warren and Beattie, on whom he could depend. Twitchell, the
fifth ministerial member of presbytery, was friendly to Scott at first but
finally shifted his support to Stanton.

Scott wanted nothing more than to be free to carry on the important
work of his parish. Stanton, however, was looking for opportunities to
embarrass Scott. His great opportunity came when five members of the
Clay Club of New Orleans, who were also members of Scott's church,
signed a memorial on July 4, 1845, addressed to the Presbytery of New
Orleans. In this memorial the five requested an investigation of "certain
rumors injuriously affecting the character of the Rev. Dr. Scott." The
memorial was presented at the July 7th meeting of the presbytery held
in Dr. Scott's church. Scott found himself in an embarrassing situation as
he was then moderator. The report was referred to a committee consisting of Beattie as Chairman, and Elders Alfred Hennen from First
Church and John A. Steele from Second Church. A special meeting of
the presbytery was called for the 10th of July.

The committee brought in a divided opinion. The majority report,
signed by Beattie and Hennen, stated that "they do not see how this
Presbytery can entertain said memorial without violating the directions
so clearly laid down in our excellent Book of Discipline." This report
further stated that the charges lacked proof and therefore recommended
that the memorial be returned to the signers. The minority report,
signed by Stanton's elder, claimed that the charges were of such major
importance that the memorial should be referred to the Synod of Mississippi for investigation.

A second special meeting of the presbytery was called for the next
day, July 11th. At this meeting Scott offered to step aside as moderator
but his friends urged him to remain in the chair saying that he was not
then on trial. Only Stanton favored Scott's suggestion. The first motion
offered was to adopt the minority report which meant that the memorial
would be referred to the synod. The vote was a tie, three to three;
Stanton and two elders voted for it while Warren, Beattie, and Elder

Maybin voted against it. Scott, as moderator, declined to vote and thus the motion was declared lost. It was then moved to adopt the majority report and again the vote was divided the same way. The official minutes read: "There being a tie, the Moderator gave the casting vote, and the question was decided in the affirmative." Scott in effect cast the deciding vote for himself in this decision to return the memorial to the signers. All of these meetings of the presbytery, even after periods of bitter debate, closed with the same formula as recorded in the minutes: "Closed with the doxology, prayer, and benediction." No doubt Scott had good reason to sing the doxology that day with some zest as it appeared that the whole unhappy controversy had now been given a decent burial.

Unfortunately for Scott, an unexpected development occurred in August when Warren became seriously ill. He died on August 13, 1845. His death greatly weakened Scott's side. Feeling that the absence of Warren was to their advantage, the opposition requested a special meeting of the presbytery for August 12th. A complaint signed by the same five laymen who endorsed the memorial of July 4th was submitted to this meeting with the announced intention of carrying the whole case to the Synod of Mississippi. Scott then presented his formal request for "an immediate and patient and full and thorough investigation into the nature, extent, and evidences of the said rumors in order that the truth may be elicited, my innocence established, and the precious cause of our holy religion sustained." If there was to be an investigation, Scott wanted it done by the presbytery and not by the synod. But the opposition refused to accede to Scott's request.

The Presbytery of New Orleans called a series of eighteen special meetings between July 7th and October 10th, some of which were not held because of lack of a quorum. The presbytery could come to no decision as the membership was evenly divided. Beattie stood with Scott while Twitchell sided with Stanton. There was considerable wrangling over procedures. The manuscript record of the minutes runs to 323 pages! The strain began to tell on Scott. He was confined to his bed during the first week of September.

The approaching meeting of the Synod of Mississippi scheduled for the last week of October forced a compromise. With both Scott and Stanton in agreement, the presbytery voted to petition the synod for the dissolution of the Presbytery of New Orleans and the absorption of its members and churches into the Presbytery of Louisiana and that the Scott case be referred to this presbytery for adjudication. This recommendation was accepted by the synod on October 24, 1845.

Scott's trial before the Presbytery of Louisiana began in the First Presbyterian Church of Columbus, Mississippi, on October 28th. The following four charges were made against him: 1. Deliberate and wilful falsehood; 2. Conduct highly unbecoming his official character as a member of the late Presbytery of New Orleans; 3. Unchristian and unclerical conduct;　and 4. Having uttered and preached sentiments which are contrary to the constitution of the Presbyterian Church in the United States. The last charged arose out of some advice Scott gave at the time Stanton was installed as pastor of Second Church in New Orleans and referred to the distribution of benevolence monies. This charge had nothing to do with the Clay controversy but had been dragged in by Stanton as a further embarrassment to Scott. Stanton served as prosecutor in the trial and Elder Joseph A. Maybin conducted Scott's defense. Although blind in one eye and with impaired vision in the other, Maybin was gifted with a keen analytical mind. He knew Presbyterian law and had a deep affection for his pastor.

The opening days of the trial took place in Lyon's church in Columbus. Lyon was the first witness and was subjected to a gruelling cross-examination by Maybin. In his final summary for the defense, Maybin accused Lyon of being unguarded in his speech and consequently "a rash and unsafe witness." Lyon was deeply troubled and hurt over the whole affair. He claimed that he was absolutely sincere in thinking that Scott had stated that he had seen Clay play cards and gamble on Sunday. When informed of his mistake, he had tried to correct the false impressions he had given. After the church court had adjourned to meet in New Orleans to continue its deliberations, Lyon wrote Scott a long letter on December 12, 1845, which contained nearly 2,500 words. The whole unhappy affair spoiled what had been a warm friendship between Lyon and Scott. Never again did Scott permit himself to be on the cordial terms which had sweetened the fellowship of earlier years.

The sessions of presbytery extended over three weeks in New Orleans and then after the turn of the new year, another week was spent hearing further evidence in Baton Rouge. Maybin made an eloquent appeal for an acquittal in his final summary. "Mr. Moderator," he said, "for months has this pious and zealous minister . . . been held up to the world as a foul calumniator, an atrocious libeller . . . held up to public scorn and contempt. . . Idolized by his church, his congregation clings to him now."

The final vote came on January 10, 1846. Scott, Stanton, and Twitchell refrained from voting. Seventeen ballots were cast and all delegates voted "not guilty" on all four charges except one, the Rev. James Smylie, who voted "guilty" on the first two charges. The vindication was almost unanimous. The vote revealed how much Scott had suffered from the animosity of one man, R. L. Stanton. The full proceedings of the trial were published in New Orleans in 1846 and the transcript ran to 357 pages. Previous to this publication, two other documents had appeared. The first was entitled: *Documents relating to certain Calumnies against the Hon. Henry Clay and ascribed to Rev. W. A. Scott of this City.* Although anonymous, it was evidently the work of some members of the Clay Club. This numbered 107 pages and appeared in New Orleans in 1845. The second document was the *Memorial to the*

Presbytery of New Orleans Concerning the trial of Rev. Scott and Three Citizens of New Orleans. This also was printed in New Orleans in 1845. The total number of pages in these three publications amounted to 530.

But the story is not finished. Stanton, thoroughly discredited, discontinued his attacks, but, the Rev. James Smylie carried on a one-man crusade against Scott for "principle's sake" by appealing the decision of the Presbytery of Louisiana to the Synod of Mississippi at its fall meeting in 1846. When his appeal was summarily dismissed by the synod, Smylie then carried his case to the General Assembly of 1847.

Smylie was some thirty years Scott's senior and had spent his entire ministry as a home missionary on a small salary in Mississippi and Louisiana. While serving as stated clerk of the Presbytery of Mississippi in 1836, he received a communication from the Presbytery of Chilicothe in Ohio which contained a series of resolutions adopted by the northern ministers urging their southern brethren to forsake "the sin of slavery." Smylie, irritated by what he considered a "violent abolition letter," decided to reply. In 1836 he published an eighty-seven page pamphlet under the title: *A Review of a Letter from the Presbytery of Chillicothe to the Presbytery of Mississippi on the Subject of Slavery.* This publication is usually considered to be the first of a series by various southern ministers on the divine origin and Scriptural justification of slavery. Smylie declared that if it were a sin to own a slave, he wanted proof from the Bible. The pamphlet was extensively circulated through the South in the pre-Civil War days and the author's views widely quoted. At the time of Smylie's death in 1853, the Synod of Mississippi eulogized him for "giving the true exposition of the doctrine of the Bible in relation to slavery in the commencement of the abolition excitement." This was the man who, picking up the standard of the opposition which Stanton had dropped, pressed the case against Scott with fanatical zeal to the church's highest court and even beyond.

According to the *Minutes of the 1847 General Assembly,* the Judicial Committee appointed to receive the complaint of James Smylie against the decision of the Presbytery of Louisiana in the Scott case was appalled at the magnitude of the printed and manuscript testimony it was expected to digest. "The bare reading of the records of the Presbytery," the Committee reported, "would consume four or five days." The committee came to the unanimous opinion that "if the case could be disposed of, consistently with the rights of Mr. Smylie, without remanding it to either of the inferior courts, and without the Assembly's adjudicating on it, all of the ends of justice would be gained and the peace of the Church would be promoted." Smylie was called before the Committee and was induced to drop his complaint.

After returning to his home, Smylie was persuaded by some of Scott's bitter opponents to publish a seventy-four page pamphlet which appeared under the title *Brief History of the Trial of the Rev. William A. Scott, D.D.* Much of the material in this pamphlet had been previously published but a few new items were included such as copies of some letters from Lyon to Maybin. Smylie dedicated the pamphlet to Dr. Charles Hodge of Princeton with the explanation: "My object is not that you may take it under your special patronage, but that you may give it your special attention."

When a copy of the *Brief History* came to Scott's attention, he hastened to write to Dr. Hodge who had been one of his professors in his year at Princeton. Under date of December 22, 1847, Scott wrote: "It abounds in misrepresentations, errors & bitterness. It is doubtless a joint production. It is an after thought. While he was at the Assembly he did not design this course, but on coming back into this heated atmosphere, he was prompted to this publication. Where I am personally well known & where this whole shameful business is understood, it can do no harm. . . I presume the object is to worry me & provoke me to do something & get the case before the next Assembly." Scott asked for advice. He admitted that in his "correspondence with the President and another member of the Clay Club of New Orleans, I fell into a hasty temper & used too violent language." He stressed how he had exercised the greatest restraint upon himself. "I have made no publications since the trial began," he wrote, "I have made no oral address to my people. I did not open my mouth in my own defence before the Presbytery. I have made no replies to the nameless newspaper attacks & pamphlets, anonymous & otherwise. . . *Personal enmity and jealousy* have kept it alive."

Scott summarized the nature and intent of the opposition by writing: "The number of persons engaged in this attempt to destroy me is very small . . . nothing but my total ruin, disgrace & removal from my Church will ever satisfy them . . . yet I have never alluded to my personal trials in the Pulpit. I love my country, but I seldom vote. I never attend public political meetings, not even to open them with prayer."

It is amazing to realize how much time and money were spent on what now seems to be so trivial a matter. No criteria are available to measure how much harm the controversy did to the work of the Presbyterian Church in New Orleans and throughout the whole Southwest or to appreciate the mental anguish suffered by Dr. Scott. The rise and continuance of the controversy seems to rest upon an unfortunate combination of factors. Lyon in his letter of December 1845 tried to explain the "inflated magnitude" of the affair by referring to the "astonishing credulity" of some and to the "impulsiveness and excitability of the Southern character in general." To this must be added the bitter passions aroused by the Clay-Polk Presidential campaign. The *Dictionary of American Biography*, in its sketch of Clay, has the following comment: "No man in American public life has had more ardent supporters or more bitter enemies than Clay." And finally we must remember the professional jealousy which motivated a few of Scott's associates in the Presbyterian ministry.

In her brief reminiscences of her husband, Mrs. Scott wrote: "Husband often remarked that he could not for the life of him understand the fuss that was made about a remark to a friend in private, made without malice and with no expectation of it ever being repeated and he always scouted the idea that it could have had any influence on the Presidential election."

Evidence of his great popularity with his people is found in the following news item taken from the April 17, 1846, issue of the New Orleans *Evening Mercury*. The reference is to a service conducted by Dr. Scott in his church the previous Sunday evening after a short absence from the city.

> The commodious church of Dr. Scott contained a large and genteel congregation, deeply absorbed in the contemplation of the subject presented to their consideration by the talent of *no ordinary man*. The mantle of the Apostles did not descend on shoulders unable to bear it gracefully and with dignity when Dr. Scott wrapped himself in its sacred folds. Bold and fearless, he is ever more dear to his congregation and church than formerly, in consideration of the fiery ordeal through which he has passed.

The last sentence carries a clear reference to Scott's trial by the Presbytery of Louisiana over the Clay affair. The above quotation contains in italics the phrase used by the author as a subtitle for this book.

FIRST TRIP TO EUROPE, 1846

The strain of the Clay trial told on Scott's health. Never of rugged constitution, he now became aware of soreness in his throat and sometimes pain in his chest. The elders of the church offered a six months' leave of absence with full pay and recommended that he visit Europe. They felt that such a trip would have therapeutic value. Mrs. Scott also urged him to go, assuring her husband that with the help of several servants, including faithful Mila, she could get along very well during his absence. Their five children were then of the following ages: Robert, 9; Martha, 7; Calvin Knox, 5; William, 3; and Chalmers who had joined the family circle on May 9, 1845. Somewhat reluctantly, Scott accepted the generous offer.

Since Scott had been elected a commissioner by the Presbytery of Louisiana to the Presbyterian General Assembly scheduled to meet that year at Philadelphia beginning on May 21st, he found it necessary to make the first part of his journey by river steamer up the Mississippi and Ohio rivers. He left New Orleans on Wednesday evening, April 29th, and on that day he started another diary which he kept with fair regularity during his travels. He began by describing the farewell scene with his family. "At half past four of the clock this day in the afternoon," he wrote, "took leave of my dear little family. I assembled the children in my wife's room and designed to talk a little with them and give them each some words of advice and pray with them. But I could not. My very soul was in agony. Tears gave no relief. The dear little faces. My sobbing wife. . . I kissed them amidst flowing tears and departed."

A group of friends were at the dock to see him depart. His diary continues: "At tea found we have about 150 souls in the cabin and a large number on deck. Observed countenances, wondered if my sons would resemble any of the young men I saw on board. Hope none of them will make themselves *goats* as many around me have. Some indeed resemble boars out of the woods."

The steamboat reached Memphis on Sunday, May 3rd. Familiar scenes summoned a parade of memories out of the past. He commented on some of the most vivid of these recollections in his diary. He recalled his first view of Memphis when he was a ten-year-old boy in the spring of 1823. Then it was nothing more than a tiny frontier settlement surrounded by a peach orchard. As he looked upon the bluff by the landing place, he remembered how he had raced down that hill in the spring of 1830 to join others in welcoming Henry Clay. How attitudes had changed during the years! Now the very mention of Clay's name brought up the most unpleasant memories. "Felt a degree of melancholy creeping over me," he mused, "at the passing so near the home of my boyhood and the graves of my departed parents." He marvelled at the changes which had taken place in the intervening years. Once he wore homespun and lived in a log cabin. Now he was pastor of one of the most influential Presbyterian churches in the nation. "What am I now?" he asked himself, "God only knows. I have seen changes, toil, labor, study, perils by water and land, sea and flood, in the wilderness and in the city." The intimate glimpses into his boyhood revealed in these reminiscences have provided some of the material used in an earlier part of this book.

Scott reached Pittsburg on May 9th. He continued his journey by stage and rail to Philadelphia via Baltimore and Washington, doing some sightseeing along the way. On Sunday, May 17th, Scott heard Dr. Thomas Smyth of Charleston, South Carolina, preach in one of Philadelphia's churches. Smyth was then reputed to be one of the most prominent of the southern Presbyterian ministers and Scott felt drawn to him. The two dined together a few days later at which time a friendship began which continued through the rest of their lives. Smyth was also planning a trip to England that spring and summer and the two arranged to meet in London and travel together.

The General Assembly of 1846, with 179 commissioners in attendance, elected Dr. Charles Hodge of Princeton as moderator. Scott called on his former professor at his hotel and the two took dinner together. Hodge's views on slavery became a molding influence in Scott's attitude to the same explosive subject. On May 25th, Scott made a brief appearance before the assembly when he spoke on foreign missions and that evening he commented in his diary: "Was dreadfully embarrassed. O, that I could think and speak to more purpose before my fellow men."

Twelve years later, Scott was to be elected moderator of the assembly but in 1846 such a possibility was still too far in the future to be imagined. Scott's presence at the assembly was cut short by the fact that he had booked passage for England on a steamer leaving Boston on Monday, June 1st. He left Philadelphia on May 27th, although the assembly continued in session until June 11th.

Scott was in Boston by Sunday, May 31st. His fame as a preacher had preceded him and he was invited to speak in the Park Street Church. The "Britannica" sailed at noon on Monday. "Rather melancholy at leaving my own native land," he commented in his diary, "and all its precious ones. . . There was not a familiar face in all the long lines on the wharf to tell me farewell. . . Quite sea sick." Within a few days the ship was moving cautiously through a tremendous field of icebergs. He described them as being "pure white, some 150 to 200 feet high, of all varieties of shape and position." Seventy-eight were counted in one afternoon. "When the sun broke out just before going down," Scott wrote on June 5th, "its glistening on the floating mountains of ice surrounded by foaming waves was a most magnificent sight. I have no words to express my admiration of the scene. It was grand. Three whales were to be seen."

On June 12th, the rocky shores of Ireland were sighted. "The native land of my dear blessed wife," he noted and added, "Have I really crossed the Atlantic? Yes, it is really so. The old world is now before me with his hoary antiquities." He looked forward with eagerness to the privilege of visiting historic sites and scenes made familiar by extensive reading. Few of his generation could have visited Europe better informed than he as to the history and significance of the places he wanted to see.

Scott disembarked at Liverpool on Sunday morning, June 14th, and attended church that day at St. Jude's. While away from home, he took every opportunity to hear good preaching, taking notes not only on the content of the sermons but also on the homiletical and oratorical techniques of the preachers. He carried with him letters of introduction to well-known ministers in the cities which he intended to visit. Deliberately he sought out and met important and interesting people. Over and over again he had to ask himself whether it was really true that he, a former backwoods lad from western Tennessee, was visiting the famous places of which he had read so much and his diary reflects the thrills he experienced. On June 19th, he was in Oxford and on that day wrote: "Is it really so that I am in Oxford, Old Oxford?" He made a pilgrimage to the spot where Cranmer, Ridley, and Latimer were martyred. He mentioned hearing discussions about the high church movement in the Church of England and about Newman entering the Roman Catholic Church. Always interested in church history, these firsthand contacts with people, places, and events made it even more fascinating.

On Sunday, June 21st, Scott was in London. "My feelings on finding myself in London, the greatest city on the globe, were truly indescribable," he wrote. He attended church three times that day. In the morning he heard the Rev. W. Henry Melville in St. Botloph's; in the afternoon he went to Westminster Abbey where "Rev. Dr. Wordsworth, said to be a brother or nephew of the poet" preached; and in the evening he listened to the Rev. Thomas Dale in St. Clement's.

On Monday, Scott spent some time in bookstores on Paternoster Row and "looked at silks and satins for my dear wife." He spent four hours in St. Paul's Cathedral inspecting the building from the vaults to the dome. The greatness of London overwhelmed him. "There is a feeling of dread & fear in a strange city like this," he wrote, "such a vast wilderness of houses & oceans of men. London is a world—months & months may be spent here & nothing known then. I greatly prefer the country." He visited the British Museum, the National Gallery of Art, and returned to Westminster Abbey. His observations gave him an unfavorable opinion of the British people as he commented caustically on their "venality and avarice." He could not help but notice "the street whores, finely dressed, painted & impudent as Satan himself."

"Thursday, June 25. Fifty seventh day from home." Each day was thus numbered. "Left London for Birmingham." There he spent a night. Nineteen years later, while in exile from his home land during the Civil War, Scott was to serve a church in Birmingham. But on the occasion of this his first visit to the city, nothing was further from his mind. Taking ship at Liverpool for Scotland, he landed in Glasgow on the 27th. In his diary he wrote:

> I feel akin to Scotland & Ireland, but a heathen & publican to England. The Englishman is as sour & sulky as a *castrated* bull, or a virile man disappointed. . . The people are crushed, spiritless, venal, avaricious, any thing for money. My impression of female chastity among the English is very bad, though God knows I have not touched one of them—but their manners are extremely disgusting. . . No modesty. The word is obsolete. The poor grow poorer, the rich richer. It is a fine country for the very rich. America is a chosen land. God be praised my children are there.

Smyth was with Scott in Edinburgh. Together they visited St. Giles Church, Holyrood Palace, Arthur's Seat, and places mentioned by Sir Walter Scott in some of his novels. His diary reads: "In all there was pain to me, my wife, my blessed wife was not at my side to enjoy it too. . . Effie Deans . . . Heart of Midlothian . . . Greyfriars Chh." On Sunday Scott and Smyth met the famous Dr. Thomas Chalmers who had led the schismatic Free Church out of the Church of Scotland in 1843. Scott carried a letter of introduction to Chalmers who at once urged Scott to preach for him that evening. Scott did so. One of Scott's sons was named for Dr. Chalmers.

While in Edinburgh, Scott wrote a long letter on July 2nd to his congregation. These pastoral letters were often sent when he was on an extended absence from his church. The following quotation from the Edinburgh letter is a typical example of how he mixed his travel experiences with pious exhortations:

> When I stood the other day in the very church in which Knox preached and hung over the tombstone in Greyfriars Schoolyard of 1800 martyrs for the testimony of Jesus, from Argyle to Renwick, my very soul was stirred within me. These are those who have gone to glory through great tribulations. . . Let us all strive for the higher degrees of knowledge, for more love and humility. O let us live for God, for the souls of men, labor for eternity.

After touring the chief points of interest in Scotland, Scott went to Belfast. On July 11th, he made the following comment on that city in his diary: "Walked about town for 2 hours—80,000 to 100,000 inhabitants, some beautiful streets. But the poverty, dirt, and degredation that I have seen in the cities and towns of Great Britain is heart sickening. I see so much of filth & ragged wretchedness that I have no appetite for my food."

Ann had urged her husband to visit her birthplace, Kilkeel on the Irish coast, to see what could be done about some property which she had inherited from her father. When Ann's father and mother migrated to America in 1817, their home was left with her father's brother. The house was then rented but the brother never sent any of the rent money to Dr. Nicholson. Later the house was sold even though Robert Nicholson had the title deed. Scott went to Kilkeel but could get no satisfaction from the occupants of the house. He got a lawyer but being pressed for time and, as Mrs. Scott later wrote, "seeing nothing before him but expense and annoyance, after spending some forty or fifty dollars in the investigation, continued his journey." When Scott was in England in 1851, he again tried to clear up the matter but without success. In a letter written by Mrs. Scott on April 15, 1876, to a lawyer in Kilkeel, she stated: "I stand bereft of my property. . . Truly as the proverb says—'The absent person is never the heir'." As a result of his investigation in 1846, Scott felt that since the property was valued at not more than eighty pounds, it was not worth the expense of a lawsuit to regain possession.

From Ireland Scott went to Germany, Switzerland, and France. He was in Coblenz on August 1st. He took a boat trip down the Rhine and visited Maintz, Frankfort, and Geneva. On August 18th, he was in Paris. "Two things have greatly surpassed my expectations," he wrote, "the Alps & Paris." He was moved by the grandeur and magnificence of Versailles. He was back in London by August 30th eagerly looking forward to his return trip home. Passage had been booked on the "Great Western," one of the most famous passenger ships of that day, leaving September 7th from Liverpool. On Sunday, August 30th, while returning to his hotel room from another visit to Westminster Abbey, he was accosted by a prostitute. The following is his account of what happened:

> Coming home had an adventure that made me tremble for nearly an hour after I go to my room—simply this, in walking up the Strand, as my boots hurt my feet; I was walking slowly— when to my astonishment a young lady to all appearances, finely dressed, blushing cheeks, came up behind & took hold of my arm, saying familiarly "How do you do. It is a long time since I have seen you." When she touched my arm, I did not see her, had no idea who or what it was—upon discovering her, I was frightened. She kept talking, saying I do not know what & I kept walking, turning my head away from her & began to think I should be compelled to call a policeman. At last she let me go & I greatly rejoiced.

Scott felt that the solicitations of street-walkers was much more in evidence in London than in any Continental city he had visited, even Paris. "It is enough to make a man curse his mother for being a woman to see the depravation of the sex in England," he wrote. "They are utterly devoid of all sense of shame, decency or modesty."

The "Great Western" ran into a terrifying storm while making its westward crossing, and Scott vowed that never again would he attempt a trans-Atlantic voyage in September. The "storm-riddled" ship docked in New York on September 30th. The next day he was cleared through customs and after saying good-by to Smyth, took the train for Baltimore. He noted in his diary receiving a letter from "my ever blessed wife & also one from Mr. Franklin." Commenting on his European experiences, he wrote: "I denied myself the pleasure of attending any concerts while in Europe. I was not inside of any opera theater or the like during all my travels abroad." Although we have no evidence that Scott did not enjoy musical concerts, he no doubt considered the theater sinful.

Scott spent Sunday, October 4th, in Baltimore where he preached for Dr. John C. Backus, pastor of the First Presbyterian Church. Here another friendship began which continued throughout their lives and resulted years later in Backus giving his fine library to the infant theological seminary which Scott was so largely instrumental in founding in San Francisco in 1871. On Monday he took the train for Montgomery, Alabama, from which place he took a river steamer for Mobile and then another ship for New Orleans. He was back in his pulpit on Sunday, October 14th.

The members and friends of First Church welcomed their pastor back with enthusiasm. Among the miscellaneous items found among Dr. Scott's papers was a card, $2\frac{1}{2}$ x $3\frac{1}{2}$ inches, which carried the following words:

THE PASTOR'S RETURN
(Sung after Sermon)

1

Great God, we thank thee for this hour
Of happy meeting given;
For all the care on *him* bestowed,
Who guides our steps to heaven.

2

What wonders on the mighty deep,
Thy powerful hand displayed!
But thou did'st lull the storms to sleep;
The waves thy voice obeyed.

3

Now to his blissful home—his flock—
The temple of thy grace,—
And to our hearts,—we welcome him;
O, fill our souls with praise.

4

For these kind tokens of thy love,
Let every heart rejoice;
Joined with the organ's solemn notes,
Be every tuneful voice.

Evidently these words were composed especially for the first Sunday after Scott's return and were no doubt sung to some familiar tune. The second stanza clearly refers to the great storm which Scott encountered on his voyage across the Atlantic.

Although Scott had taken the long trip abroad with the hope that travel and a change of climate would benefit his health, yet in the secrecy of his diary he confessed that he often suffered pain after his return. Still there is no doubt that the contacts he made with leading churchmen both in this country and abroad were of great value to him, and he found the whole experience tremendously stimulating.

SCOTT'S ATTITUDE TOWARD SLAVERY

Before we can understand Scott's attitude toward slavery, we must review the pronouncements of his church on the subject and become acquainted with some of the contemporary developments pertaining to the problem. The Presbyterian General Assembly of 1818 took a strong stand against slavery by declaring that it was "a gross violation of the most precious and sacred rights of human nature" and "utterly inconsistent with the law of God." The assembly urged all Christians "as speedily as possible to efface this blot on our holy religion, and to obtain the complete abolition of slavery throughout Christendom." This was the last pronouncement by the assembly on slavery until 1845. The long silence of the Church on the explosive subject of slavery is but another example of how oftentimes the pocketbook takes precedence over the prayer book. The growing economic importance of the cotton trade with England, following the invention of the cotton gin in 1792, called for cheap labor. Slavery was the answer. Although various northern judicatories of the Presbyterian Church made anti-slavery pronouncements after 1818, the General Assembly remained cautiously silent.

During the 1820s and 1830s, there was a stirring of the church's conscience throughout New England and the Western Reserve, due largely to the influence of the New England theology with its strong emphasis upon the human or social aspects of the Gospel. In 1817 the American Colonization Society had been founded for the purpose of sending freed Negroes to Liberia. The first emigrant ship to carry such colonists back to Africa sailed in March 1821. William Lloyd Garrison, perhaps the most outspoken of the abolitionists, launched his *Liberator* in January 1831. He maintained that slavery was a sin and that the only solution to the problem was complete abolition. He considered the objectives of the Colonization Society totally inadequate and felt that this movement was nothing more than a sop to the Christian's conscience. Under the leadership of such men as Garrison, the abolition movement spread rapidly throughout the northern states. By 1836, when Smylie published his defense of slavery, there were 250 branches of the American Anti-Slavery Society in existence in the North.

Although sharp differences of opinion regarding matters of doctrine and polity were primary reasons for the 1837 division of the Presbyterian Church into its Old and New School branches, the slavery issue may also be considered an important factor leading to the disruption. The increasing support given the abolition movement among the New School men was paralleled by a defense of slavery as a divinely ordained institution by some Old School ministers. One of the spokesmen for the more moderate position of the Old School was Dr. Charles Hodge of Princeton, the editor of the *Biblical Repertory*. In 1836 he argued through his magazine that the Scriptures did not condemn slavery as being sinful. Although admitting that the system as practiced in the South had many evils, he maintained that abolitionism was not the solution. Hodge wrote: "When southern Christians are told that they are guilty of a heinous crime, worse than piracy, robbery, or murder, because they hold slaves, when they know that Christ and His apostles never denounced slaveholding as a crime, never called upon man to renounce it as a condition of admission into the church, they are shocked and offended, without being convinced."

Twelve memorials on the subject of slavery were brought before the General Assembly of 1836 and a special committee was appointed to study the proposals. The majority report recommended no action since the whole subject of Negro bondage was "inseparately connected with and regulated by the laws of many of the States of this Union, with which it is by no means proper for an ecclesiastical judicatory to interfere." They who held that opinion quoted Section IV of Chapter XXXI of the Presbyterian *Confession of Faith*, which is still a part of the Confession, and which reads: "Synods and councils are to handle or conclude nothing, but that which is ecclesiastical: and are not to intermeddle with civil affairs which concern the commonwealth, unless by way of humble petition in cases extraordinary; or by way of advice for satisfaction of conscience, if they be thereunto required by the civil magistrate." More and more the moderates retreated to the position that since the slavery question was a political issue, it was not proper for the church to rule on the subject. However, a minority of the committee returned a vigorous dissent in which it stated that the "buying, selling, or holding a human being as property in the sight of God [was] a heinous sin."

Following the division of 1837, the Old School Assembly refrained from saying anything on the subject of slavery until 1845. In the assembly of that year, by a vote of 168 to 13, a pronouncement was passed which included the following statements: "The church of Christ is a spiritual body, whose jurisdiction extends only to the religious faith, and moral conduct of her members. She cannot legislate where Christ has not legislated, nor make terms of membership which He has not made. . . This Assembly cannot, therefore, denounce the holding of slaves as necessarily a heinous and scandalous sin." In brief, the assembly refused to make the holding of slaves a bar to communion.

When Scott was traveling in England in the summer of 1846, a number of people queried him about conditions in the United States and also about his attitude to the whole subject of slavery. England had abolished slavery in the West Indies in 1833. Scott noted in his diary some of the questions being asked and his answers. Some people wondered whether the Negroes of the South would rise in insurrection. Scott answered: "I don't believe a word of this." Others asked whether slavery would eventually be abolished. In reply he said: "This I believe would be done by gradual emancipation. The South will accomplish this. The time has not fully come." Still others, more prophetic in their analysis of the situation, wondered if there would not be a civil war when the government would fail and the union would be dissolved. Scott scoffed at such a fantastic notion. "This I do not believe," he said. "I believe that a century hence the United States will stretch from sea to sea & the same glorious stars & stripes wave over a hundred free and sovereign states."

In the early months of 1847, the Rev. Ebenezer Davis, an Anglican clergyman from New Amsterdam, British Guiana, made a tour of 4,000 miles through the southern states, and up through the Mississippi and Ohio valleys. He was investigating the slavery situation as it prevailed in the South and the attitude of northern people to Negroes. His sympathies were humanitarian. He considered the Negro to be a human being entitled to the same degree of respect as that given a white person. His findings appeared in a book entitled *American Scenes and Christian Slavery* which appeared in London in 1849. In it we find stirring accounts of slave auctions, mistreatment of slaves, and his appraisal of the prevailing attitude of people in both South and North to the whole slavery question. The author was a keen observer and skillful reporter. His volume must have been joyously received by the abolitionists.

The book is important to our study of Scott as Davis spent some time in New Orleans and attended the services conducted by Scott in the First Presbyterian Church. Incidentally, Davis throws some light upon the tobacco chewing habits of some of Scott's church members. On Sunday, February 1, 1847, Davis and his wife attended First Church. Here is what he wrote:

> Curious to know how people did really pray and preach with slavery and slave-trading in their vilest forms around them, I set off in search of the First Presbyterian Church. It is a beautiful building; seldom, if ever, had I seen a place of worship the exterior of which I liked so much. . . The church I found as beautiful inside as out . . . a very neat and graceful structure, capable, as I learned, of accommodating about 1,500 people. But the floor —the floor! What a drawback! It was stained all over with tobacco juice! Faugh! Those Southern men are the most filthy people in that respect I ever met with. They are a great 'spitting' community. To make it still more revolting to luckless travellers, this nasty habit is generally attended with noises in the throat resembling the united growling of a dozen mastiffs.
>
> While the congregation was assembling, a grey-headed, aristocratic-looking old negro came up into the gallery, walked along "as one having authority," and placed himself in a front pew on the right-hand side of the pulpit. . . Others succeeded, till ultimately there were from forty to fifty of the sable race in that part of the gallery. Not one white was to be seen among the blacks, nor one black among the whites. There, then, was the "Negro pew." It was the first time even my West India eyes ever beheld a distinction of colour maintained in the house of God!
>
> At eleven o'clock precisely, a man of tall but stooping figure and dark complexion, about forty years of age, muffled up in a cloak, took his stand at the bottom of the pulpit or platform stairs. It was Dr. [Scott].

Somewhat to the visitor's surprise, Dr. Scott called upon one of his elders to lead in prayer. Such informality would never have been part of a British service. Davis' account continues: "During the whole of the service, I may here remark, there was a good deal of going in and out, talking, whispering, spitting, gutteral turbulence, &c." It so happened that a visiting minister had been invited to preach that morning. Regarding the message, Davis wrote: "It was thoroughly evangelical and good; but I listened to it with mingled feelings. It was painful to think that such a ministry could co-exist with slavery. The creed it is evident may be evangelical, but there is a woful neglect of the duties of practical piety."

Davis returned to the church in the evening. Commenting on Scott's prayer, which was seven or eight minutes long, Davis called it "admirable." "I wished some dry, prosy petitioners in England could have heard it," he wrote. "It was devout, comprehensive, and to the point. All classes of men—but one—were remembered in it. The slaves were not mentioned,—their freedom was not prayed for!"

Regarding the evening sermon, Davis wrote: "This masterly discourse was read, but read in such a manner as to lose none of its effect. It occupied upwards of an hour. My irresistible impression as I listened was, *There is a man of God.* Truly a light shining in a dark place; for, as I returned to my lodgings, I found the coffee-houses, oyster-saloons, and theaters all open, just as on any other day, only more thronged with customers. How much such discourses are needed in this place."

Davis attended a prayer meeting at the church on Monday evening following, at which time between sixty and seventy were present. "After the address," wrote Davis, "the pastor called upon 'Brother Franklin' to 'lead in prayer.' The phrase was new to me, but I liked it." Franklin's prayer was "scriptural and good." During the week, Davis visited a slave auction and penned a stirring record of what he saw. He told of a man and wife selling for $600, and with the auctioneer crying: "Really, gentlemen, it is throwing people away—going for 600 dollars; going—once—twice—gone for 600 dollars!" The couple must have been getting old for at the same auction, a Negro blacksmith, 30 years old, sold for $790; a 16-year-old boy for $625; an 18-year-old girl for $580; a 10-year-old boy for $425; and a 17-year-old mulatto girl received a bid of $545 which was refused.

Davis gave the following summary of his impressions of Dr. Scott:

> He is a Southern man, born and bred amidst the wilds of Tennessee, whose early educational advantages were very small. He is, in a great measure, a self-made man. Brought up in the midst of slavery, he is (I rejoice to hear) a cordial hater of the system. As a minister, he is "thoroughly furnished—a workman that needeth not to be ashamed." His knowledge of the world, as well as of the Word of God and of the human heart, is extensive, and is turned to the best account in his ministrations. In leaving New Orleans I felt no regret, but that I had not called upon this good man.

Prior to the Civil War it was customary in most of the Protestant churches of the South for both colored and white people to worship together in the same service. The segregation of the races within the church was by the seating arrangements, as noted by Davis. The whites had the pews on the main floor; the colored went to the galleries. When Scott was abroad in the summer of 1846, he was surprised at first to see white people seated in the galleries. On June 28, 1846, he wrote in his diary: "Ladies & gentlemen sit here in the gallery pews as well as in the body of the house. This is the case in all the churches I have seen in Europe & in the northern states. Why may it not be so in ours?" Even if Scott had tried to induce some of his white hearers in New Orleans to take seats in the gallery, he would have failed. Accepted custom had decreed certain taboos and these could not easily be broken.

Prior to the Civil War we find Protestants throughout the South sensitive to their obligations to do what they could to evangelize the Negroes but they were seriously handicapped by restrictions of both their respective states and of the society which surrounded them. When the newly-organized Presbytery of New Orleans met on April 7, 1845, it heard a report on the spiritual condition of "persons of color" within its bounds. According to this report, of the 100,000 Negroes living within their jurisdiction, "nearly all of whom were slaves," about 40,000 "belong to our Roman Catholic friends." The remaining 60,000 were "more or less accessible" to Protestant ministers. The report states: "It is indeed true that there are Protestant planters in Louisiana who are opposed to the religious instruction of their slaves. They have been alarmed by the movements of a certain class of men at the north, and under an honest apprehension on the subject, they have felt it their duty to exclude all ministers of the Gospel from their plantations."

"It is due to the members of this Presbytery to say," the report continues, "that all of them are accustomed to preach to this class of our population, and as often as is practicable. . . In nearly all our houses of public worship, seats are provided for the colored people, and seldom is an assembly of Christian worshippers seen among us which does not contain more or less of the children of Africa." Beginning with the 1847 issue of the *Minutes of the General Assembly,* a separate column showing the number of colored communicants was included for Presbyterian churches in the South. That year First Church of New Orleans reported having forty such members. Thereafter as long as Dr. Scott remained as pastor, the number listed varied from thirty to forty-six out of a total membership of from 600 to 780.

The sessional records of the First Presbyterian Church of New Orleans carry many references to slaves being baptized, married, or received into the church. The elders tried to exercise some oversight of their colored members. The following minutes for March 7, 1843, are typical: "Whereas a report has reached the Session that Thos. Miles, a cold. member of this church has been acting in a manner calculated to injure his Christian character. Resolved that the Pastor be a Comme. to wait upon him in regard to this affair." No Negro was received into membership without the written consent of his owner. Among the Scott papers in Bancroft Library is a note which reads: "Rev. Dr. W. A. Scott. Will you be kind enough to call over to the house . . . this Wednesday, the 22nd Dec. [1852] and marry my slave Ann to Alex. Long at half past eight o'clock and oblige, Yours truly, E. C. Pamly." When Scott was abroad in 1851, he sent letters back to be read not only before the white people but also before special meetings of the colored people held on Sunday afternoons.

The Scotts owned several slaves while living in New Orleans. Mila was a beloved "mammy" for the children. Since Scott kept a stable, he needed a man to take care of his horses. According to a record in Scott's day book, he purchased a Negro named Albert in 1843 for $600, plus $6.50 "expense in purchase." Albert was sold on August 9, 1844, for $650. The day book carries the following notations of money expended on Albert: "May, 1844, gave him $2.50; shoes, $2.00; for his round-about coat, $1.25; 4 Aug. gave him $1.00." Writing to her husband on July 30, 1846, when he was abroad, Ann stated: "The boys have brought me their wages regularly. I have received $50 from Mr. Sweet three times and $40 once, making $190."

Among the letters in the Scott Collection is one from Allan Mac-Farland of Cheraw, South Carolina, who wrote on April 16, 1850, regarding a mullato girl he owned by the name of Hannah, twenty-four years of age. For some reason MacFarland found it necessary to send her away from his community and begged Scott to take her as a gift. "I am inclined to hold the opinion," MacFarland wrote, "that freedom is no blessing to Hannah's caste. I wish her well and should prefer she had a protector—a master rather than turn her loose on a selfish world. . . . In this dilemma, will you, my dear Sir, come to my aid and accept of her as your servant?" With the letter was a bill of sale by which "a mulatto female slave named Hannah" was sold for one dollar. Scott delayed until July 22nd before replying. He then wrote: "It is our wish to diminish rather than increase our responsibilities towards slaves; but under the circumstances we will take the woman Hannah and do the very best we can with her & for her, with the understanding that she is to be subject to all the casualties that our own other slaves are." Hannah was given her liberty before the Scotts left for California. Years later while going through his files, Scott came across this correspondence and added a note to the effect that he paid her travel expenses to Cincinnati "and this is the last I know of her."

This experience with Hanah suggests the idea that the care of an attractive mulatto woman was often a matter of real concern. In her brief biographical sketch of her husband written after his death, Mrs. Scott stated: "He disliked slavery but could not see the way out of it. He said it was a much greater evil to the white man than to the colored man and kept the South in bondage to the North." Descendants of Dr. Scott say that he gave all of his slaves their freedom before moving to

California. They also report that he sent one couple back to Africa under the colonization plan but that they were very unhappy in Liberia and begged to be returned.

The consciences of good Christian men throughout the South were sorely troubled as the abolitionists increased the tempo of their campaign against slavery. There were so many tangent issues involved that it was easy to rationalize away the central issue of slavery by talking about states' rights or some other problem. By 1850 some people in the South were discussing the possibility of secession as a solution to the whole slavery question. In October 1850 when Scott was on his way to Europe for his second visit, he stopped over in Boston. He was both amazed and distressed at the extent and vehemence of the abolition sentiment. Writing to his wife on the 28th, he said:

> There is considerable excitement all through Yankeedom about the Fugitive Slave Law. Many of them don't know any thing about the subject at all. But I verily believe that the Union will be dissolved or slavery will be abolished. . . My opinion is strong, the contest is for & will really result either in the abolition of slavery or the dissolution of the Union, & much as I love the Union, & much as I wish the negroes all to be free, yet I am for dissolution rather than dishonor & shame to the South & a forced emancipation.

And on November 1st, he wrote: "I believe the Union is on the brink of dissolution. . . The danger has been brought about by the North. It is their fault if the Union is dissolved." Thus nearly eleven years before the first southern states seceded, Scott foresaw the inevitable event and had already cast his lot with the South.

A further expression of his views on the slavery problem is to be found in his address, "Emigration of Free and Emancipated Negroes to Africa" which was delivered at the annual meeting of the Louisiana State Colonization Society held in his church on March 7, 1850. This address appeared as a pamphlet with a New Orleans imprint of 1853. The following quotations have been taken from the pamphlet:

> The only hope of the free black man is his removal to another Continent, beyond the barriers of those prejudices and circumstances that oppress him here, and to a soil and climate for which he is suited. . . The free people of color are not at home amongst us. The All-wise Creator has placed upon the black man the mark of separation. Man being gregarious and social in his habits, it was necessary for the subduing of the earth to the arts of peace, that men should be dissociated, segregated. . . The black man, socially and politically, can never mingle with the white man as his equal, in the same land. It is worse than visionary; it is vain and mischievous to labor to bridge the gulf that the Almighty has made impassable.

Scott maintained that the same means which had brought hundreds of thousands of Irish to America could with equal efficiency transport a like number of Negroes to Africa. He proposed that the free colored people should be the first to be sent back and then the "increase of the slave population." "As soon as the existing generation should die off," he said, "not a black man would be found on American soil."

The whole proposal was both visionary and impractical. The cancerous growth of slavery could not be cured by any temporary medication. A major operation was necessary.

AT HOME AND AT WORK

In order to round out the story for the years 1846 to 1854, a number of events need to be mentioned. There were changes in the Scott family circle. Calvin Knox, whom his father called "our dear little boy," died on November 13, 1847, a few months before reaching his seventh birthday. The family record does not give the cause of his death. A second daughter was born on May 12, 1848, who was named Louisiana after her native state. Her nickname was "Lou." Two more sons arrived before the Scotts left New Orleans. Ebenezer was born on June 5, 1851, when Dr. Scott was on his European trip and Paul Eli arrived on December 24, 1853. Thus eight children, one of whom had passed away, had been born to William and Ann before their move to California in 1854.

The Scott family lived on Magazine Street until after Calvin Knox's death in 1847. They then moved to 96 Prytania, a section of the city which is now in the commercial district. We have no evidence that Dr. Scott took part in any such outdoor activities as riding, boating, or fishing. Seemingly he had no love for gardening or for any special hobby. He did not draw or paint, nor did he play any musical instrument. His one absorbing leisure time activity was reading. We know that the Scott family had dogs and cats as pets. Among the family traditions is the story of how a big cat used to sit on his desk as he wrote and how sometimes the swishing tail would upset the sand-shaker.

In Presbyterian terms, Dr. Scott was "bishop of the First Presbyterian Church of New Orleans." He was also by virtue of his ability and interests the unofficial bishop of Presbyterianism for the whole city and surrounding territory. In addition to the two new churches started with groups from First Church in 1843 and 1844, another organization, called the Third Presbyterian Church of New Orleans, was launched on March 7, 1847, with a nucleus of eighteen members out of First Church. Scott tried to induce the Presbyterian Board of Foreign Missions to start work for the French-speaking people of New Orleans but in this he was not successful.

Following the outbreak of the Mexican War in 1846, Scott saw new opportunities for his church. In a letter to Dr. John C. Lowrie of the Foreign Board dated November 16, 1847, he said: "The whole Rio

Grande country is ripe for schools, books, & missionaries. While our armies are there, impressions may be made that cannot be withdrawn even if our forces are recalled." And on another occasion he urged that a minister be sent to Tampico, Mexico, where there were several thousand American troops in addition to many United States citizens engaged in commercial pursuits. "There is no Protestant minister in the place," he stated. "The call is an urgent one."

Scott's Thanksgiving sermon received flattering attention by several of the New Orleans papers. The *Weekly Delta* of November 17th said: "We shall not attempt to report this masterly effort of Dr. Scott's. We trust we are incapable of doing him the gross injustice of pretending to present the methodical arrangement of its divisions . . . the beautiful train of thought running through the whole." The *Courier* of the same date commented: "Several gentlemen who heard the sermon of the Rev. Dr. Scott assured us that it was everything his friends could expect or desire. The church was crowded with worshippers of both sexes who for one full hour seemed spell-bound by the eloquence of the preacher." Scott believed in long sermons. He once remarked that he never heard a sermon shorter than forty-five mintues "which was not seriously defective in either its exposition, division, discussion, or application."

In 1847 a prominent member of the New Orleans bar, J. S. Whitaker, published his *Sketches of Life and Character in Louisiana* in which he commented on Dr. Scott's pulpit ability as follows:

> Dr. Scott . . . [is] a bold and fearless advocate of principle and of truth, teaches the faith without fear, without reproach. . . Earnestness, fervent zeal, and energetic language characterized the manner and style. . . He is a perfect embodiment of modern Calvinism. . . He can scarcely be termed eloquent, though his manner is too impressive not to hold the attention captive and to arrest the wandering thoughts. His style is characterized by nervousness, strength, and perspicuity.

Scott was conservative not only in doctrine but also in tradition. In her summary of her husband's life and work, Mrs. Scott mentioned the fact that he never permitted a woman to lecture or to preach in his church. He accepted Paul's injunction literally: "Let your women keep silence in the churches." He never dreamed that the Presbyterian Church, U.S.A., would ever authorize the ordination of women, but such action was taken in 1956.

Scott's fame as a preacher naturally attracted the attention of other churches within his denomination. The Duane Street Church of New York City sent overtures to him to be its pastor in the fall of 1849. There is no longer a Presbyterian church by this name in the Presbytery of New York, but then it was the fifth in size in the presbytery with a membership of over four hundred. The church offered a salary of $3,000 per annum. This was but one of several calls from other congregations that came to Dr. Scott during the years of his greatest popularity.

During this period events were taking place which in time induced Dr. Scott to move to San Francisco. As one of the results of the Mexican War of 1846, the United States flag was raised over the customs house at Monterey, California, on July 7, 1846, and two days later over the sleepy little village of Yerba Buena on San Francisco Bay. Thus California passed under the jurisdiction of the United States. In January 1847 the name Yerba Buena was changed to San Francisco.

Little interest was shown by the people of the United States in the new territory until news of the discovery of gold reached the East. American civilization on the Pacific Coast began in Old Oregon. Until 1846 California was a foreign land, where the Roman Catholic faith was the official religion and Protestant missionaries were not permitted to enter for the purpose of carrying on their work. Beginning with 1843 when the first great wagon train of about one thousand people crossed to Oregon, the primary objective of the westward bound emigrant was the Pacific Northwest. Very few Americans settled in California during the first two years after the raising of the United States flag and not a single Protestant missionary. The discovery of gold at Sutter's mill on January 24, 1848, changed everything. The first announcement of this era-marking event appeared in a San Francisco newspaper dated March 15th. The news did not reach the eastern states until July or August and the first printed reports aroused little more than a ripple of excitement.

The need for more rapid communication with the west coast induced the United States Government to enter into contract with two steamship companies to inaugurate sailings during the latter part of 1848. The United States Mail Steamship Company operated between New York and other ports, including New Orleans, and Chagres on the Atlantic side of the Isthmus of Panama. The Pacific Mail Steamship Company commissioned several ships including the "California" and the "Oregon" to ply between Panama and San Francisco. The "California" sailed from New York on October 6, 1848, and after rounding the Horn, anchored at Panama on the following January 17th. She was followed by the "Oregon". Any passengers bound for California had to cross the Isthmus by canoe and horseback. The railroad connecting the two ports was not opened until January 1855.

On December 1, 1848, the "Falcon" left New York for Chagres via New Orleans. She carried only twenty-seven passengers bound for California among whom were two New School Presbyterian missionaries, the Rev. Samuel H. Willey and the Rev. John W. Douglas. They had been commissioned by the American Home Missionary Society and were the first missionaries to be sent by any Protestant society to California. Although these men, as well as the society, were aware of the reports of the gold discovery in California, this fact had not entered into their selection or appointment.

The "Falcon" reached New Orleans on December 11th. In a letter to his board, Willey described the great excitement which was stirring the city at the time of their arrival. A man had just come from the gold fields of California with a bag of nuggets worth $212 which, so he claimed, he had gotten "by a couple of weeks' work." No doubt his account of the ease with which one could pick up gold from the ground was somewhat embellished with repeated tellings. Here was tangible evidence, though, that all the rumors about the gold discovery were true; these were not just fairy stories. Hundreds of New Orleans residents clamored for passage on the "Falcon" but only about two hundred additional passengers could be accommodated. The gold rush had begun! Through the years that immediately followed, New Orleans remained an important halfway point between the Isthmus and eastern ports. Because of this strategic location, hundreds of the city's residents were among the first to migrate to California.

It is altogether probable that while the "Falcon" was in port, Willey and Douglas called on Dr. Scott. Willey was destined to become one of the most influential of all the pioneer Protestant missionaries who went to California. Among other accomplishments, he was one of the founders in 1855 of the College of California in Oakland. In 1868 this became the University of California with Willey as the first acting president. As will be told later, Scott was the chief founder of San Francisco's City College in 1859, an institution now defunct which bears no relationship to the present day City College. It is easy for us from our vantage point to imagine the two young Presbyterian missionaries calling on Dr. Scott, and the three talking about far away California. But then, with the future a closed book, it was impossible for either Scott or Willey to foresee how their mutual interest in higher education would someday clash. Scott was Old School, deeply committed to the idea of working within his denominational framework; Willey was New School, a firm believer in interdenominational cooperation.

Beginning with the March 10, 1849, issue of the *New Orleans Presbyterian*, news stories about California began to appear. The first such account carried a reference to the Rev. Timothy Dwight Hunt, a New School Presbyterian minister who arrived in San Francisco from Honolulu in October 1848. He was the first Protestant pastor to settle in California to devote full time to religious work. He was entirely independent of any missionary board. On January 9, 1849, Hunt conducted the first Protestant communion service in California after the raising of the United States flag.

In the March 31, 1849, issue of his paper, Scott made brief mention of Sir Francis Drake's visit to California in June 1579. A copy of the *London Examiner* of unknown date had come to Scott's attention which had carried a quotation from John Pinkerton's *A General Collection of the Best and Most Interesting Voyages and Travels in all Parts of the World*, published in London in 1812. Quoting from volume XII, page 156, of this work Scott wrote: "Pinkerton, in an account of Drake's discovery of a part of California, to which he gave the name of New

Albion [i.e., New England], states—if we can depend upon what Sir Francis Drake or his chaplain says . . . the land is so rich in gold and silver, that upon the slightest turning it up with a spade or pickaxe, these rich metals plainly appear mixed with the mould." There is some mystery as to where such a reference to gold and silver occurs in the writings of the Rev. Francis Fletcher, who was Drake's chaplain, and we have no extant writings of Drake regarding his famous voyage. Incidentally Fletcher was the first Protestant clergyman to conduct religious services and to administer the Sacrament of the Lord's Supper to Englishmen on what is now United States soil. Also, he was the first to bring an English Bible to this country. However, the item in the *London Examiner* which caught Scott's attention was the reference to the abundance of gold in California.

A third reference to California in the *New Orleans Presbyterian* appeared in the issue of December 9, 1849. Scott then commented on the arrival in New Orleans of the "Alabama" with $300,000 in gold dust from California. He mentioned two other ships that had carried $1,500,000 and $750,000 in golden treasure out of San Francisco a short time before. Such fabulous wealth! No wonder the cupidity of men was aroused. What an alluring subject to dream and to talk about! With the passing of the months, more and more of the residents of New Orleans left for the land of gold.

The sessional records of the First Presbyterian Church of New Orleans show that on December 9, 1851, five asked for letters of transfer to the First Presbyterian Church of San Francisco. An examination of the membership roll of this latter church shows that by 1854 fifteen out of a total of 101 had come from Dr. Scott's church in New Orleans. In addition there were others from the New Orleans church who were in the gold mines where there were no churches, or who for various reasons had not asked for letters of transfer. Among these was Stephen Franklin, once an elder in the New Orleans church, who went to San Francisco in 1849. His wife, Eliza, and their daughter, sailed from New Orleans on January 1, 1851, to join him. The ever growing number of southerners in San Francisco, and especially the former members of Dr. Scott's church or congregation, prepared the way for him to follow. In this move, Stephen Franklin played a prominent role.

SECOND TRIP TO EUROPE, 1850-51

On Monday morning, October 7, 1850, the readers of the *New Orleans Delta* found the following news item in their paper:

> We understand that the respected pastor of the First Presbyterian Church on Lafayette Square is about to make a tour of Europe and the Holy Land. After religious service yesterday, the subject was brought before Dr. Scott's congregation. In consideration of the eminent services and long devotion of Dr. Scott, his congregation passed a series of resolutions highly honorable to

themselves and to their beloved pastor. They gave him leave of absence for nine months,—agreed to pay his expenses, and to supply his place during his absence by some competent minister. We are gratified to hear of this arrangement. We know of few persons who will make the tour of the Old Continent with more advantage to themselves and to the society in which they move, than Dr. Scott. His intellect is a remarkably sagacious and vigorous one, and his mind and memory are stored with valuable knowledge. . .

For years Scott had suffered from ill health. His doctor had prescribed travel for its therapeutic value in 1846 and for this reason he had made his first trip abroad. The records of the session meetings of First Church show that during the late spring and summer of 1850, Dr. Scott was often unable to attend because of illness. For instance, the minutes for May 7th state: "No meeting of session. The Revd. Moderator being too unwell to attend." Looking back on this summer while abroad, Scott in a letter to his wife dated May 5, 1851, wrote: "I am astonished to think back on what I have suffered in ill health at home. I wonder how I got along. I was feeble. I was scarcely ever free from some pain or ache." The nature of his trouble was not explained.

Concerned over their pastor's continued ill health, the elders consulted with his doctor and again a trip abroad was recommended. Someone suggested Palestine. Such an idea was received with enthusiasm for few, if any, could gain so much from such a trip as Dr. Scott. His extensive knowledge of Biblical history combined with his alert, inquiring mind, was excellent preparation for a leisurely tour of the Holy Land. Naturally the question of expense arose. The elders assured their pastor that funds would be available to cover all expenses, that his salary would continue as usual, and that his pulpit would be supplied during his absence. One by one that various objections which at first appeared to block such an ambitious project melted away.

There was his family. Ann was consulted, but she quickly agreed with the session. She assured her husband that she could manage very well during his absence. Robert, their eldest son, then thirteen, was already in a private school conducted by a Mr. and Mrs. Bird in Hartford, Connecticut. At home were the four little children, Martha, William, Chalmers, and Louisiana. She had servants including the mulatto girl, Hannah, who had joined the household sometime that summer and who seemed reliable. Mrs. Scott enjoyed excellent health and there was no doubt about her ability to run her household with efficiency. Plans were well matured for Dr. Scott's departure when a new complication arose. Mrs. Scott discovered that she was pregnant. If her husband were to be away for nine months, the baby would be born during his absence. William was hesitant to leave but Ann was insistent that she could manage and that he must go. All this preceded the congregational meeting of Sunday, October 6th.

Passage was booked on the United States Mail Steamship "Ohio" leaving October 14th for New York. Scott described her as being "a magnificent ship." This is the line which carried passengers to and from Chagres and it is most probable that Scott found among his fellow travelers some who were returning from California. By this time it was common knowledge that California had been admitted on the preceding September 9th the thirty-first state to the Union.

The "Ohio" got underway at 8:30 Monday evening, the 14th. With a heavy heart Scott retired to his cabin to begin the first of a series of fifty-nine letters to his wife, all of which are now a part of the Scott Collection in Bancroft Library. "Our present situation is painful," he wrote, "but it is the best thing we could do on the whole, so far as we can see. We are always safe in the discharge of duty. . . The expense of this journey does not diminish your support a single dime. Nothing is abstracted from you or our dear children. They have been provided by our dear people freely, liberally & much more easily than before."

The ship touched at Havana, Cuba, on Thursday, the 17th, and dropped anchor in New York harbor on Tuesday, the 22nd. Except for getting seasick, Scott's only complaint about the voyage was that he could not find a set of chess aboard. In New York, he took a room in the Astor House, and on Thursday evening he heard the famous Swedish soprano, Jenny Lind, sing before an audience of some 3,500. In a letter written that evening to his wife, he gave the following impressions of her: "She is pretty—but walking or curtsying or turning her back to you, she is ordinary. . . I was pleased with her and yet disappointed. The great wonder to me is not that she sings well—that she is even the first of singers, but that people should make so much of her. She is an extraordinary woman."

Scott left for Hartford by rail on Friday. Taking his son Robert with him, he went to Boston where they spent Sunday. The two were in New York by the 31st and there he found a letter from Ann. He was homesick. "If I could find any honorable excuse," he wrote, "I certainly would return home." He added: "I am well. I feel so anxious to be preaching. . . I wish I could return. I cannot linger here. The only way for me to do is to shut my eyes & plunge ahead & away, never looking back." In another letter to his wife written a few days later, he reported hearing of Jenny Lind's plan to give a concert in New Orleans. "You must hear her at any price," he wrote. "Remember I say so, & God says, 'Wives obey your husbands.' "

While in New York, Scott secured a number of letters of introduction to leading churchmen, United States consular officials, and others abroad. Among these was one to the leading French church historian of the day, Dr. Merle d'Aubigne. Passage for Liverpool was booked on the "Asia" due to sail on November 6th and Robert sent back to Hartford.

His farewell message to his wife was written late on the evening of the 5th: "I bless God for having given you to me & for all the happiness I have had in you. I thank you—all my body & soul thank you for your care of me & tenderness towards me." He commented on the fact that the New Orleans church had given him $2,500 for expenses and outlined his trip. "My plan now is, as I am so early in the season, to go via Marseilles, Genoa, Pisa, Florence, Rome, Naples, Malta, to Egypt. I design resting a few days in England." Reporting on the state of his health, he said: "I have had no pain in my side since leaving Havana. The very disagreeable feeling that annoyed me so much is wholly gone. The only thing about now, is the weakness or partial loss of my voice . . . [it] is feeble, like it was when I was sick at home. . . Necessity is laid upon me. I cannot go back with honor. Exile and dirt and the discomforts of foreign travel are the tribulations Providence has laid upon me at this time. These are my cross now." The next morning Scott, with a heavy heart, boarded his ship and set sail for England.

Writing from Liverpool on November 18th, he referred to "the awful Atlantic between me and you" and again confessed to his deep longing to be back home with his family. "But after all that has been said, & all that our people have done, I am ashamed. It would argue weakness —a want of manliness—to return without seeing Egypt. Well necessity is laid upon me, I will try. . . And never again will I, in my right mind, consent to leave you on such a journey."

Scott's letters written while abroad give us a vivid commentary on travel conditions of that day. For instance, it took him thirteen hours on November 23rd to go the three hundred miles that separated London from Paris. About this time Scott met three gentlemen from the United States who were likewise planning to tour Egypt and was invited to join their party. He referred to them as "Col. Walker of the U.S. Army, Mr. Davis of Phila., & Mr. Taylor also of Phila." When traveling alone, Scott often practiced economies, as going second class on the trains, but with others, he found it necessary to travel first class.

On November 30th, the party visited Lyons and the grave of Irenaeus, bishop of the city in the latter part of the second century. They took a boat down the Rhone River stopping off to see the residence of the antipopes of the "Babylonian captivity," 1309-78, at Avignon. Writing from Marseilles to his wife on December 5th, Scott said: "It would astonish you how I can scold & quarrel & bargain in French. It is the way. We can't help it." He mentioned the fact that he had found no soap in any hotel.

Taking ship from Marseilles, the party of four men arrived in Genoa on the 7th. From there they continued by sea to Leghorn where they took a railroad to Pisa and Florence. Along the way they visited palaces, churches, and museums. Being with others was a good thing, for congenial fellowship lessened the feeling of loneliness. Weeks passed without the receipt of a single letter from his wife. "I know you have written," he wrote on December 7th, "but the fact is I travel so fast that I keep ahead of my letters." Writing from Florence, he told of how the four took their meals in their hotel rooms. "We have a good fire," he wrote. "We have just eaten our dinner at 8 p.m. which consisted of mutton chops, roasted chicken, roasted duck & pigeons, rice, pomme de terre, bread, grapes, pears, apples, and figs dried." He told of visiting the famous cathedrals. A Pisa, he climbed the leaning tower, "330 steps without stopping to breathe." This was no small accomplishment for a person with a crippled foot and shows that he was then enjoying good health.

Scott revelled in the great museums of Florence, especially Pitti Palace. The men spent several days there and in his letter to his wife of December 13th he told of how in some ways he had been able to economize on expenses because he was with others. "We have engaged a servant man to go with us to Rome and Naples who understands everything here," he wrote. "We are to pay him one dollar per day which is 25 cts each . . . speaks English." He described their fellowship around the table at night when "4 big bougies" would be lighted and each would be busy writing letters. According to the dictionary, a bougie is a big wax candle, but it might also be the nickname for a cigar. Among other letters, Scott wrote to his church giving long accounts of his travels which were usually read at the midweek meeting.

The party was in Rome on the 18th where the men found accommodations at a cost per person of $2.50 per day. Writing that evening to his wife, Scott described his first visit to St. Peters. He wrote: "The size & height from without did not meet my expectations, but soon after I entered I was almost overpowered by its elegance and immensity. It surpassed my expectations. It is grand, sublime. If wealth, genius, and the fine arts could make a temple worthy the worship of the God of Heaven, this is the temple. But alas! It is a temple of the grossest idolatry. The Gospel is not seen in it." Scott saw people kissing the toe of the statue of St. Peter, which, he said, was originally "an old heathen Jupiter."

Christmas eve found Scott still in Rome. He wrote to his wife: "O this thing of being far from home at Xmas is martyrdom equal to that of San Sebastian. . . It shall never befall me again." The big event of the day was the opportunity to be present at a "pontifical mass in Saint Peters" where he saw Pope Pius IX, who occupied the papal throne from 1846 to 1878. Scott's attitude to the Roman Catholic ceremonies reflects the anti-Catholic spirit so common among Protestants of his generation throughout the United States. He wrote:

> We were required to appear in dress suits, so I put on my best clothes . . . and appeared in my place at 9. After waiting awhile, the immense church filling up with strangers, soldiers and saints, the grand procession came in. First a long line of soldiers with drawn bayonets, then the Swiss guard, then noble guards, then a long cordon of cardinals, patriarchs, abbots, bishops &

priests & then the Pope, borne on his chair on the shoulders of eight bishops. . . The procession passed through the great nave of the chh. I was near enough to the Pope to have pulled his nose or to have kissed his toe, but I did not do either. He appears to be a good natured man of about 60 years. Has a good voice—chants well. . . He looks something like Dr. Manly [president of the university] of Tuskaloosa.

The Pontifical Mass occupied today three hours & a half. It is a wearying heathen ceremony, dressing and undressing the Pope, bowing & marching . . . burning incense & washing hands, kissing each other & the Pope, the most absurd & impressively ridiculous affair for religious worship I ever saw. It surpasses all my ideas on the subject. As a pageant it is doubtless the height of human effort. It is a grand affair and a show. . . Romanism in Rome in the XIX [century] is nothing but heathenism modernized. It is true the Pope's toe is kissed. I saw it today.

After visiting Naples and Pompeii, they ascended to the top of Mt. Vesuvius—3,572 feet, according to Scott's report to his wife. In a letter from Naples to Ann, dated January 2, 1851, he wrote: "I am so homesick that I know not what to do. If I could return with honor & in justice to the expectations of my congregation, I would now do so. . . You ask how I liked New York. I did not like it at all. . . I want you to see New York but I have no idea of living there. . . I think New York is the most wicked city in America." Within about twelve years however, William and Ann, impelled by circumstances over which they seemingly had little or no control, were living in New York. But more about this later.

The four men left Naples on January 3rd. The ship made a short stop at Malta and then proceeded to Alexandria. "I am now in Africa," Scott wrote on January 12th. "How strange! How wonderful are God's ways. A Tennessee boy from the plough." At Cairo, the four men got donkeys and rode out to the pyramids, a $12\frac{1}{2}$ mile round trip. They crossed the Nile "donkey and all in a sort of tub boat," and they climbed the Gizah Pyramid. Scott was appalled by the unsanitary conditions he saw. "Dirt, filth, fleas, as I never saw before," he wrote. And again: "Fleas, lice & flies can only be measured in Egypt by bushels and acres." Referring to the people, he commented: "The present race of Egyptians are beyond redemption."

The four men decided to take a boat trip up the Nile to the first cataract, the present site of the Aswan dam. This was a most unusual excursion for tourists to take in that day. "The Pasha does not allow steamers to run on the Nile," Scott wrote to his wife. "It would leave the boatmen without anything to do." The men rented a boat for $150 which price included the services of a crew of twelve. All were Nubians. In a letter to his son Robert, Scott stated: "Our boat is called a Dahabish. It is 70 feet long & 13 across the middle. It has two masts. The kitchen is a very small affair in the center. Then from the kitchen to the cabin is our lounging, sitting and talking place, which is covered with awning. Our cabin consists of two rooms with a narrow passage in the middle. . . I brought an air pillow from home & bought a quilt, blanket & sheets. We bought also a table, cooking apparatus, chairs & such things." The boat was propelled by the sails when the wind was favorable; when it was not, the crew had to row or tow. The estimated time for the round trip was about six weeks, allowing ten days for sight-seeing. Together with the dragoman, the cook, and two servants, the total party aboard numbered twenty.

Provisions, including food, candles, etc., were stowed aboard and the great adventure began on Monday, January 20th. Before leaving Cairo, Scott rented a double barrel gun for $6.50 for the trip. In writing to his wife, he said that he planned to walk on the bank of the river and hunt for pigeons. "These," he explained in a letter to Robert, "are almost as numerous as the sands of the desert. I never saw so many." Since the birds were destructive to crops, the peasant farmers were happy to have them killed. Thus pigeon hunting provided both exercise and food. With no refrigeration then available, the party had to depend largely on what fresh food they could purchase or shoot along the way. After the trip was over, Scott in his letter of March 6th, said: "On the Nile we four ate 1,600 eggs & 175 chickens besides geese & turkeys & an occasional mutton." This meant an average of nine eggs per person per day, but no doubt the eggs were small. The men were also able to get water buffalo milk.

For six weeks the four men were cut off from the outside world. During this time, no letters could either be mailed or received. They had an abundance of time to read, walk, or write. Scott took advantage of the leisure time to improve his knowledge of Arabic. His letters describing his experiences during these six weeks are unusually rich in anecodote and detail. After the novelty of the first few days wore off, Scott found the scenery along the Nile dull and monotonous.

> The voyage up the Nile is a humbug. Thebes is about as far from Cairo as Vicksburg is from New Orleans. It [the Nile] has the same mud & sand banks. . . The climate is the best for invalids I ever saw. The mornings are cool but the sun of noon is withering, melting, burning. . . I am very well. I have no aches or pains—no head ache or sour stomach or nervousness . . . take a good deal of exercise. But I am so home sick that I do not know what to do. . . It will be near the 1st of May before I shall be able to get to Beyroot.

Some idea of the slowness of Nile travel in those days is to be found in the fact that it took Scott's party nine days to go the 125 miles from Thebes to the first cataract and return. They were back in Thebes on Sunday evening, February 16th.

At a little past 4 Monday morning, I got up, dressed & went out alone to take a moonlight view of Luxor, which is one of the great temples of mighty Thebes. . . On my right and before me were the remains of the walls, of the massive gate towers, and the grand colonnades. The shadows of the moonlight, the twinkling of the stars, and the fiery light of a planet, and the solitariness of the scene—almost bewildered me. I was dumb, silent, thoughtful, and it was not until I found myself suffering from the cold that I could abandon the view.

Scott was overwhelmed with the majesty and wonder of the ruins at Karnak. "It was grand, magnificent, absolutely stupefying overwhelming at first. . . Far surpassed my imagination." And he called the day spent there "the most memorable view-seeing day on record." On February 26th, when the boat was about one hundred miles from Cairo on the return trip, Scott wrote another long letter to his wife.

It is now three months since I have had a word from you, & it will be 3 months the 2nd March since I have heard from our city. . . Why did I leave you to bear all your burdens alone— God forgive me. I thought I was doing my duty. . . You know I have never left your side before in all your hours of trial after the manner of women. God forbid I should ever do so again. The fact is, I was so much out of health, was so much pressed with public care, during the last summer at home, that I scarcely knew what I was doing. . . I am exceedingly anxious about you. . . Last night I lay on my hard dirty couch & wept & wept & sobbed until a very late hour and every night my dreams are of you . . . know this then my precious wife, that you never were so priceless in my sight as you are now.

Scott and his fellow travelers, all heavily bewiskered, as they did not shave on their six-weeks journey, returned to Cairo on Saturday, March 1st. They got rooms in Shepherd's Hotel and to Scott's great joy he found a number of letters awaiting him including three from Ann. These were dated December 16 and 24, and January 4. He replied the next day, March 2nd with a long letter.

The four men separated at Cairo. Mr. Taylor, the Quaker business man from Philadelphia, agreed to go with Scott on his trip to Mt. Sinai and the Holy Land. "He is an excellent man," wrote Scott, "& as good a traveling companion as can be found in a year of Sundays." He outlined their plans: "We hope to leave by Thursday next and to reach Jerusalem by Suez and Mt. Sinai in 30 days. . . The Arabs are all now at peace. We have an experienced dragoman. . . Our trip up the Nile cost me $146 for 39 days. This is cheap & well spent. . . I have seen all I came to see." The dragoman was the same who was with the party on the Nile trip. "He is kind and acquainted with his business."

There was no other way to make the trip to Mt. Sinai except on

camel back across the desert, spending the nights in tents as did the
Arabs. Scott faced with some dismay the prospect of another long period
without a chance of getting a letter from his wife. "Think of it," he
lamented "from 1st March to perhaps 10th May I shall hear nothing
from you." He was more pessimistic than subsequent events proved for
he found a letter from Ann dated January 20th when he reached
Jerusalem on March 31st.

Scott and Taylor left Cairo on March 4th riding about eighteen
miles that day on donkeys, pausing briefly to see some of the sights in
Heliopolis, about seven miles from Cairo. On the 5th they completed
arrangements for their journey across the desert, and on the 6th they
started. That evening Scott began a long letter to his wife. He wrote
at seven o'clock in the evening just after dinner at the end of "one day
in the wilderness." The letter deserves to be quoted at some length.

My dear precious wife. . . To start on a journey any where
is troublesome. Think then what it must be to start on such a
journey as this with Arabs. But the agony is over. We are fairly
out on our "ships of the desert" and we are very glad of it. Our
Sheikh is a young man of about 30 years & bears the highest character. . . We have eight camels, one for Mr. Taylor to ride,
one for me, and one for the Sheikh & one for the dragoman &
the rest for our tent, water casks, and provisions. We have 2 kegs
& 2 skins, say 70 gallons. We have 50 chickens in a coop that
ride on the top of our canteens. Then we have 4 cases of crackers
& 2 jars of real Irish butter—which I bought in Malta, plenty of
vermicelli, macaroni, rice, sugar, coffee & tea, besides prunes,
apricots & 300 oranges. We have tobacco and pipes & segars,
and a double barrel gun & a large brace of pistols, powder & shot.
And we have I don't know what else.

With God's blessing, we shall be very comfortable. We have a
carpet & quilts, 2 chairs & a little table & candles & a lamp—
maps & books. I am able to talk & ask & tell almost anything I
want in Arabic. My knowledge of Hebrew helps me. I am perfectly well & there is no sickness in the country, and nothing to
fear; but we have essence of ginger, & brandy, laudanum, paregoric,
calomel, blue pills, camphor, cologne, pain extractor, . . . &
eye water, etc. As to the camels, they are exactly as you see them
in the pictures. We tried several & I selected a young female that
walks very easily, but trots pretty hard. I have been accustomed to
hard trotting you know. I got English stirrups & fixed my saddle
and rode about the city. . . I got so accustomed to my camel
that I could manage her with the halter & my stick with the aid
of the Driver.

Our ride today has not been half so fatiguing as I expected. . .
We are on the route of the Israelites & hope to be at Mt. Sinai in
10 days, perhaps 11. The air of the desert is most delightful. It is

thus far a rolling, sandy, pebbly world with scarce a green or living thing. I forgot to say that I have called my camel Jenny Lind & Mr. Taylor calls his Susannah. We pay $12.50 for each camel from here to Nakhl, a place 6 days beyond Mt. Sinai. There it is probable we may change camels. From Nakhl to Jerusalem we have to pay $6.00 more for each camel.

The next day they were up before dawn and were on their way by seven o'clock. In his account to his wife, Scott reported that he rode "10 long hours on the camel without stopping." He explained that the one-humped Arabian camel, such as he rode, was called a dromedary. His letter continues:

Jenny Lind, as you know I call mine, is already badly spoiled. . . We take lunch riding along, & as soon as she hears me chewing bread, she turns back her head & lays her head on my knee and looks so beseechingly in my face, that I can't refuse to divide my last crust with her. . . Do not be jealous, she is the only female that has taken any liberties with me since I left home . . . & I don't think Jenny will go with me to America.

The mornings are cool. We ride all day with an overcoat on. The wind has chapped our faces & we are awfully sun burnt. . . We stopt at 5, put up our tent. I made my quilt bed & rested a little & our man got dinner. We had boiled chicken, pilau, vermicelli soup, stewed apricots, oranges, a glass of sherry & tea. Our dinner was by candle light.

On Sunday, March 9th, the men rested at Suez near the northern end of the Red Sea. The animals were sent around the end of the sea while the men crossed the water in a boat. "We expect to sleep tonight," wrote Scott that day, "at Ain Musa, wells of Moses." The camel journey from Cairo to Mt. Sinai usually took from ten to twelve days but Scott and Taylor made it in eight and a half days. This meant hard riding. They reached St. Catherine's monastery at the base of the mountain early Saturday morning and spent two days there sight-seeing, which Scott described as being "days of deep, almost wild, intense excitement. The crowd of holy associations that clusters here is almost overwhelming."

On Sunday evening Scott, in another long letter to his wife, summarized his latest experiences. He told of how he and Taylor decided to ride on ahead of the rest of the caravan in order to have more time at Mt. Sinai. So they arose at midnight on Friday, March 14th, and after the necessary preliminaries of eating and packing, they were on their way by three o'clock. "The glorious moon was directly behind us," Scott wrote, "perhaps yet an hour high. Just after we started, the bright morning star appeared directly before us. It reminded me of the star of Bethlehem. . . Then the knowledge that we had been & were still on the very track along which the Israelites had been led by the pillar of cloud & of fire. The whole was grand—it was sublime. It was awful." His thoughts, leaping both space and time, carried him back to his boyhood days in western Tennessee;

> I remembered many of the solitary morning rides I had taken on a bag of corn to the mill through the unbroken forests of my own native state. I remembered how then I used to sing or repeat to the listening stars scraps of hymns & verses of Scripture as I rode on—and how even when a lad I used to preach & pray on my horse until I would weep. In the deep forest shades, I have passed many of the most interesting moments of my religious life. . .
>
> At 8 o'c my faithful dromedary kneeled at the Convent gate of Mt. Sinai for me to descend & enter. On our first entrance we were presented with some sugar plums & . . . date brandy. We got some breakfast and began our ascent of the 'Mountain of God' about 10 o'c A.M. It took us 2½ hours to ascend to the top. The mountain is 700 feet above the monastery and about 9,000 feet above the sea. We took lunch on the top—made coffee—& spent two hours & descended. Then we examined the monastery, chh., cemetery & gardens, burning bush, [Exodus 3:1-3].

No doubt the two men were shown some of the manuscript treasures of the convent. It was there a few years earlier, in 1844, that the great German Biblical critic and scholar, Constantine von Tischendorf, had discovered one of the oldest Greek manuscripts of the Bible in existence. He secured some of the pages, but it was not until 1859 that the full codex was obtained. This manuscript is now one of the great treasures of the British Museum. It is possible that the monks showed a part of this manuscript to Scott and Taylor but if so they would have had no idea of its importance.

This visit to Mt. Sinai was the fulfillment of one of Scott's dreams. He wrote: "I consider this journey worth ten times its cost in money." In a letter to his son Robert, written from Hebron on March 28, 1851, Dr. Scott gave some more details regarding the monastery at Mt. Sinai. "It contains 20 monks & 20 cats & an unknown quantity of vermin. . . The monks are ignorant, lazy, & dirty. But one or two can read."

The two men left Mt. Sinai on Monday, March 17th, for Hebron. By riding ten hours a day they were able to reach their destination on Thursday, March 27th. Thus they made the journey from Cairo in twenty days, not counting the time for sight-seeing. Usually thirty days were taken for such a trip. At Hebron the two men were confined in quarantine for three days and it was not until the 31st that they were permitted to rent horses and continue their travels through Bethlehem to Jerusalem. They found the ride most fatiguing. "Our Turkish horses were rough," wrote Scott.

To his great joy he found a letter from his wife awaiting him in Jerusalem. It was dated January 31st, two months earlier. This letter is among those on deposit in Bancroft Library. Again and again Scott had urged Ann to meet him some place in the East upon his return from Europe. Ann, however, knowing that her confinement was due early in June refused to consider leaving New Orleans. "Indeed, my dear husband, I cannot see how I can leave my comfortable home and start on such a journey without you at my side, to direct and care for us all. My courage quails at the thought of landing on a strange wharf . . . the more I think of it the more I dread it." She quoted Elder Maybin as saying that: "You should prolong your stay in Europe so as not to reach home before October 4th." Ann confessed that she was not enthusiastic for such a delay but yet felt that her husband should not return before the middle or latter part of August when the worst of the summer's heat would be over. This was her recommendation even "though my eyes ache to see you and my heart yearns to be with you."

Scott replied on April 1st. "Your last letter distracts my thoughts," he wrote. "I don't know what to do—my elder and wife urging me to stay away!—and until October!!" He added that if she would only meet him some place in the East, he would be quite willing to stay away from New Orleans "as long as you say I must." He noted that he had been away from home five months on March 14th. "If I thought it would take me as long to return, I would be almost crazy."

Scott made some comments on her personal appearance and his wardrobe. "I assure you that I am very well," he wrote. "My whiskers have not been touched since I left Paris. I intend they shall grow till I get back to Paris." His letters often sparkle with touches of humor. The turn of a phrase suggests a smile on his face or a twinkle in his eye as, for instance, when he wrote about his wardrobe. "I am literally all in rags. My buttons, every one on my pants have been off, some of them several times. Three of my red drawers have lost the throne of honor. My shirts are more holy than righteous."

Ann had written about the possibility of his visiting Kilkeel, Ireland, again to see if he could get possession of her property. She felt that it was worth at least $1,000. On his previous trip abroad he had been unsuccessful in clearing up the legal difficulties, and was reluctant to make a second effort. "You are mistaken about the value of your house in Kilkeel," he wrote. However, for her sake, he promised to make inquiry when he returned to England.

Scott and Taylor spent a week in Jerusalem. For Scott, the preacher, this was a never-to-be-forgotten experience. The holy city became a living commentary on the Bible. Hours were spent in the temple area, in the Garden of Gethsemane, and in the Church of the Holy Sepulchre. They climbed the Mount of Olives and rode around the walls of the city. Mindful of the coming days when he would be preaching or lecturing again, Scott eagerly stored away in his mind and notebooks the impressions and information he gathered from his visits to the sacred sites. He wrote long letters not only to his wife but also to his congregation and begged Ann to save all of his letters for future reference.

The men started north from Jerusalem on horseback on April 7th. They visited Mizpah and stopped for a short time in Nablus and afterwards in Nazareth. They arrived in Beirut on April 14th where they met Walker and Davis. Here Taylor parted company with Scott and joined his former traveling companions. The three sailed from Beirut on April 17th and Scott was alone again. Reporting on events in a letter to Ann dated April 15th, he said that he planned to go to Damascus. He had weeks and months to spend yet in traveling. "I am consumed with anxiety about you! The care of my people. . . And yet after all, my people—even my heart's life, my precious wife, says 'don't show your face here till autumn.' " Defying such advice, he added: "I think I shall be home by the last of July at any rate."

Scott turned to United States Consul, J. Hosford Smith, in Beirut for help in making arrangements for his Damascus trip. The Scott Collection in Bancroft Library contains a document dated at Beirut on April 16, 1851, which reads as follows:

> It is agreed that Altoon Sherif shall furnish two horses and one mule to W. A. Scott to perform a journey to Damascus & thence to Baalbeck and return—the said journey is to occupy eight days & for each horse and for the said mule, Mr. Scott is to pay 120 piastres, making 360 piastres in all for the trip—the half of the said sum is now paid in hand to the said Sherif. . . The horses & the mule are to travel when and where the said Scott desires, but he is not to be responsible for them or their food in any way. The remaining half is to be paid on completion of the journey in Beirut.

On the back of the agreement appears a notation about supplies, including a tent, which were to be taken. Scott was back in Beirut by Thursday, April 24th, for on that day he wrote from that place to his wife.

> I have just returned from Damascus and Baalbeck, & I am very tired." He summarized his experiences: "Last Thursday, the 17th inst., all my friends having gone in the steamer, as I wrote you, I set out alone with my dragoman & muleteers for Damascus. It is usually a three days' journey; but I made it in 2, the distance is 75 miles & the last day I rode 42—was in the saddle 14 hours—such distances are nothing with us in America, but here, and especially over the mountains of Northern Syria, Mt. Lebanon & Anti-Lebanons, they are something. I remained in Dalaqcus two days. It is beautiful, surpassingly beautiful viewed from the mountain top, but it does not bear inspection. . . The bazaars are poor. . . I am deeply disappointed in Damascus.

Whenever Scott spent a Sunday in a city where there were English and American missionaries, he was invariably asked to speak. His reputation as one of America's greatest preachers was known in Damascus with the result that on Sunday, April 20th, "the largest English and American congregation ever assembled in that city" gathered to hear him. In his letter to his wife of April 24th, he confessed: "I have no objection to preaching but don't like to have so many clergymen as hearers . . . in Damascus half the male part of the congregation was clergymen."

The ruins at Baalbeck inspired the same awe he felt when viewing the monuments of Luxor and Karnak, and words failed him as he tried to describe their stupendous magnificence. Back in Beirut after his grueling ride, he felt physically exhausted. "For 4 months," he wrote, "I have been making my own bed & living as a wayfarer. . . I am tired, almost tired to death of travel."

On Saturday, after his return from Damascus, he made an excursion to the cliffs at the mouth of Dog River about nine miles north of Beirut to see "some Phoenician, Persian, Roman & Saracemic inscriptions." The narrow strip of land between the mountains and the sea was an important link in the highway which connected the two civilizations of the Euphrates and the Nile valleys. The cliffs carry inscriptions of conquering rulers who passed that way, beginning with Rameses ii, spanning a period of over three thousand years. After Scott's day, new inscriptions have been added including that of General Allenby of World War I fame. Even he who has but a limited knowledge of ancient and modern history will find his emotions stirred as he notes the roster of famous names and visualizes the passing and repassing of many armies from many nations at that place. Few visitors to Dog River would have appreciated the historical significance of the series of inscriptions more than Dr. Scott.

Taking ship at Beirut on the 29th, Scott arrived in Smyrna about five days later but was kept in quarantine with the other passengers for five days. While in Smyrna he was entertained by an old friend, then United States consul, T. P. Johnston. Writing to Scott on June 11, 1852, Johnston said: "Your visit to Smyrna though short was one of the most interesting to me that I have had since leaving my native land more than 18 years ago. . . It was a rare pleasure to me to see one who had been baptized by my uncle, Thomas Hall." It was this reference to Thomas Hall which provided the clue to the identification of him as the pastor of the Bethbirei Church in what is now Marshall County, Tennessee. This in turn pinpointed within a few miles the birthplace of William A. Scott.

By May 10th, Scott was in Constantinople which he described in a letter of that date to his wife as being "a wonderful city." This was the city of Chrysostom, the golden-mouthed preacher of the 4th century. Here again the English-speaking residents prevailed upon him to speak. In a postscript to his letter of May 10th, he added: "I preached to some 150 English & American residents & travellers. My whiskers are grey & hang down into my bosom & my mustache covers my mouth." On May 22nd, he wrote to Ann from Athens. He was distressed by not hearing from her. "The last letter I got before coming to Athens was written 22nd Feby. & now [it is] 22 May, three months. Surely, surely, my beloved wife, you have written me oftener than once a month." Possibly some of her letters were lost in the mails but it also appears that she was so engaged with her household duties that she had little time for writing. In a letter written to his father about this time, Robert said: "Ma dont write to me now once in a coon's age."

After leaving Athens, Scott moved on to Trieste, Venice, and Milan. He was at the latter city on June 5th, the date his wife gave birth to a boy who was named Ebenezer. But of this event he had no word until sometime in the first part of July when he was in England. From Milan, he went to Lake Como and then crossed the Alps through the Splügen Pass, a road now rarely used by travelers. "We travelled for hours through banks of snow higher than the top of our diligence [i.e., stage coach]," he wrote in a letter to his wife dated June 9th. "It stands like a wall on either side." From Zurich, he took a boat down the Rhine, perhaps to Cologne, whence he went by train to Paris. He was then back in familiar territory.

To his great joy Scott found a number of letters, including several from Ann, awaiting him in Paris. Her last letter was dated April 29th. Writing to her on June 17th, he said: "Mr. Maybin argues very strongly that I must not return till October. Says *you* concur with him. . . If I had not been accustomed in my youth to Indian warfare & forest-startling yells from painted savages, I verily believe you and Mr. Maybin would have frightened me out of all my senses." Scott heard some disquieting reports from several friends about the condition of his church due to the lack of pastoral oversight. This made him all the more eager to be back home.

Scott was in London on June 21st and made arrangements to sail for America on the "Pacific" on July 9th. With plenty of time on his hands, he attended the World's Fair then being held in Hyde Park in London. One of the outstanding attractions was a great exhibition hall constructed largely of glass and known as the Crystal Palace. In his letter of June 28th to his wife, he told of visiting the fair. "I walked and walked," he said, "until I could scarcely stand up." After returning to New Orleans, Scott had occasion to draw upon his European experiences for sermon illustrations. On January 15, 1854, he spoke before the South-Western Bible Society on *The Bible, God's Crystal Palace*. His address was shortly thereafter published as a pamphlet.

Scott had written to a lawyer in Ireland about the Kilkeel property but to his disappointment received no reply to his letter. By this time he was, as he said, "exceedingly tired of travelling." His one great desire was to get back home. In his letter of July 2nd, written from Liverpool, to his wife, he said that he had given up any idea of going to Kilkeel. "I married you and not your old house in Kilkeel," he wrote. "The fact is, I care for nothing on earth but to get home & find you well. Fear I shall hardly find the skeleton of my congregation." The lack of information about Ann and the birth of the baby, which he knew was then long past, drove him almost frantic. It seems probable that some word about the arrival of his son reached him shortly before he sailed on July 9th.

By the 23rd of July, Scott was back in New York. Writing that day to Ann, he reported that he had made arrangements for Robert to join him and that the two were sailing from New York on the 26th. He and Robert returned to New Orleans on Tuesday August 5th. No extant record remains telling of the joyous family reunion which must have taken place. A brief note in one of Scott's journals reads: "Arrived at home this morning, Tuesday, 5th August 1851. Have travelled more than 20,000 miles—absent 9 mos., 3 wks. & one day. Oh the goodness of God. It is overwhelming. I fear & tremble at the responsibility & labors that are upon me." We can well believe that Scott vowed to his wife that never again would he leave her for such an extended period. And we can only imagine the emotion that welled up within his heart when he held his newly born in his arms. He also made a notation that the total expenses for the extended journey "will be all of $3,000." This the church paid.

Scott was back in his pulpit on Sunday, August 10th. A brief note in his diary reads: "Congregation very large—preached on Isa. 61:1-3. Intro. was all I could reconcile to myself to spend in reference to my travels. Presume many people expected a very different kind of discourse. Can't help it. It would have been foolish, out of taste, wicked to have made a display of myself on my travels in such a place & at such a time."

Naturally, however, he drew upon his travel experiences for some of his sermon illustrations. Sunday after Sunday, the church was filled with hearers. The *Daily Delta* for October 21st, reporting on a sermon entitled "The Crystal Palace," commented:

> We have never heard from the pulpit a more instructive and eloquent discourse than that delivered by Dr. Scott of the First Presbyterian Church on Sunday last, to the largest congregation we have seen this season. The Doctor has recently returned from a very extended tour through the Old World, and has been a close observer of the conditions of affairs there. The result of these observations, as far as they relate to the political conditions of the leading nations of Europe was given in the discourse of Sunday. Dr. Scott is a thorough, hopeful democrat, a believer in the capacity of all people to govern themselves—who holds that the republican system must eventually triumph over all the other forms of government. . . Dr. Scott gave a very beautiful and graphic description of the Crystal Palace, in its influence on social advancement and international feeling.

Sometime during the early part of the summer of 1852, Dr. Scott succumbed to an attack of "malignant typhoid fever." In a letter written from Middlebury, Vermont, on July 26th to his friend Walter Lowrie, Scott said: "It left me exceedingly feeble. My Physicians have ordered me to the mountains of New England for quietude & rest during the summer." Scott was back in his pulpit in October and the *Daily Delta* reported that "this eminent divine" had returned "with his health thoroughly established." On November 28, 1852, this newspaper devoted its full seven-column front page to the text of his Thanksgiving sermon delivered a few days earlier.

YELLOW FEVER

Among the treasured heirlooms belonging to descendants of Dr. Scott are pieces of a large silver service which, according to a family tradition, was presented to him by the city of New Orleans for distinguished service rendered in a yellow fever epidemic. The complete service was divided among the members of the family following Dr. Scott's death in 1885, and then subdivided again among his grandchildren. It is now impossible to know how large the original service was. Facts regarding the exact time or the special occasion for the presentation have been forgotten with the passing of the years. One of the older descendants believes that a Roman Catholic priest was given similar recognition at the same time, but all efforts to document the recognition have failed. The original minutes of the City Council of New Orleans and contemporary New Orleans newspapers covering the years when the epidemics were at their worst were examined without finding any mention of such a presentation. But, on the other hand, these individual pieces of the large silver service remain as tangible evidence to support the family tradition.

Yellow fever first appeared in New Orleans in 1794 and thereafter took its annual toll of lives during the summer and fall for over a century. It was not until 1900 that scientists proved that the virus causing the fever was transmitted by certain mosquitoes. Out of this important discovery came a vaccine for immunization and mosquito control measures which in time completely stamped out the disease in the United States.

The symptoms of the fever included a hot and dry skin, pulse of one hundred or more, violent headache, pains in the back and limbs, coated tongue, fetid breath, and nausea. Often there was black vomit of coagulated blood. Sometimes there were hemorrhages of the nose, gums, or bowels. The fever began on the fourth or fifth day and then the skin and eyes turned yellow giving rise to the name yellow fever. The doctors were almost helpless. The bowels were kept open and patients were advised to stay in bed. Some doctors prescribed quinine; others favored the common remedies of the time as blood-letting and calomel. The disease was deadly, as less than ten percent, according to reliable estimates, of those afflicted recovered. If one survived an attack, he had immunity from a second. Thus both Dr. and Mrs. Scott, who had the disease shortly after moving to New Orleans, became immune.

People did not know if the disease was infectious; there was much speculation as to whether the contagion could be transported in persons or goods from one place to another. Some noted that people with yellow fever were landed from steamboats at Memphis where they died or recovered "without communicating the disease in a single instance." Of course nothing was then known about Memphis being beyond the range of the mosquito causing the trouble. Some felt that the accumulation of putrifying matter and foul stagnant waters gave rise to the disease. Such a theory was close to the real source of the trouble as these conditions often provided breeding places for the mosquitoes.

Three major yellow fever epidemics struck New Orleans during the years the Scotts lived there. More than 1,500 died in 1843; about 2,700 in 1847; and over 11,000 in 1853. The epidemic of the latter year began on May 28th when a patient in the charity hospital spewed up black vomit. The dread killer was back again. William L. Robinson in his *The Diary of a Samaritan*, published in 1860, has the following description of conditions in the stricken city:

> The whole city was a hospital, and every well man, woman, and child were instrumental . . . in relieving the sick. . . Such was Death's harvesting that, to keep pace with the call for interments, trenches of seven feet wide and one hundred feet long were constantly being dug, into which the coffins were closely packed, three to four deep, without intermediate earth. The morning train of funerals, as was the evening's, crowded the road to the cemeteries. It was an unbroken line of carriages and omnibuses for two miles and a half.. . . The sun's heat and putrid exhalations were sickening to the sense.

The stench was so bad that wages up to $5 an hour were paid to Negroes to do the burying.

Another and slightly different account of the burials is found in the August 13, 1853, issue of the *Christian Advocate*. This report stated:

> Long ditches were dug across the great human charnel. Wide enough were they to entomb a legion, but only fourteen inches deep. Coffins laid in them showed their tops above the surface of the earth. On these were piled dirt to the depth of a foot or more, but so loosely that the myriads of flies found entry between the loose clods, down to the cracked seams of the coffins, and buzzed and blew their ovaria, creating each hour their new hatch swarms.

One morning the grave diggers were astounded to hear moans coming from one of the coffins which had been imperfectly covered the day before. On opening it, they found a man who had been picked up for dead and buried but who was actually in a drunken stupor.

As the weeks passed the toll of the dead mounted with frightening rapidity. Out of a total population in 1853 of about 154,000, nearly 30,000 fled to safer localities inland. August was the worst month. Reports show that 1,186 died of the fever during the first week; 1,526, the second; 1,534, the third; and 1,628, the fourth; making a total of 5,874 for the month. The epidemic was so severe that it caused serious curtailment of business. Many ships refused to call at the port. All manner of supposed remedies were tried including the firing of cannon throughout the city "to disturb the atmosphere." We also read of some tar burning to combat the putrid odor of decaying flesh.

Robinson in his book mentioned above reported: "The clergy of all denominations did honor to their calling during the epidemics. . . So much were they in request that it was impossible to meet every demand of their time." Many were buried without benefit of clergy. Sometimes a layman would read a few prayers at the graveside. In the introduction to his *Daniel*, Dr. Scott commented on the ravages of the epidemic. "Many of the precious youth who listened to these lectures," he wrote, "have fallen its victims." He also explained: "It may be readily supposed that in filling my pulpit, and in visiting the sick, in burying the dead, and in attempting to instruct, encourage, and comfort the living and the bereaved, and alleviate the miseries of the suffering poor, I have had but little time or heart for the work of revision." The introduction was dated September 20, 1853.

Since the 1853 epidemic was by far the worst which struck the city during Dr. Scott's residence there, we may assume that the award of the silver service by the city council came in the fall of 1853 or shortly thereafter. A second heirloom owned by one of Dr. Scott's granddaughters is a ring which, according to another family tradition, was given to him by the Masonic order of the Knights of St. John of Jerusalem in recognition of his services to the sick. The stone set in the ring is reputed to have come from the wall of Jerusalem. Around the stone is the design of a cord worn by a monk, with an inscription in Hebrew "Jehovah guard and keep thee." There is no evidence as to the time or the occasion when such a presentation was made but it is possible that this too came during or shortly after the 1853 yellow fever epidemic.

Sometime during August 1853, a number of letters came to Scott from people in San Francisco asking whether he would consider accepting a call to a new Presbyterian congregation to be formed in that city. Among these was one from his former elder, Stephen Franklin. Such a prospect could not have come at a more favorable time. Scott felt exhausted both physically and emotionally as a result of the unceasing demands upon his time and strength arising out of the epidemic. When he had first considered accepting a call to the New Orleans church, he visited the city and had hesitated to make the move because of the dangers that he and his family would face. New Orleans was a "sickly" place. Yet he accepted and in the fall of 1843 almost paid for the decision with his life. He had spent over eleven years in New Orleans. Twice he had been obliged to travel abroad to regain his health. If ever he had to face another summer like that of 1853, he felt certain his strength would fail again.

California with its sunshine and invigorating climate was calling. There was no yellow fever there! Only the yellow fever of gold seekers.

ACCUSED OF PLAGIARISM

In the spring of 1853 Scott made arrangements with Harper's of New York for the publication of his first book with the title, *Daniel, A Model for Young Men.* "It has been my custom," wrote Scott in the preface, "for more than ten years to devote my Sabbath evenings, during the winter and spring months, to young men. On such occasions I have delivered one hundred and fifty different discourses." He prided himself on his ability to appeal to the young men of his generation and the repeated invitations that came to him to speak to such groups is evidence of his popularity. Out of this series of lectures he selected a number for publication.

Among the chapters included was a lecture delivered before the Young Men's Christian Association of New Orleans on January 16, 1853. The Y.M.C.A. was first launched in London in 1844. The first association in the United States was formed in Boston in 1851. This became a model for most of the other Y.M.C.A.s founded in this country in the years immediately following. Active membership was limited to young men who were members in good standing of an evangelical church. Seven cities including New Orleans had an association before the end of 1852. Scott was keenly interested in the movement and gave the Y of his city his wholehearted support.

In his address to the Y members of his city, Scott sought to interpret Christianity in a way that would appeal to young men. The following is a quotation from his lecture: "The Bible does not tolerate a lukewarm, lopsided, segmented Christianity; but a deep, equable, and ever-flowing, circumferential, whole-bodied piety, a piety that is in strong sympathy with our individual [needs] in this up-and-down world, that seizes the soul and fastens upon it the great vitalized convictions of truth, as it flowed from the lips of the Divine Saviour, and carries them out into the parlor and the highways of life."

Scott asked the Rev. William B. Sprague of Albany, New York, to write an introduction for the book. Sprague was then at work on his great nine-volume *The Annals of the American Pulpit* and had previously asked Scott to furnish information about some early Cumberland Presbyterian ministers. This Scott had done. Sprague wanted to read the text of Scott's book before writing an introduction, so proof pages were sent to him sometime during the summer of 1853. On the day before Sprague sent his introduction to the publishers, a disastrous fire destroyed Harper's publishing establishment and both the manuscript and the stereotype plates of Scott's book were destroyed. Since Sprague had the proof pages, the work was transferred to Robert Carter & Brothers, also in New York, which brought out a handsomely bound volume of Scott's *Daniel* in the fall of that year. A second edition of this work appeared in 1856.

A review of Scott's book appeared in *Norton's Literary Gazette* in the spring of 1854. The reviewer was sharply critical of Scott and accused him of taking material from a work on Daniel published a few years earlier by a Dr. Cummings of London, "without the least acknowledgment." Stung by the charge of plagiarism, Scott in September 1854 issued a four-page folder in which he stoutly defended himself. He claimed that due acknowledgment had been made in the introduction of his book to all authors consulted. He confessed that because of the pressure of pastoral duties, connected in part with the yellow fever epidemic of that year in New Orleans, he had not been able to revise the manuscript as he had wished. The text had gone directly to the publisher from its use in the pulpit. Scott explained how in his original manuscript the quotations taken from the book by Cummings had been inserted in their proper places, but when the type was reset after the fire, from the proof pages, many of these quotation marks had been omitted. This, he claimed, had occurred without his knowledge as he trusted another to read proof the second time. Whereas Scott can justly be criticized for carelessness in permitting his work to be published without personally checking the proof, the charge of deliberate plagiarism seems to be unfounded. In later years some of Scott's critics in California republished the charge of plagiarism, to his great embarrassment.

CALVARY CHURCH, SAN FRANCISCO, FROM AN ARCHITECT'S DRAWING, 1854
Courtesy of San Francisco Theological Seminary.

San Francisco, Calvary Church

As a loyal Old School Presbyterian, Dr. Scott was an enthusiastic supporter of the benevolences of his denomination. In his several parishes, statistics show that he was aggressive in inducing his people to give liberally to both home and foreign missions and to the other programs of the national church. Very wisely, he felt that an informed people would be a giving people. Therefore when the official boards of his denomination launched the *Home and Foreign Record* in January 1850, Dr. Scott went before his elders in the New Orleans church and persuaded them to enter two hundred subscriptions for the church families in the parish. The cost was taken out of the church's budget.

Through the columns of this magazine, Presbyterians were kept informed of the progress of their work throughout their home land and in many countries overseas. During 1852 and 1853, the *Record* gave considerable attention to California. Such reports carried special interest to Presbyterians in New Orleans. As has been stated, New Orleans by virtue of its strategic location on the main route linking the Isthmus of Panama with eastern ports, was immediately drawn into the orbit of the California gold rush. Beginning with December 1848, an ever increasing stream of its citizens were leaving for San Francisco, the main port for all of northern California. The first to go were the riffraff, men without family or property responsibilities, and the adventurers. Upon arriving in California, they scurried to the Mother Lode country in the foothills of the Sierras. According to figures compiled by the California State Mining Bureau, the yield of gold in 1849 was about $10,000,000. By 1852 this had risen to $81,000,000. Such riches inevitably stimulated commerce, and San Francisco boomed while fortunes were made in real estate. Beginning in 1850 a more substantial type of immigrant began arriving in the city. These were young business and professional men such as merchants, doctors, lawyers, and skilled craftsmen. A high percentage were well educated, and within another year they began sending for their families. So great was the influx of Americans that California was admitted to the Union as a state on September 9, 1851, without first having been a territory.

Among the correspondents who wrote from California, none was more faithful than the Rev. Albert Williams, pastor of the First Presbyterian Church of San Francisco. An Old School Presbyterian, he had arrived in the city on April 1, 1849. A number of letters from Williams were published in the *Home and Foreign Record* in which he repeatedly pleaded for greater support from Presbyterians for the work just beginning in California. The June issue carried one of his letters under the title: "California, A Presbyterian Missionary Field." In the April 1853 number appeared another of his appeals under the caption: "A Voice from California."

The June 1853 issue contained still another letter from Williams under an introductory editorial on "Present condition and obligations of Protestantism in California." The editor, drawing upon an unpublished section of Williams' letter, wrote: "The entire population of California by the late census is 224,435, and the increase in two years more than ONE HUNDRED THOUSAND! San Francisco has a population of 34,876! It must now be about 40,000." In general the Protestant work throughout the state was reported to be spotty and very weak. Most of the Methodist preachers, including both northern and southern branches, were unordained laymen with little or no support from their respective denominations. Appointees of the different Presbyterian or Congregational missionary boards found that their stipends, geared to living conditions in the East, were wofully inadequate to meet the inflated prices of California. Unless these men had private means, they were forced to turn to other occupations, usually schoolteaching, to supplement their meager income.

The subject of California was again emphasized in the July 1853 *Record* when the editor quoted at length from a letter from an unnamed Presbyterian layman who wrote on March 10th of that year. It seems that the writer hailed from New Orleans for he made the comment: "The Sabbath is pretty well observed, better than in New Orleans."

The layman had some penetrating observations to make about San Francisco based upon a two years' residence in the city. "Within the last year," he wrote, "a very large emigration of families has occurred, and there are now some twenty-five hundred children in the Public Schools, where, when I came, not a *child* was to be seen in the street, or if met, was a sight so rare as to startle one." He mentioned the fact that one of the two Episcopal churches in the city was paying its rector an annual salary of $6,000 and that the First Congregational Church, of which the Rev. Timothy Dwight Hunt was pastor, was erecting a handsome brick edifice at a cost of $50,000.

Regarding the number of Christians among the incoming population, the layman wrote:

> A most remarkable feature of the emigration is that numbers of converted men are here, and coming here; and what is truly a blessing, the churches are sending not only their converted young men, but their converted young women also, as daughters, sisters, and wives; and a very marked feature is, that a very large number of these are *Presbyterians!* You will at once ask, "How is this? If so many are Presbyterians, why have you but 120 church members?" It is even so; hundreds roam the streets, or go to other churches, forgetting that which forgets them.

At the time the layman was writing, Old School Presbyterians had but three churches in the state. The oldest was that at Benicia founded on April 15, 1849, by the Rev. Sylvester Woodbridge, Jr. This was the first Protestant church with a resident ordained pastor to be established in California. Next came the First Presbyterian Church of San Francisco organized on May 20th of that year by the Rev. Albert Williams. The third church was at Stockton where the Rev. James Woods established a church on March 17, 1850. These three ministers, often referred to as the three "Ws," erected the pioneer Presbytery of California on February 20, 1850. This judicatory was then attached to the Synod of New York. Upon the arrival of a few more ministers, General Assembly in 1852 authorized the division of the Presbytery of California into two parts, the second to be called the Presbytery of Stockton, and that these two with the Presbytery of Oregon should constitute the Synod of the Pacific. This was done on October 19, 1852.

In February 1853 the Rev. William Speer, D.D., who had spent four years as a missionary in Canton, China, arrived in San Francisco to open a mission for the Chinese of the city. There was also in San Francisco a "feeble" congregation for the Welsh-speaking Presbyterians. But on the whole, the author of the letter had good reason to bemoan the weakness of the Old School work. He gave credit to a more aggressive activity being carried on by the New School brethren and their Congregational associates. The layman's letter continues:

> But, perhaps you ask me, "What kind of men do you need?" Let me state a case, and you will see. Suppose that to-day, even while you read my letter, in Kentucky, that all the old men, all, or nearly all the women and children were suddenly abstracted from your State, and none left you but the young and the ardent, the energetic and the enterprising; suppose that an influence should suddenly fall on these to wake their energies, and tax them with a power to will, that had never before been seen; and each man with his hands full of money, and accustomed to have every thing his heart desired, regardless of cost, and willing and ready to pay for it at five times the accustomed rate; and withal, suppose seven-tenths of that population educated, and you have a picture of California! What kind of ministers would you send them? What kind would they listen to? None, but the very best! None, but such as could make them think—or as one wished the other day, "who could drive him up in the corner of his pew."

The whole implication of the letter was that the Old School Presbyterians had sent not only too few ministers to the booming state but also that these were of mediocre ability. The rare combination in San Francisco's population of youth, money, talent, and education presented a challenge such as could not be duplicated in any other city of the nation. What San Francisco needed was the very best of the country's ministers. If such a person of superior ability and proved experience could be found, wrote the laymen, he could be assured of finding "a hearty welcome and a satisfactory support." This issue of *The Home and Foreign Record* was delivered to Dr. Scott's home about the time the letters arrived from San Francisco asking whether he would consider a call to that city.

CALLED TO CALVARY, SAN FRANCISCO

Some time in July 1853, a number of business men met in San Francisco to discuss the possibility of establishing another Presbyterian church in the city. The fact that First Church was not measuring up to its opportunities was too apparent to be denied. There were literally hundreds of Presbyterians in San Francisco who had not transferred their membership to First Church. Among these was Stephen Franklin, for years an elder in First Church, New Orleans, who had been in California for about four years, presumably all of this time in San Francisco, without transfering his membership. In all probability it was he who called the small group of men together to discuss what could be done. According to an early record in the first session book of Calvary Presbyterian Church, these men "feeling deeply the need for further & more vigorous efforts for the spiritual welfare of our rapidly increasing population, invited the Revd. Wm. A. Scott, D.D., of New Orleans to visit San Francisco with the view of establishing another Presbyterian Church."

Meticulous care was taken to conform to Presbyterian law and tradition. The elders and pastor of First Church were consulted. In 1882 Albert Williams published his *A Pioneer Pastorate and Times* in which he made mention of the fact that his session gave full approval to the proposed establishment of another Old School Presbyterian church in the city. "An official letter, embodying this assent," wrote Williams, was sent to Dr. Scott. "And, upon an intimation that a personal letter from me was desired on this subject, I wrote to Dr. Scott, assuring him of my acquiescence and cordiality in the plan." This was a gracious move as both the session and Williams were fully aware of the inevitable competition that such a magnetic personality as Dr. Scott would create.

Unfortunately the Scott Collection in Bancroft Library does not contain the original correspondence which passed between the self-appointed committee in San Francisco and Dr. Scott. It is clear that Scott was immediately receptive to the idea. The heavy responsibilities he was carrying, increased by the demands of the yellow fever epidemic of that summer, added to the heat and humidity of the New Orleans climate, had again brought on ill health. Lawyer Franklin, never one to lose sight of a good argument, had no doubt extolled the merits of San Francisco's wonderful climate. The question of the salary arose. The men promised $8,000 a year and even agreed to pay most of Scott's moving expenses should he be willing to visit the city to obtain firsthand knowledge of the opportunity. This Scott agreed to do but said that he would be unable to get away until the late spring of 1854. The Scott Collection in Bancroft contains only one letter from Franklin dealing with these negotiations. This is dated October 20, 1853, and contains the sentence: "I am delighted with the hope of seeing you here."

The promised salary of $8,000 was twice that being paid by the New Orleans church. After taking into consideration the extent to which the dollar has been devaluated since 1853, the amount would have to be multiplied several times to be comparable to present day values. In all probability this was the largest salary ever offered to a Presbyterian minister of his generation in the country. On the other hand, it should be remembered that San Francisco was then experiencing an inflated economy and that prices were, by all eastern standards, fantastically high. Most of the necessities of life were still being imported.

We may assume that the preliminary negotiations between the committee in San Francisco and Dr. Scott were strictly private. He naturally would not wish to disturb the tranquillity of his relationship with his people in New Orleans with a possibility that might not materialize. But the calm was suddenly shattered when the October issue of *The Home and Foreign Record* reached New Orleans. Therein under the caption "California" was the following news item:

> Our readers are aware that the Board of Missions has been desirous of re-inforcing our missions in California, but have had serious difficulty in obtaining suitable men. That they may know the feelings of men in that far off State towards our Church, and their great anxiety to be supplied with a suitable ministry, we give an extract from a correspondent of the *Journal of Commerce, New York*, dated San Francisco, August 1st, 1853:
>
> "The Rev. Dr. Scott of New Orleans, has had a call sent him by a number of our first citizens—prominent members of the Old school Presbyterian Church—with an urgent request for him to come to this city and labour among this people. A wide field, and one full of promise, is here open to a man of his talent and ability in the Church, and it is hoped that he will at once signify his acceptance. These gentlemen guarantee Dr. Scott a salary of eight thousand dollars per annum."

The premature announcement of a possible move to San Francisco no doubt caused Dr. Scott considerable embarrassment. He was quick to disclaim any attraction of the $8,000 salary. Instead he stressed the fact that his continued ill health in New Orleans was the chief factor for even thinking of leaving the city. Since no immediate action was contemplated, he quieted their fears and carried on his usual duties. On December 24, 1853, William and Ann welcomed their sixth son and eighth child into their home. He was named Paul Eli. Since one of their children had died, this left seven children ranging in ages from sixteen down to the newly born baby. The large family demanded a correspondingly large income.

FIRST VISIT TO SAN FRANCISCO

After making arrangements for a four-month leave of absence from his New Orleans pastorate, Dr. Scott left for San Francisco on April 22, 1854. According to a San Francisco newspaper report, he crossed the isthmus through Nicaragua and then took passage on the "Sierra Nevada" which arrived on Friday, May 19th. Cornelius Vanderbilt had opened the Nicaraguan route in 1851. Until the railroad was completed across Panama in 1855, this longer way was popular with many travelers.

When Scott landed in San Francisco, the city was poised on the brink of a serious business depression, but of this few had any suspicions. The spirit of bubbling enthusiasm characterized the adolescent city. A series of five fires, some of which were incendiary, ravaged the city beginning in December 1849 and ending in June 1851. Following the last fire, the central part of the city was rebuilt with such fireproof materials as stone and brick. Around this central section were frame structures and tents which sprawled out over the sand hills. When Scott landed in May 1854, he still could see some building activity but it was beginning to slow down.

The committee sponsoring Dr. Scott's coming had given due notice of the event through the daily press. The Musical Hall, located on the southeast corner of Montgomery and Bush Streets, in what is now the heart of the financial district of the city, was rented for three Sundays. Among those present for the morning service on Sunday, May 21st, was the Rev. James Woods, founder of the Presbyterian church in Stockton, who happened to be in the city on that day. Following the death of Dr. Scott in 1885, Woods wrote an eulogy for the *Occident,* a Presbyterian weekly then being published in San Francisco, in which he gave the following description of that first service:

> I was present at his first service in San Francisco. It was in the largest hall in the city and the hall was crowded. It would have melted a heart of stone to have witnessed the weeping and sobbing of an old lady of eighty, one of the Lord's poor who had been a member of his church in New Orleans. Nor were hers the only weeping eyes. Most of the congregation wept tears of joy and sympathy. Then in the prime of his years and strength, the power and pathos of his preaching moved the hearts and consciences of strong men, and made them tremble.

Scott spoke that Sunday evening in the new First Congregational Church, whose pastor, the Rev. Timothy Dwight Hunt, was out of the city at the time. Again every seat was taken, some stood throughout the service, and others were turned away. During the week following several of the city's newspapers gave glowing reports of Dr. Scott's services. The following editorial from the *Daily Evening News* for May 27th is an example:

We hope that none of our readers will forget that Dr. Scott of New Orleans is now in our city. . . Those who have been favored in listening to this eloquent preacher in the sunny South, need not be told to go and hear him, and thus revive and quicken old associations, which carry us back to the days when we were charmed and edified by the luminous thoughts of his heart. When he, with humble and fervent piety, but eloquent and magnificent language, warned us to "flee from the wrath to come." And then, too, his earnest and touching appeals to the throne of grace, in the framing of which Dr. Scott has never been excelled . . . will never be forgotten by those who have knelt with him.

We are well satisfied that there are few minds now found in the pulpit that possess all the requisite qualifications for a great religious teacher to such a degree as Dr. Scott; and there is no one more calculated by simplicity of manner, and attractiveness of deportment, to take hold of the affections of his people, and to dissipate the mistaken impression which unfortunately prevails that a life of piety is one of gloom.

The editor mentioned Dr. Scott's ability to appeal to young people and especially to young men. He concluded his editorial by writing: "We think the future morality and welfare of our city is involved in the question of his remaining among us, and hope that he may be induced to direct his labors permanently in the great field which California lays open to the spiritual instruction."

It is well to remember these encomiums when we note the abuse poured out upon Dr. Scott two years later by some of the city's newspapers because of his stand against the Vigilance Committee. Perhaps the most striking example of this change of attitude is seen in the *Pacific,* a New School Presbyterian and Congregational weekly which was launched in August 1851 and which, therefore, had the distinction of being the oldest religious periodical to be published in California. Scott in after years was the frequent object of the paper's wrath but in its May 26th, 1854, issue, there was nothing but praise. The editor wrote: "It is with great pleasure that we welcome to our shores this eminent Divine, whose name and praise is known throughout our country." In commenting on the evening service which Scott conducted in the Congregational church, the editorial continued: "The house was filled to overflowing, while crowds went away unable to gain admittance. . . Thus ended Dr. Scott's first Sabbath in California which was extremely pleasant and gratifying to the friends of this new church enterprise."

New Orleans papers republished some of the news stories about Dr. Scott which had appeared in the San Francisco papers. There was considerable speculation among Scott's friends in the Crescent City as to his plans. After giving the full story which appeared in the May 26th issue of *The Pacific,* the editor of the *Semi-Weekly Creole* in his June 24th number wrote:

In response to numerous inquiries, we state distinctly that we are not able to learn from any of Dr. Scott's correspondents, what his purposes are, in regard to the invitation of the Californians. He has gone for a short season, as a Missionary, in response to the earnest appeal of his brethren there—"Come over and help us. . ." Without doubt, his prospects of a brilliant career of usefulness on the Pacific [Coast] are very flattering; but it is well known that his heart is with the people of New Orleans.

The facts are that Dr. Scott himself did not know whether he should remain in California. In a letter to his wife dated June 15, 1854, he commented first on the state of his health: "My health has greatly improved. I scarcely ever have any trouble in my head now. . . I dread the homeward voyage very much." Regarding the response he was receiving, he said:

Already I have the most important congregation of any in the city. The leading men, "outsiders" are going to have a public meeting next Monday evening to see if a church can be built for me like ours in New Orleans. The results of this meeting will have an important bearing on my visit. If it is successful, then I will endeavor to organize a church, & if God bless this attempt also: & especially if any of the impenitent are awakened—I shall then begin to feel that I am called to this field at least on *furlough for two years.*

Scott felt that there were many disadvantages connected with moving his family to California. "The future of this whole country is extremely uncertain," he wrote. "And more than all, I love New Orleans tenderly. But I cannot live there." He debated the idea of a two-year furlough. Let the New Orleans church call a colleague who would carry on there. He could move his family to San Francisco in December or January and, after a permanent congregation was well established, they could decide whether they should stay or not. Scott assumed that such an indefinite pastoral relationship would be agreeable to his New Orleans congregation. Later, when faced with the possibility of losing their pastor, this was exactly what the New Orleans church proposed. Writing on July 14th to the Rev. W. McClung, who was supplying the New Orleans church during his absence, Scott explained that he had gone to California for "the double purpose of trying to establish a church here & of regaining my health." He mentioned the possibility of requesting a furlough of eighteen months or two years and pointedly asked whether McClung would welcome a call from the New Orleans church if such were offered.

CALVARY CHURCH ORGANIZED

After three Sundays in Musical Hall, Dr. Scott and his congregation moved to the First Unitarian Church which at that time happened to be without a pastor. To the great delight of the committee responsible for inducing Scott to visit the city, his popularity increased with the passing of weeks. Many of the leading citizens of the city, even some not linked up with any church, felt that it was highly important for a minister of Dr. Scott's ability to remain in San Francisco. A public meeting of all interested in the organization of a new Presbyterian church and in calling Dr. Scott to be its pastor was called for Monday evening, June 19th, at Musical Hall.

The official records of the Board of Trustees of Calvary Church tell the story. "A large meeting convened . . . on motion of S. Franklin, Esq., the Hon. C. F. Garrison was called to the chair." Garrison was mayor of San Francisco. Although not a Presbyterian, his willingness to serve as chairman of the meeting is indicative of the interest many of the leading citizens were showing in the project. Franklin then outlined the steps that had been taken to get Dr. Scott to visit San Francisco, making mention of the tentative promise of an annual salary of $8,000 should he be willing to stay. Having heartily endorsed all that had been done, the meeting adopted a resolution which included the following: "We hereby renew the invitation that was given him to take charge of a Presbyterian Church . . . and we do now pledge ourselves to erect for him a new and suitable Church Edifice with the least practicable delay."

A Committee of Twenty was appointed, with Garrison as chairman, to solicit subscriptions for the purchase of a lot and the erection of a building. Among some of the prominent men on this committee were Thomas H. Selby, later an elder in Calvary Church and also once a mayor of San Francisco; James B. Roberts, later an elder in Calvary and one of the most active members of the church; Stephen Franklin; H. Channing Beals; and Fletcher M. Haight, father of Henry Haight who later joined the church, became an elder, and in 1867 was elected governor of California. These were men of standing in the community and reflect the kind of people Scott drew within the circle of his friendship and influence.

The Committee of Twenty met on June 21st and set a goal of $75,000. They agreed to solicit pledges on the basis of 25% on demand; 25% when the foundations of the new church were laid; 25% when the roof was placed; and the last 25% when the building was completed. The current expenses of the new congregation were to be raised by the sale of pews at public auction. Within two weeks the committee had raised $25,000. On July 14th the committee members addressed a letter to Dr. Scott in which they reported that "notwithstanding the extreme depression of trade and general stringency of monetary affairs," they had met with "encouraging success." The committee begged Dr. Scott to effect a formal organization of a church "at some early date." Scott replied the next day expressing his willingness to proceed with the organization of a church based on the following five-fold conditions:

1. That a house of worship be built according to plan, and that when it is dedicated to the service of Almighty God, it shall be considered free from debt. 2. That all the expenses of my removal be paid say 2,000 or 2,500 $. 3. That a suitable dwelling house be provided in addition to the salary named. 4. That premiums on my life policies be also paid by the congregation here . . . probably about 600 $ per annum. . . 5. That at the end of 18 months or by the meeting of the Genl. Assembly of 1856, should it please God so long to spare my life, both parties to this engagement shall respectively be considered as at full and perfect liberty to make whatever changes shall then in the fear of God and according to the leadings of His Providence seem to be best.

I am constrained to say that on many accounts I have come to this result with much painful hesitation and with no small degree of fear and trembling. I am thus tearing myself away from the best and most devoted people, I verily believe, in the world, and on no other account than that of health could I feel myself right in leaving them.

No time was lost in speeding the formal organization of the new church. Public announcement was made on Sunday, July 16th, for a meeting of all interested parties the next evening in the Unitarian Church, located on Stockton Street near Sacramento, and for the formal organization to follow the morning service on the next Sunday. The Committee of Twenty reported to the meeting held on Monday evening. To that date $30,000 had been raised but the committee was optimistic as only "a very partial canvass of the City" had been made. Scott's letter of the 15th was read. Those present pledged themselves to guarantee the erection of the new building if he would accept the call to be pastor. A board of nine trustees was elected which included Mayor Garrison. A constitution, which evidently had been prepared in advance, was submitted and adopted.

At the morning service on Sunday, July 23, 1854, Dr. Scott invited all persons desirous of uniting in the formation of a new Presbyterian church to stay after the dismissal of the congregation. About seventy remained. With Dr. Scott as moderator and Stephen Franklin as secretary, the meeting proceeded with the formal organization of Calvary Presbyterian Church of San Francisco. The sixty-three charter members all came by letter of transfer. Only a minority of these came from the other Presbyterian churches of the city. Eleven transferred from First Church and two from Howard Presbyterian Church (New School) of San Francisco. Several, including Stephen Franklin and his wife, came direct from First Church of New Orleans. Colonel Redick McKee and Stephen Franklin were elected elders. The strength of the new church lay in the fact that Dr. Scott had rallied sufficient support from the unattached Presbyterians in the city to warrant its establishment.

On August 10th, Elder McKee, representing Calvary Church, appeared before the Presbytery of California and requested that the newly organized church be received by Presbytery. This was done. At that time there were only three resident Presbyterian ministers within the bounds of the Presbytery. This was the minimum constitutional number required for a quorum. These three were Albert Williams, William Speer, and Frederick Buel. The latter was secretary of the American Bible Society. After being seated as the official delegate from Calvary Church, McKee presented the request from his church "for the pastoral services of the Rev. W. A. Scott, D.D., of New Orleans." Initial steps were then taken to effect the transfer of Scott's membership from the Presbytery of Louisiana, but this proved to be a more complicated process than any then imagined.

In the meantime the trustees were busy. On August 9th a lot was purchased for $20,000 on the north side of Bush Street, between Sansome and Montgomery and diagonally across from Musical Hall. The lot had a frontage of 67' 9" and a depth of 137' 6". The site is now occupied by the Mills Station of the United States Post Office. In consultation with Dr. Scott, the trustees drew up plans for the construction of a rectangular building "in the Roman Corinthian style," 62 by 110 feet, with a semi-circular apse and a central pulpit. The basement, which extended the length of the building, was almost if not entirely above ground which meant that there was a flight of stairs, the lower part of which was divided, leading up to the front doorways. The central entrance was flanked on either side by two imposing Corinthian columns which supported the narrow roof of a porch. The main body of the auditorium contained 185 pews capable of seating 1,075 persons. The pews in the galleries could seat another five hundred. The pulpit was to be of white marble. Four steps on each side of the pulpit connected the platform with the floor of the auditorium. The communion table, in strict accordance with Puritan tradition, was on the floor of the auditorium immediately before the pulpit.

Bids were called on August 23rd for the erection of the new building and a contract was let for $33,000. The final cost proved to be considerably more. The new building was supposed to be completed by Christmas, and would be larger than that of any other Protestant church in California. On October 27th the trustees authorized the printing of some lithographs of the new building, a copy of which is included as an illustration in this book.

During his stay of a little more than ten weeks in California, Scott was in great demand as a lecturer. He made one trip, beginning on July 2nd, to the "northern mines" during which he addressed large audiences in Grass Valley, Marysville, and Nevada City. He returned from this excursion in time for his Sunday services on July 8th. As a result of his observations, he preached a sermon on "Woman in California" in which he claimed that one of the main reasons for the prevalence of crime in new states and frontier districts was the absence of women.

I am well satisfied that nothing is more imperatively needed in California than the softening, purifying and elevating influence of women. . . . The two great wants of California are, not a railroad to the America [i.e., the East] nor a steamship line to Japan and China, though these are important, and will I hope soon be accomplished; but the two greatest wants of this State are the presence of mothers, wives and sisters, and a thorough American home education.

In a letter to a friend describing his experiences in San Francisco, Scott claimed that he had "delivered fifty discourses" during his ten weeks' visit. No doubt this number included the twenty sermons preached for the new church congregation. Scott said that his lectures were given "before various literary and benevolent associations that sold tickets & realized handsome sums, but I never charged nor received a cent from them." Those interested in the establishment of Calvary Church paid all of his travel and living expenses while absent from New Orleans.

Scott started back to his home on August 1st. This time he traveled via the Isthmus of Panama and was back with his family on August 21st. During the weeks immediately following, Scott experienced a turmoil of soul. He looked back with great satisfaction upon the cordial, even enthusiastic, reception he had received in San Francisco. A new church had been organized. A campaign for $75,000 was well under way and responsible citizens had promised to see that the new building was completed by Christmas and ready to be dedicated free of debt. He was tremendously impressed with the outlook for California and especially for a fruitful ministry in San Francisco. Above all the climate promised to be beneficial to his health. This latter factor was of the greatest importance.

On the other hand, Scott dreaded breaking the ties which bound him to a loyal and devoted people in New Orleans. How could he tell them that he must go? The idea of a temporary absence as a furlough had some merit. Suppose prospects did not work out in California as they now promised? Might it not be well to have some place to which he could return? Although some opposition on the part of a church to the announced plans of its pastor to resign in order to accept another call is often pleasing and sometimes flattering to the individual concerned, Scott seemed to have been entirely unprepared for the intensity of the resistance which he faced in his New Orleans church when he announced his intention of accepting the call to San Francisco. There were many tears shed and hearts were heavy. On none was the emotional strain greater than upon Dr. Scott himself.

Before relating the sequence of events which closed Scott's ministry in New Orleans, it is well to note some of the heartaches which he inadvertently left behind in San Francisco.

TWO EMPTY PULPITS IN SAN FRANCISCO

The enthusiastic reception given to Dr. Scott and the prospect of his residence in San Francisco as pastor of the newly organized Calvary Church were the compelling reasons, added no doubt to other factors, which led to the resignation of two of the pioneer ministers in San Francisco from their respective pulpits. The first was the Rev. Timothy Dwight Hunt, pastor of the First Congregational Church, and the second was the Rev. Albert Williams, pastor of the First Presbyterian Church. Certainly there was no conscious involvement on Dr. Scott's part in either instance. It is true in every generation that whenever a minister of outstanding ability comes to a new community, he will draw to his church some members from other congregations. He will also attract the unattached, the non-church members, and those who drift from church to church eager to hear some new voice. So it was, and even more so, in the summer of 1854 in San Francisco. Dr. Scott's tremendous magnetism in the pulpit had a devastating effect upon the size of the congregations in all of the other Protestant churches of the city.

Timothy Dwight Hunt was the first Protestant minister to settle in California after the raising of the United States flag at Monterey on July 7, 1846. Hunt, a New School Presbyterian, went out to the Hawaiian Islands in 1844 as a missionary under the American Board of Commissioners for Foreign Missions. After serving in this capacity for several years, during which time he learned the native language, Hunt left the mission and became pastor of an independent church for English-speaking residents of Honolulu. When news of the discovery of gold reached Honolulu in the late spring and early summer of 1848, so many of his congregation left for the gold fields, that Hunt decided to follow. Leaving his family temporarily in Honolulu, Hunt sailed for San Francisco where he landed on October 29, 1848. As has been mentioned, Scott carried a reference to Hunt in the March 10, 1849, issue of his *New Orleans Presbyterian*.

At first Hunt held his interdenominational services in the school house on Portsmouth Square. Following the organization of the Old School Presbyterian, the Methodist, the Baptist, and the Episcopal churches, Hunt on July 29, 1849, organized the remnant of his congregation into the First Congregational Church of San Francisco. In 1852 his people purchased a lot at the corner of California and DuPont street on which they erected a new building large enough to seat seven hundred at a total cost of $57,000. The building was dedicated in June 1853 about a year before Dr. Scott visited the city. Since the church had only about 130 members, the whole building project was somewhat beyond their financial resources and they were burdened with a heavy debt.

On May 16, 1854, just a few days before Dr. Scott's arrival in the city, Hunt left on one of his semiannual visits to the Hawaiians, or the Kanakas as they were sometimes called, in the mining districts. Since he knew their language, he felt he had a special responsibility to keep alive their Christian faith. On this trip he preached to a group of seventy who had gathered at Bidwell's Bar on the Feather River to hear him. Hunt returned to San Francisco on Saturday, May 28th, and the next evening he had opportunity to hear Dr. Scott. Hunt was faithful in keeping a diary, which is now in the archives of San Francisco Theological Seminary. After hearing Dr. Scott for the first time, he wrote: "Was pleased with his solemn & impressive manner & matter. Glad that one so attractive is also so evangelical. May he stay & do good work for our common Master." Before going to church on the following Sunday, June 4th, Hunt was a bit apprehensive over the size of his congregation but was pleased to know that all of his faithful members were in their places. "Encouraged to find," he wrote, "that the old though young pastor was not deserted for the new though older whose prestige was drawing crowded houses."

On June 11th Hunt attended the dedication of the first public school house in the city "pronouncing the benediction on a large number of bright children, proud parents, delighted spectators, devoted teachers." And that evening he called on Dr. Scott. He commented in his diary that night on how much he had enjoyed the interview and then wrote prophetically: "I am now ready for the next thing." A week passed without an entry and then Hunt wrote:

> Monday, June 19, 1854. "The next thing!" How little did I dream what it would be! How little ready was I for it! Had it been the sudden death of my beloved wife, or an unlooked for arrest of myself for alleged crime, I could not have been more surprised. Nor could I have been much more grieved. For that "next thing," for which at the close of my record a week ago today I said I was "ready" was *no less* than the painful certainty that *I must resign my charge & leave my people!*

Writing in retrospect, Hunt told of how four of his trustees had waited on him the previous Wednesday and began "by speaking of the bankrupt state of the Church" and the vain efforts that had been made to remedy the situation. "Allusion was made to the necessity of some thing decisive being done immediately inasmuch as the friends of Dr. Scott were soon to canvass the city for funds to carry out their purposes. Remarks followed with reference to his 'decided ability' & to the popular enthusiasm connected with the whole movement designed, as I perceived, to disparage myself & my own congregations. . ." Hunt was told that the officers of the church were of the unanimous opinion, "though arrived at with great & painful reluctance that a *change of pastor would be necessary in order to liquidate the debt.*" The committee informed Hunt that they were moved from "a business point of view solely," confessing that but for the debt they would not have thought of the change. Hunt's account continues:

The principle on which they acted was this, that a greater man coming to them from the East, with prestige to his name, would attract larger audiences & so divide the burden of the Church expenses among a greater number. Especially would the prospect of some renowned D.D. as the preacher enable them to raise more money on a subscription paper! . . . The idea of pecuniary relief which they imagined would come from a great man with a great name blinded them to every moral obligation which bound them to their pastor.

Hunt was stunned and heartbroken. He turned to his friend, Rev. Samuel H. Willey, pastor of Howard Presbyterian Church, for advice. Although Willey felt that the whole affair was "an outrage on all ministerial rights and feelings," yet "it was finally agreed between us that a resignation was inevitable as well as advisable." Hunt tendered his resignation on June 26th. Many of his congregation, astounded at the action taken by their officers, objected. For a time Hunt was persuaded to withdraw his resignation, but the tie which united a pastor with his people had been cut. Hunt finally resigned on December 11th and accepted a call from the national Congregational Church to become superintendent of Home Missions for California as an agent of the American Home Missionary Society. His new duties began January 18, 1855.

The second San Francisco minister to resign as a result, at least in part, of the enthusiastic popular support given to Dr. Scott, was the Rev. Albert Williams, founder and pastor of the First Presbyterian Church of the city. On July 1st, less than a week after Hunt wrote his letter of resignation, Williams notified the session of his church of his intention to leave after the fall meeting of the Presbytery. In all probability Williams would have found it necessary to resign about this time even if Dr. Scott had never gone to San Francisco. For one thing, his health was poor and this was given as the main reason for his resignation. Although much credit deservedly goes to Williams for his pioneer labors in establishing the first Protestant church in the city (prior to the organization of the First Congregational Church, since Hunt's congregation in the schoolhouse was never considered a formally organized denominational body), yet the evidence is clear that he did not have the ability to meet the challenge of that pulpit.

Even though those interested in establishing Calvary Church were very careful to observe Presbyterian protocol, and even though they had the outward approval of both the session of First Church and of Williams himself, yet Williams was sensitive to the tremendous success of the project and in the end became bitterly critical of Scott. In a letter to Scott dated August 15, 1854, Franklin told of the action of the Presbytery of California in receiving Calvary Church and in proceeding with the call. "Mr. Williams seemed to think," wrote Franklin, "there had been some informality in our proceedings which he proposed to waive however & let us in without further delay." Elder McKee pointed out that they had moved most cautiously and that "our enterprise had been sanctioned in the outset by himself." After some discussion, Williams withdrew his objections and, according to Franklin, "we were received with 'clean papers.' The animus of a certain party was thought to have shown itself in a small way . . . but I trust it will soon be forgotten."

When Williams published his *A Pioneer Pastorate* in 1882, he claimed that: "Of the sixty-three original members of Calvary Church, nearly every one had been connected for a longer or shorter period with the First Church, either enrolled in its communion or enjoying its privileges." A study of the original membership roll of Calvary Church shows that only eleven of the charter members transferred from First Church. Others transferred later. Williams explains in his book: "A crisis in my incumbency of the pastorate, which was for months foreseen, at length arrived. Labors of such continuance and degree . . . with their imposed burdens, had issued in extreme bodily prostration." His doctor advised him to resign. All of this is part of the background which prompted Williams to send in his resignation on July 1st. He preached his farewell sermon on October 8th and left soon afterwards for his old home in New Jersey. He returned to California in the spring of 1859. Records of the Presbytery of California show that after his return he always aligned himself with the opponents of Dr. Scott in the several controversies which harassed the members of the small presbytery. Seemingly Williams could never forget that Scott had succeeded where he had failed.

THE SCOTTS MOVE TO SAN FRANCISCO

When Scott landed in New Orleans on August 21, 1854, and felt the hot humid atmosphere enveloping him, he was acutely conscious of the superior qualities of San Francisco's climate. There the summer days were delightfully cool. At night one and sometimes two blankets were needed while sleeping. When the summer sun scorched the interior valleys, a thick fog would roll in from the Pacific covering the city with its billowy folds and protecting it from the sun's rays. Often people in San Francisco had to wear overcoats in July! How different from New Orleans where there was no escape from the heat and humidity day or night. San Francisco was so healthy, so free from epidemics. New Orleans lay in the heart of the yellow fever belt. Another epidemic had struck the city in 1854, not as bad as that of the previous year, but still severe. The toll of dead mounted to over 2,500. An appreciation of the contrast in the climates of the two cities deepened Scott's resolve to move. His health and physical efficiency demanded it.

Scott called a meeting of his session for the evening of the 22nd. In a letter to the elders of Calvary Church dated September 6th, Scott said: "My beloved people ask me on every side, Do the newspapers say truly that you are removing to California? My uniform answer is, that it is true that I have promised to return to California for a year or a year and a half, provided a church is built and placed out of debt by December next." Some of his friends comforted themselves by saying that this condition could never be met. Others said that even if the new building were completed by December, Dr. Scott as a Presbyterian was subject to the rules of presbytery. He could not leave without the consent of the New Orleans church and this they said they would never give. Scott commented on his health and told of how much better he felt in California. In reply "The elders argued that if I travelled about, and took the same degree of exercise here that I did in California, I should have as good health." They reminded him that since New Orleans was a much bigger city than San Francisco, it was therefore a greater missionary field.

Summing up developments, Scott wrote: "The sentiment of the Congregation and of the City, I believe I may say without vanity (from which may God of his infinite mercy ever save me) is very strong, united and earnest against any idea of permanent removal. Much more so than I expected to find it. . . On the plea of health, however, I think I can get a furlough according to my proposition to you, and then God will make the rest plain." Scott felt that unless he and his family were able to get away in November, they would have to wait until spring. "If the Nicaragua steamers on this side resume their trips in October, as it is said they will, I prefer to take my family that route." Resisting all appeals to remain, Scott insisted on obtaining a leave of absence from the church. Reluctantly the session called a congregational meeting for Wednesday, November 1st, to consider what should be done.

A new and unexpected development occurred early Sunday morning, October 29th, when a fire completely destroyed the First Church building on Lafayette Square. The *New Orleans Crescent* the next day reported: "The scene was the most grand and imposing that we ever beheld. . . About 6 o'clock the steeple and belfry fell out into the street with a crash that caused the ground to vibrate as with the shock of an earthquake. . . The silver-ware, books, and some of the property in the church were saved. . . Dr. Scott's congregation worshipped yesterday at Odd Fellows' Hall." There was evidence that the fire was the work of an incendiary. The building was insured for $40,000 which permitted the congregation to plan at once for a new church on the same site. This new building was dedicated in 1857. Here the First Church of New Orleans remained until 1939 when a new building was erected at 5401 South Claiborne Avenue, near Tulane University. The present site on Lafayette Square is now occupied by a government building.

The officers and members of the First Presbyterian Church of New Orleans at the meeting held on November 1st took action as follows:

WHEREAS, our pastor, Rev. Dr. Scott, has during his late visit to California, much to our regret, made conditional arrangements with a newly organized church . . . to sustain a missionary

enterprise for a limited time in that city, and since his return to
New Orleans received a call to become their pastor, which call he
declines to entertain:

And whereas, Dr. Scott considers himself bound to fulfil his conditional pledge to said Calvary Church, and in a letter addressed
to the officers of this church under date of September last, requests
a leave of absence from this congregation, to repair to California
for that purpose. . .

Be it Resolved, That we, the members of the First Presbyterian
Church of New Orleans, do, with the greatest reluctance, and more
especially at this time, in consequence of the destruction of our
church edifice by fire, grant to our pastor . . . a leave of
absence from the duties of his charge here until the first day of
January 1856, when, God willing, we expect him to resume his
place over this congregation.

Resolved 2, That under no circumstances, not provided for by
the special leadings of God's Providence, will we entertain a call
from the brethren of the congregation . . . in San Francisco or
elsewhere to sever the pastoral relation, which has so happily and
profitably subsisted between Dr. Scott and his people during the
twelve years of his residence among us.

A third resolution emphasized the missionary importance of the New
Orleans field and stated that pastors who had "nobly and cheerfully
borne the dangers and trials of acclimation, and on that account, should
be held in 'double honor' by the whole church, and left undisturbed
over their respective flocks. . ." A fourth resolution stated in part:
"That we have perceived with deep and painful regret the various efforts that have been made, since the invitation to San Francisco was
made, in various ways at the North and elsewhere to induce our Pastor
to dissolve his pastoral relation with us. . ."

The reference seems to refer to some articles which appeared in
various religious periodicals in the North which applauded the idea of a
man of Dr. Scott's stature going to San Francisco. The October 1853
issue of *The Home and Foreign Record,* previously mentioned, is an
example. The resolutions, signed by all the officers of the church, were
published as a broadside and copies sent to Dr. Scott, to Calvary
Church, to several northern religious periodicals, and to some of the New
Orleans papers. A copy is in the Scott Collection in Bancroft Library.

Sensitive to the difficulty the New Orleans church might experience
in finding a suitable supply if there were the possibility of his return,
Scott on October 27th sent in his resignation to the session. The elders,
however, refused to accept it and withheld the information from the
people. The last reference to Scott's presence at a session meeting is
for November 21st when he served as moderator. At this time letters
of dismissal were granted to Stephen and Eliza Franklin to Calvary
Church, San Francisco.

Thus Dr. Scott's ministry of twelve years as pastor of the First Presbyterian Church of New Orleans came to a close even though the congregation clung to the tenuous hope that he would return. A review of membership statistics for this period tells only a part of the story of growth. When he began his ministry there, the church had 341 members. A peak enrollment of 779 came in 1852. During his pastorate, three new Presbyterian churches were organized each with a nucleus of members out of First Church. In 1854 the church reported 607 members, making First Presbyterian Church of New Orleans the largest church in the South and fourth in size in the entire nation of that denomination. In that generation membership totals were usually much smaller than attendance records. Today the reverse is usually the case. One of the Presbyterian historians of the South, the Rev. J. R. Hutchinson, in his *Reminiscences* published in 1874, characterized Scott's ministry in New Orleans as being "exceedingly productive." The deep hold that Dr. Scott had upon the affections of his people is further evidence of the effectiveness of his ministry.

After moving to San Francisco, Scott realized that he never could resume his New Orleans pastorate. There were many reasons for this decision, health being but one. Twice in February 1855 and once in April, Scott wrote to the New Orleans church requesting that his resignation be accepted. Each time the request was rejected. History often repeats itself. So it was in this case for some twelve years earlier the Tuscaloosa church was reluctant to sever its pastoral relations with Scott. Now the New Orleans church was in the same position. On June 19th, the elders of First Church again voted not to accept the resignation and again they renewed their faith that their pastor's health would so improve as to permit "his return to his pastoral duties with us on or before Jany. 1856." They declared: "Our devoted attachment to Dr. Scott remains undiminished." The church remained adamant in its refusal to grant any dissolution of the pastoral relationship until September of that year. Finally on September 14th, the reconstituted Presbytery of New Orleans voted to dismiss Dr. Scott to the Presbytery of California, and the pulpit of First Church was declared vacant.

Dr. Scott's successor was the Rev. Benjamin M. Palmer, D.D., formerly of Charleston, South Carolina, who began his ministry in New Orleans in December 1856. Palmer was a staunch supporter of the Confederate cause throughout the Civil War. He was one of the most active of southern Presbyterian ministers in the formation of the Confederate Presbyterian Church which, after 1865, became the Presbyterian Church in the United States, often known today as the Southern Presbyterian Church.

Scott secured reservations for himself and his family on the "Prometheus" scheduled to sail from New Orleans on Wednesday, November 29th, for Nicaragua. A multitude of things needed to be done in those last few weeks. All of their household belongings, including Dr. Scott's books, which they wanted to take with them to California, had to be shipped by sea around South America. Only their hand luggage could be taken with them across Nicaragua. Even though Calvary Church had guaranteed all moving expenses, Scott found himself financially embarrassed. It became necessary for him to borrow $1,500 in order to clear all obligations before leaving New Orleans. Their home on Prytania Street was rented. Later this was sold. As has been mentioned, all of the servants who did not already have their freedom were given it as, according to family tradition, the Scotts took no colored help with them to California.

Scott's last Sunday was November 26th. No account remains describing the farewell events. The church was doubly afflicted in losing both its building and its pastor within one month. Scott confessed that the circumstances lay heavily on his heart but there was no turning back. No record has been found of their travel experiences from New Orleans to San Francisco. There must have been many difficulties in traveling with seven children ranging in age from one to eighteen years even though Robert and Martha were old enough to help care for the five younger ones. Scott, having previously crossed both by the Nicaraguan route and that of the Isthmus of Panama, chose the former. On the west coast they boarded the "Uncle Sam" which carried them to San Francisco where they landed December 21st. The slowness of travel in those days as compared with conditions in this jet age is seen in the fact that Scott spent some seventy-two days, or about two and a half months, in his travels to and from San Francisco in 1854.

Before leaving San Francisco in August 1854 to get his family, Scott had requested the trustees of Calvary Church to rent a house for him which would have four bedrooms, study, stable, and a carriage house. A suitable place was rented beginning January 1st at a monthly cost of $160. The 1856 *City Directory* lists Scott's address as "South Park, east end of Gordon's Row." South Park lay at the edge of Rincon Hill, about three blocks up from the waterfront on Second Street and about two blocks from the present Southern Pacific depot. The area was described as a fashionable residential district especially for families from the Deep South. In May 1857, Scott took his $2,000 annual rental allowance, and, possibly with funds realized from the sale of his New Orleans house, purchased a home on the west side of Second Street between Folsom and Harrison. This was also in the Rincon Hill area. The site is about a block from the present bus depot serving the East Bay area.

CALVARY CHURCH

During Dr. Scott's absence of nearly five months, the officers of the newly organized church tried to keep up regular Sunday morning services. Since neither the Unitarian Church nor the Musical Hall was available, they were obliged to turn to the modest Chinese Mission Chapel which had shortly before been erected at the corner of Sacra-

mento and Stockton Streets for a meeting place. Supply preachers were
difficult to find. Among those who assisted was the Rev. Sylvester Woodbridge, Jr., of Benicia, whom Scott first met as a fellow student at
Princeton Theological Seminary. Since both were southerners, a strong
friendship bound the two together which lasted throughout their lives.
In the meantime construction of a handsome new building on Bush
Street was pushed forward with all possible speed.

The first session meeting after Dr. Scott's return was held in his home
on Friday evening, January 5, 1855. In view of the fact that the new
building was to be ready for occupancy "in a few days," the elders felt
it wise to recommend some "general rules . . . for the observance
of this Congregation." They agreed that beginning with the first Sunday
of February, communion services were to be held every alternate month.
Bibles were to be placed in every pew. "In singing the praises of God,"
they decided, "it is recommended that the Congregation be seated except in the closing stanza or Doxology, when all will rise. During public
prayer the Congregation will arise & remain standing."

The dedication of the new building was held on Sunday, January 14,
1855. All of the 1,500 seats were taken and people were standing.
Their fondest dreams, less than two years old, had come true. A new
church had been planted in the very heart of San Francisco with one
of the nation's greatest preachers in the pulpit as its pastor. Dr. Scott
in his dedicatory sermon had opportunity to reaffirm his philosophy of
the church, saying:

> We set this church apart to the worship and praise of the one
> living and true God, and to the work and glory of the great
> Redeemer. Rather than that these walls should witness the teachings
> of any other doctrines than those of true religion, let them crumble
> into ruins. Rather than that anyting but loyalty to the great dis-
> tinctive national institutions of our fathers, and of good will to men,
> and the way of salvation through the Cross, should be taught here,
> may there not be one stone left upon another. The chief design of
> the gospel is to save the soul through faith in Christ, but in doing
> this it scatters along its path innumerable blessings . . . edu-
> cation, an orderly government, the advance of freedom, and works
> of charity. Its teachings are to infuse into man's bosom a princi-
> ple fitted to subdue the ferocity of the savage . . . to repress
> the excesses of luxury, and the wantonness of power, peculation,
> fraud, and corruption; to control the fury of passion and restrain
> the shedding of human blood . . . to minister consultation to
> the widow and protection to the fatherless.

The Gospel which Dr. Scott preached was, according to the best
standards of that day, thoroughly Biblical and heavily doctrinal, but
at the same time linked with the problems of the world about him.
Religion to him was not just the mental acceptance of a creed. Religion
was life itself. The principles of Christ were to permeate all of day by

day living. His preaching was both personal in its application and practical in its interpretation.

A business recession was beginning to be felt when Dr. Scott first visited San Francisco in the summer of 1854. According to John S. Hittell in his *A History of the City of San Francisco:* "Out of a thousand business houses in the middle of 1854, more than three hundred were unoccupied. . . There were two hundred voluntary bankrupts, with deficits of forty thousand dollars each." Over speculation in real estate had led to the bursting of the get-rich-quick balloon. Interest rates soared in some instances to ten percent per month! The business conditions of the city continued to worsen until the term "panic" was used to describe the state of affairs in 1855.

The construction of the new church building had gone forward during the fall of 1854 with the expectation that payments on pledges made would be received as the successive stages were reached. But this did not prove to be the case. As a result the trustees were greatly embarrassed when they realized that they would be unable to fulfill their promise of providing a building for Dr. Scott which would be free of debt. Although the full extent of the unfortunate financial situation was not revealed to Dr. Scott when he returned to San Francisco, he could not have been entirely unaware of the problem. The officers of the church felt that when he was once on the field, the magnetism of his personality and the attractiveness of his preaching would soon lift them out of their financial trough.

The first step taken to remedy the situation was the holding of a public auction on Monday evening following the dedication of the church to sell the pews. The trustees had placed a tentative value of $1,000 on twenty pews and other sums graduated downwards according to desirability of location. If all pews had been sold at these tentative values, the church would have realized $70,000. All sums paid for pews would be considered as payments on a building pledge. After the purchase of a pew, the holders were expected to pay an annual assessment for current expenses. In addition to such income would be the Sunday collections. There was nothing unusual in this method of raising the necessary funds for building and yearly expenses. This was the common practice of the time.

The church realized a total of only $22,263 from the sale of the pews. The total debt still remaining was about $35,000 or approximately half the total cost of lot, building, and furnishings. The trustees had taken out a mortgage for $15,000 on which for a time, at least, they were paying $2\frac{1}{4}\%$ interest per month, or 27% per annum. The balance of the indebtedness was held by two members of the church. An item in the minutes of the Board of Trustees for March 3rd reads: "Moved and passed that Mr. Roberts be allowed interest at the rate of $2\frac{1}{2}\%$ per month up to the 1st March on his account against the church for monies advanced." The reference is to James B. Roberts, one of the most active men in the organization of the church. At this time he was serving as a trustee, but later he became an elder.

A complicating factor arose when San Francisco papers copied items from New Orleans papers which reported on the refusal of the First Presbyterian Church of the latter place to agree to a dissolution of pastoral relationship with Dr. Scott. The possibility of Dr. Scott's returning to New Orleans caused many prospective givers to hesitate in their support of Calvary Church. What would happen to the church if Dr. Scott left? After considerable discussion of the issues involved, the trustees finally decided to address a letter to Dr. Scott and tell him frankly the financial situation and ask him whether or not he intended to remain in San Francisco. Under date of April 18, 1855, they wrote:

> Among the pledges made was an agreement to erect a convenient church and place it free from debt. Trusting in the promises of many persons, more or less definitely made and hoping also for the continuance of prosperity to our city, we have caused the church to be erected. We regret to say however that up to this time . . . there is now a debt upon it of about $35,000. We regret particularly to have learned that this condition of our affairs is the occasion of great anxiety and annoyance to your mind, and we desire for this as well as for other reasons, to settle all as soon as possible upon a safe and permanent basis.

The trustees asked Dr. Scott if he would not regard what they had accomplished as being "nearly the same as though we have literally fulfilled the promise." They felt that the measure of success thus far realized would not "permit us of despair if we may be assured of the continuance of your aid." The trustees frankly asked their pastor whether or not he would release them from their promise to provide a debt-free building. They asked: "What would be your inclination, all other things pertaining to the respective churches concerned being equal, in choosing between this city and New Orleans as a place for residence? What is the probability of your being able to obtain a dismissal from the Presbytery of New Orleans?" They wanted to know just when he would make his decision whether to return or remain. Dr. Scott replied on April 20th. He reminded the trustees:

> I broke up my household in New Orleans and came cheerfully and promptly to fulfill my promises to Calvary Congregation under the belief that the lot was paid for and was free from and in every way clear of all debt. And that the proceeds of the sale of pews were to pay for the building and that rents of pews would meet all current expenses. It was therefore with the greatest surprise & with much mortification that I have been recently acquainted with the state of your finances as given in your letter of the 18th inst. Had I known there was a mortgage on the lot, or been fully acquainted with the condition of the finances of the enterprise, I would never have left New Orleans.

Taking note of the "unforseen and unprecedented reverses" suffered by the business community, Scott indicated his willingness to extend the time when the church should be entirely free of debt to August 1, 1856. Scott wrote in warm terms of his New Orleans church. At the time of his departure, he said, his salary was $6,000 which included house rent. "I am still willing to return and labour and die among them if such shall seem to be the will of God," he added. He was frank in stating that he felt that if he remained in New Orleans, he should not live long. His health could not endure the climate.

> I believe that while they still think I have made a great mistake in coming to California, that now if I urge them to release me, on the plea of health and from a conviction that it is my duty clearly to remain here, that then and in that case they will acquiesce. . .
> If the door is closed against me here, I will cheerfully and happily return. If on the contrary it is still the wish of Calvary Congregation and of the citizens of San Francisco to have me remain and they shall prove that wish by carrying forward your enterprise, then I believe the way will be open for me to remain.

A congregational meeting was held on April 24th to consider the financial situation and Dr. Scott's new proposal. The treasurer reported total receipts of $41,398 to apply against a total expenditure of $82,-121.28. The interest item alone amounted to $2,377.57. The debt totaled $40,813.28. After deducting the $15,000 mortgage which was not due and some $5,000 considered collectable pledges, a balance of $21,000 remained which was needed "immediately." A special effort to raise this sum was made in June which would have been successful if all pledges had been paid. On June 29th Scott sent a letter congratulating his church officers and then announced: "With God's help I will now endeavor to effect my ecclesiastical transfer to San Francisco without delay. . . For some weeks ago, believing that I could not stand that climate [i.e., in New Orleans] without serious peril, I wrote to them that I wished to be released on account of health, whether I remained in California or not. At all events I believe there will now be no serious difficulty or delay in obtaining my ecclesiastical transfer to California." Although the full amount of the original mortgage was paid by May 31, 1856, there still remained some other obligations.

Scott was welcomed into the Presbytery of California as a corresponding member at its March 1855 meeting. He was received by letter of transfer from the Presbytery of New Orleans in August 1856. Due to some technical difficulty in his papers, he was not then installed as pastor of Calvary Church but listed only as its stated supply. Then because of several unhappy controversies in which Scott became involved during the years 1856 and following, he was never installed as pastor of Calvary Church. The official records listed him as "pastor elect" or stated supply.

According to the annual reports published in the *Minutes of the General Assembly*, Calvary Church had two hundred members at the end of 1856. The number increased steadily year by year until 363 were listed by the end of 1861, which year marked the close of Scott's first period of residence in San Francisco. Since the church began with sixty-three charter members, this meant a six-fold increase in eight years. An item in the *San Francisco Times* for January 19, 1857, states that the average Sunday attendance at Calvary Church was then one thousand. It is not known whether this referred only to the Sunday morning service or to the combination of morning and evening. The *San Francisco Daily News* for December 1st of that year reported the fact that Calvary Church had "received a new Sunday School library of 1,000 volumes." Only two other Protestant churches in the city had similar libraries at that time. Since San Francisco did not have a public library before June 1879, there was real need for the church to provide good reading material for its young people.

In 1858 Calvary Church ordered a cathedral pipe organ from a New York firm. The instrument contained forty-five stops and was custom built. *The San Francisco Daily Times* in its October 12th issue reported the arrival of the organ and claimed that it was the largest on the Pacific Coast. It was not however, the first pipe organ to be owned by a Protestant church in San Francisco. In 1852 Howard Presbyterian Church had installed a much smaller organ, which it is still using. The claim has been made that the Howard Church pipe organ was the first to be installed by any Protestant church on the whole Pacific Coast. It took two weeks to install the organ in Calvary Church during which time the congregation had to meet for the Sunday services in the basement or lecture hall. The organ was heard publicly for the first time in a grand concert on Tuesday evening, November 16th. *The Alta California* reported in its issue of the next day that even though the admission price was high, the church was filled. All proceeds went toward paying for the instrument.

Calvary Church used this organ for about seventy years. After fifteen years on Bush Street, Calvary Church relocated in 1869 on the northwest corner of Powell and Geary, a site now occupied by the St. Francis Hotel. The organ was moved to this building. After thirty-two years on this corner, the church moved a third time to its present location at Jackson and Fillmore and again the organ was reinstalled. Some modernization work was done on it at this time, and it was used until 1928 when a new organ was presented to the church.

PERSONAL AND FAMILY AFFAIRS

When Dr. Scott began his ministry as pastor of Calvary Church, he was in the prime of life. He celebrated his forty-first birthday on January 30, about a month after he and his family arrived in the city. San Francisco's climate proved to be most beneficial to his health and he was now at his best in the pulpit. The combined results of years of extensive and intensive reading, of travel, and of preaching were bearing a bountiful reward for his hearers. A reporter for the *Sacramento State Journal* commented as follows after hearing Scott preach twice in his city on Sunday, November 8, 1857: "His style is pleasant and forcible, and he possesses the rare gift of being able to engage the attention of his hearers from the commencement to the close of his discourse." Both services were held in Philharmonic Hall. All seats were taken at the evening service and many were obliged to stand. "So much interest was taken in the words of the preacher," wrote the reporter, "that they continued to stand throughout the entire service." And Dr. Scott was not noted for his short sermons!

What was the secret of such pulpit magnetism? There can be no doubt about his forceful, dynamic personality. But added to this were acquired abilities of speech and presentation. A penetrating glimpse into his homiletical methods is found in a letter he wrote on March 12, 1855, to Dr. G. Van Arsdalen who was then supplying the pulpit of the First Presbyterian Church of New Orleans. It appears that Dr. Van Arsdalen had written to Dr. Scott and in his letter had made some remark about the advantage of moving into a new parish and being able to reach into the proverbial preacher's barrel and pull out an old sermon. In his reply Dr. Scott wrote:

> The difficulties, then, in my way of using old sermons are these: 1st. Although I always write on every subject I investigate, as far as my health and time will allow me to do, still many of my discourses are mere fragments of what I actually uttered in the pulpit. They are written out only in part. In former years, I wrote more fully than I do now. Of late years, much of what I say in the pulpit does not exist on paper, nor anywhere out of my own mind, so far as I know. To repeat such discourses without relaboring them all over is not expedient; and this relaboring is about equivalent to a new production, and then there is hope that the new one would be better than the old one reproduced. So that, as a general rule, I throw the old one away, and try for a new one. I fear my mind or feelings would become contracted, sour, mouldy, or apathetic, if I were to allow myself to go round and round in the same old circles. *I love a change of scenery—I am always looking for a wider horizon.*
>
> "2d. *I am dissatisfied with every sermon or discourse I have written or preached. I have never in my life been able to copy one of my discourses exactly. Never in a single instance. Even those that have been printed, have existed in but one manuscript. It is only by an iron rule that I can succeed in copying a letter. . . I am not, therefore, happy in preaching old discourses, except when I have strength and time to remodel them.*
>
> "3d. *Old sermons are not up to the times. They always want*

freshness and the pointed illusions that give vivacity and power to a public speaker. I am aware that many admired preachers so polish and expurgate their discourses, that they will suit any age and any country—which, in my judgment is to make them fit for no age nor country. They might as well have been preached a hundred years ago as in the present *living* century. There is no moving life, no colored pictures in them by which, from internal evidence, it could be known *when* and *where* they were preached, or who their authors were. This machinery and automation kind of patented sermon-making may satisfy others. . . But it is not my idea of successful oratory.

An examination of the sermon manuscripts stored in the once water-soaked chests in Scott Hall at San Anselmo clearly shows that Dr. Scott did use old sermons, but always with revisions. Many sections of the manuscripts would be eliminated by large "X" marks. New notes would be inserted between the pages of the manuscript. Frequently he would tear open an envelope and use the inner side for his notes. Often those old envelopes still bore the original stamps and among the United States stamps salvaged from the manuscripts in the chests was one from the first issue which appeared in 1845.

During the first part of Dr. Scott's second residence in California, i.e., after 1870, he was in demand as a commencement speaker by many of the church-related or privately conducted academies scattered throughout northern California. At the close of such events, he would often pick up and take back to his study the unused programs in order to use the blank sides for notes. This parsimonious habit of salvaging these odd pieces of paper goes back, no doubt, to his youth when such acts of thrift were encouraged. Often, when revising an old sermon, Dr. Scott would write on these pages and insert them between the leaves of his manuscript. Incidentally, these old programs throw considerable light upon early education in California before the state had begun to support high schools as they often give such incidental information as the cost of board and room, tuition, and other relevant information.

Scott's willingness to write and rewrite and then to depart from his manuscript and strike out in free, direct speech reflects that great inner urge which restlessly prodded him forward to do his best. Out of his early youth came that compelling desire to excel. He never could be satisfied with less than his best efforts.

Scott's letter to Dr. Van Arsdalen on his homiletical habits closes with the following tribute to his former New Orleans congregation: "You will have to travel round this globe and back again to New Orleans seven times seventy before you will find another such congregation. They are a precious people."

Scott was a great believer in the power of the press. This conviction is expressed in the first line of the introduction to his *Esther:* "There is no more powerful auxiliary to the pulpit than the Press." The first five

years of his residence in San Francisco were marked by extraordinary
literary activity, especially when one remembers that everything published was first handwritten. During these years he published five
pamphlets and four books. In addition he wrote an article for a
California magazine and had two of his lectures included in annual
reports. The titles of his pamphlets follow:

A *Lecture delivered before the Mercantile Library Association of
San Francisco on the Influence of Great Cities, in Musical Hall,
June 16, 1854.* San Francisco 1854.

A *Discourse for the Times, delivered in Calvary Church, Sunday,
July 27, 1856.* San Francisco, 1856. This came out of the vigilante controversy to which reference will later be made.

*The Pavilion Palace of Industry, a lecture delivered on August 23,
1857, before the Mechanics' Industrial Exhibition.* San Francisco,
1857.

*Two Worlds United, the Atlantic Submarine Telegraph, a sermon
preached in Calvary Church, September 19, 1858.* San Francisco, 1858. This sermon was inspired by the news of the suc-
cesful laying of the trans-Atlantic cable. Scott was tremendously
impressed by the achievement. He said in this sermon: "Time,
distance and impossibilities seem blotted out from the dictionary
of the nineteenth century. I have often read the Arabian nights,
the oriental tales of the genii—in fact, I confess to a fondness
for oriental literature, in all its extravagances of Olympian
divinities and supernatural beings, who could assume or lay off a
body and travel through ocean depths or mountain caverns, or
fly on the clouds at will. . . But we have entered upon a new
reading of physical possibilities. *Realities are stranger than
fictions.* We have now to rejoice over the greatest triumph of
human genius."

Scott ventured to look into the future and make prophesies.
He claimed that not more than five years would pass before
"the *celestial* merchant of Sacramento Street will be able to
read over his morning dish of tea the news from Pekin of the
preceding evening." In conclusion he said: "I have had a
greater desire to have twenty-five years added to my life, since
the successful termination of this telegraph cable, than I have
ever felt before, just that I might see what great things God will
yet do in this world of ours for His church and His people."
Scott's wish came true for he did not die until 1885 and he did
live to see a multitude of new discoveries and inventions.

The Bible and Politics. San Francisco, 1859. This pamphlet also
arose out of controversy to which mention will be made later.

The Wedge of Gold: or Achan in El Dorado. San Francisco, 1855,
was the first of Scott's four books published during these years.
This small volume contained a series of Sunday evening sermons

preached especially for young men. Beginning with the story of Achan in Joshua 7:1 who gave way to temptation and stole a wedge of gold, Scott drew some pertinent applications to the young men of his generation who had gone to California to make their fortunes. He warned against the sins of covetousness and gambling but at the same time praised the right use of money. "Repeatedly has it been declared from this pulpit," he said, "that true religion is not a declaration of war against wealth, refinement or elegance of taste and manners. Repeatedly have we shown that riches are in themselves blessings. Money is a good thing. A man may be very rich and yet be a saint. The power to get riches according to the Bible is God's gift. Christianity does not therefore authorize any crusade against rich men. But both the Bible and common sense teach that the responsibilities of riches are great—that it is a great sin to abuse wealth."

Trade and Letters: Their Journeyings Round the World, New York, 1856, contained three discourses delivered before the Mercantile Library Association of San Francisco. Here Scott stressed one of his favorite themes, the great and good influence of commerce on society. He showed how trade fostered civilization and culture.

The Giant Judge: or the story of Samson, the Hebrew Hercules, San Francisco, 1858; and *Esther: the Hebrew-Persian Queen*, San Francisco, 1859, contain a series of expository sermons on the lives of Samson and Esther. Explaining his selection of Old Testament characters for the subjects of his books, he wrote: "The Old Testament is not a mere Hebrew ritual, nor a mere political hand-book of the ancient Jews. It is as much a part of the word of the living God as is the New Testament, and we are to study it as well as the New Testament, if we desire to know the will of God."

The March 1855 issue of *The Pioneer*, a California monthly magazine, carried an article by Scott entitled: "Some hints on the moral influence of the commercial spirit of the age." This was a lecture delivered before the Mercantile Library Association in Calvary Church on January 25, 1855, on the occasion of its second anniversary.

The Young Men's Christian Association of San Francisco was organized on July 18, 1853, the year before Scott's first visit to the city. Even as he had been a strong believer in the Y in New Orleans, so he gave the same support to this association in San Francisco. He was invited to speak at the second anniversary meeting of the San Francisco Y on August 6, 1855. His address was printed in the Y's *Second Annual Report*. In his remarks Scott censured the cheap, sensational literature of the day. Commenting on the statement of a large publishing house that "the worse works sell best" and that "mere rubbish has the best sale," Scott said: "Works of this class gratify a bad taste where it is already formed, and create it where it does not already exist." He bemoaned the fact that such a degrading type of literature was so easily available to young men. "Indulgence in such worthless and vile publications," he said, "consumes their time, corrupts their thoughts, heats their passions, dissipates and enfeebles their minds, and wholly unfits them for mental application and the toil of every day life."

On October 21, 1855, Scott delivered the oration on the occasion of the first anniversary of the College of California in Oakland. This was published in the 1856 *Catalogue*. This college had been founded by the Congregationalists and New School Presbyterians. The Rev. Henry Durant, a Congregational minister was the first president and at this time was cordial to Dr. Scott. Later Durant became one of Scott's most caustic critics. There were few subjects on which Scott took more delight than that of education for at heart he was always a teacher.

Scott edited a manual for Calvary Church which was published in 1860. This included the rules adopted by the session, the form of covenant, a list of members, and the liturgies used in the administration of the sacraments. Also included is the marriage service and here we note some interesting emendations to the form usually used in that day by the Presbyterian Church. Whereas in the denominational service the bridegroom promised to be "a loving and faithful husband," in Scott's version the word "affectionate" was added. In the former service, the bride promised to be "a loving, faithful, and obedient wife." Scott changed this to read: "a loving, faithful, and dutiful wife." Scott also added the following words in the vows made by the groom: "[to] love, and comfort, and cherish her." And the bride promised "[to] love, comfort, and honor him."

The wonders of Yosemite Valley were first seen by white men in 1851. Among those who did much to publicize the marvels not only of the valley itself but also of the giant redwoods and awe inspiring beauty of the high Sierras was James Macon Hutchings. He was an artist as well as a writer and was thus able to illustrate his text. In 1886 he published his *In the Heart of the Sierras* in which he gives the following incident involving Dr. Scott. It appears that Hutchings and some friends had made a trip to the Yosemite Valley in the spring or early summer of 1855. He wrote:

> Upon the return of our party to San Francisco, the writer being in pleasant intimacy with the late W. A. Scott, D.D. [who had died the previous January], and family paid them a visit, when the subject of the scenery of the Yo Semite was discussed, and sketches shown. The doctor manifested remarkable interest in the theme, and added: "Mr. H. I am badly in need of a vacation, and if I can induce a number of my friends to join me, I should like very much to visit such a marvelous locality. I shall esteem it a personal favor to myself if you will dine with us at an early day, on which

occasion I will invite a few intimate friends to join us, and discuss the subject of visiting that astonishingly magnificent creation." This invitation was cordially accepted, and in due time and order the proposed dinner party assembled, when the matter was thoroughly canvassed, and a company formed for making the journey.

There is some question as to the exact time when Dr. Scott and his friends made their first trip to the valley. It might have been during the summer of 1855 or possibly the following year when it is known that Dr. Scott was in the Sierras during May when the vigilantes hanged Casey and Cora. A newspaper clipping from the *Mariposa Gazette,* now in the Scott Collection in Bancroft Library but without date, states that the Rev. Samuel Willey of San Francisco and the Rev. Lewis Hamilton conducted religious services on Sunday, July 1, 1860, "at Peck's Hotel in Yo Semite Valley." The account adds: "This we believe is the second observance of the Sabbath in the Valley. The first occurred in August 1856 when the Rev. Dr. Scott of San Francisco, assisted by the Rev. Mr. Speer, preached at the Mariposa Camp Ground, as it was then known, to a party of perhaps twenty. The impressive remarks of the Doctor, the singularity of the occasion,—it being before public notice was much attracted to the Valley—combined with the awful grandeur of the place, made the occasion one to be ever remembered by those present." It seems probable that the writer of the news item made a mistake in the year and that this first religious service to be held in Yosemite was in August 1855 rather than 1856. We have clear evidence that Scott was in San Francisco during most if not all of August 1856.

Hutchings in his account of Dr. Scott's first visit to Yosemite adds: "After a very satisfactory and soul-satisfying jaunt, Dr. Scott upon his return to San Francisco, gave several eloquent discourses, and published some tersely written articles upon it. His magnetic enthusiasm largely contributed to the development of an interest in the minds of the public, to witness such sublime scenes as those he had so graphically portrayed." Hutchings links Scott's name with those of Horace Greeley and the Rev. Thomas Starr King, the noted San Francisco Unitarian minister, as being among the most prominent in advertising the wonders of the valley. According to a family tradition, it was Scott who named Vernal Falls. When he first saw the giant sequoias, he is reported to have said: "I never expect to see a grander sight than this, this side of heaven." He often returned to the valley in after years, sometimes with his wife and members of his family.

A few changes in the family circle took place during these years under review. Their seventh son, and their ninth child, was born on September 3, 1856. He was named Benjamin Francisco. When the Scott family settled in San Francisco, Robert the eldest son, was nearly eighteen years old. He entered a law office in San Francisco, possibly that of Stephen Franklin, where he studied law with the intention of entering that profession. Although the training there received proved later to be of inestimable value to him, Robert turned to a military career. In the summer of 1856, Dr. Scott wrote to the Hon. Lewis Cass to see if he could obtain an appointment to West Point for his son. Cass saw President James Buchanan and on January 1, 1857, wrote to Scott: "I have the pleasure to inform you that I have seen the President and that he has authorized me to say that he will appoint your son to the Military Academy." In the meantime, however, Scott had also gotten in touch with the secretary of war who offered young Robert a commission as second lieutenant in the Fourth Infantry. This he accepted and on February 21, 1857, was commissioned. In those days it was possible for a young man with good family connections to become an officer in the army without any previous military experience. Robert was sent to Washington Territory where he saw duty at several frontier posts. Evidently his mother was solicitous over his welfare for once she wrote to him urging him to go to bed early every night. In a letter to his father written while on duty near Port Townsend on July 13th, Robert commented: "It would be rather hard to comply with Ma's wish for me to go to bed early every night when as 'Officer of the Day' must, according to Regulations, sit up every night (when my turn   .   .   . comes around)   .   .   .   to visit my guard."

The first of the children of William and Ann Scott to be married was Martha who became Mrs. Nicholas Kittle on June 6, 1859. She and her husband moved to Elizabeth, New Jersey, where they lived for several years. Nicholas had an office in New York City. The Kittles were back in San Francisco in 1869 and were active in the movement which called Dr. Scott back to California after a voluntary exile of more than eight years.

FIRST HANGING IN EFFIGY

William Anderson Scott has the dubious distinction of being the only clergyman in California's history who was hanged not once but twice in effigy. The first time was in October 1856 as the result of his opposition to the Vigilance Committee. The second time came five years later, in September 1861, because of his southern sympathies. The two events are not unrelated.

One of Dr. Scott's great assets was a personality which drew to him a host of friends whose love and devotion were seemingly without bounds. At the same time he occasionally aroused in others deep animosities. The Rev. James Woods, in his *California Recollections,* tells of remonstrating with some of the members of Calvary Church over what he considered to be the extreme adulation given to their pastor. Woods wrote: "I said to one of his leading church members, 'God is jealous of his glory and will allow no idols. Beware, lest your church make an idol of your pastor.' Dr. Scott had not, nor has ever had, a more sincere friend than myself. And I used to tremble for him when I saw so much of what seemed to me a spirit of idolatry among his people." In sharp contrast to such devotion was the emotional heat engendered by those who differed with him in several controversies in which Dr. Scott became involved during his first San Francisco residence, 1854-61. In these unhappy experiences his opponents, including some of his fellow Protestant ministers, were as deeply committed in their hostility to him as his friends were in their attachment. Whereas he could count his friends by the hundreds, actually those who took an active part in denunciations or in the two effigy-hangings were few.

San Francisco attracted a rough and lawless element almost from its very beginning. In 1849 a band of ruffians, mostly from Australia, who called themselves "The Hounds" or "Regulators," so terrorized the town that in self-protection a band of citizens summarily seized, tried, and banished the leaders. In 1851 lawlessness again became so rampant that a Vigilance Committee took the law out of the hands of the weak and corrupt elected officials and by some quick decisive steps cleaned up the situation. Ninety-one persons were taken into custody; four were hanged after being tried in the courts of the vigilantes; and at least twenty-eight were banished. In addition hundreds of others fled the city or went into hiding. For a time safety of life and property returned to normal in San Francisco.

No voice of protest was raised among the city's clergy against what appears to have been the necessary but still unlawful activities of the first Vigilante Committee. On the contrary, we find approval. One of the four criminals hanged by this committee was John Jenkins. On the Sunday following the Rev. Timothy Dwight Hunt preached a sermon in the First Congregational Church which was subsequently published under the title: *Sermon Suggested by the Execution of Jenkins on the Plaza by the 'People' of San Francisco during the night of 10th June, 1851.* Incidentally this happens to be one of the first sermons to be published with a California imprint. Hunt defended the hanging of Jenkins by the vigilantes.

> Actual incapacity, or gross corruption, on the part of rulers, may sometimes justify, and even require, a people to overthrow and change the administration, or, during the exigency of the times, to take the power into their own hands. . . I cannot censure a people, if having been long and needlessly outraged by a gang of villains, they rise in their sovereign majesty, and quietly, and by orderly procedure, seize upon, try, condemn, and execute one, even though they have to set aside the authority they dare not trust with the culprit.

Five years after the first Vigilance Committee was disbanded, another wave of lawlessness and corruption engulfed the city. Stuffed ballot boxes insured the election of weak and dishonest officials. Albert Williams, in a letter published on July 12, 1856, in the Philadelphia *Presbyterian*, stated that through a period of seven years "many assassinations and murders had been committed, and yet only one instance of

capital punishment, under the constituted authorities, had occurred."
Any person with money could buy his way out of jail.

San Franciscians were shocked on November 19, 1855, to hear of the
murder of General Richardson, a United States marshal, by Charles Cora,
a gambler. Cora was apprehended and imprisoned. A trial was held
but because the jury could not come to agreement, another trial was
ordered. While awaiting his second trial, Cora became unhappily involved in the Casey case.

The real occasion which resulted in the organization of the Vigilance
Committee of 1856 was the fatal shooting of James King of William by
James P. Casey on the afternoon of May 14, 1856. King had the custom
of signing himself "of William" thus referring to his father. As editor
of the *Daily Evening Bulletin,* King had exposed some of the corruption
existing in the city's life and in the course of such reporting had
incurred the anger of Casey. The brazen attempt on the life of King
took place in the presence of many witnesses on the corner of Montgomery and Washington Streets, in the very heart of the city. Casey
gave himself up and was incarcerated, no doubt with the thought that
for the time being a jail was a good place of temporary refuge.

San Francisco was stirred as it had never been before. The news of
the shooting spread throughout the city with astonishing rapidity. A
crowd quickly gathered before the jail and clamored for the life of
Casey. Some of the business and professional men hastened to band
themselves together into a Vigilance Committee. Many of these men
had belonged to the 1851 committee including the well-known merchant, William T. Coleman, who was also a pew holder in Calvary
Church. Within a few days the forty-one member executive committee,
of which Coleman was chairman, had enrolled between five and six
thousand men. They were quickly organized into military companies,
given arms, and were being drilled. Headquarters were established on
the second floor of a building which stood on the southeast corner of
Front and Sacramento Streets. A barricade made out of gunny bags
filled with sand was piled in the street around the entrance to the building. The name Fort Gunny Bags was given to the corner.

An intimate look into the exciting events of those days is to be found
in the diary of the Rev. William Caldwell Anderson, D.D., who was
called to the pulpit of the First Presbyterian Church of San Francisco in
the fall of 1855. In this diary, now in the archives of San Francisco
Theological Seminary, we find the following entries:

> MAY 15, 1856:   Vigilance Committee organizing. Hundreds are
> joining, as I am informed. A most terrible excitement in the com-
> munity. Casey has escaped to the jail where he is strongly guarded
> or protected by the Sheriff & a party of his friends—all of the
> same kidney.
> MAY 18. SUNDAY. 3,000 armed men, members of the
> Vigilance Committee to day took Casey & Cora, two murderers

out of jail & confined them in the rooms of the Committee—will probably hang them to night. Seems hard to let the people rise & yet it is necessary here. We have no law—no power in our courts—all in the hands of gamblers & villains.

19. Vigilance Com, it is said, are trying Casey. His chances of life are as one to one hundred—and should King die, his chances are not one. He dies as surely as King dies.

TUES. 20. Kind died to day at half past One P.M. Stores closed. Fearful agitation of the masses. How it will end, I cannot devise. Cora on trial today for the murder of U.S. Marshal Gen. Richardson last fall. The Court does not convict him & he was in jail awaiting another trial. But the V.C. have taken him in hand: he deserves death, but I wish it was done by law.

With but one exception, and that was the San Francisco *Herald,* all of the newspapers of the city, including the Congregational-New School Presbyterian *Pacific,* enthusiastically endorsed the Vigilance Committee and their activities. The *Golden Era* in its issue of May 18th carried an editorial under the caption "The Reign of Terror" which said:

> It is worse than useless—it is criminal—to longer shut our eyes to our moral rottenness, and talk of order and justice, when murder stalks openly upon our highways and crime and corruption rule our Judicatory. Year after year have we seen the sacred rights of the ballot-box trampled upon by armed cut-throats and bullies and hell-hatched villains raised to officers of honor and trust; year after year have we seen cold-blooded assassinations and butcheries perpetrated in the broad glare of noon-day and the murderers escape unpunished. . . What then remained to be done? It is a fearful alternative, but there is nothing left but for honest men to arm, meet these ruffians with their own weapons, set aside for the time the authority of our legal tribunals of perverted justice, and strike terror to evil-doers by speedy trials and the rope! There is the work for the Vigilance Committee and we hope they may not shrink from the task.

The May 22nd issue of the *Pacific* carried heavy black lines between each of its seven columns on the two inside pages. In a long editorial under the caption, "Death of Mr. King," the editor threw his full support behind the Vigilante Committee. "The re-organization of the Committee," he wrote, "was a matter of necessity apparent to every unprejudiced mind. . . Conviction for any crime, when the accused had money, was clearly a moral impossibility." And he called the committee: "The truest and most direct representation of the people." For several weeks following, the *Pacific* continued to carry editorials in favor of the vigilantes.

The Vigilance Committee seemed to have had the unanimous support of all of the Protestant pastors of the city. Several preached sermons endorsing the movement. Among these was the Rev. Benjamin Brierly of the First Baptist Church whose sermon appeared in the May 29th issue of the *Pacific* under the title: "Thoughts suggested by the present crisis." It was subsequently reprinted as a pamphlet.

The overwhelming majority opinion of the public as expressed through the activities of the Vigilance Committee and through the press and the pulpit was in favor of the movement. But there was a minority who composed the Law and Order party. Among these was William Tecumseh Sherman who happened to be in San Francisco at the time in a civilian capacity. Shortly before the Casey-King incident occurred, Governor J. Neely Johnson of California, prevailed upon Sherman to accept the commission of major-general of the Second Division of the State Militia which included San Francisco. Although Sherman had received his commission, he had not accepted it by the time the trouble broke out. Even if he had been officially inducted into his office, he would have been without soldiers as the entire body of militiamen aligned themselves with the Vigilance Committee. Governor Johnson arrived in San Francisco on Friday, May 16th, two days after the shooting, but found it impossible at that time to reestablish law and order.

Following the death of King on May 20th, there was no doubt in any one's mind about the outcome of the trial being held secretly by the vigilantes. Casey was sentenced to be hanged. A like sentence was given to Cora who cursed Casey for the deed which directed the attention of the vigilantes to both of them. A gallows was prepared adjacent to an upper room of the Vigilance Committee's headquarters on Sacramento Street by extending a beam from the roof from which ropes were hung. The funeral of King was held at the Unitarian Church on Thursday, May 22nd. The Vigilance Committee decided that this would be a good time to execute the two men. The report in the *Pacific* for May 23rd reads: "Yesterday, at twenty minutes past one o'clock, about the time of the conclusion of the funeral exercises over the remains of Mr. King, the two felons were launched into eternity. The time was well chosen, when the attention of the multitude was elsewhere bestowed. While thousands were waiting to form in the procession that escorted a good and great man to his grave, . . . in another portion of the city the two convicts were suffering the last penalty of justice." The bodies were left suspended for about an hour before being taken down. The news of the hanging, according to the story in the *Pacific*, "spread like wild-fire throughout the city, and there was an immense rush of people to see the bodies."

Among those who witnessed the execution were Governor Johnson and General Sherman while standing on top of a neighboring building. There was nothing they could do to prevent the hangings. Two days later, the *Herald*, speaking for the Law and Order party, declared:

To-day we have a government based on no single principle which the American people have ever acknowledged or with which they have sympathized; nay, more than this—a government the worst in form, the most unjust in tendency and most liable to abuse, the most irresponsible, the most absolute, the most passionate, with fewer checks and safeguards, the worst organized for deliberation. . . It is not an American government; it owes no allegiance to the constitution of the United States nor of the State, but acts in defiance of both.

With great boldness and with incisive arguments, the editor pointed out the grave dangers of turning the government over to a self-appointed committee with absolute power. Members and friends of the vigilantes showed their displeasure by cancelling advertisements and subscriptions. For a time the *Herald* appeared in a much reduced size.

It so happened that Scott was enjoying a short vacation in the Sierras when the trouble broke out in San Francisco. He returned on Saturday, May 24th, at which time he found the city, as he later described it, "glowing like a furnace." Scott's reaction to the events was quick and incisive. Even though there were men of high integrity at the head of the vigilantes, yet it was mob rule, and as such it was politically dangerous and morally wrong. Better a poor government with duly elected officials than a temporary good government by a mob. In reviewing the exciting events of those days, Scott wrote on September 18th of that year:

> My church was crowded on Sunday to hear what I would say in behalf of the Vigilance Committee. It seemed to be the opinion that as all, or almost all, the Protestant clergymen had committed themselves to their measures that I should do so likewise. Several had said they would not miss hearing me on that occasion for hundreds of dollars. I was advised on both sides. I was threatened if I did not favor the Committee. I did not inform any one what I would do. But when the Lords Day came, and the church was crowded to overflowing, I preached a plain, solemn, old fashioned orthodox sermon on God's love to sinners in the mission of Christ. I did not say a word about the Committee. . . My course gave great offence to some. Several left my church. I know not how many, but still by God's blessing, we were full—more crowded than ever. . . [It was not] the hour for invective or even reason. I sought to moderate the violent passions of men by pointing them to the love of God and the sufferings of Christ.

Scott's refusal to endorse the vigilantes was disconcerting to many of his own congregation. His silence was more eloquent than any open denunciation of their lawless act ever could have been. Although Scott had been friendly with the Rev. Isaac H. Brayton, a New School Presbyterian and editor of the *Pacific,* prior to this time, now a coolness began to develop between the two. Scott was greatly disturbed over the series of editorials that appeared in the *Pacific* in favor of the vigilantes. In a letter to the *Daily True California* dated October 4, 1856, Scott declared: "I also remonstrated in three letters to the Rev. Mr. Brayton. . . . I also wished him to publish our correspondence at the time in his paper, if he thought it would do good." But Brayton refused to take public issue with Scott. In fact all through the summer of 1856, the *Pacific* completely ignored Scott.

Because his silence was being misconstrued and much harmful gossip was being circulated, Scott felt it wise to issue a public statement regarding his views of the Vigilance Committee. In his letter of October 4th, he explained: "As such themes did not come, according to my views, within the proper sphere of the pulpit and the Lord's day, I invited all the officers of my congregation to meet me in my study. They did me the kindness to come, and I laid before them in as full and plain a manner as I could, what my views were—showing that my *education, antecedents, conscience, principles,* and *relations* to the Church of Christ were such that I could not for one moment approve of the proceedings of the Committee." He told his church officers of his desire to publish a statement on the subject and asked for their approbation.

All but two of the eleven officers of his church were members of the vigilantes. They were among the church's largest contributors and were the leaders in that large congregation. Yet Dr. Scott had the courage to confront them and denounce as sinful the principles and acts of the vigilantes. Stung by their pastor's condemnations, the men urged caution and delay. "They advised me wait until the excitement might subside," wrote Scott. "They told me that it would do no good to attempt to reason on the subject then. A few days afterwards they requested me in writing, for the sake of the public good, not to say anything on the subject. Out of regard to their wishes, as the representatives of a generous people, who had treated me with great kindness, I did not then publish my letter."

Four weeks after this meeting with his officers, Scott felt that he could hold his peace no longer. On Sunday, July 27th, he preached his famous sermon "A Discourse for the Times" which was the boldest and strongest condemnation of the vigilantes which was ever spoken or published in San Francisco during those emotion-charged days. His theme was: "Education, and not Punishment, the true remedy for the wrong-doings and disorders of society."

Scott began with an admonition to parents and teachers who had an unescapable responsibility in giving right training to the children committed to their care. "The right beginning," he said, "is the first and chief preventive in our power of the moral and social disease that is preying with such dreadful ravages upon us." He emphasized the supreme importance of religious and character education for the young in the home, the church, and the school. Scott stabbed the consciences of his hearers. In giving the following penetrating diagnosis of the ills of California society, he painted a grim picture of his times:

> The immediate causes and actual developments of human depravity among us that have made us a hissing and a terror in the civilized world, are to be found in the corrupting influences of gold and of riches accumulated suddenly, and often by dishonest means —speculation and fraud—idleness—too many seeking to live by their wits, and not by honest labor—the aggregation here of the depraved and adventuring of many lands—the absence of family ties—husbands and fathers and brothers congregated here without their wives, daughters, and sisters—the presence of swarms of bad women from almost all parts of the known world in our cities and throughout our mountain towns—and hard drinking, and gambling, and working on the Lord's day, and the carrying and using of deadly weapons, and lawlessness in a thousand ways—the idea and the feeling too that this was not our home—that this country would do to trade in—to speculate in—to scrape gold out of—but not to make one's home—and the consequent shipping out of the country of large sums of treasure, and recently more than ever— and the sending away of our children to be educated—and the prolonged absence of citizens and capitalists from the country— the indifference of some to the support of Home institutions, and the absorption of others in their own affairs, and *their refusal to perform the duties of good citizens in upholding the laws of the country, and their neglect of public affairs,* and the consequent leaving of them to fall, in some instances, into the hands of incompetent, unprincipled or bad men. These and the such like are the immediate causes of our present melancholy state of affairs. As a result of these things we are overwhelmed with corruption.

In clear unmistakable terms, he warned his hearers: "We may erect a citadel on every street, and plant cannon on the top of every warehouse, and convert every man and boy into a dragoon, and scour the country from the sea to the mountains for gamblers and thieves, but until the work of education is rightly done, and all have reverence for God and for his laws, we shall never have a home here fit to rear our children, nor a more and religious, peaceable and well to do city."

Dr. Scott's remedy for the ills of the time were very practical: "We must elevate and purify public sentiment by the principles of the ten commandments, and of the sermon on the mount. . . I would not have you go to chaos. We have some good things left. Our fundamental laws are good . . . and we have some honest and able men among us. . . What we want then is not externals, but internals. We want the people to fear God and keep his laws. We want law and not lawlessness." In his closing remarks, he summed up his convictions:

You may depend upon it, the stream of blood will never be staid while men take the law into their own hands, and while the fierce brutal passions are excited under the pretext of supporting the laws, and revenge is mingled with the maintenance of justice. Never shall we have peace while gambling and lewdness and murder are allowed to reign in our city and defiance of our statutes. Nor can we expect freedom from violence while the practice of carrying deadly weapons is continued, and the intoxicating glass is used to keep up brute courage. And never will men be virtuous until they are governed by principle and not by brute force— never will they be happy until they fear God and love their fellow men. This is my testimony concerning our evils and their remedy.

Never before during the reign of the vigilantes had anyone in San Francisco spoken so boldly against them as did Dr. Scott. In the author's judgment, this was the most courageous act in a career marked by many conflicts and controversies. Dr. Scott was not a man who, for expediency sake, would seek to avoid meeting head-on a moral issue.

A few days after that memorable Sunday in Calvary Church, the sermon was published in an edition of three thousand copies as an eight-page pamphlet. "A number of bookstores and newspaper stalls," later commented Dr. Scott, "would not allow it to be sold at their counters because it was anti-Vigilante." Today this pamphlet has become a choice item of rare Californiana.

A chief criticism of Dr. Scott's proposed remedy for the ills of the time was that it would take years to effect. His opponents felt that an emergency situation demanded immediate and drastic action. As though in answer to Scott's plea for moderation and for the restoration of law and order, the vigilantes hanged two more men on July 29th, just two days after Scott had preached his "A Discourse for the Times." This brought the total of hangings to four by the vigilantes of 1856.

If Scott had been satisfied with the protest made through his sermon against the vigilantes, probably nothing more would have happened. A new factor, however, was injected into the unfolding drama when a letter from Brayton appeared in the *New York Evangelist* under date of July 3, 1856. In his strong endorsement of the vigilantes, Brayton wrote:

One of the most marked features of the present movement in this State, is the unanimity with which the clergy have approved of it, and the churches have engaged in it. With scarcely a single exception in the whole State, the pastors have approved of the action of the Committee. Most of them have preached on the subject. They have animated the people to go forward in the reform, as the work of religon—the work of God. The Church throughout the State is with this movement. It is part of her religion to make pure the body politic.

Although Brayton did not mention Scott by name in his letter, the following barbed bit of sarcasm was hurled in his direction: "It is an object with the enemies of this movement to misrepresent the position of the Church. They have not attempted it, save in a single instance, unworthy of notice." It should be remembered that Brayton wrote several weeks before Scott preached his famous sermon.

The issue of the *Evangelist* which contained Brayton's letter reached San Francisco about August 1st. When Scott read it, he became indignant and then angry. He felt that he had been unjustly assailed. On several occasions during the summer of 1856 Scott had written to Brayton explaining his position in regard to the vigilantes with the hope that the letters would appear in the *Pacific*. This Brayton had not seen fit to do. Scott was ignored. But now since Brayton's letter had appeared in an eastern periodical, the issue was not longer local but national. Scott felt that the way was now open to him to explain in some detail the reasons for his opposition to the vigilantes. His reputation among his eastern friends was involved. The very honor of the church had been besmirched. To Scott, the position taken by Brayton and his clerical friends was nothing less than betrayal of true Christianity. The church had no business to become involved in politics. Being thus aroused, on August 4th Scott wrote a letter of about four thousand words to the *Philadelphia Presbyterian* which was published in the September 6th issue under the caption: "The Church and Lynch Law."

Scott addressed his letter "To the Editors of the *Pacific* in San Francisco." In other words, he was directing his remarks to Brayton. "I address you by the way of Philadelphia," he explained, "because I wish to escape, as much as possible, from local prejudices and momentary excitements, and to speak of principles and things beyond the influence of passion." With logical arguments, he challenged some of the claims Brayton had made regarding the basic assumptions of the vigilantes. "And to my mind," he added, "it is perfectly preposterous to contend that the many thousands of men and money wielded by the Committee, could not have secured in a lawful manner the purity of our elections and the faithful execution of the laws, as far as perfection in such things can be obtained in human courts. If they could not, then our republican institutions are a failure." Scott accused Brayton and his associates on the *Pacific* of stirring up the people "to contravene the laws of the land."

> It is the opinion of some of the most intelligent men of this city, that the example of the ministers which you commend, and the cry of the press of the city for blood, have contributed greatly to our present disorganized state. The newspapers that have laboured most violently, and called the loudest for the reign of lawlessness, have quoted the *religious papers* as sanctioning their course, and in support of the movement. Now, if the religious

teachers and leaders of the people have set such an example, the people are almost excusable.

Scott referred to the pressure which had been brought to bear upon him "to pray for the Committee, and preach in their behalf." He was told that he would "lose my congregation" if he refused.

> It may be I have no power to do any thing more than to *pro-test* against your views of the Church and of the duty of ministers of the gospel in this crisis, but I do most earnestly and solemnly *protest* against your placing the Church of Christ in any such position. And I protest against your teaching church members to support lynch law. . . Nor are there bayonets enough in the State, nor gold enough in its mountains, to compel me to introduce such themes into my humble pulpit ministrations.

Scott in this letter clearly defined his philosophy of the relationship of church and state, a philosophy which he consistently followed a few years later when the tremendously important issues of slavery and secession were claiming public attention.

The issue of the *Philadelphia Presbyterian* with Scott's letter arrived in San Francisco the last of September and it at once aroused the ire of all who supported the vigilantes. The *San Francisco Daily Sun* in its issue of October 2nd commented: "The Rev. Dr. Scott of Calvary Church has brought down on his head the anathemas of the organs of the Vigilance Committee, because he was possessed of the true Christian spirit which frowns upon lawless acts of mobocracy. . . The alleged offence has been the publication of a letter in the Philadelphia Presbyterian condemnatory of the acts of the Vigilance Committee, but more especially of religious papers and orthodox preachers." Scott's letter stabbed the consciences of many. Some read it and were troubled. Others, and no doubt they were in the minority, read and became angry. The vigilantes could and did search without warrant and arrest without charge, but how could they handle a recalcitrant minister?

Since Dr. Scott could be neither frightened nor silenced, there remained in the minds of his aroused opponents but one course of action, that of harassment and insult. They would pour out their scorn by hanging him in effigy. There was no mob. Only a few, who were never identified, took part and they worked in the darkness of the night of October 4th. According to a report in the *Golden Era* for October 12th: "The figure was cut down at 6 o'clock by a party of well-dressed gentlemen before it had attracted much attention. The artists are not known, as the clothes could not be identified, although the position and peculiar color of a patch on the most exposed portion of the pantaloons go far in fixing the suspicion upon an old bottle merchant."

As could have been expected, the *Herald*, in its report of the incident on the following Monday expressed deep indignation. The editor wrote under the caption "HUNG BE THE HEAVENS IN BLACK! YIELD DAY TO NIGHT!"

On yesterday morning—the morning of God's Holy Day—was perpetrated in the streets of this city an outrage so damnable and disgraceful that as Californians we are pained and humiliated to be compelled to report it. The Reverend Doctor Scott, a clergyman of the Presbyterian Church, was hung in effigy from a lamp-post opposite the church, of which he is the reverend pastor, on Bush Street near Montgomery. . . An act of vandal malice more atrocious—an act of meanness more revolting—an act of cowardly ruffianism more utterly, more unspeakably disgraceful, we have never in the long course of our journalism in a city where outrages and atrocities have been by no means unfrequent, been called upon to chronicle.

In those days San Francisco had a plethora of newspapers. On October 12th, the *Golden Era* in an article under the caption, "Horrible! Most Horrible!" presented a pithy review of the editorial reactions of the city's newspapers to the incident. Quoting the *True California* of October 6th: "We blush to be called upon to chronicle one of the most disgraceful and outrageous acts against public decency and decorum that has come to our notice." The *Post* declared: "We are most heartily ashamed to record such an act of indecency and outrage." The *Bulletin* reported: "There are no words sufficiently strong to express our condemnation of the deed . . . or the contempt and detestation we feel for its perpetrators. The fact was sacrilegious and cowardly, and merits the severest reprobation." The *Herald,* the *Sun,* and *Town Talk* likewise condemned the act, the latter saying that it was "one of the most dastardly vandalisms which has ever disgraced this community."

On the other side, the *Alta California* did not "consider the matter of sufficient importance to demand serious attention." And to this judgment, the editor of *Golden Era* wrote:

> Just our opinion to a dot. We heartily condemn the whole proceeding, and could wring the noses of the mischievous rascals who perpetrated it; but we neither "blush" at the thought of it, nor consider the community irretrievably "disgraced" in consequence of the misdemeanor. Dr. Scott's religious preferences had nothing to do with it. He left the pulpit and made himself the champion of an opinion which has assumed but little else than the form of a political issue, and therefore laid himself liable to all of the consequences of party hatred. The "outrage" was not intended for Rev. Dr. Scott, pastor of Calvary Church, but for plain Mr. Scott, the politician. Viewed in this light, the affair looks considerably less "heinous, sacrilegious, and damnable." Better men have been hung in effigy and for less reason.

Scott was hurt, deeply hurt by the insult. His officers rallied immediately to his support and, on the very day the hanging took place, signed a joint letter expressing their indignation. Among the fifty who signed were Fletcher M. Haight, Stephen Franklin, W. C. Ralston, Thomas H. Selby, James B. Roberts, H. P. Coon, Redrick McKee, and Nicholas G. Kittle, his future son-in-law. This was heartening but on the other hand there was a surprising amount of space devoted to the Scott affair in both the religious and secular press of the city following the October 5th incident. Brayton had an editorial nearly four columns long in his *Pacific* of October 9th. The *Pacific* refrained from making any direct reference to the hanging. The October 16th issue carried a letter from the Rev. Benjamin Brierly in which he expressed sympathy with Dr. Scott "in the wanton and vulgar method resorted to last Sabbath morning." Brierly felt that he was speaking for all of the clergy of the city. On November 16th the *Golden Era*, referring to some local celebrities, commented: "Rev. Dr. Scott, . . . has within the past month, figured in more newspaper paragraphs than that of any other individual we know, save Kennevan, the pedestrian, and the Sacramento 'snake charmer.' "

All of this publicity became increasingly distasteful to Scott until he began to consider the advisability of resigning. He wondered if the wide divergence of opinion over the whole vigilante affair between himself and the majority of the men of his church would undermine his usefulness as their pastor. He talked with one of the trustees of the church, James B. Roberts, who was one of the most prominent of the younger business men of the city. Roberts was also active in the vigilantes. Alarmed over the possibility of Scott resigning, Roberts hastened to communicate with the other members of the Board of Trustees. A special meeting was called for Thursday evening, October 16th. Scott was not present but Roberts presented his views.

According to the minutes of the meeting, the trustees were unanimous in their "feelings of the deepest indignation of the outrage committed" and felt that Dr. Scott had every right "to entertain and express feelings and views" regarding the vigilante movement which differed from "the prevailing sentiment of this board and Congregation." The men also expressed themselves in saying that "such opposite views & feelings should not be allowed to alienate the confidence and affection of his people." A committee was appointed to draft a letter to be sent their pastor which would embody the sentiment of the board. Another meeting was called for the following evening when the final draft of the letter was approved. "We avail ourselves of this occasion," the letter reads, "to assure you of our high regard for you as a man and a Christian pastor. Our confidence in your piety and your eminent capacity for usefulness and our sympathy with you in your labors as an ambassador of Christ . . ." were reaffirmed. Moreover a special meeting of the congregation was called for the Monday evening following when the letter of the trustees was read to the church.

For a fortnight, Dr. Scott carried on. His unhappiness, however, increased to such a point that on November 8th he addressed a letter of resignation to the church. In this letter he reminded his people that he had never been officially installed as their pastor. He was still only the pastor-elect or the stated supply of Calvary Church and according to Presbyterian polity, such a relationship was easily dissolved. No action of presbytery was necessary. In explaining the reasons for his decision, Scott wrote:

> It is now perfectly clear to me that there are divisions among you and considerable dissatisfaction with me and my labors in the pulpit on account of my well known views of the Vigilance Committee which has so unhappily agitated this community for the last several months. Both in my regular reading and preaching of the Word of God just in the same manner that I have always done and in using as I sometimes do an old discourse or sermon written ten years or more ago, I find myself *hindered* or *fettered* and oftentimes, though wholly unconscious of making any "flings" or allusions to the late local troubles, I am frequently so misunderstood that great offense is taken at my preaching and expounding of the Holy Scriptures.

Under the circumstances, he felt that "the peace and prosperity of this Congregation which we all love so much at heart may be the better secured by my withdrawal from it. I do hereby decline to act or to be considered any longer as pastor elect."

The letter was received first by the session which called a congregational meeting for Monday, November 17th. The threatened loss of their pastor erased differences which had arisen over the vigilantes. Moreover, the political scene itself was changing. The Vigilance Committee had been dissolved late in August. Fort Gunny Bags was dismantled. City and county elections were held which brought into office a complete slate of vigilante men. Law and order gradually replaced the rule of the Vigilante Committee. Members of the church were asking: "Now that the political situation is clearing, why should our pastor leave us?"

Six resolutions were heartily and unanimously adopted at the congregational meeting. The first was an expression of regret that Dr. Scott had been moved to send in his letter of resignation. Number two stated: "That while we appreciate the motives of honor and delicacy which have induced Dr. Scott to tender his resignation, we beg to assure him that howevermuch many of us may differ with him in opinion concerning recent local events—we feel united to him by an attachment too sincere and strong to be dissolved with our consent by any differences that have yet occurred. . . ." The third resolution expressed detestation of the "gross indignity" which was directed against their pastor. This, they said, was not only an insult against Dr. Scott, it was also an insult "to ourselves." The fourth resolution was an expression of warm gratitude for all that Dr. Scott had done for the church. Number five stated that his "withdrawal from this city would be a public loss." Resolution number six called upon the elders and trustees to inform Dr. Scott of the "earnest desire" of the church for him to remain and directed the officers to urge him to be duly installed as their pastor as soon as possible.

On the same evening that the congregational meeting of Calvary Church was being held, W. T. Sherman addressed a letter to Dr. Scott from which the following has been taken:

> It may be impertinent for me, a stranger to you, to address you on a subject apparently purely personal: but from my estimate of your character, I believe you will receive from me kindly what is offered in that spirit.
>
> To night your congregation meet to receive your resignation. I cannot realize that you will under the circumstances press it on them, beyond what you in your conscience deem just to your sense of the delicate relations between pastor and flock. Other important considerations enter into this matter, which I know you must feel, but in the doubt whether some who are more capable than myself will express them to you, I must do it.
>
> You alone among the Protestant clergy of this City opposed in feeling and actions the principles too long practiced in this State, of the Peoples rising up under excitement & apparent cause to break the laws and constitution of their own making and to insult and tread upon the officers of their own choice after having forced them to swear to obey and execute that constitution and those laws. Now if you leave us and your congregation agree to part with you at this time, it will form an additional link in that chain that seems to threaten to bind us in the future to make the unascertained will of the People the law.
>
> Believing in the doctrines of Government bequeathed to us by Washington, and having our lots cast in this city, we all owe it to our common country, and common history to vindicate in the future the wisdom of those principles of government and if we succumb to the opposition, or seem to succumb, we may in fact be a partial cause to break up our great constitutional Government. . . I admit my faith in these principles is somewhat shaken and fear that to reestablish the Executive offices of this State and City in their confidences in the majesty of Law and its capacity of self vindication, we may be compelled to witness further violence; but to this end and to lessen the prospective danger of such collisions, we need just such men as you who think for themselves, who drink their principles of action from a more holy source than the Evening Bulletin or such trashy newspapers as purport to represent our public opinion. We need men to teach moderation, patience, and submission to the Law, not inconsistent with the most perfect freedom. . .
>
> San Francisco must become a Great City, when the arts &

literature will be encompassed—when life & prosperity will be safe, and when manufactures and commerce will vie with each other in contributing to the wants & luxuries of life. This result cannot come unless the Law is made and enforced as nearly perfect as the machinery we must use is capable of. If we who live in San Francisco cannot do this, the world will justly scorn us as men unworthy the destiny imposed on us by Providence. For myself I am willing to stand by the task and I should like to know that Dr. Scott was at his task according to his wisdom working in the same Cause.

Representing such principles at this time and occupying as I do a peculiar relation to the mercantile public, my duties are like yours somewhat delicate. And I assure you I appreciate the nice position in which you stand but representing as you do a noble principle, let me join your other friends in asking you to meet them more than half way; remain with us, and let us convince our opponents and thereby confound them, better than victory of arms and blood. This may seem to you like hypocrisy on my part, but I repeat that those who obey the Law from principle cannot spare you from California *now*. Your Master bore taunts, ignominy, and death itself to establish on earth the Rule of charity and kindness. I know if you can, you will follow His example.

> Yr. friend & servant, W. T. Sherman.

The resolutions unanimously adopted at the congregational meeting, combined with such appeals as that made by the Roman Catholic soldier turned merchant, W. T. Sherman, induced Scott to withdraw his resignation. In a letter to Lowrie dated December 1856 Scott reported that his congregations continued to be as large as ever. "Many go away from my evening services," he wrote, "for the want of seats." In spite of such outward evidence of his continued success as a preacher, Scott was discouraged. This letter to Lowrie is steeped in pessimism, an attitude most unusual for him. "The whole country and existing state of things is supremely disgusting to me, except the soil & the climate," he wrote. "There is no permanency or confidence here in any body or in any thing. . . I believe this will become a populous & mighty country, but not in my lifetime. . . We shall not live to see the Railroad and if we did its influence upon California we predict is a hundred times overrated." Scott frankly stated that "I should prefer a field of labor in N.Y. because it is a larger city."

In this same letter he summarized the financial condition of Calvary Church. "It is probably not known to you," he wrote, ". . . that I am out of pocket six thousand dollars for this Chh. I have just paid the last of a $2,000 subscription. The money has been raised again and again, but always comes short, and in order to get through & save the enterprise, I have subscribed myself and have paid. . . I know not how often it has been published that Calvary Chh was out of debt. I have thought so myself. But it never has been out of debt and now owes $4,000." On the brighter side, he reported that "My salary including house rent is $10,000 & promptly paid."

Scott was puzzled as to whether he should stay in San Francisco. "*I can stay,*" he wrote and underlines the words, as he did also for the following: "*I can sleep on the field of battle. The victory is on my banner. . . The State is with me.*" He asked his friend:

> Is it best for me to keep on the armor and fight on? Could not another of God's servants against whom such an army of vigilantes would not be arrayed, do more for our Zion & for Christ here than I can now reasonably hope to do? And might I not labor more comfortably and successfully in a field where such violent prejudices would not exist? . . . My way is neither clear nor dark. I do not as yet even see men as trees walking. . . I have many bitter, very bitter enemies here. But I am able to maintain my post with God's blessing. *Ought I to do so?* I am in great doubts. I am fettered in reading & preaching the word of God. When I am not thinking of the Committee, I am supposed to be flinging at it—and that too when the Chief men of the Congregation—all the officers but two, nine out of eleven are strong Vigilantes.

He claimed that he had to be extremely careful in what he said in his sermons as the most innocent remark would be twisted.

There were stern realities which had to be faced. Scott had a family of eight children, the youngest of whom was only a little more than a month old when he wrote out his resignation. There was no other Presbyterian congregation in California which could have supported him. The only possible change meant taking a church in some eastern city and this in turn involved the heavy expense of transporting his family the long way across the Isthmus. Another factor that both William and Ann took into consideration was the problem of giving their older children a good education. Institutions of higher learning in California in 1856 were still hardly more than academies.

Sometime during the summer of 1856, when the vigilantes were in full power, Scott had written to his friend, Dr. John Backus, pastor of the First Presbyterian Church of Baltimore, and indicated a desire to leave California. Backus replied on October 3rd saying that he stood ready to recommend him to the Central Presbyterian Church of Baltimore, then vacant, if Scott were truly wanting a change. He indicated interest, and a formal call was issued on December 2nd. The church then had a membership of 257, being the second Presbyterian church in size in the city, and offered a salary of $4,000. Its auditorium was large enough to seat 1,200.

About the same time the West Arch Street Presbyterian Church of Philadelphia learned of the possible availability of such a famous preacher and likewise extended a call. This church had a membership of 330 and likewise offered a salary of $4,000. It boasted a new building which had cost over $100,000 which it claimed was "decidedly the most beautiful church of our City of any denomination." Somehow the news of the two calls became known to the San Francisco papers. On January 3, 1857, both the *Alta California* and the *Chronicle* ran news stories about them.

Scott was in a quandary. On February 16, 1857, he wrote a long letter to his friend, Walter Lowrie, and poured out his troubles. He felt that there was a possibility of the vigilantes being revived at "any hour." He repeated his conviction that far more harm than good had come from the movement. "Time and reflection only enhance the monstrousness of the whole outrage," he wrote. "No good has been done, not a particle, but awful wrong. See our papers for wholesale robberies & murders in every part of the State . . . suicides & insanity crowd our columns. . ." After painting a dark picture of social conditions in California, he asked: "Is it right then for me to keep *eight children in the mouth of such a volcano? Or can I hope that my preaching the Gospel will do any good among such a people?* My hope is indeed almost all gone. There is no sympathy between the members of my Chh who are Vigilantes & myself. I see not how there can be."

After weeks of indecision Scott declined both calls. He decided to remain in San Francisco. The Philadelphia church, however, refused to accept Scott's reply as final. New and more liberal terms were offered which reopened the whole subject. Scott was on the point of accepting the call when an unexpected event changed the whole picture. On Thursday night, March 19, 1857, a fire broke out in the basement of Calvary Church which burnt through the main floor and spread up to the roof before it was brought under control. The newspaper accounts differ as to the amount of the loss. The *Chronicle* and the *Bulletin* claimed that the damage amounted to $20,000. The *Fireman's Journal* estimated it at $5,000. There was also a difference of opinion regarding the cause. The *Alta California* stated that the fire was undoubtedly accidental while the *Bulletin* was positive that it was arson. Insurance covered most of the loss. An interesting sidelight is found in the March 28th issue of the *Fireman's Journal* which stated that on Sunday, March 22nd, three days after the fire, Dr. Scott "offered one of the most eloquent prayers in behalf of the firemen of this city ever listened to."

The fire, like some magic coalescent agent, united the discordant elements within Calvary Church. With one accord the members joined in their support of both the church and their pastor. In a letter to Lowrie dated May 18th, Scott described what had happened.

> The West Arch church made a *second* invitation after I had closed the first. This was every thing I could have desired. Liberal, earnest and putting every thing into my own hands—and financially, even more than I had asked as to money—and what was more, an earnest appeal to come & *save* or gather an Old School church.

And I was on the eve of accepting, when our church edifice here was laid in ashes, though not wholly destroyed. The incendiary did his work on the night before the sailing of the steamer that was to carry my acceptance to Phil. *Such a man as I could not flee* when the enemy was thus triumphing. I could not leave *the flock here without either fold or shepherd.* I reconsidered the whole matter. The congregation seemed as though they would not let me go. Even some who were for *vanishing me* a few months ago were now ready *to keep me by violence.* And on the whole I thought Providence had interposed to keep me here for the present. And though *personally* I am free to confess I did not wish to stay, yet I yielded most cheerfully. I declined Phil. & all other overtures. And having sold my home in New Orleans, purchased one here.

Scott in his letter to Lowrie of the previous December made reference to some "patrimonial property." It is probable that his wife received some property from the estate of her father, the late Dr. Robert Nicholson, and that some if not all of such funds were used to purchase their home in New Orleans. Having sold this property, money was available for the purchase of a home in San Francisco. In his May letter Scott wrote that he bought a home "chiefly for its *moral* effect on the city. It is my offering to inspire confidence in the community. Not one dollar of all this however is from my salary."

In the light of the changed situation, Scott decided to remain at his post "for one or two years, therefore, but not longer as I now think. . . This is the *sowing time* I know, but will the *reaping ever come?*" The crisis was over. Gradually tensions lessened and life in the city and in the church returned to normal.

The question has often been asked: Did the vigilante movement of 1856 do more harm than good? The *San Francisco Herald* of October 20, 1857, looked back over eighteen months and summarized its convictions as follows: "The truth is that for all purposes of good, the Committee has been a sorry and tragical failure. During the last six months, crimes against life have been more frequent in San Francisco than in twice that length of time in any previous period of its history. Murders, robberies, and all sorts of ruthless violence have run riot in our midst."

On the other hand, California's great historian, H. H. Bancroft in the sixth volume of his *History of California,* published in 1888, declared that as a result of the work of the vigilantes: "Crime never again reached dangerous proportions in the city. . . A people's reform party was organized, which for at least ten years did good service in maintaining an honest administration, and urging the people to a performance of their political duties so disastrously neglected."

Among Dr. Scott's papers in the archives of San Francisco Theological Seminary is a collection of notes made with the evident intention of publishing a book or pamphlet on "The Church of God, a Witness against Lynch Law." The following are a few quotations from these notes:

Two years since the organization of the Committee of Vigilance of San F. Time has shown that it was a most unfortunate organization of "unmitigated evil." I shall deem it one of the most happy things in my life if I am so fortunate as to deserve the esteem of my friends and to retain it; but if I am not, then my duty is only the more plain: *Truth before friends.* I am well persuaded, that *Where there is no law, there is no liberty.* I regard the Vigilance Committee as a deplorable catastrophe for the cause of Freedom, a terrible episode in our social history.

I do not believe any sudden or revolutionary movement can remedy our social or public evils. We cannot multiply statute laws so as to reach every action of life. Social evils do not come upon us in a day, nor can they be removed in a moment. They are of gradual growth, and it is only by substantial industry, virtuous economy, general intelligence, rigid morality, and spiritual religion, that the stability of our Institutions can be secured. Private worth & vital piety are essential.

Thus Dr. William Anderson Scott by example and by spoken and written word bore his testimony against mob rule and for the orderly procedures of a democratic government.

MODERATOR OF THE GENERAL ASSEMBLY, 1858

Within two years after going through the valley of trouble, persecutions, and despair, Scott reached the peak of success in his professional career when he was elected moderator of the Old School Presbyterian Assembly in 1858. The Presbytery of California met in Calvary Church on December 29, 1857. Three ministers were present including William C. Anderson of First Church, William Anderson Scott of Calvary, and Frederick Buel of the American Bible Society. Both First and Calvary sent elders. Thus the total attendance was only five. Scott was elected moderator and also commissioner to the 1858 General Assembly scheduled to meet in the First Presbyterian Church of New Orleans on May 6th. It was most fitting that he should have been chosen to go to this particular assembly.

Scott sailed from San Francisco on April 5th for Panama and crossed the Isthmus on the railroad which had been opened in January 1855. People likened it to a wedding ring slipped on the finger of the Isthmus binding the two oceans together. He arrived in New Orleans on April 28th.

For the first time he saw the handsome new building which replaced the one which on October 29, 1854, had burned just before he left New Orleans for San Francisco. And perhaps for the first time he met his successor, Dr. Benjamin M. Palmer, who graciously invited him to occupy the pulpit of First Church on Sunday, May 2nd. The June 1st issue of the *San Francisco Bulletin* carried a news item from its New Orleans correspondent regarding the enthusiastic reception given to Dr. Scott.

The reporter wrote: "I do not know that I ever saw a greater crowd assembled in a church than went the first morning after his arrival for the purpose of shaking his hand."

The Old School Presbyterian Assembly began its sessions on Thursday, May 6th. Three, including Dr. Scott, were nominated for the moderatorship. He was elected by 106 ballots on the first roll call. The combined total for the other two candidates was ninety six. Thus at the age of forty-five William Anderson Scott was awarded the highest honor within the power of his church to bestow. He was the first moderator to come from the Pacific Coast and it was not until 1877 that the Presbyterian Church conferred a like honor upon another minister from the far west.

In commenting on the events of the 1858 Assembly, the *Southern Presbyterian Review* reported that this Assembly enrolled 149 ministers and ninety nine elder commissioners, making a total of 248. They came from 157 different presbyteries which were constituent parts of thirty three synods scattered from New Hampshire to California. The total membership of the Old School Church was 259,335 that year. At the same time the New School branch had 143,510 members. Commented the editor of the *Review:*

> It was a matter of interest that they were presided over by the distinguished brother from San Francisco, most of whose life has been spent in frontier cities, who, at home, looks upon Asia across the Pacific, who had travelled more than 5,000 miles to reach the place of meeting, and who was called upon to occupy the Moderator's chair, in the city and the church of his former residence and labors—a source of gratification doubtless to himself, and to the people of his former charge.

The editor of the *Presbyterian Magazine* in its December 1858 issue wrote that Dr. Scott "discharged the duties of his office with great ability, and with Christian affection and simplicity."

The 1858 Assembly met during a time when the slavery issue was becoming increasingly important in ecclesiastical as well as in political circles. Lines were being sharply drawn between slavery and anti-slavery states. Tensions were mounting. Zeal-inflamed consciences inspired extremists on both sides. In the South, an increasing number of Protestant ministers felt moved to defend the whole institution of slvaery. It was God-ordained. The Negro belonged to an inferior race and needed a white master. In the North, the abolition movement grew both in and out of church circles. As the issues became more demanding for a permanent settlement, many of the southern church members tried to relegate the whole question to the political arena and thus to exclude it from ecclesiastical jurisdiction. Such a rationalizing process, however, failed to suppress the moral issues involved. Good people were troubled; angry people refused to debate; tempers hardened; and events rushed to a crisis.

The Methodist Episcopal Church split into its northern and southern branches in 1845. In the same year the Southern Baptist Convention was organized. The New School Presbyterians, with about eight-ninths of their membership in the North, felt the impact of the controversial slavery issue several years earlier than did the Old School branch which had at least one-third of its membership in the South. Also to be remembered is the fact that the New School was more liberal in its theological outlook having accepted much of the so-called New England Theology with its social emphasis. For years anti-slavery memorials, overtures, and resolutions, had disturbed the peace of the New School Assemblies. A strong and vocal southern minority prevented the Assembly from taking a decided stand before 1857. In the Assembly of that year the Presbytery of Lexington, South, frankly stated that "a number of ministers and ruling elders, as well as many church members, in their connection, hold slaves 'from principle' and 'of choice' believing it to be according to Bible right." This statement forced the New School Assembly to declare itself. "We deem it our duty," the Assembly replied, ". . . to disapprove and earnestly condemn the position, which has been assumed by the Presbytery of Lexington, South, as one which is opposed to the established convictions of the Presbyterian Church. . . Such doctrines and practice cannot be permanently tolerated in the Presbyterian Church." The vote to condemn stood at 169 to 29. On April 1, 1858, commissioners from twenty-one southern New School presbyteries, representing a total membership of about 15,000 organized the United Synod of the Presbyterian Church. The division in the New School was complete.

All of this was common knowledge to the commissioners who gathered in New Orleans in May of that same year to transact the business coming before the Old School General Assembly. Even though there was a strong sentiment among the men from the North to have the Assembly take a definite stand against slavery, nothing was done. How could one expect otherwise when the Assembly met in a southern city and when so many strong pro-slavery men were present as commissioners? Among these was the Rev. James Smylie of the Presbytery of Louisiana who in 1836 had published his famous pamphlet, *A Review of a Letter from the Presbytery of Chillicothe to the Presbytery of Mississippi on the Subject of Slavery.* As has been previously stated, this was one of the earliest, if not the first, attempt on the part of a southern minister to prove the divine origin of slavery. Smylie was also the one who carried the case against Scott in the Clay controversy to the General Assembly of 1847.

Another important Southern churchman known for his strong pro-slavery views, who was a commissioner to the 1858 Assembly, was the host pastor, Dr. Benjamin M. Palmer. After the southern element of the Old School Presbyterian Church broke away from the Assembly of 1861, the Presbyterian Church in the Confederate States of America was organized on December 4th of that year and Dr. Palmer was elected its first moderator.

With commissioners like Smylie and Palmer and many others holding the same convictions in the Assembly of 1858, no pronouncement on the slavery issue was possible. Moreover, the commissioners who held anti-slavery views had but to look at the vote which had shortly before divided their New School brethren to realize that the same might happen to their church if they insisted on some anti-slavery declaration. So they bided their time. Although Scott never took the extreme stand taken by Smylie and Palmer, yet he did hold that slavery was a political and not a moral issue and therefore the church had no business making pronouncements on the subject. Without a doubt, the strategic role he played in this Assembly as moderator explains in large part the complete silence of that body on the most crucial issue of the day.

The Assembly closed its sessions on May 18th. Scott found it necessary to go to Philadelphia and New York before returning to San Francisco. On his way up the Mississippi River, he stopped over at St. Louis where he visited his brother Eli Davis Scott. While in the east, he was invited to speak in several churches. This moderatorial tour, if it could be so designated, was very short as compared to present day expectations of a moderator of the Presbyterian General Assembly for he was back in his pulpit in Calvary Church on Sunday, July 18th. The July 15th issue of the *Pacific* noted Scott's return "after an absence of three months" but made no mention of his election to the highest office within his denomination. The great honor which had come not only to Dr. Scott but also to Calvary Church was ignored.

THE LIKENESSES OF DR. SCOTT

So far as is known the first likeness of Dr. Scott is an exquisitely wrought cameo cut, as he explained in a letter to his wife dated December 21, 1850, "by the best artist in Rome." Scott was then on his extended European trip and when he saw the beautiful work being done, he ordered two cameos bearing his likeness, one for his wife and the other for his daughter Martha. He explained to Ann: "The two cost $33 without settings which I will leave for your own taste. I hope you are not angry at my prodigality." On the 22nd he referred to the cameos again in another letter to his wife and told her that one of his traveling companions, Mr. Davis, "says my cameo is going to be a perfect likeness & a magnificent thing. If there be sin in this, may it be forgiven." He was pleased with the finished product. Writing on Christmas eve, he added: "They are certainly exquisite pieces of work & my companions say they are admirable likenesses." In answer to his letter of December 21st, Mrs. Scott wrote on January 31st saying: "You could not have decided on any thing that would please Martha & myself so much as to have your cameo likeness for a breastpin. The thought is admirable."

When the author came across these references to Scott's likeness

WILLIAM ANDERSON SCOTT

(*above*) The earliest oil portrait, about 1853, by an unknown artist. Original in First Presbyterian Church, New Orleans.

(*below*) The cameo likeness, carved in ne in December 1850. From the original in San Francisco Theological Seminary.

WILLIAM ANDERSON SCOTT

(*above*) Oil portrait of an unknown date; possibly by the same artist who painted New Orleans portrait. Original owned by Mrs. Paul Foster of Ross, California.

(*below*) The earliest known portrait, about 1853. From an engraving in the 1854 issue of *Cohen's New Orleans Directory*.

being carved in cameo for breastpins, he made inquiry among the Scott descendants to see if one or both of the pins could be located. At first there was complete ignorance on the subject. No one had ever heard of the cameos, but several of the granddaughters did make search. Finally Mrs. Anna Draper of San Francisco, a daughter of Louisiana Scott Foster, showed the author a cameo which she had found among some of the family heirlooms in her possession. She had no idea whom the likeness was supposed to represent. The cameo, beautifully mounted, measures about two by two-and-a-half inches and gives a man's likeness in profile.

A comparison of the cameo with a picture of an oil painting of Scott in the First Presbyterian Church of New Orleans, both made within a few years of each other, shows identical characteristics. The similarity of the hair line over the right forehead, the dimple in the right cheek, and the general contour lines of the face give unmistakable evidence that this is one of the original cameos. Further identification is found in references in several of the letters Scott wrote to his wife during his European tour of 1850-51 to the fact that he was letting his beard grow. The artist who cut the cameo shows a beard, whereas the oil painting does not. Since cameo jewelry was a vogue of the Victorian era, Scott was up-to-date in getting cameo breastpins for his wife and daughter.

Three oil portraits of Scott are in existence. One hangs in a parlor of the First Presbyterian Church of New Orleans; a second is in the home of Mrs. Paul Foster of Ross in California; and the third is in San Francisco Theological Seminary. The first two were by the same artist although neither is signed nor dated. It is possible that the church made arrangements for the first painting to be made and that Dr. Scott then requested a second for himself. In all probability these were painted some time before or during 1853. They show a middle-aged man with dark hair, a strong masculine face, clean-shaven except for long side-burns. The New Orleans portrait shows him standing with an open Bible on the pulpit before him.

An oil painting of Ann Scott, possibly by the same artist who painted the portrait of her husband, is in the home of Mrs. Anna Draper. This shows a woman of about forty years, a brunette with an attractive oval face and dark eyes. The portrait suggests a person of intelligence and strength of character. She is pictured wearing on her breast a broach with a man's profile which was, no doubt, that of her husband. Among the Scott family heirlooms is a miniature portrait of Dr. Scott on an oval breastpin, which measures two-and-a-half by three inches, framed with small pearls. This is in the possession of Louisiana Foster, now living in Carmel.

The first known photograph of Dr. Scott was taken in 1851, an engraving which appeared in the 1854 issue of *Cohen's New Orleans Directory*. He was then wearing a short beard with low cheek whiskers. Another portrait worthy of special mention is a lithograph made by

Charles (or Carl) Fenderick in 1856. The November 1957 issue of the Library of Congress *Quarterly Journal* carries an article nearly four pages long about this artist and his work. The Library owns a collection of twenty-seven watercolors, drawings, sketches and some early lithographs by Fenderick belonging to the period 1837 to 1848. Fenderick specialized in making portraits of prominent people. According to the *Quarterly Journal*, he drew likenesses of "Presidents, members of the Supreme Court, the Cabinet, Members of Congress, and other notables of the day." Among his lithographs are those of President Van Buren and General William Henry Harrison. In 1849 Fenderick joined a company of gold-seekers who went overland to California under the leadership of J. Goldsborough Bruff. While in California, Fenderick pursued his art and included among his portraits of this period is a lithograph of Dr. Scott, which he signed and dated 1856. Only two copies are known to exist. One is in the California Historical Society in San Francisco and the other is in San Francisco Theological Seminary. Since Fenderick was always selective in the choice of his subjects, his willingness to make a lithograph of Scott is evidence of the artist's high regard for the minister.

Scott had a number of photographs taken after he left San Francisco in 1861. A picture taken in 1866, when he was fifty-three years old, shows that his hair was then beginning to turn gray. A third oil painting of Scott was executed by a well known artist of that day, S. W. Shaw. The exact date of the painting is not known except that it was after 1875. According to the late George Otis, a popular painter of California landscapes who lived in Marin County, this portrait of Scott once won a prize in an art show in the Louvre in Paris shortly after it was painted. This report could not be verified. Today this painting is a prized possession of San Francisco Theological Seminary.

THE BIBLE IN PUBLIC SCHOOLS

Elated by his election to the moderatorship of the General Assembly, Scott returned to San Francisco in the summer of 1858 never suspecting that the three most turbulent years of his life lay before him. Controversy was to follow controversy with his opponents, for the most part, being fellow members of the small Presbytery of California together with the continued critical attitude of the *Pacific*. Three major issues came up for debate. The first dealt with the proposal to have the State of California pass a law requiring the reading of the Bible in the public schools; the second centered around the establishment of an Old School Presbyterian college in San Francisco; and the third came to a sharp focus in the correlated problems of slavery and the rebellion. The controversies dovetailed into each other. Before the echoes of the acrimonious debates of one issue died down, the clamor of another was engaging popular attention. The troubled years came to a dramatic climax on September 22, 1861, when Dr. Scott was hanged in effigy for the second time. A few days later he and his family left San Francisco on a self-imposed exile which kept them out of California for over eight years.

Following the resignation of Albert Williams as pastor of the First Presbyterian Church of San Francisco in the summer of 1854, the Rev. William C. Anderson, D.D., was called to be his successor. Dr. Anderson, an able man, arrived in the early fall of 1855. Born in Pennsylvania in 1804, he was, therefore, some nine years older than Scott. He was well educated and had traveled twice to Europe. He had occupied pastorates and teaching positions in Pennsylvania and Ohio and for the five years preceding his call to San Francisco had served as president of Miami University at Oxford, Ohio. He held strong anti-slavery views. Herein lies the basis of the antipathy which quickly developed between Scott and Anderson. From the very beginning of their association in the Presbytery of California, there was a lack of rapport between the two men. One was a southerner and the other a northerner, each with all of the strong convictions and prejudices characteristic of the two sections of the nation on the eve of the Civil War.

Added to this fundamental difference of outlook were some other factors which contributed to the strained feeling which developed between the two. Anderson had been called to rally a congregation which had suffered a great loss in members and financial support to the newly organized Calvary Church. After the initial loss of about ten percent of its members who became charter members of the new organization, another twenty percent subsequently withdrew. Thus about one-third of the members of First Church in 1854 transferred to Calvary Church that year or shortly thereafter. The weakened financial position which resulted did not permit First Church to pay more than $3,500 a year when it extended a call to Dr. Anderson, whereas at the same time Dr. Scott was drawing his $8,000. In addition, of course, each was getting a rental allowance.

Dr. Anderson kept in a desultory manner a diary for these years of his residence in California. This diary is now in the archives of San Francisco Theological Seminary. Some of the entries he made throw considerable light upon the problems he faced. Here, for instance, is his notation for Sunday, October 5, 1856, following a service when only fifty-two were present: "I am nearly hopeless in this church. If God has a work for me here, I wish to do it; but the external evidence seems to be that I am in the wrong place." Rarely was the attendance at a morning service in First Church up to one hundred, while at the same time, ten times as many were crowding into Calvary Church. In face of these facts, it is easy to understand why those still loyal to First Church, and their pastor, should be sensitive to and envious of the spectacular success of Calvary Church. All that was needed for an open break between the two men was for some issue to arise outside of their local churches on which they would take opposite sides. Such an issue arose in the fall of 1858 when most of the Protestant clergy of the State of California united in calling for the passage of a law which would require the reading of the Bible in public schools. Anderson argued vehemently in favor of the proposal; Scott with equal force was against it.

According to Ray Allen Billington's *The Protestant Crusade, 1800-1860* (Chapter VI), a movement was started in Maryland as early as 1838 to require by law the reading of the Bible in the schools of that state. In 1840 and 1841 this was a heated issue in New York State. The question, widely debated in various parts of the nation, did not capture the attention of the Protestant churches of California until the mid 1850s. The chief proponents of making Bible reading in the schools compulsory by state law were the New School Presbyterians and the Congregationalists who argued their cause through their weekly paper, the *Pacific*. Petitions calling for such a law and addressed to the legislators of the state were circulated through most of the Protestant churches. Even though Scott was repeatedly requested by his fellow clergymen to lend the great weight of his support to such a campaign, he steadfastly refused to do so. In this he stood at that time almost alone among the Protestant clergy of the state.

Beginning October 17, 1858, Dr. Anderson delivered a series of four Sunday evening discourses on "The Bible in Common Schools." These were published in several issues of the *Pacific* during the following December and in an abbreviated form as a thirty-one page pamphlet early in 1859. Anderson's approach to his subject consisted in answering four common objections to the proposed law.

In the first place, Anderson denied that the Bible was a "Sectarian Book" because no one sect could claim exclusive rights ot it. The Bible was "the heritage of humanity." Secondly, the Bible was not exclusively "a Protestant Book" because "the fidelity of the translation to the original" made the King James version "almost perfect." Anderson said: ". . . our English Bible *is not a Protestant Book*, unless the original itself be Protestant." In answer to the criticism, "The rights of conscience are trampled on by the use of the Bible in the schools," he argued: "Shall the conscience of one sect, numbering two or three millions, govern, or shall that of all other sects numbering twenty millions?" And he asked why the "millions who compose the evangelic church of America" should take the Bible out of the schools "where their fathers placed it, and subordinate their consciences to the dictates of the Romish church?" And finally, in reply to the argument that the use of the Bible in the public schools was unconstitutional, he claimed that "by no fair construction can the constitution be made to prohibit, or even discountenance, its free and unrestricted use in the schools." A little more than one hundred years later the Supreme Court of the United States ruled to the contrary.

Moved no doubt by Dr. Anderson's discussion of the subject in his pulpit, Dr. Scott on Sunday, November 28, 1858, preached a sermon on "The duty of catechizing our children in the doctrines of our holy religion." In its December 10th issue, the *San Francisco Times* carried a brief review of Dr. Scott's sermon with its hearty endorsement of his position. The paper quoted him as saying: ". . . most of our children will be educated in the Public Schools. Religion cannot be taught to them there; it ought not to be; yet they need religious truth. Then we must have Denominational Schools." Dr. Scott made no mention, according to this newspaper account, of Dr. Anderson or of any other clergyman who differed from him on this subject. Rather he discussed the subject from an objective point of view and emphasized his conviction that religious training should be the responsibility of the home and the church rather than the public school.

Sometime in the latter part of 1858, the *Sacramento Union* carried a reference to the *Pacific* as "an organ of the Presbyterian church." On December 28th, Dr. Scott wrote to the editor of the *Union* correcting the impression which had been given. The editor published the letter. Scott claimed that the *Pacific* itself did not claim to be the organ of any church and added: "Having the honor to be Moderator of the General Assembly which met in New Orleans last May . . . I know whereof I affirm, and have a right, if, indeed it be not my official duty to protest against any such journal as the one above named being considered and appealed to in the future history of this noble state as an organ of the Presbyterian church."

In the January 6, 1859, issue of the *Pacific*, the editor, then the Rev. J. H. Warren, a Congregational minister, took note of Scott's letter to the *Sacramento Union* and devoted thirty column inches to reply. After acknowledging the fact that the *Pacific* had also sent in a correction to the *Union*, the editor with considerable sarcasm rebuked Scott for not being more specific. Which Presbyterian Church was he representing, the Old School or the New School? It was well known that the latter was friendly to the *Pacific*. Warren then added: "The entire country knew our position. . . What need there then, of the Moderator of the last General Assembly of the Presbyterian Church, coming up in the wrath of a Hebrew Hercules or in the frowning majesty of a Giant Judge, to enter a solemn protest against a newspaper mistake?" The mention of a Hebrew Hercules and of a Giant Judge were to two of Scott's books. The editor dipped his pen again into his well of sarcasm and wrote: "No one would ever think of taking such a responsibility unless he had long been a member of Gen. Jackson's family, and had become thoroughly imbued with the daring spirit of the old hero, or else he were infatuated with the idea, that in him, bodily dwelt the *Presbyterian Church*. . . The Pope virtually makes himself the church. Have we a Pope in the Presbyterian church?"

The tone of the editorial stung Scott deeply. He replied in a long letter dated January 12th which Warren published in the January 20th issue of the *Pacific*. The text ran to about twenty-two column inches of fine type. "Some of these statements," wrote Scott referring to the editorial of January 6th, "I deem it due to truth to correct. The tone and style and personal abuse you have seen fit to indulge in, I cannot imitate." Scott touched on the issue of the compulsory reading of the Bible in the public schools. Here is evidence that this was the real reason for the editor's attack on Scott. Scott explained his position: "There is no objection that I can see to the use of the Bible in common day schools; but I do not think it wise, best, expedient and constitutional to force the reading our Bible in our 'free Public schools'—schools that are supported by our public monies. I do not believe it is right under our Constitution to use the State treasury to teach any kind of religious creed or uphold any form of worship."

Editor Warren replied to Scott in the January 20th issue of the *Pacific* in an editorial which extended to forty-eight column inches! Condemning Scott's views on the disputed Bible in the public schools question, he wrote: "These are ideas that Catholics, Romanists and Jesuit, will fight for to the last—ideas which are now at issue in the East and sooner or later must be here." Warren also criticized Scott for his refusal to sign petitions urging the passage by the state legislature of stricter Sunday laws.

Scott's attitude on these questions was incomprehensible to his brethren in the Protestant clergy not only in California but elsewhere throughout the nation. In the December 18, 1858, issue of the Methodist *Christian Advocate* of Portland, Oregon, the editor informed his readers: "You will be surprised to hear that Dr. Scott of the Old School Presbyterian Church preached against the use of God's holy word in public schools. His position, it is said, was defined a few days ago, and leads the public to conclude that on this question he has joined the Atheists, Deists, and Roman Catholics." The editor of the San Francisco *Christian Advocate* on January 28, 1859, likewise accused Scott of "Jesuitism" and wrote: "He has announced a ruinous and destructive heresy on the subject of education . . . such is the system advocated in a leading pulpit in this city. . . The Jesuits, Infidels, and Dr. Scott!" An unidentified newspaper clipping in the Scott Collection in Bancroft Library contains comments from the San Francisco correspondent of the *Boston Recorder* who wrote: "We are at a loss to know what kind in his logic could have thrown him so far off the track. . . Dr. Scott takes ground against the Bible in schools, against chaplains in the Legislature, against all Sunday laws, and generally goes in for the largest liberty on religious subjects, insisting that ours is not a Christian country or Government." William Anderson Scott was a century ahead of his generation.

The Presbytery of California met on March 27, 1859. Only five were present. Dr. Scott was there with his elder, Judge H. P. Coon. Elder Nathanial Gray of First Church came with Dr. Anderson. Also present was the Rev. John Anderson, son of Dr. W. C. Anderson, who, in 1857 at the age of twenty-three, became pastor of the First Presbyterian Church of Stockton. John usually voted with his father on controversial issues.

The main business to come before the March meeting was the election of a commissioner to attend the Old School General Assembly which was to meet the following May in Indianapolis, Indiana. Speaking on the floor of the Synod of the Pacific on October 3, 1860, Dr. Scott explained what happened: "The Reverend Dr. Anderson and myself differ about the compulsory use of the English Bible in the Public Schools. Both of us publish our views; and thereupon Dr. Anderson asks the Presbytery to sustain his and condemn mine. Nor would Dr. Anderson allow me to be appointed delegate to attend the General Assembly of 1859, which as retiring Moderator it was my duty to open and preside over according to the usage of the Church, until he had obtained the vote of the Presbytery condemning my opinion." Evidently after some discussion, Judge Coon introduced the following: "Resolved that in the opinion of Presbytery the subject of the Bible in the Public Schools is one of great importance, and that this Presbytery is in favor of what is commonly understood as the use of the Bible in said Public Schools." The vote was four to one, Dr. Scott alone dissenting. He gave notice of his intention to file a protest at a future meeting. Having passed the resolution, Presbytery then proceeded to elect Scott as its commissioner to the Assembly.

For various reasons, according to a notice which appeared in the *Philadelphia Presbyterian*, Dr. Scott chose not to attend the meeting of the Assembly that year. In Dr. Benjamin Palmer's review of the events of the 1859 Assembly, which is to be found in the *Southern Presbyterian Review*, we may read: "Considerable disappointment was felt in consequence of the absence of the Moderator, the Rev. Dr. Scott of California, whose arrival was anxiously and vainly expected up to the moment when the sessions were to open." Scott explained that his absence was due to the great distance involved and "family reasons." The latter evidently refers to the marriage of his daughter, Martha, affectionately known within the family circle as Mattie, to Nicholas G. Kittle on June 6th.

In her brief sketch of her husband following his death, Mrs. Scott commented: "Husband was so worried and beset with certain people teasing him to sign petitions to the Legislature for Sunday laws, temperance laws, to force the Bible in public schools, &c. and his objections to moving in such matters were so misunderstood or misrepresented that he decided to express his true views in the form of a tractate. Its publication excited a great deal of opposition." She was here referring to her husband's 146 page, paper-bound pamphlet *The Bible and Politics: or, an Humble Plea for Equal, Perfect, Absolute Religious Freedom, and against all Sectarianism in our Public Schools.* The item was published in May 1859 by the H. H. Bancroft & Company of San Francisco. This company was founded by the great historian, Hubert H. Bancroft, whose collection of western Americana forms the nucleus of the present Bencroft Library in the University of California. Bancroft was a member of Calvary Church.

Scott wrote a one page advertisement dated May 5, 1859. Under the Latin title: *"Audi alteram partem*—Hear both sides," he wrote: "I understand the compulsory use of the Bible in our schools to mean teaching religion by stress of law, and this, in our country, I consider fanatical, unconstitutional, unjust, and tyrannical. While I believe, with all my heart, in the Word of God, *I am opposed to any statute to compel me or my child to read or hear the Bible read anywhere, or that shall compel my neighbor, or his child, to hear or read the Bible anywhere contrary to his wishes, and the honest convictions of his own conscience."*

He began his pamphlet by referring to the many personal invectives used by his opponents against him over a period of many months, without mentioning names. The following are a few of the examples he quoted: "He (Dr. Scott) has joined the Atheists, Deists, and Roman Catholics." "A Jesuit in an evangelical Protestant pulpit." "A Jesuit in disguise." And "A high church functionary, a D.D., thundering forth his egotistical anathemas against the Bible as a school book; pointing, as with a finger of scorn, at its pages, as containing matter not proper to be read in schools by the youth of our land." Dr. Scott admitted that he had not attained "to such a sublimity of character as to be wholly indifferent to the good opinion of the religious public." He was frank in saying that he coveted "the suffrages of enlightened and pious and patriotic men." Therefore, in order to answer "These odious flings, innuendoes, misrepresentations and absolute falsehoods," he had decided to set forth his views in the tractate. In doing so, he avoided all invectives, personal references, and sarcasm. Rather, in clear objective language he stated his position.

Here are some quotations from his pamphlet: "I hold that no man is to be taxed for the support of the religious services of another, whether they are performed in a schoolroom, meeting-house, or cathedral." "Ought the Legislature to tax a Catholic to have the Protestant Bible read to or taught to his child; or ought the Legislature to tax a Protestant to have his child taught the Catholic's Bible?" "I deny that the State has any right to take my child from my arms and educate it without my consent." And "If ever the liberties of America perish, it will be by the hands of quasi-religious demagogues. Only sacerdotal hands can ever ply the torch to the temple of our liberties."

The publication of Scott's pamphlet brought an immediate response from Warren and Anderson. Beginning with the May 12th issue of the *Pacific*, a series of editorials and long articles appeared which continued week after week through the next three months. Warren often devoted from three to six full-length columns of the *Pacific*, which had the dimensions of the present day *New York Times*, to the controversy. Among the contributors was a member of Scott's church, a lawyer, Fletcher M. Haight, who wrote at some length on the "Constitutional Review of Dr. Scott's Bible and Politics." Haight was a personal friend of Dr. Scott's and wrote in a calm, objective manner. He sought to prove that there was no constitutional barrier to a law requiring the reading of the Bible in the public schools. A longer series of articles came from Anderson's pen. These same articles also appeared in the San Francisco *Christian Advocate*. Subsequent to their publication in the religious press, Anderson brought out a ninety-two page pamphlet which included both his articles and those of Haight's under the title: *Notes on Dr. Scott's Bible and Politics.* The total number of pages of the three pamphlets published during this controversy was 269, about one-third of the total number of pages in the pamphlets issued during the Clay controversy.

Whereas the limited number of religious periodicals then being published in the West seems to have been united in opposing Dr. Scott's position, the secular press with equal unanimity praised his stand. The *Daily Alta California*, for instance, in its June 24th issue, commented: "We cannot but admire the frankness with which the Rev. Dr. Scott expresses himself, and at the same time the freedom from all sectarian bias which he shows in his discussion."

When the Presbytery of California met on September 12, 1859, Scott was ready to submit a protest against the action of the Presbytery taken at its March meeting. In order to bring the unhappy controversy to an end, Scott called on Anderson and proposed a settlement. He would withdraw his protest if Anderson would cease seeking further action by any of the ecclesiastical courts. At least this was Scott's understanding, so he withdrew his protest. Much to his surprise, Anderson brought up the matter again before the October 7th meeting of the Synod of the Pacific. The synod adopted a resolution calling for the "introduction of the Bible in the Common Schools." Scott, finding that he had some unexpected support for his position among the members of the other presbyteries, then introduced the following which was adopted by a small majority: "Resolved, That this Synod in the adoption of this resolution in relation to the introduction of the Bible in Public Schools, does not intend to favor its compulsory introduction by law into such schools." With this action, Scott was, as he later wrote, "fully satisfied."

For about a year the issue remained dormant. When the synod met on October 4, 1860, Anderson, finding that he had enough support to pass a resolution of his own wording, introduced the following: "Resolved, that in the judgment of this Synod it is the duty of the State to introduce by law the Bible into all Schools." This was adopted by a vote of eleven to six. Dr. Scott submitted a protest in writing. He claimed that the synod did not have the right to dictate to the state. Moreover, he said that the Dr. Anderson had broken his promise to drop the whole matter and that personal issues had become more important than the original proposal of having compulsory reading of the Bible in the public schools. In other words, Scott maintained that the real purpose of the resolution was to condemn him and to "sustain and endorse" Anderson.

As far as the Presbyterians were concerned, this action of 1860 brought the unfortunate controversy to a close. The state legislature did not pass any law regarding the compulsory reading of the Bible in public schools or for a stricter observance of Sunday. The most important consequence of the controversy was the deepening of the rift which separated the two strongest men of the Presbytery until it became a chasm. Other important issues, as that of founding a denominational college, were beginning to arise in the presbytery. Again and again, Anderson and Scott were pitted against each other, but of this further mention will be made later.

THE PACIFIC EXPOSITOR

The extended controversy over the Bible in the public schools convinced Scott that he needed some periodical through which he would be free to express his opinions. Other denominations in California as the Northern and Southern Methodists, the Baptists, the Jews, and even the Mormons had their respective organs. The New School Presbyterians and the Congregationalists cooperated in publishing the *Pacific,* but the Old School Presbyterians had no paper. Scott felt handicapped and frustrated. Because of the ill will existing against him on the part of some of his brethren, he knew that there was no chance that either the Presbytery of California or the Synod of the Pacific would endorse such a venture. If there were to be a periodical for Old School Presbyterians, he would have to accept full responsibility for both its financing and its editing. He knew from his three years' experience with a denominational paper in New Orleans how much work would be involved. Yet he felt that he had no alternative. His opponents held a great advantage over him because they had an effective organ for the dissemination of their views. He felt the situation demanded a new periodical.

Under date of July 18, 1859, Dr. Scott issued a prospectus which began with the statement:

> It is believed there is no portion of our continent where a religious monthly, such as we now offer to our friends and the public, is so much needed as in California. The power of the Press is beyond all calculation. Eternity only can reveal its influence on mankind. All sects and denominations, schools, creeds and parties have their organs, from the daily sheet to the stately quarterly. It is not our wish, however, by this publication to interfere with any other, but to supply what seems to us to be a special and pressing want on this coast.

The name of his monthly magazine was to be *The Pacific Expositor.* The subscription cost was $3.00 per annum.

Dr. Scott planned an octavo sized publication of about fifty pages. It seems probable that he modelled his new magazine after one of the "stately" quarterlies which were being published in the East as the *Biblical Repertory and Princeton Review*, edited by his former professor and friend, Dr. Charles Hodge, and the *Southern Presbyterian Review*, published at Columbia, South Carolina, and edited by the leading spokesman of southern Presbyterians, Dr. James H. Thornwell. Undoubtedly Scott was a subscriber to both of these magazines. He designed to make his periodical somewhat of a combination of the scholarly journal and the weekly newspaper. Each issue would carry a sermon. An examination of the first twelve numbers shows that eight of the sermons were his and four were from other California ministers. Each number would also contain informative articles on religious subjects, book reviews, and brief news items about church events on the west coast and especially in California. Scott outlined the purpose of his new periodical in the prospectus:

> We would, if possible, furnish sermons to be read on the Lord's day, in the lonely places of our valleys and mountains, where there is no pastor or evangelist to open his mouth and show the way of salvation; and into the crowded villages of miners, farmers and travelers, where as yet there is no house of worship. . . It is well known that a large number of the half million souls that are on this coast, do not attend any church or meeting-house; many thousands of them never hear a sermon preached from year to year. . . We hope to make the Expositor *a missionary* that may preach everywhere the colporteur and the evangelist do not go.

In an editorial in the September 1859 issue of the *Expositor*, Scott repeated his hope that the new magazine would be "indeed a paper-pulpit for the family and the solitary."

In an editorial which appeared in the February 1861 issue, he wrote: "We aim at *an original California* journal calculated especially to do good on our coast in our own times. . . We indulge in no personal abuse. We attack nobody. We make but few personal explanations. Our aim is to produce an original California journal that may contribute something towards forming the right kind of a public sentiment, and of a Christian literature for our times." Frequent appeals for subscriptions show that he was experiencing difficulties in making the venture self-supporting. He alone was responsible for any deficit that might have occurred.

Scott issued a special appeal for increased support in the August 1861 issue of the *Expositor* when he reported: "Until the present troubles came upon the country, our circulation was steadily increasing both East and West, and it is still increasing on this coast; but by the cutting off of the mails to the South, we lose over *two hundred subscribers*." Here is evidence that many of his friends throughout the South, especially no doubt in New Orleans, were taking his magazine. All of these subscriptions were lost to him.

In a letter dated April 5, 1860, Dr. Burrowes, who arrived in San Francisco in 1859 to engage in educational work for the Presbyterian Church, wrote a letter to the *Philadelphia Presbyterian* which appeared in its May 12th issue. Dr. Burrowes paid the following tribute to his colleague:

> The Congregationalists, with the New School, the Methodist Church North, and the Methodist Church South, have each a weekly religious newspaper . . . we have nothing but Dr. Scott's *Expositor,* and this has been got up by his personal influence, energy, and toil. Were it not for this, our Church would have no organ on this coast. The Church at home have little idea of the struggle Dr. Scott has been maintaining here in her behalf. No man on the roll of her ministry is more deserving of her sympathy, her support, and her prayers.

An undated newspaper clipping in the Scott Collection likewise bears tribute to his indefatigable labors. This states: "Another characteristic of Dr. Scott is a wonderful facility of doing many things at the same time. . . Instead of having but one iron in the fire . . . he keeps poker, tongs, shovel, and all in a glowing forge at the same time."

The launching of the *Expositor* rather unexpectedly plunged Scott into more and deeper troubles. Shortly after his new periodical appeared, he advocated through its columns the importance of Old School Presbyterians having a denominational college in San Francisco. This aroused immediate opposition from those who favored Old School support for the Congregational and New School College of California which had been founded in Oakland in 1855. A second cause for criticism came from Scott's cautious but evident support of the South in the explosive issues leading up to the Civil War. His writings on the relationship of church and state through his *Expositor* contributed directly to the events which came to a climax when he was hanged a second time in effigy.

The *Pacific Expositor* appeared regularly every month from July 1859 through April 1862. Dr. George Burrowes took over the editorship after Scott left the city on October 1, 1861, and brought out the last six issues.

CITY COLLEGE, SAN FRANCISCO

Old School Presbyterians manifested an interest in the establishment of a denominational school in California from the very beginning of their work. The Rev. Albert Williams went to California in the spring of 1849 under the joint sponsorship of the Board of Missions [which was later called the Board of Home Missions] and the Board of Education. He landed in San Francisco on April 1st and two days later arrived in Benicia at the northern end of the bay where the Rev. Sylvester Woodbridge, Jr., was at work trying to rally support for a Presbyterian church. At that time some real estate promoters had visions of Benicia becoming the main metropolis of the bay and in fact it did have the distinction of being the state capital in 1851-52 and again for a time in 1853. Robert Semple, one of the proprietors of the townsite, offered a plot of land to Williams for a college to be established there under the sponsorship of the Presbyterian Church. His partner, Thomas O. Larkin of Monterey, refused to go along with the idea so the proposal failed to materialize. Williams returned to San Francisco where he saw his greater opportunity in the ministry of the First Presbyterian Church which he founded on May 20th. No doubt the idea of establishing a Presbyterian college at that early date was premature. In the light of later developments, it is well to remember this early interest taken by Williams in an Old School Presbyterian college in California.

Dr. Scott's interest in the establishment of a Presbyterian college dates back to the time when he first arrived in California and looked upon the hills surrounding the magnificent bay. He then resolved that with God's help he would establish both a college and a theological seminary somewhere in that vicinity. His keen interest in education may be due in part to his several years experience teaching before giving full time to the parish ministry, and also to the fact that he had seven children to be educated.

Early in 1855 Dr. Scott wrote a letter which was published in the Philadelphia *Presbyterian* in which he lamented the seeming lack of interest by Old School Presbyterians in establishing a school or a college in California. The criticism moved Dr. Cortlandt Van Rensselaer, secretary of the Board of Education with offices in Philadelphia, to reply. Writing on March 13th, Dr. Van Rensselaer mentioned the fact that the Board had sponsored in part Albert Williams' going to California and that "we have been disappointed beyond measure at the turn things have taken." He wrote: "In the autumn of 1849, brother Williams wrote to us that he was engaged in securing a site for a college at San Jose, and that he designed making it, not denominational, but evangelical. . . We disagreed with him as to the propriety of this course." Nothing came of this proposal. Van Rensselaer's letter points to a basic difference in policy. Williams was interested in an interdenominational institution while the board wanted it to be strictly Old School Presbyterian.

Scott and Van Rensselaer continued to correspond on this subject. On January 25, 1856, Van Rensselaer wrote again about "that California College." He raised the question as to whether the two local presbyteries in California—namely the Presbytery of California and the Presbytery of Stockton—could undertake the establishment of a college. He wrote: "California can only be supplied with ministers in sufficient numbers by raising up men on her own territory for the work," and he asked whether there would be "a demand for a theological department at no distant day in such an institution." In a reply dated March 4, 1856, Scott wrote:

> I perceive you do not see clearly our weakness on this Coast. It is true there is nominally a Synod and three Presbyteries, [one

of which was in Oregon]. The Presbyteries can scarcely meet once a year for want of a quorum. The Synod has never had but one meeting. . . When I first visited this side of the world, I found the Baptists, the Methodists both North and South, the Episcopalians, and New School and Congregationalists on the ground and in strong forces and well fortified and sustained liberally with men & money from home. Each one of the above denominations had a paper (New School & Congregationalists united) & a college, either built or building. Some of their papers have died. . . The Methodist College is flourishing, they have a large brick building at Santa Clara. . . The same course is pursued by the New School & Cong. . . The Baptists I believe have not done much. The Episcopalians have a girls school in this city. . . Other denominations have thrown very serious impediments in the way of establishing an Old School Presbyterian College.

In order to make it easier for the Synod of the Pacific to secure a quorum for its meetings, the General Assembly of 1856 erected the Presbytery of Benicia. The synod met on October 21st of that year with eight ministers and three elders present. Each of the four presbyteries was represented. Dr. Anderson was elected moderator. Among the items of business discussed was that of education. After some debate, the nature of which is not disclosed, the synod authorized the appointment of a board of regents consisting of five ministers and five elders to see what could be done about establishing high schools and a college within the bounds and under the care of the synod. The synod stipulated that four members of the board would constitute a quorum, thus making it easier for meetings to be held. Anderson was made chairman. The synod did not meet again for want of a quorum until the fall of 1859, three years later. In his report of that meeting published in his *Pacific Expositor*, Scott said: "For three years Dr. Anderson has been Chairman of a Board appointed for that purpose by the Synod, but for various reasons the Board was never called together, and nothing was done." Scott was on the board but was unable to do anything through this channel without Anderson's cooperation.

When the Presbytery of California met in April 1858, the subject of the establishment of a denominational school again came up for discussion. Scott, mindful of his correspondence with Van Rensselaer, was pressing for action. To Scott's great satisfaction, the presbytery unanimously voted "that the time had come for the establishment of an Institution of learning under its care." Even Anderson, who was present, assented. Later Anderson claimed that he was thinking only of a grammar school and not of a college. The presbytery appointed Scott and Anderson to a committee to see what could be done and Scott was asked to communicate with the board of education asking for its financial assistance.

Following the meeting of the General Assembly of 1858, Scott made a trip to Philadelphia to intercede directly with the board. Writing on June 18, 1858, Dr. Van Rensselaer said to Scott: "Education in California is a great subject. It has become greater in our view, since the interview you had with us." The board began looking for a suitable man to send to California for this work. Lack of funds was a serious handicap, and during the months that followed, a number of letters passed between Scott and Van Rensselaer on this subject. The latter reported on several possible candidates who had been investigated but for various reasons all had been rejected. On December 4, 1858, Scott suggested the idea of a "female academy in California," which Dr. Van Rensselaer thought was "admirable." "We must take care of the girls," he wrote. "Female Academies are an essential part of Zion's institutions."

Because of the controversy over the use of the Bible in public schools which began in the fall of 1858, antipathies between Anderson and Scott made cooperation between the two practically impossible. Thus the more Scott argued for a denominational college, the more inclined Anderson was to object.

Sometime in the fall of 1858, probably in November, the Rev. George Burrowes, D.D., called on Dr. Cortlandt Van Rensselaer and offered his services to the Board of Education. He had heard of the need for an educator in California and indicated his willingness to go there. He tells us in his journal that while a student in Princeton Theological Seminary he had "determined to devote myself to the life of a foreign missionary." Circumstances had arisen after his graduation in 1835 which led him to abandon this purpose. But with the passing of the years, he had become increasingly conscience stricken over his failure. According to his journal, the words of Ecclesiastes 5:4 haunted him: "When thou vowest a vow unto God, defer not to pay it; for he hath no pleasure in fools: pay that which thou hast vowed." When Dr. Burrowes walked into Dr. Van Rensselaer's office, he also walked into the life of Dr. Scott.

George Burrowes was born in 1811 and was therefore about two years older than Scott. The two were together in Princeton Theological Seminary in 1834 but there is no evidence to show that they were then more than acquaintances. Burrowes kept a diary with more or less regularity from April 1827 to April 1892. Ten of these manuscript volumes are in the archives of San Francisco Theological Seminary. In 1889 Dr. Burrowes wrote a journal, as he called it, in which he reviewed in some detail his connections with Dr. Scott and City College of San Francisco. Following his death on April 19, 1894, the journal was sent to the Presbyterian Historical Society in Philadelphia which published it in three issues of the *Journal of Presbyterian History* in 1955. From the diaries and journal of Dr. Burrowes we gain a wealth of detailed information regarding the troubled events connected with the endeavor to establish an Old School Presbyterian college in California.

A perusal of the Burrowes' diaries reveals a soul, deeply mystical and intensely devoted to Christ. His *A Commentary on the Song of Solomon,* published in 1853 is characteristic of his mystical outlook. Burrowes had an irenic disposition and would never engage in controversy if he could possibly avoid it. In a letter to Dr. Scott dated March 15, 1859, Dr. Van Rensselaer described him as being "a lovely unpretending Christian, of gentlemanly manners & of some experience in teaching. He is moreover a good preacher. He has a wife but no children."

Burrowes had served as pastor of the West Nottingham, Maryland, church from 1835 to 1850. He then became professor of languages in Lafayette College where he remained until 1855. He was as proficient in reading Latin and Greek as he was in English. According to a statement made in his diary in his old age, he had read the Greek New Testament through a total of 373 times.

Following his service as a member of the faculty at Lafayette College, Burrowes accepted a pastorate at Newtown, Pennsylvania. But at heart he was a teacher and soon longed for the classroom again. This is why he called on Dr. Van Rensselaer who immediately felt that he was the very man for the proposed San Francisco school. After some deliberation, Burrowes came to feel that the opportunity opening up in California was in truth a call from God and by the end of December 1858 had made his decision to go. There was some delay because of a severe illness which continued through the first part of 1859.

On June 13th, Dr. Van Rensselaer informed Dr. Burrowes that the board had allotted $500 for travel expenses for him and his wife to California. He also said: "We advise you to consult with Dr. Scott, who has written to us many letters on this subject, and who was the means of our opening the matter to your own mind. You will find in him a noble counsellor and a generous friend. Dr. Anderson will, I doubt not, also sustain you with all his strength." Dr. Van Rensselaer was far too sanguine in his opinion of Dr. Anderson's cooperation. Although Burrowes may have known something of the tangled situation in San Francisco, he later discovered that it was far more complicated than he had been told. Dr. and Mrs. Burrowes sailed from New York for their new appointment on July 5th and arrived in San Francisco on the 24th.

In the meantime the Rev. Albert Williams had returned to San Francisco. Williams, after resigning his pulpit in First Church, had gone back to his former home in New Jersey. On March 8, 1859, one of Scott's friends at Princeton wrote to him saying: "Mr. A. Williams is about breaking up here for a return to California. His mind is bent on laying the foundation of some educational institution." Knowing that he was not in good standing with the Board of Education, Williams realized that whatever he did along educational lines in San Francisco would have to be on an independent and self-supporting basis. Burrowes wrote in his journal that when he arrived in San Francisco he found "the Rev. A. Williams at work with a school of four boys in the Chinese Chapel" on Stockton Street. And he added: "The first time I went to the Post Office in San Francisco, I saw a frame with a glass in it hanging in the thoroughfare containing the Rev. A. Williams' circular for San Francisco University Grammar School." It was dated July 12, 1859.

Burrowes received a warm welcome from Dr. Scott who invited him to occupy the pulpit of Calvary Church on Sunday, July 31st. Since Williams had already started his school, Scott advised Burrowes to wait until the fall meeting of the synod when the whole matter would come up for review and decision. Scott even suggested the possibility of Burrowes going to some other place and "leave Mr. Williams in peaceable possession of the city for his school." This proposal Burrowes refused to accept. "I told him," he wrote, "the Presbyterian Board of Education had spent $500 in getting me here, and I felt bound as an honest and honorable man to go to work in that cause and in this city." He did consent to wait until the synod met in October before starting a school. In the meantime he agreed to supply the pulpit of Westminster Presbyterian Church of Sacramento.

When the Presbytery of California met on October 3, 1859, a few days before synod, Dr. Burrowes was received as a member. By this time it was evident that Williams was unable to start a school. The action taken by presbytery at its April meeting regarding the establishment of "an Institution of learning" came up for discussion. Dr. Anderson and his elder, Judge R. H. Waller, stated that since "the word Institution is now intended to mean college," they were opposed to such. Anderson explained his stand by saying the Old School Presbyterians were too weak in numbers and resources to support a denominational college. He favored cooperation with the New School Presbyterians and Congregationalists in their College of California in Oakland. The presbytery finally voted to refer the whole matter to the synod.

The Synod of the Pacific in 1859 had four presbyteries, twenty churches, and twenty-seven ministers. Present at the meeting which began on October 4th were thirteen ministers and five elders. The October issue of the *Pacific Expositor* contained a brief summary of the actions of the synod including the following: "After mature deliberation, the Synod by a large vote resolved to establish *a Grammar School, as the beginning of a College or University in this city,* and recommended Rev. Dr. Burrowes as Principal, and the Rev. Albert Williams as general financial agent. It is expected that the school will begin in a few weeks, at least by the first Monday of November." In the November issue of the *Expositor,* Dr. Scott gave more details. As chairman of the Committee on Education, he submitted a series of eight resolutions which "were discussed at considerable length." Describing what happened, Scott wrote: "Rev. Dr. Anderson opposed these resolutions from beginning to end and was supported in whole or in part by Judge Waller, ruling elder of his church, and by his son, Rev. J. Anderson of Stockton . . . but on the final vote adopting them, we heard but one negative, that of Dr. Anderson."

Dr. Anderson inserted a "card" in the newspapers following the meeting of the synod in which he gave reasons for his opposition. He argued that the Old School Presbyterians were "utterly unable to establish a college" and that the venture proposed "would certainly prove a failure." He said that "the only possible hope of successful issue 'of such an attempt was found in the union of lovers of learning of different denominational views, and that the strictly sectarian form of the proposed college would prevent such a union." And in the third place, he argued that since the College of California was "already in successful operation, free from all *ecclesiastical control,*" this was sufficient "for the wants of the Presbyterians of our Synod." Scott also quoted Anderson as having said that if Dr. Burrowes wanted to have a grammar school, that was all right but that if this were intended to become a college "he would have nothing to do with it, good, bad, nor indifferent."

On the evening after the Synod of the Pacific closed its sessions, the Congregationalists and New School Presbyterians held a meeting in the First Congregational Church of San Francisco. Anderson attended and in a public statement identified himself with the College of California. He said in part:

> I came to this coast believing in the ecclesiastical control of Colleges. At the first meeting of our Synod that I attended, we appointed a Board of Regents. We cast about to see what could be done—could do nothing—could not build a College. . . I have changed my views, and come to the conclusion that the true idea for building a College in California is to unite. I have no doubt this is the basis of a successful work. I have had experiences in colleges. It is impossible to found a denominational College under ecclesiastical control in this State. All the Protestant denominations must be represented. Away with the Shibboleths and Sibboleths! Let them sink. The Devil made them. I am happy, I say, to identify myself publicly with this College of California.

The Congregationalists and New School Presbyterians were so delighted to see a prominent Old School minister come over to their side that they made him not only a member of the board of trustees for the college but also president of the board. He was serving in that capacity when on April 16, 1860, the trustees selected the site for a new campus in what is now Berkeley. When these grounds were consecrated to learning, he offered the prayer. A bronze plaque may be seen today on Founders Rock, near what was once the northeast corner of the campus, which bears the names of those who selected the site, and Dr. Anderson's name heads the list. About five years after Anderson left California, the trustees of the College of California found themselves faced with difficult financial problems. They finally decided that the only way out of their dilemma was to turn the college over to the state. This was done in 1868 and thus the present University of California came into being. The Rev. Samuel H. Willey was the first acting president.

At one time Dr. Scott was invited to become a trustee of the College of California. This he declined. Dr. Anderson was mistaken in his prophecy that no denominational college could survive in the state. The Methodist College of the Pacific, founded in 1851, now the University of the Pacific at Stockton, is but one institution under ecclesiastical control which has proved him wrong.

Answering Dr. Anderson's position, Dr. Scott in the November issue of the *Expositor* argued at some length in favor of a denominational college. He wrote:

> We do not believe that it is practicable to build up an efficient institution under the government of a number of different sects. A mixed neutral concern for the training of youth is an impossibility. . . We must have a State University in which as such no sect or denomination can be known, like the University of Virginia. And such an Institution must be under the direction of the Governor and Legislature, and not under the control of a quasi-ecclesiastical or denominational Board of Trustees. . . For ourselves we are frank to say that we prefer a College with a *positive* religion, and not one that is any thing or nothing. We are in favor of the Public Schools and of a State University, and at the same time we are in favor of denominational Schools; but we do not believe that any religion or sect or denomination, should be supported in any way by law. . .

Dr. Burrowes in his journal has the following comment on the college issue:

> The truth is—Dr. Anderson and Dr. Scott were in deadly antagonism. Dr. Anderson had been won over by the friends of Oakland to the interests of their institution; they were determined that no other college should be started, if they could help it . . . and they were using Dr. Anderson for drawing off the Old School influence to feed their undertaking. The controversy between Dr. Scott and Dr. Anderson on the questions of Sunday laws and of the Bible in Public Schools was then in its vigor.

Several weeks after the meeting of Synod, Dr. Anderson chanced to meet Dr. Burrowes and said to him:

> Now, I wish to give you a piece of advice as a friend. I have been several years in California; I know it and I know San Francisco well, and the state of public sentiment. There is great opposition felt to this undertaking of yours. It can never succeed. It can prove nothing but a failure; and as a friend I would advise you to have nothing to do with it. If you do go on with it, you will utterly fail; and you will find that in a year or eighteen months, it will leave you bankrupt in purse and character.

According to Burrowes' journal, the Rev. John Anderson said to him about a year later: "I will fight you—that is, your institution as long as I live."

Dr. Burrowes opened his boys' school in the large basement room of Calvary Church on Tuesday, November 1, 1859. He never forgot the unpromising beginnings, for in his old age he wrote:

> The morning was foggy and gloomy. So violent had been the opposition to our undertaking that I supposed the beginning would be small. But even my humblest expectations were above the mark. After all the resolutions of Synod, and the advertisements that had been published for four weeks, there were present only four small boys, William and Chalmers Scott, Prentiss Selby, and Freddy Henderson, the last not yet six years old. The average age of the four could hardly be more than ten years. Every thing was gloomy and discouraging in the extreme. Dr. Scott and three or four others were the only ones to bid us God speed.

When asked by a friend before leaving the East what he planned to do after his arrival in San Francisco, Dr. Burrowes had replied: "Any thing necessary for pushing forward the object of my Mission, even though it be necessary for me in doing this to teach children the alphabet." And then in his 1889 journal he commented: "At the time, I did hardly suppose it would come to this; yet this it was necessary for me at the beginning to do." The two Scott boys, ages sixteen and fourteen, were old enough to take high school work including Latin and Greek in which Dr. Burrowes delighted.

There was no school furniture. "The only desk I had to sit at," wrote Burrowes, "was a table found among the rubbish in another room, which, having been thrown aside as useless, had only three legs, and had a fourth leg supplemented by my splitting off a piece from a pine box and nailing it on in the place of the fourth leg." The enrollment slowly increased to eleven by Christmas time. Six more entered after New Years and by May 1st the number totaled twenty-six. By this time assistant teachers had been hired. Although Dr. Burrowes got some financial help from the board, the school was conducted almost entirely on the income received from tuition fees. The public examination held in June at the end of the first year's work received much favorable comment. By this time Dr. Burrowes' ability as a teacher and school administrator was recognized.

By July 1st it was clearly apparent that new quarters had to be secured. Dr. Scott found a lot for sale, $137\frac{1}{2}$ feet square, at the corner of Stockton and Geary Streets in what is now the very heart of San Francisco. The site is located at the southeast corner of Union Square and is now occupied by the store, The City of Paris. The price was $10,000. Scott paid the first $1,000 and with the help of two of his elders, Judge H. P. Coon and Henry H. Haight, raised the balance

City College and Chapel at Geary and Stockton Streets, San Francisco
From the *Pacific Expositor*, July 1861. In 1864 an extension of sixty-four feet was added
to the main building. In 1876 the building was moved to Haight Street.

largely from members of Calvary Church. Even though Williams had been appointed by synod to be the financial agent for the new church, he failed to render any assistance.

An account of Dr. Scott's report before the October 1860 meeting of the synod appeared in the November issue of the *Expositor*. Although the report was headed "Dr. Burrowes' School," we meet here for the first time the new title CITY COLLEGE. He told of the plans that were then being made for the erection of "a College Hall" on their new site. He stressed the fact that: "This College will be open alike to all creeds and religions," and that: "Though controlled by Old School Presbyterians, no religious test will ever be required." He pointed out the financial advantage to parents of having such an institution in their midst. "It is much cheaper to send our sons from our own doors to college," he argued, "than to board them away from home." And he shared his dream: "We are now trying to lay the foundations of a College that shall be to San Francisco and the whole Pacific world, what the University of Edinburgh has been to Scotland and to Christendom."

In the December issue of the *Expositor* appeared an article under the caption "Our City at Present" which included the following statistics: "White male population, 49,343; white females, 23,985. Total white population, 73,328. Chinese, 3,150; Colored, 1,605. Total population, 78,083." It was also stated that "Whole number of scholars attending public schools, 6,201," and that 1,988 scholars were enrolled in the nineteen Sunday Schools conducted by the various Protestant churches.

The prospect of a new building for the college lifted the attendance from fifty-five in the fall of 1860 to over eighty at the beginning of the new year. Of this latter number forty-three were under fourteen years of age and presumably all in the grammar school grades; twenty-two were fourteen to sixteen; and fifteen were over sixteen. Out of the latter group the first college freshman class was formed.

The new two-story building, which measured forty by sixty feet, fronted on Stockton Street and had its longer side parallel with Geary Street. On Tuesday morning, February 5, 1861, the student body of about eighty, led by Dr. Burrowes and the other four teachers, marched from the basement of Calvary Church to their new college home. Both Dr. Burrowes and Dr. Scott spoke at the dedication ceremonies. Their addresses were published in the March *Expositor*. In his old age, Dr. Burrowes recalled how the sand dune on the south side of the building crowded upon them and how this "had to be shoveled away from the side every few days to enable us to get out into the lot."

The sand was gradually cleared away and a chapel erected by Calvary Church which was designed to be used both by the college and also by a mission Sunday School. In April 1861 an elaborate twelve-page prospectus advertising the college was issued which carried a picture of the two buildings. By that time the college had been incorporated under the ambitious title "The Collegiate School of the City College of San Francisco." This was the first college to be established in the city. It has no relationship to the present day institution of the same name in San Francisco. The prospectus gave the names of the fifteen members of the board of trustees. Scott was listed as president. Other ministerial members included included Dr. Burrowes and the Rev. Sylvester Wood-bridge, Jr. Among the elder members were several from Calvary Church including H. P. Coon, H. H. Haight, F. Henderson, Thomas H. Selby, and J. B. Roberts. The names of the 127 students who had been enrolled during the previous year were also listed.

In May 1861 a Female Seminary was opened in the basement room of Calvary Church under the direction of the Rev. C. R. Clarke. This was another of Dr. Scott's projects. In the report of the educational activi-ties of the synod submitted to its October 1861 meeting, Scott said: ". . . the Rev'd C. R. Clarke, a licentiate of our church, and gradu-ate of Princeton with the assistance of his wife has established a collegiate school for girls in the city of San Francisco. There are between 30 and 40 pupils in this school, and its prospects are considered good." This Female Seminary, which had hardly been started before Dr. Scott found it necessary to leave the city on the following October 1st, was still in existence when he returned in 1870. In a letter written to Scott by Stephen Franklin on October 27, 1861, the following reference was made to Clarke's strong sympathies with the Northern cause: "Poor Brother Clarke was invited to preach a Sabbath or two since & prayed so earnestly that the Lord would crush out rebellion that he is not likely ever to be called upon to preach again. There was a rebellion in the church at once. The sensitiveness of the people to anything which they consider adverse to your views is a gratifying indication that their hearts are in the right place." Clarke was ordained by the Presbytery of California in 1866 and is listed in the *Minutes of the General Assembly* as a teacher and evangelist in San Francisco for the years 1862-70. It is possible that he conducted a private school for girls during these years.

On September 14, 1861, shortly before his resignation, Dr. Scott wrote out the second annual report of City College for the fall meeting of the Synod of the Pacific. In reviewing the events of the year, he mentioned the erection of the two buildings, the publication of the first catalogue, and the fact that the college had 102 students enrolled. A freshman class had been organized, thus the actual work of college instruction had been begun, and seven instructors were "constantly employed." Within one year the attendance had increased fourfold. The college was an eminent success and all signs pointed to ever increasing usefulness.

Difficult days came following Dr. Scott's departure from the city. Friends of the college were hesitant to give financial help because they did not know what action the Synod of the Pacific might take in regard to the institution. Burrowes in his journal explained the situation. "The Synod had done us no good; they had done us much evil. From the Spirit manifested we could not tell what might be yet done. From every meeting of Synod our friends came home harrassed and worried,—at last disgusted. The College was a bone of contention and kept our meetings in constant disturbance. I have remarked, and without exaggeration, that if I had been a robber let loose on this coast, I need not have encountered more opposition in my undertaking." Finally the board of trustees of the college decided that it was best to sever all connection with the synod. Request to this effect was made at the October 1862 meeting of the synod. With but one dissenting vote, that of Albert Williams, the synod acceded to the request of the trustees. Thereafter the board of trustees of City College was self-perpetuating and the college itself was entirely free of ecclesiastical control.

In a letter to Scott dated November 11, 1862, H. H. Haight commented on the action taken by the synod by writing: "Mr. Williams made an hour's speech against the resolution & voted alone in the negative." It is somewhat difficult to understand Williams' position unless it be that he felt he would have a better chance to work into the administration of the college after Dr. Scott's removal from the city if it remained under synod's control. Haight felt relieved. "So we are finally through with that quarrel," he wrote, and added: "The College lot is worth today about $30,000 & will be worth $75,000 in a very few years if no calamity befalls us here." He also reported that steps were being taken to acquire a twenty-five acre campus at University Mound about three miles south of the site at Stockton and Geary Streets. But of this more later.

We can but speculate as to what would have been the history of City College if Dr. Anderson and Dr. Scott could have worked together in harmony during the critical years of its beginning. After Dr. Scott's guiding hand was removed from the administration of the college and the institution itself was cut loose from church control, its fortunes gradually declined. In spite of the valiant efforts Dr. Scott made to save the college after his return to San Francisco in 1870, the school was lost to the church. Thus the Presbyterians missed their great opportunity to have a college or a university in what is now Northern California.

THE PRESBYTERIAN CHURCH
AND THE APPROACHING CRISIS

The years leading up to the outbreak of hostilities in the war between the North and the South were troubled and difficult years for the religious, as well as for the political leaders of the nation. While debates on the vital issues of the day were being carried on in Congress and through the editorial columns of the nation's newspapers, similar deep differences of opinion were being expressed in the various ecclesiastical courts of the land and in the religious press. The Old School Presbyterian Church was deeply involved as the whole basic theory of the relationship of the church to the state was under discussion.

Following the division of the Presbyterian Church into the two bodies in 1837, the Old School Presbyterians found themselves with a large membership in the South. This fact accounts for the hesitancy of the Old School to make pronouncements against slavery. The subject did come up for debate in the Assembly of 1845 which declared: "The Church of Christ is a spiritual body, whose jurisdiction extends only to the religious faith and moral conduct of her members." The Assembly dismissed the whole slavery question by saying that it could not "denounce the holding of slaves as necessarily a heinous and scandalous sin." But with the passing of the years after 1845, there was an increasing sensitivity on the part of the Northerners regarding the moral implications in slavery. At the same time a parallel tendency arose among the Southerners to take refuge in the argument that slavery was a political rather than a religious question and should not, therefore, be discussed in church courts. The stronger the abolition movement grew in the North, the stronger and more determined was the conservative reaction in the South to maintain the *status quo*.

The extreme sensitivity of the Southerners to any pronouncement by the assembly on any issue considered by them to be extraneous to the "spiritual" message of the church is reflected in some actions taken and not taken in the 1859 and 1860 assemblies. Dr. Scott as the retiring moderator of the 1858 assembly was supposed to open the sessions in 1859 but, as has been stated, was unable to attend. During the course of the meetings, an elder commissioner from the North introduced a resolution which called for a commendation of the American Colonization

Society. Many of the Southerners were in full sympathy with the main purpose of this society, which was to send freed Negroes to Liberia in Africa, and Dr. Scott had in 1850 published an address that he had made endorsing the endeavor. But the introduction of the proposed resolution into the assembly aroused some of the Southern commissioners to object. The merits of the plan were not questioned but rather the right of the assembly to take action either pro or con on such a subject.

Dr. Benjamin M. Palmer, Dr. Scott's successor in the New Orleans church, wrote a review of the actions of the 1859 Assembly which appeared in the fall issue of the *Southern Presbyterian Review*. Commenting on the debate which centered about the proposed resolution, Palmer wrote: "The interest of the debate turned simply upon the views brought out as to the true nature of the Church of Christ." Among the commissioners present was Dr. James H. Thornwell, a member of the faculty of the Presbyterian Theological Seminary at Columbia, South Carolina, and one of the most influential of all of the southern Presbyterian clergy. In 1847, when he was only thirty-four years old, Thornwell was elected moderator of the Old School Assembly. When Dr. Thornwell rose in the Assembly of 1859 to oppose the resolution endorsing the Colonization Society, all listened with rapt attention. Of this Palmer wrote:

> We have often heard Dr. Thornwell in the conduct of an argument far more elaborate than the present, but have rarely heard him in a more brilliant and rhetorically effective speech than this. . . The Church of God, he said, is exclusively a *spiritual* organization and possesses none but *spiritual power*. It was her mission to promote the glory of God and the salvation of men from the curse of the law. She had nothing to do with the voluntary associations of men for various civil and social purposes, they were outside of her pale. . . The question of colonization is a question of worldly policy.

Thornwell swung the Assembly to his views. The proposed resolution was rejected.

Scott in an editorial entitled "Mission of the Church" which appeared in the July issue of his *Pacific Expositor* applauded the action of the assembly in regard to the Colonization Society. Again Scott quoted the section from Chapter xxxi of the Westminster Confession of Faith which reads: "Synods and councils are to handle or conclude nothing, but that which is eccliastical; *and are not to intermeddle with civil affairs.*" Scott italicized the last clause. Commenting on Dr. Thornwell's speech, he said: "It is not a new doctrine that the Church is purely a spiritual body, and is not to meddle with any secular or civil affairs. It is the doctrine of the Bible and of our Confession of Faith." Scott was deeply committed to this theory of church-state relationship and in full consistency with this view wrote in his editorial: "For this reason we have declined to have anything to do with the Presbyterian Historical Society as a church. Drive out of the Church, colonization societies, abolition societies and pro-slavery societies." Such an expression of opinion in the very first number of the *Expositor* was most disturbing to members of Calvary Church who held contrary views.

The Presbytery of California at its March 1860 meeting re-elected Dr. Scott a commissioner to the General Assembly. James B. Roberts, an elder in Calvary Church, was selected as the lay commissioner. The session of the church on April 5th took the following action: "Resolved, That in view of the Pastor's health, and the importance thereto of some relaxation from pastoral duties, as well as his recent appointment   .   .   . as a delegate to the General Assembly to meet in Rochester [New York] on the 17th of May ensuing, leave of absence is hereby accorded   .   .   . in order that he may make the journey contemplated leaving about the middle of April and returning D.V. [Deo volente] about the middle of July."

The Scott Collection in Bancroft Library contains some notes made by Mrs. Scott about her husband after his death. Included is the following brief description of his travels by overland stage to St. Louis:

> He attended the Gen. Assem. at Rochester just before the war by going overland by the Butterfield Route, through Indian territory, Arizona, and Texas. He was 21 days in a small mail wagon —the sides lined with fire arms, from S.F. to St. Louis. They traveled day and night—only stopping to change horses and get food. Husband complained of aching limbs from long confinement. But said he got a good idea from the horses that quite relieved him. So when they stopped, he would get out, stretch himself on the ground and roll over until his circulation was quite restored.

According to a letter dated June 19, 1962, and addressed to the author from Waddell F. Smith of San Rafael, a descendant of one of the founders of the pony express and an authority on the overland route, the total distance covered by Dr. Scott in 1860 was a little less than 2,800 miles. Smith wrote: "The eastbound stage left San Francisco, crossed Pacheco Pass and on to Los Angeles where it picked up mail and passengers. From there the route went through Fort Yuma, California; Tucson, El Paso, and on up to Tipton, Missouri, which was the terminus of the railroad, 230 miles west of St. Louis.   .   . The schedule, as provided by the mail contract, was 25 days and the operation was semi-weekly and pretty steadily on schedule, so to have made it in 21 days would have been 'a record.' " Of course, Mrs. Scott, writing many years later, could easily have been mistaken as to the number of days involved. After deducting the 230 miles of railroad travel, this means that if Scott spent twenty-four days on the road he would have had to average about 110 miles each twenty-four hours or a little more than four miles an hour day and night. This must have been a gruelling experience, especially for one who was not considered to be in robust health.

An undated clipping from the *St. Louis Presbyterian* in the Scott Collection in Bancroft Library reported that: "The Rev. W. A. Scott, of San Francisco, passed through this city on his way to Rochester. . . He came through the Southern Land Route, and notwithstanding the excessive fatigue of continuous travel, day and night, he looked remarkably well. He spent several days at the residence of his brother, E. D. Scott, Esq., in this city, so that he had an excellent opportunity for recruiting his exhausted strength." He preached twice on Sunday, May 13th, in two of the city's Presbyterian churches "to overflowing audiences." He evidently completed his journey to Rochester by railroad.

When the commissioners gathered at Rochester on May 17, it was discovered that the retiring moderator of 1859 was not present, so Dr. Scott, as the retiring moderator of the 1858 Assembly, was asked to preside until a new moderator was elected and to preach the traditional opening sermon. He selected for his text 1 Cor. 2:2: "For I determined not to know anything among you save Jesus Christ and him crucified." The July 1860 issue of the *Pacific Expositor* carried a brief summary of the sermon including the following: "The minister of the Gospel who would preach Christ as Paul preached, must preach him experimentally —he must be a truly converted man. There is something fearful in the idea of an unconverted man being a minister of the Gospel." In this rare privilege of preaching before a Presbyterian General Assembly, Dr. Scott was majoring on that which had always been central in his pulpit presentations ever since the days when he was a circuit rider in northwestern Tennessee.

The *Southern Presbyterian Review* for July 1860 commented: "It was an able, eloquent and earnest discourse on the work of the ministry. Dr. Scott set forth, with unction and power, the subject, and manner and method of true Gospel preaching. . ." An undated item from a Rochester paper, reprinted in the July 31st issue of the *San Francisco Herald*, reported: "About the preacher, I will only say that the prominent marks of his pulpit exercises are earnestness and unaffected simplicity. . . There is no attempt at creating sensations—no mannerisms—no affection of learning or oratory—but a simple and earnest endeavor to convey the truth of which he is treating to the minds of his hearers."

Among the commissioners present at this assembly were the leading advocates of the theory that the church was "purely a spiritual body" and should not meddle in political affairs. Among them were Dr. J. H. Thornwell and his colleague on the faculty of the seminary at Columbia, South Carolina, Dr. John B. Adger. Dr. Thornwell was another of the Southern ministers who had argued for the divine sanction of slavery. In a report on this subject given to the Synod of South Carolina on November 6, 1851, Thornwell stated: "The Scriptures not only fail to condemn—they as distinctly sanction slavery as any other social condition of man. . . What Scriptures have sanctioned, she does not condemn." Although we have no evidence of Scott taking such an extreme position as this on the subject of slavery, he was in full sympathy with Dr. Thornwell's stand against any pronouncements by the church on social or political issues.

Also present at the 1860 Assembly were such outstanding leaders from the North who held opposite views, as Dr. Gardiner Spring, pastor of the Brick Presbyterian Church of New York City. Dr. Spring assisted Dr. Scott in the worship services at the opening of the assembly. A year later it was Dr. Spring who introduced the resolution which called for an endorsement by the assembly of the federal government, the adoption of which was the cause for the division of the Old School Presbyterian Church into its northern and southern branches. But of this more will be said later. In between the opposing views as represented by Thornwell and Spring was Dr. Charles Hodge of Princeton who was also present at the 1860 Assembly. Dr. Hodge sometimes supported and was sometimes critical of each point of view.

Writing in the July 1860 issue of the *Princeton Review,* Dr. Hodge had the following comment to make on the tension which was felt at the assembly over the explosive issue of the church making pronouncements on social or political problems:

> More apprehension was felt in reference to this subject than any other which was expected to come before this Assembly. The ground understood to be taken last year at Indianapolis was that the church was bound to restrict her deliverances to her own members, and to matters under her control; that organizations outside of her pale, however objectionable or praiseworthy, could be neither recommended nor objected to; and the action of the state, however inconsistent with the word of God, could not be testified against. . . Very great and very general dissatisfaction was excited by this new doctrine concerning the right and duty of the church. It was felt that this would put a muzzle over her lips, and forbid her exercising one of the highest and most important prerogatives.

Dr. Scott occupied a key position in the Assembly when he was made chairman of the Committee on Bills and Overtures. Dr. Hodge was one of the members. This committee was the largest and most important committee of the assembly. Each state in which Old School Presbyterians were at work was represented and an effort was made to include men of divergent points of view. The September 1860 issue of the *Pacific Expositor* carried the following quotation from the *Presbyterian Banner* regarding the type of men present as commissioners:

> They were industrious men; they came from the Presbyteries to do the business of the Church, and neither cared to make speeches,

nor allowed themselves to be influenced by the speeches that were made. I cannot, perhaps, have selected a better type of this class of members than William A. Scott, D.D., of California, the Chairman of the Committee on Bills and Overtures. He is a man of few words, and those are always well chosen; a man of action, and his actions are guided by sound judgment. The business which passed through his hands, as Chairman of the above mentioned Committee, was immense; and it was, for the most part, reported to the Assembly with admirable judiciousness.

Reporting on the work of the assembly in the August *Expositor*, Dr. Scott commented on the number of "inflammatory" overtures which came before his committee. One such overture sought the assembly's endorsement of the Colonization Society. A number dealt with the slavery issue. Others agitated for temperance reforms. Another requested that the assembly endorse the recently organized Presbyterian Historical Society. After what must have been many hours of debate, the committee finally adopted the following compromise statement: "Resolved, That while the General Assembly on the one hand, disclaim all right to interfere in secular matters, and on the other [hand], assert the right and duty of the Church, as God's witness on earth, to bear her testimony in favor of truth and holiness and against all false doctrines and sins, wherever professed and committed, yet in view of the oft repeated action of the Assembly in reference to the subjects above referred to, it is inexpedient to take any further action in relation thereto." Scott reported that the resolution was adopted by the Assembly "without debate and with entire unanimity."

As is usually the case with compromise statements, differences of interpretation at once arose. Dr. Scott in the August issue of his *Expositor* showed relief when he editorialized: ". . . it is the settled policy of the Church to keep itself within its proper jurisdiction, and to leave all outside matters to *citizens*—all secular, social and political affairs to citizens—rendering to Caesar the things that are Caesar's, and to God the things that are God's." Dr. Hodge on the other hand, in the July issue of his *Princeton Review* came to a different conclusion. He wrote: "It is now clear that the advocates of what was regarded as a new and revolutionary doctrine, and that the action of the last Assembly [i.e., 1859], has been misapprehended. The above resolution, which distinctly asserts the right and duty of the church, as God's witness on earth, to bear her testimony in favour of truth and holiness, and against all false doctrine and sin . . . was received without the least opposition." Although Dr. Hodge never denied that the church was essentially spiritual, he would never agree that the church should be denied the right and even the duty of speaking on social and political matters.

After his return from the Assembly of 1860, Dr. Scott began to insert articles and editorials in his *Expositor* which more and more indicated his deep sympathy for the South. The following extracts from an editorial entitled "The Unholy Crusade" which appeared in the *Expositor* in September is indicative of this attitude: "We are deeply pained at the tone of some of the so-called *religious* papers of the East. They are not only prone to violence, but have actually engaged in the avowed work of arraying the North against the South for the purpose of electing their candidate. . . We are wholly opposed to the mixing up of religion and party politics. The Church of Christ is too holy to be identified with politics." The presidential campaign was then reaching its emotional crisis. Although Scott did not mention Abraham Lincoln in his editorial, there is no doubt but that he deplored the activity of some religious periodicals in the East in his behalf. Scott was not only a Democrat, he was a Southern Democrat as well.

THE YEAR OF CRISIS, 1861

Scott's conscience was always getting him into trouble. By nature he was a peace-loving soul. He shunned sensationalism. He yearned for the good will of his brethren, but when he came face to face with what he considered to be a principle, he never wavered. He took his stand on what his conscience said was right, cost what it may. Looking back upon those days from the perspective of a hundred years or more, we must conclude that in the controversies in which he was involved, he was more often right than wrong. We applaud his stand against the vigilantes and against the compulsory use of the Bible in public schools. We feel that if he had only had the undivided support of his brethren in the Presbytery of California, and if he had not felt obliged to leave California in 1861, the Presbyterian Church today would have either a college or a university in Northern California. On the Civil War issues, however, we feel he was wrong. But, while passing this judgment, we must remember that he was a Southerner, a son of his generation, and that there were hundreds of thousands of good men who conscientiously held the same views.

Long spans of Dr. Scott's ministry in New Orleans and in San Francisco were marred by controversies. There were some significant differences between the Clay controversy which covered about three years, 1844-47, and the series of controversies which spread over five years of his California ministry, 1856-61. The former was more personal. His honesty and integrity were questioned. The San Francisco controversies were on a different plane. There the issues were bigger with denominational or national implications. In both cities deep personal animosities were aroused which affected his relationships with his brother Presbyterian ministers.

In reviewing the events of the five troubled years in San Francisco, we are reminded of the story of Job. The prologue of Job tells of how one messenger after another came with tales of disaster. Three times we meet the refrain: "While he was yet speaking, there came another. . ."

So it was with Scott during this first period of his residence in San Francisco. He hardly got through one controversy before he was dragged into another. Of the several in which he became unhappily involved, the one with the largest issues and the most direct consequences upon himself and his family was that connected with the Civil War. The year 1861 was a time of crisis not only for the nation but also for William Anderson Scott. Indeed for the Scott family it was more than a year of crisis, it was a year of upheaval.

As has been pointed out, the gold rush, as far as the eastern states were concerned, began in New Orleans in December 1848 when some two hundred excited men crowded aboard a ship bound for the Isthmus of Panama. They were the advance guard of a steady flow of Southerners into California. On the eve of the Civil War, California was largely democratic in its political affiliation. The California delegation to the 1860 Democratic Convention stood solidly with the ultra pro-slavery wing. There was a strong secessionist sentiment in Southern California, notably in Los Angeles and San Bernardino, although there was also considerable strength in San Francisco, Sacramento, and throughout the San Joaquin Valley. In the presidential election of 1860, Lincoln won the four electoral votes of California by a narrow margin and only because the Democratic vote was divided. The final results gave Lincoln 38,734; Douglas, 38,023, and Breckinridge, who was the choice of the South, 33,975. Thus about two-thirds of the votes cast were against Lincoln. This shows that many of Scott's fellow Californians shared his Southern sympathies.

The one man who played a major role in swinging California into the Lincoln camp during the elections of 1860 was the Unitarian minister, the Rev. Thomas Starr King. Although he was only thirty-five years old when he arrived in San Francisco in April 1860 to be pastor of the First Unitarian Church of the city, he had the reputation of being one of the most eloquent orators of his generation. Scott went to hear him preach and wrote his impressions for the June issue of the *Expositor*. After carefully explaining that he did not agree with King theologically, Scott frankly said: "As an intellectual effort, his discourse surpassed our expectations, and was worthy of praise."

King threw himself into the political arena with enthusiasm. He hailed from Boston and shared the anti-slavery convictions of most New Englanders. He was indefatigable in his support of the Northern cause and travelled from one end of the state to the other pleading for the election of Abraham Lincoln. Many felt that if it had not been for King, Lincoln would have lost California. So significant were his patriotic endeavors that when California selected two of its most distinguished sons to be represented in Statuary Hall of the capitol building in Washington, D.C., it selected the famous Roman Catholic pioneer missionary, Father Junipero Serra, and Thomas Starr King. The latter's statue was dedicated on March 1, 1931.

The zeal and emotionalism of some of the Northerners throughout the nation was matched by an equal intensity of devotion by many Southerners. The secessionist spirit became evident even in ecclesiastical circles. During the meetings of the Old School Synod of South Carolina at Charleston, beginning November 28, 1860, a series of resolutions was introduced aimed at a separation of southern synods and presbyteries from the Presbyterian Church, u.s.a. The second resolution read: "Resolved, That fidelity to the South requires us to sever all connection with the Northern portion of the General Assembly." After considerable debate the matter was laid on the table by a vote of seventy-seven to twenty-one. The incident, however, was but a foreshadow of what was to come within a year.

On December 20th South Carolina seceded from the Union being the first of eleven states which finally constituted the Southern Confederacy. Six other states quickly followed her example and on February 9, 1861, Jefferson Davis was elected president and the Confederate States of America became an actuality.

It seems evident that Dr. Hodge of Princeton heard of the resolutions which were to be introduced into the Synod of South Carolina before it actually met. He deplored the move. In the same November he wrote an article entitled "The State of Our Country" which appeared in the January 1861 number of his *Princeton Review*. The whole tone of the article was to placate rising tempers by showing that the complaints of the Southerners were largely unfounded. He referred to the abolitionists, for instance, and claimed that they did not represent the Presbyterian Church. "Of the three thousand Old-school Presbyterian clergymen in the country," he wrote, "we do not believe there are twelve who deserve to be so designated." He looked upon secession in either the nation or in the church as being morally wrong. To him disunion was "only another name for destruction."

After writing this article, a copy of a Thanksgiving sermon preached by Dr. Palmer in New Orleans on November 29, 1860, came to Hodge's attention. Several thousand copies of the sermon were printed and distributed. Stressing his belief that "with the destiny of a great people waiting upon the decision of an hour, it is not lawful to be still," Palmer said: "In determining our duty in this emergency it is necessary that we should first ascertain the nature of the trust providentially committed to us. . . If then the South is such a people, what, at this juncture, is their providential trust? I answer, that it is *to conserve and to perpetuate the institution of domestic slavery as now existing*." And he added: ". . . in this great struggle, *we defend the cause of God and religion*. The abolition spirit is undeniably atheistic."

Hodge was stirred to write a stinging reply. Never before had he come out so strongly against slavery. In answer to the assertion that Palmer had made regarding the duty of the South to conserve and perpetuate the institution of slavery, Hodge wrote: "Is not this monstrous perversion of the nature of the trust confided to them?" He bluntly said that the main theme of Palmer's message was "to perpetuate the inferiority and dependence of four millions of human beings and their descendants indefinitely. What can this mean, if it does not mean that they must be kept in their present state of ignorance and semi-barbarism? This is the light in which the doctrine of this sermon is generally regarded. It has, therefore, given a fearful shock to the public mind. It has alarmed the North, as though a great gulf does exist between the North and South. . ."

Dr. Hodge's article in the January 1861 issue of the *Review* brought consternation to its southern readers. Hodge had been known for his irenic, compromising spirit, but now it appeared that he had joined the anti-slavery party. When Dr. Scott read Hodge's article on "The State of Our Country," he was moved to write a reply. This appeared as an editorial in the March 1861 issue of the *Pacific Expositor*. Scott wrote:

> The article . . . has caused us great grief. No man living has a greater regard for Princeton and for Dr. Hodge, than we have cherished for now nearly thirty years. . . The tendency of the article is to rend asunder both the church and the State, and, as far as its influence goes, to excite to civil war. The author did not so intend, but this is the bearing of the article. Its spirit is bitter, and the arguments all from a northern point, and in our poor judgment, for the most part, incorrect. We protest against such views being received as the sentiments of the Old School Presbyterian Church. Our grief is unspeakably great at beholding narrow and one-sided views from any section of our country, for all such representations increase our troubles, and if not corrected, will produce a division in our beloved Church. . .

The April 1861 number of the *Princeton Review* carried another article by Dr. Hodge on "The Church and the Country." By this time the confederacy had been formed and all signs pointed to a civil war. Dr. Hodge argued that this did not necessarily mean that the Presbyterian Church should be divided. "We are, moreover," he wrote, "historically one church. . . The North needs the South, and the South needs the North. . . A church which regards itself as commissioned to conserve and perpetuate slavery, and a church instinct with the principles and spirit of modern abolitionism, must both alike be offensive to God and injurious to men." And in one of the most amazing passages of the articles, Dr. Hodge split some fine hairs by writing: "We do not believe slaveholding to be sinful, but we believe slavery to be an evil and a burden; to be disastrous in its influence, especially on the non-slaveholding whites." In other words, slavery was not a sin but had evil results! The main theme of this article was ". . . with the blessing of God, our church may survive this conflict, and present to the world the edifying spectacle of Christian brotherhood unbroken by political convulsions." Thus weeks before the Old School Assembly of 1861 met, in which Dr. Hodge was destined to play such an important part, his position on the importance of keeping the church united was made plain. To him this was more important than taking a stand on a moral issue.

In the brief biographical sketch of her husband, written after his death, Mrs. Scott commented:

When the news came of the attack on Sumter, Husband was more depressed than I ever saw him. He walked the floor incessantly. It seemed to him just madness, unless they had assurance of recognition from the European Powers. He deplored the adoption of a new flag, saying that the old flag was theirs as much as anyone else's and they should have fought under it for their rights. He did not like slavery—thought it more injurious to the white man than to the colored man and kept the South in the bondage of the North. He saw no right way to get rid of the evil but that of purchase by the Government, as was done in the West Indies. But still he recognized their *Right of Revolution* and deeply sympathized with their courage and sufferings.

Dr. Scott returned to this troubled subject in the May number of his *Expositor*. Even though war had already started and blood had been shed (but of this fact he may have been unaware when he wrote), Scott insisted that "there is no cause for war . . . everything can be better settled by negotiation before and without war, than after the shedding of blood. We are positively opposed to *civil war* between the American States for any cause, or under any circumstances. And as to our Church, we see no cause for it . . . to be at all disturbed. We hope and pray that no agitation on this subject may ever find a place in our Presbyteries or Synods. Let the Church remain united, even if the States are divided."

San Francisco was a Union city. Since Dr. Scott's Southern sympathies were well known, his patriotism was under suspicion. He knew that he occupied a delicate position and conscientiously sought to avoid giving offense. His lifelong policy of never mixing politics with religion was now an asset for no one would ever have the chance of hearing him discuss such issues in the pulpit. His opponents had to look elsewhere for points to criticize.

The editor of the *Pacific* took the lead in the attack. On December 6, 1860, that paper carried an editorial entitled "Dr. Scott, The Pacific, and the College of California." In his promotion of the Old School City College, Dr. Scott had frankly stated his faith in a denominational rather than an interdenominational institution. The editor claimed that Dr. Scott "sneers at the idea" of men "of various religious denominations" successfully conducting a college. Time proved Dr. Scott to be right in this instance for in 1868, as has been stated, the College of California was turned over to the state and became the nucleus of the University of California. City College struggled along a few years as an independent institution apart from denominational control.

Someone with a long memory dug up the charge of plagiarism which had been levelled against Scott in 1853 when his *Daniel* was published After making long quotations from Scott's book, an editor paralleled them with quotations from Dr. Cummings book with the same title. The article appeared in the December 17th issue of the Sacramento *Union* and was spread over three long columns. Three days later the *Pacific* drew the attention of its readers to the article and commented that "the coincidence of thought, style and *language* is amazing—very wonderful indeed." The editor expanded on the thought. ". . . for two minds to take up identical subjects, in identical language and style, if not equal, it is at least next to one of the seven wonders of the world. . . We will not take it upon us to say that it is one thing or the other—a wonder or a plagiarism. If it is the first, it will outlast a nine days' wonder; if the latter, it is *awful.*"

Scott promptly wrote to the editor of the *Union* denying the charge of plagiarism and explained how he had answered the same criticism more than six years previous. He told about the fire which had destroyed the original plates of his books and the manuscript and how the work was reset. Because of the difficulties of communication, he explained he had been unable to read proof and as a result many quotation marks had been omitted. The editor of the *Pacific* in his December 27th issue caustically remarked: "We cannot understand how a fire could have burnt out all the quotation marks so essential to a work so extensively compiled from others as the one in question. Dr. Scott has failed to clear the record against him."

A vitriolic attack on Scott appeared in the spring of 1861 in a thirteen octavo page pamphlet entitled *Divided.* It was written by the Rev. Henry Durant although his name does not appear on the title page. Durant, a Congregational minister, arrived in San Francisco in 1853 and was actively associated with the College of California from its very beginning, serving for a time as president. Durant Street in Berkeley is named after him. He and others interested in the College of California were greatly troubled and at times angered by Dr. Scott's promotion of City College. We do not know just what happened to have raised Durant's wrath to the explosive point that inspired such a vituperative attack.

In *Divided* Durant characterized Scott's writings as "supercilious . . . like another little head which also vibrates a forked tongue, and hides a venomous tooth." He called the *Expositor* "a great humbug" in which, he said, Scott "fulminates his old trash." He warned: "In the minutest secretions of the insects, and lesser reptiles, among beasts; of weeds, and shrubs, and fungi, among plants, lie her deadliest poisons. . . The *great things* of the *Expositor* are comparatively harmless. . . But the squibs; the flings; the slender needle-like little arrows that spin like gossamer in the ventilations of the *Expositor;* look out for these." Even though we are aware that Durant was incensed over

Scott's stand on the college issue, it is difficult to understand why a clergyman of his standing should have published such a sarcastic and bitter denunciation of a brother minister.

Scott in the May 1861 issue of the *Expositor* reported on the contents of the pamphlet to his readers and commented: "We verily believe, that Fort Sumter was not a greater annoyance to the South Carolinians than *Calvary Church*, the *Expositor* and its humble editor and 'the City College' are to certain well known parties on this coast."

Scott continued to draw large audiences at Calvary Church. During his absence from San Francisco in order to attend the 1860 General Assembly, his friend and co-worker, Dr. Burrowes, edited the *Expositor*. The June number carried a tribute to Dr. Scott by Burrowes, who wrote: "No other clergyman in California preaches to such a congregation. . . His church is always full, evening and morning. He preaches Jesus Christ and Him crucified. There is not a pulpit in the United States, where this is done with more fulness and faithfulness. . . No pulpit can be more entirely free than his from things which should be foreign to the pulpit."

Two issues arose during the spring and early summer of 1861 in which Scott found it difficult if not impossible to separate religion from politics. The first involved praying for the rulers of the nation and the second centered about flying the national flag from the church. Scott had long felt it his Christian duty to pray for those in authority in the government. He published a pamphlet on this subject in 1843. The October, 1860 number of the *Expositor* carried a twenty-two page article on this theme. "To pray for our rulers is an act of true patriotism," he wrote. "As it is our duty to reverence and obey them, so it is our duty to pray for them."

Among Scott's papers in the archives of San Francisco Theological Seminary is a seven-page manuscript dated February 10, 1861, entitled "A Prayer for the Times." This is evidently a pulpit prayer. He remembered all in authority and prayed for peace for the land. "Restore brotherly love between the people of all our States. Lord God of our Fathers, look down in great mercy upon our beloved country and save us from all insurrections, animosities and blood shedding." Included in the prayer was the following: "Sit thou at the right hand of our governors and the President & Vice President. Bless the heads of Departments of our Army & Navy."

When Dr. Scott learned of the election of Jefferson Davis as president of the confederacy, he was placed in a quandary. Should he pray for Jefferson Davis as well as for Abraham Lincoln? He decided that he would but he knew that it would not be wise to mention the head of the confederacy by name. He accomplished his purpose by the simple expedient of changing the word "president" from the singular to the plural form. The Scott Collection in Bancroft Library contains an unidentified clipping from some San Francisco newspaper which reads: "Dr. Scott, we understand, during a prayer at Calvary Church last

Sunday, invoked a Divine blessing upon the Presidents and Vice Presidents of both Confederacies. His auditors opened their eyes in amazement, and looked at each other inquiringly, but the Doctor concluded his prayer as calmly as though it was his duty to pray for treason." This item was copied in another San Francisco paper, also unidentified, to which the editor added the following comment:

We have always been inclined to credit Dr. Scott with being a man of sound sense, though rather egotistic in his opinions. He is entitled to an expression of opinion as a private individual but when he deliberately desecrates the sanctuary of the most High by invoking Divine blessing for the thieving traitor Davis, he forgets that he should have some slight respect for the existence of a government under whose benign influence he has been enabled to amass riches. If he continues to insult the Union sentiment, so nearly allied to religion, he must expect to be disgraced by being stripped of the power to do mischief.

Here was an implied threat of being run out of the city. San Francisco was still a frontier town where many of its leading citizens were among those who took an active part in the vigilante movement of 1856.

The single letter "s" at the end of the word "president" touched a sensitive nerve in many of Dr. Scott's hearers. He was praying for Jefferson Davis! Sunday after Sunday he repeated the petition. The full prayer appeared in the June 1861 issue of the *Expositor* where we read: "We do especially beseech Thee to bless . . . all that are in authority throughout our land . . . whether they be governors, presidents or vice-presidents." The following item from the San Francisco *Daily Call* for May 10, 1861, reflected the growing criticism: "What is worse, to commit treason or to pray for treason? Or is there any difference? Dr. Scott, a famous divine of this city, it is said makes a regular practice of praying for the success of traitors against the U.S. Government. He might as well make public speeches on behalf of Jeff. Davis' cause. Treason enunciated from the pulpit in the form of prayer loses none of its criminality on account of the sacredness of its surroundings."

Patriotism became more emotional as the war progressed. Led by Thomas Starr King and enthusiastically supported by William C. Anderson, many of the churches began flying the United States flag from their edifices. The following news item appeared in the June 27, 1861, issue of the *Pacific* under the caption "The Flag on the Churches:"

We are informed that quite a general movement is on foot to unfurl 'the Stars and Stripes' on the churches of this city on the Fourth of July. The flag already waves on the First Presbyterian Church [Dr. Anderson's] and on the Unitarian Church [Rev. T. Starr King's]. Flags have been secured for the First Congregational Church and the Howard Street Presbyterian Church and rumor

has it that a flag is also to be hoisted on Calvary Church. . .
In fact, we would not be surprised to hear on that day the flag
waved on every Protestant Church edifice in the State, excepting of
course the Methodist Church South.

When Dr. Scott read this, an alarming thought passed through his
mind. Had some of his elders with unionist sympathies taken matters in
their own hands? Had they made plans to raise the national emblem over
Calvary Church without first consulting him? He called on Elder James
B. Roberts and was relieved to learn that no such action had been taken.
Yet the whole subject seemed to him to be so important that he decided
to write a letter to the "Officers of Calvary Church." The original of
this letter, dated June 28, 1861, is in the Scott Collection in Bancroft
Library. It reads in part:

> Our house of worship is for religious, not secular or civil or
> political uses. Built & solemnly dedicated to the worship of Al-
> mighty God, it is a place of divine prayer & praise for all nations
> —sacred to the religious services of the people of God & of all
> parties & of all political opinions. No sign or symbol therefore
> should be found attached to it that could offend the feelings of the
> humblest disciple of the Lord Jesus. His Kingdom is not of this
> world."

Dr. Scott said that he displayed the flag three times each year over
his dwelling; on January 8th in memory of General Jackson's victory at
New Orleans, and again on February 22nd and July 4th. "I do not wish
to see it," he insisted, "or any other flag upon our house of worship.
Let it be free from all sectional prejudice." He is also reported to have
said that he considered it just as inappropriate to fly the national flag
over a church as it would be to sing the Star Spangled Banner at a communion service. But those who held different views bided their time.
They felt that a day of reckoning was coming.

THE GENERAL ASSEMBLY OF 1861

The Presbytery of California selected Dr. W. C. Anderson and his
elder, W. W. Caldwell as commissioners to the 1861 Old School General
Assembly scheduled to meet on May 17th in Philadelphia. For three
successive years, 1858, 1859, and 1860, Dr. Scott had been the ministerial commissioner to represent the presbytery at the general assemblies. Anderson's selection for the 1861 meeting was logical as he had
not represented his presbytery at any meeting of the assembly since his
arrival in San Francisco in 1855. Although his strong Northern sympathies were well known, no one could have foreseen the dominant role he
was to play in the 1861 gathering. Thus from this small pioneer presbytery in far-away California came two of the most influential figures of the
Old School Presbyterian Church during those critical years 1858 to 1861
inclusive: Dr. Scott and Dr. Anderson.

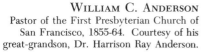

WILLIAM C. ANDERSON
Pastor of the First Presbyterian Church of
San Francisco, 1855-64. Courtesy of his
great-grandson, Dr. Harrison Ray Anderson.

Dr. Anderson's son, the Rev. John A. Anderson of Stockton, was also known for his strong unionist sympathies. John's grandson, Dr. Harrison Ray Anderson, for many years pastor of the Fourth Presbyterian Church of Chicago and moderator of the General Assembly of 1951, turned over to the San Francisco Theological Seminary some of his great-grandfather's papers including a diary kept in 1861. Even though Dr. W. C. Anderson made only brief entries, yet such as were made throw a searchlight upon the stirring events of the 1861 assembly.

From the diary we learn that Dr. Anderson sailed from San Francisco for New York on February 11th. He arrived at Panama on the 25th and disembarked in New York on March 5th. He landed in the East at an exciting time. Abraham Lincoln had been inaugurated as President of the United States on March 4th. Seven states had already seceded from the Union. On April 12th shore batteries at Charleston, South Carolina, opened fire on Fort Sumter. The Civil War had begun. On the 14th, Anderson wrote in his diary: "Have heard of the fall of Ft. Sumter," and with prophetic insight he added: "This will prove .the fall of slavery & the South." On April 15th President Lincoln issued his call for 75,000 volunteers. Anderson went to Washington, D.C. from New York and on Wednesday, April 26th, noted: "Spent day in soldiers camp." After visiting friends and relatives, he went to Philadelphia for the assembly.

Three were nominated for the moderatorship including Dr. Anderson of San Francisco. For reasons not known, Anderson withdrew his name. Dr. John C. Backus of Baltimore was elected. The Assembly, with only 264 commissioners present, was smaller in number than that of the previous year. This was due to the absence of many Southerners. Thirty-three of sixty-four Southern presbyteries were not represented. There was not a single commissioner from Alabama, Arkansas, Georgia, Louisiana, North Carolina, or South Carolina. Although some, no doubt, were absent because hostilities had commenced, others deliberately absented themselves. Dr. Hodge's article on "The State of the Country" aroused, according to an article in the April number of the *Southern Presbyterian Review,* "the profoundest emotions of astonishment and grief in the minds of all in the South." Dr. John B. Adger of the faculty of the seminary at Columbia, South Carolina, openly urged the Southern commissioners not to attend the Philadelphia meeting. In the July 1861 issue of the *Southern Review* he wrote that "Southern Commissioners generally would not go and sit down in council with the enemies of their country [who were] seeking her utter ruin and overthrow." Among the Northerners present were two who had been at the 1860 Assembly, Dr. Gardiner Spring of New York City and Dr. Charles Hodge of Princeton.

Commenting on the Assembly of 1861, Dr. Hodge wrote in the July issue of his *Review:* "The eyes of the whole country were converged on the house in which the Assembly sat. The secular press was clamorous for an open avowal of allegiance. Threatening murmurs against clerical traitors were heard on every hand. Those who resisted the action of the Assembly were denounced in the streets as secessionists, as pro-slavery, as trucklers to the South, as traitors." For the first time after the outbreak of hostilities, a national body of one of the country's largest denominations was holding its annual meeting. The great question of the hour was "What would the Presbyterians say about the rebellion?"

Dr. Robert L. Breckenridge, editor of the *Danville Quarterly Review,* was more specific in his account of the emotionally-charged atmosphere in which the Assembly met. He described the "outside pressure" in favor of some pronouncement for the Union as being "tremendous." He added: "The Assembly met in the bosom of a community prodigiously excited, and demanding that every influence, religious as well as civil and military, should be brought into the field to uphold the National Government."

According to this Breckenridge article, rumors were circulated among the commissioners regarding some resolutions introduced into the November 1860 meeting of the Synod of South Carolina which called for support of a Southern secession in the church as well as in the state. The reports were incorrect as the resolutions were tabled, but this evidently was unknown to the commissioners and to Breckenridge, for he wrote:

> It appears . . . that the excellent brethren inhabiting the "political hub of the universe," preceded the Assembly in dabbling

in the dirty puddle of politics. If the statement made on the floor
of the Assembly is to be credited, that Synod [South Carolina]
approved in advance the act of secession which it was well known
the State Convention would pass. They could not wait till the foul
deed was done. They were so fondly anxious to baptize the cocka-
trice, they could not wait till the cock's egg hatched. They antici-
pated the monstrous birth, and sanctioned it by a decree of the
church. And yet no men have declaimed more eloquently against
defiling the pure robes of the Bride of the Lamb by contact with
the world than these very brethren.

The irony of it all was so apparent! In spite of well-spun theories about
never mixing politics and religion, the two had become thoroughly hom-
ogenized in Presbyterian circles in South Carolina.

On Friday after the assembly opened, Dr. Spring introduced a resolution which called for the appointment of a special committee "to inquire
into the expediency of this Assembly making some expression of their
devotion to the Union of these States, and loyalty to the Government;
and if, in their judgment, it is expedient so to do, they report what that
expression shall be." There was immediate objection on the part of the
Southern commissioners present who were joined by Dr. Hodge and
other cautious men from the North. Dr. Hodge argued that if the
assembly took any such action it would split the church. This was a
political issue. Better say nothing and keep the church united. A
motion to lay the proposal on the table carried 123 to 102. The Southerners and the cautious party had won the first round.

On Saturday, May 18th, the Northerners, having rallied their strength,
introduced a motion calling for a reconsideration of Dr. Spring's resolution as an order of the day on the following Tuesday. The motion carried. On Tuesday the verbal battle began. Anderson noted in his diary
that day: "Stormy debate on Resolution to support Govt. Southern men
oppose it." On Wednesday, May 22nd, he introduced two resolutions,
one of which stated in part: ". . . in view of the present agitated
and unhappy condition of this country, the first day of July next be
hereby set apart as a day of prayer throughout our bounds. . ." On
that day Anderson wrote in his diary: "Stormy debate continues. I
have spoken & am kept at my post. Am regarded as a leader, must
stand up to the trust." Dr. Hodge introduced a resolution which called
for the consideration of the Spring resolutions as the first order of the
day on the following Friday. This was adopted. Dr. Spring in his
published *Reminiscences* wrote: "In the interval between Wednesday
and Friday, strenuous efforts were made by some members of the
Assembly and some who were not members . . . to induce me to
modify my resolutions, as to be more conciliating to the Southern members . . . I could not accede to their request."

On Friday, May 24th, Dr. Spring's resolutions were taken up and
again Anderson noted that there was some "stormy debate." Dr. Hodge

proposed what Anderson labelled as "Milk and water resolutions." By this time the membership of the assembly had been fairly well divided. Anderson was the acknowledged leader of the Northern party; Hodge was the spokesman for the Southern. A new factor was suddenly injected into the background of the debate when the startling news came that Colonel Elmer Ellsworth, a dashing young officer and a close friend of President Lincoln, had been killed while removing a Confederate flag from a hotel in Alexandria. The man who shot Ellsworth was himself killed. The first blood had been shed. Ellsworth's body was taken to the White House where it lay in state. Anderson made a brief reference to the incident by writing: "News of murder of Col. Ellsworth by a Virginia Secessionist. Great excitement." Some of the cautious and hesitant members of the assembly moved over to Anderson's side.

The Assembly found it difficult to carry on its routine business. On Monday, May 27th, Anderson noted: "Ordinary business part of the day & the loyalty debate the remainder." On Tuesday the assembly voted to refer the whole matter to a committee of nine, five ministers and four elders, with instructions to report at four o'clock that afternoon. Both Hodge and Anderson were members of the committee. The committee, evidently appointed by the moderator, Dr. Backus, who was in full sympathy with Dr. Hodge's position, was overbalanced with men either sympathetic to the South or too cautious to take a firm stand. Anderson was the only strong Union man included.

After some deliberation the committee drew up the following statement which was accepted by a vote of eight to one, Anderson alone objecting: "That in the present distracted state of the country, this Assembly, representing the whole church, feel bound to abstain from any further declaration in which all our ministers and members, faithful to the constitution and standard of the church, might be able safely and consistently to join." In other words, say nothing and do nothing.

Dr. Anderson, convinced that there was a moral issue involved which the church could not avoid, brought in a minority report which consisted of the Spring resolutions strengthened by some additional wording of his own. Resolution no. 2 then read, with Dr. Anderson's wording italicized by the author: "That this General Assembly, in the spirit of that Christian patriotism which the Scriptures enjoin, and which has always characterized this Church, do hereby acknowledge *and declare our obligations to promote and perpetuate, so far as in us lies, the integrity of these United States, and to strengthen, uphold, and encourage the Federal Government in the exercise of all its functions under our noble Constitution. . ."* The federal government was then defined as being the "central administration."

Dr. Anderson's brief entry for the 28th was: "Loyalty papers referred to a com. of nine of which I am one. 8 mem. com. reported a milk & water paper. I submitted a minority report, Dr. Springs paper."

As soon as the committee reported, a motion was made to accept the majority recommendation. A heated debate followed which carried the assembly up to the hour of adjournment. The matter was taken up the next day, May 29th, and it was not until six o'clock that afternoon that the matter came to a vote. The majority report lost by a tally of 128 nays and 84 yeas. The minority report submitted by Dr. Anderson was then before the assembly and it carried by a vote of 156 to 66. The decisive issue was settled but the repercussions were yet to come.

Before the Assembly adjourned, Dr. Hodge submitted a protest condemning the ruling of the assembly. In this he was joined by fifty-seven others including the moderator, Dr. Backus. The heart of the protest reads:

> We deny the right of the Assembly to decide the political question, to what government the allegiance of Presbyterians as citizens is due, and its right to make that decision a condition of membership in our Church. That the paper adopted by the Assembly does decide the political question just stated, is in our judgment undeniable. It not only asserts the loyalty of this body to the Constitution and the Union, but it promises in the name of all the churches and ministers whom it represents, to do all that in them lies "to strengthen, uphold, and encourage the federal government. . ."
> In adopting this paper, therefore, the Assembly does decide the great political question which agitates and divides the country. The question is, whether the allegiance of our citizens is primarily to the State or to the Union.

Dr. Hodge and those who stood with him claimed that the assembly violated the constitution of the Presbyterian Church by making such a pronouncement. "We protest loudly," they said, "against the action of the Assembly, because it is a departure from all previous actions. . ."

Within two years the assembly had made a complete about-face. In 1859 when the assembly adopted Thornwell's theory of the spirituality of the church, it refused to make any pronouncements on social issues or to endorse any society no matter how commendable its aims. In 1860, this theory gave way somewhat but in a compromise statement which vainly tried to preserve the "spiritual view" theory and at the same time declare the right of the church to condemn "all false doctrines and sins." But now in 1861 the assembly had made a pronouncement with far-reaching social and political implications. Seemingly the pronouncement was in direct violation to the provision still found in Section IV of Chapter XXXI of the *Confession of Faith:* "Synods and councils are to handle or conclude nothing, but that which is ecclesiastical; and are not to intermeddle with civil affairs which concern the commonwealth, unless by way of humble petition in cases extraordinary. . ." Dr. Hodge, in taking a middle-of-the-road position, condemned the judgments of the assemblies of 1859 and 1861 but approved that of 1860. In all of these controversies, the whole philosophy of the relationship of church and state was under examination and debate.

After being in session for seventeen days, the 1861 Assembly adjourned on June 1st. During those years the assembly usually met for about two weeks, so this 1861 meeting was only about three days longer than average. Dr. Anderson, feeling deeply satisfied with the results of the assembly, left from New York on his return trip on June 11th. He was back in San Francisco on July 4th, the day set for the national flag to be flown from all Protestant churches in San Francisco. No one could have been more pleased than he to see it displayed on the First Presbyterian Church. He was aware of its absence on Calvary Church.

Following the assembly came the editorial post-mortems in several of the Presbyterian publications. Dr. Hodge writing in the July issue of his *Review* gave a lengthy account of the assembly and again stated his position:

> We believe the course of the South, in its attempt to break up our glorious union, is unreasonable, ungrateful, and wicked. . . We believe that it is the duty of every man in these United States, to do all that in him lies "to strengthen, sustain, and encourage the Federal Government" in the conflict in which it is now engaged. . . But our private convictions have nothing to do with the rights of the General Assembly. . . The General Assembly had no right to decide the political question, as to what government the allegiance of Presbyterian citizens is due.

It is rather strange to note that any direct references to slavery were almost entirely lacking in the debates of the assembly and the reviews of its action. Everything but that, and yet in the background was the great moral issue which could not be buried under a torrent of words. One of the few direct discussions of slavery is to be found in the September 1861 issue of the *Danville Quarterly Review*. Therein the editor, Dr. R. J. Breckenridge wrote: "If slavery, protected though it be by the state, be a *melum per se*, the church must say so, and act accordingly: the slave-holder must be excluded from her fellowship while he continues in the practice of his sin." The editor frankly faced the great question: When do moral questions become political or when do political issues become moral? What was the Church to do when threatened with civil war? "Stand still like a dumb dog, totally indifferent to the awful realities of the hour?" The editor denied the right of the assembly to take the action that was taken. Rather it should have issued a pastoral letter "rivaling in dignity, piety and wisdom, that of their illustrious predecessors of the old Synod." He felt that if such a course had been followed, the Old School Presbyterian Church would not be facing a division.

In describing the outside pressure which was brought to bear on the assembly, the editor wrote:

> The house was crowded with ministers and members of other

denominations as well as our own . . . urging the adoption of the obnoxious resolutions; the populace demanded it with loud cries and threatening demonstrations of fearful import; the streets of Philadelphia were thronged with thousands of troops and vast trains of baggage and munitions of war, intensifying to the highest pitch the popular enthusiasm in behalf of the government. In a word, such was the strange condition of things in and around the Assembly, that no fair-minded man will hold the Church responsible for the act in question. The fact is, the General Assembly of 1861, *quod hoc* was not a free Assembly.

The Spring resolutions were debated in such an emotionally charged atmosphere that it was most difficult for men with conscientious contrary views to express themselves. How different might have been the final pronouncement if the assembly had met that year in some city other than Philadelphia. If the slavery issue were not in the background and if the secession of the southern states had resulted from some purely economic issue, as for instance an excessive tax on cotton, would the General Assembly then have been justified in demanding allegiance of all its members to the federal government? Has the church the right to dictate where one should place his political allegiance?

The focal point of disagreement involved in the secessionist movement was slavery, and slavery was a moral issue. Here, according to Dr. Anderson, the church had not only the right but the duty to speak. Another "if" invites speculation. This was stated by Dr. Breckenridge in his review of the Assembly: "Had one man from the West, who was providentially hindered therefrom, been in his seat, so as to unite with his conservative brethren in stemming the tide of radicalism, we confidently believe the Church would have escaped the disaster which has befallen her." In other words, if in the providence of God, Dr. Scott rather than Dr. Anderson had represented the Presbytery of California in 1861, the church might not have been divided.

During the summer and fall of 1861, forty-seven Southern presbyteries severed their relationship with the Old School General Assembly. They constituted parts or the whole of ten synods. The Historical Foundation of the Presbyterian Church in the United States has in its library at Montreat, North Carolina, the original Minutes of Charleston Presbytery. The following item from the record for July 25, 1861, is characteristic of similar sentiments which are to be found in the minutes of other Southern presbyteries.

Whereas, the General Assembly of the Presbyterian Church in the United States of America, by adoption of a paper known as Dr. Spring's resolutions, ignoring the establishment of the Government of the Confederate States of America, and disregarding our rights, privileges, and duties as citizens thereof, enjoined our allegiance to and support of a Government foreign and hostile to our own, and required us not only to yield obedience to a political power which we, in common with our fellow citizens of all classes and all churches have disowned and rejected, but also to act as traitors and rebels against the rightful and legal authorities of the land in which we live: . . . Therefore, Be it Resolved . . . that we do not recognize the right or authority of the General Assembly to adopt the resolutions above referred to; and that we disown and repudiate those resolutions, both in their letter and their spirit, as having no authority over us. . .

The General Assembly of the Presbyterian Church in the Confederate States was formally organized at Augusta, Georgia, on December 4, 1861, with an enrollment of fifty ministers and thirty-eight elders. They represented 1,100 churches and about 75,000 communicant members. Dr. Benjamin M. Palmer of New Orleans was elected the first moderator. He is reported to have said: "We are neither the friends nor the foes of slavery. We have no commission either to propagate it or abolish it. The policy of its existence or non-existence is a question which exclusively belongs to the State. We have no right, as a church, to enjoin it as a duty or to condemn it as a sin."

New Orleans was captured by federal forces on April 24, 1862, and occupied by troops commanded by General Benjamin F. Butler, who earned there the opprobrious title of "Beast Butler." Among those who fled the city before the occupation was Dr. Palmer, who moved to South Carolina. He did not return to his pulpit until July 16, 1865. After the war ended, Dr. Palmer was most adamant in his stand against any reunion with the northern branch of the Old School Church. In 1863 the United Synod of the South, which was the southern branch of the New School Assembly, joined with the Old School body in the South. This synod had about two hundred churches; twelve thousand members. Dr. Scott's old friend, Dr. J. A. Lyon of Columbus, Mississippi, was made the first moderator of the united body. After the close of the Civil War the name of the denomination was changed to The Presbyterian Church in the United States. It still maintains its identity as a separate body.

SECOND HANGING IN EFFIGY

The rapidly developing war situation in the spring and early summer of 1861, the growing agitation about flying the flag from churches, and the first rumors as to what was happening at the Old School Assembly cast Dr. Scott into the depths. Added to these concerns was the fact that his eldest son, Robert, now an officer in the United States Army, had let his parents know that he would cast his lot with the North. His parents were heartsick.

Much of the copy for the July issue of the *Expositor* had to be prepared in June. Although Dr. Scott tried to avoid political issues in his paper even as he did in the pulpit, he did not succeed. His deep sympathies for the South became ever more apparent. One of the editorials which appeared in the July number bore the caption "The Religious Papers on the War." "We are perfectly amazed," he wrote, "at the tone of many of the papers called religious and *pacific* as to the fury with which they have called for blood, confiscation and extermination!" He put the following in italics: *"To rush on blindly and wickedly murdering each other—for we can call it by no other name—simply because they disagree upon a question of whether a State has a right to secede or not, upon points of honor falsely so called, seem to us to be devilish and fiendish in the extreme. All good men should set themselves at once to stay the effusion of blood."* He closed his editorial by saying: "We have written from an overburdened heart. We may be in error as to what ought to be done in this fearful crisis. If so it is an error of the head and not of the heart. Perhaps we ought to have said nothing at all. From the fullness of the heart the pen will write as well as the lips speak. We proscribe no man for differing from us. He may be right and we wrong."

Dr. Scott had learned of the introduction of the Spring resolutions into the General Assembly but did not know the exact wording, only in general that they were "in favor of Mr. Lincoln and the Federal Government, and of course against the Southern States." He knew that Dr. Hodge opposed them and likewise must have known that Dr. Anderson supported them. Scott wrote: "We greatly regret that they were ever introduced. The Assembly is an ecclesiastical, spiritual Body—not a civil or political Convention."

The July issue of the *Expositor* also carried an editorial on "Chaplains" in which Dr. Scott praised the example of some southern presbyteries in underwriting the salaries of ministers who were going as chaplains. This was consistent with his previously expressed opinions on the complete separation of church and state. And in another short editorial entitled "The Church and the Crisis," he condemned "northern and eastern religious newspapers and pulpits" for the way in which they had "endorsed the coercive war of the Administration on the South." And he added: "The pulpits of this city have to some extent followed this unholy example."

The Scott Collection in Bancroft Library contains two unidentified clippings from a San Francisco newspaper, evidently from the summer of 1861, which contain the following quotations: "He [i.e., Dr. Scott] is editor of the *Pacific Expositor*, a one-horse, seven-by-nine monthly periodical, devoted to Southern Christianity and morality, and to slavery." The second reads: "THE PACIFIC EXPOSITOR—This detestable organ of treason in a black gown, for the month of August, has been laid upon our table. As we think it calculated to divide and disturb our people, and excite disaffection against our Government, and as we desire to see its editor sent out of the country as a public enemy, we have not opened it, and cannot therefore say whether it contains the usual amount of treason or not." Since the writer of this quotation had not read the

August number of the *Expositor*, it is evident that his unfavorable opinion of Dr. Scott was gained from previous issues and no doubt that for July.

Out of an inner turmoil of conflicting emotions, Dr. Scott finally came to the conclusion that he ought to resign his pulpit. In a letter to his session dated "Study of Calvary Church, Monday, 1 July, 1861," he wrote: "It has become palpable to me that there is dissatisfaction in the congregation . . . in regard to my politics & sentiments in reference to war now carried on between the Federal Government and the Seceded states. . . Forasmuch as I am unwilling to be the occasion of troubles or dissatisfaction in the congregation . . . I therefore now request that you will call a meeting of the congregation to unite with me in asking the Presbytery to allow me to return to them the call which you put into my hands. . ." Since Dr. Scott had never been installed as pastor of Calvary Church but had served as stated supply, his resignation could the more easily be made effective. None of the complications which marked his departure from his parishes in Tuscaloosa and New Orleans were now possible.

With a large family to support, he of necessity was obliged to look around for another church. He considered returning to the South. On July 2nd, the day after he had submitted his resignation, he wrote to his friend and former traveling companion, Dr. Thomas Smyth of Charleston, who years later included the letter in his *Autobiographical Notes*. Scott wrote: "With an overwhelming congregation and good health, I am nevertheless constrained to resign and leave this country, for many reasons which I would give in full if I thought you would receive this direct. My object in writing is to let you know I desire a field of labor in the South. I know not at present how to get away, but will try." Scott suggested that Smyth address him in care of his son-in-law, Nicholas Kittle, at his business address in New York or "by the British mails." Since the federal government had stopped all mail with the South on June 1st, this explains his concern about a reply. Whereas we know that Dr. Smyth received Scott's letter, we have no evidence that Scott ever had a reply or that any invitation came during the years of the Civil War for him to return to the South. Even if such an invitation had been forthcoming, there still remained the practical problem of moving from San Francisco to some southern port. If he were to leave San Francisco, where was he to go? The future was dark.

The elders of Calvary Church met on Thursday evening, July 11th, to consider their pastor's letter. After considerable discussion, they voted to seek the advice of the board of trustees. This board met the next day and voted: "Resolved that in the opinion of this Board, the peace and prosperity of Calvary Church and Congregation would not be promoted by the acceptance of Dr. Scott's resignation." The elders voted to invite any member of the church or of the congregation who had a different opinion to write a letter to the session. This was done and when the session met again on Tuesday evening, July 16th, only four letters had been received and not one of these called for the resignation of their pastor. The elders therefore took action requesting "the Rev. Dr. Scott to withdraw his resignation, earnestly desiring that he will continue his pastoral labors among us. . ."

Another meeting of the session was held on July 28th with Dr. Burrowes as moderator. A letter was read from Dr. Scott dated the 27th which said in part: ". . . in view of the fact that you do not know of any member of the Church or Congregation that wishes me to leave it, and also in view of the fact that your request *exacts no pledge from me,* I do hereby withdraw my letter of resignation. . ." At least two Presbyterian periodicals in the East published, during the first part of August, the erroneous report that Dr. Scott's resignation had been accepted and that "he proposes to seek a home in the South so soon as an opening occurs."

Things were quiet during August. In the prospectus for the third volume of the *Pacific Expositor,* which appeared in the August 1861 number, Dr. Scott included the following quotation from the famous Scottish reformer, John Knox: "I am in the place where I am demanded of conscience to speak the truth, and therefore, the truth I speak, impugn it whoso list." This same number carried in full the protest made by Dr. Hodge and fifty-seven others to the action of the General Assembly in its adoption of the Spring resolutions with the amendments by Dr. Anderson. The protest was printed without editorial comment but on a following page, Dr. Scott quoted Dr. Hodge as bemoaning the division of the Old School church and as pointing out the danger "that the Northern Church will succumb to a fanatical anti-slavery spirit and victimize conservative, moderate men." The August number also included an appeal for peace from "the Peace Society of London to the People of the United States." Only a rabid abolitionist could have found any basis in this issue of the *Expositor* for calling it a "detestable organ of treason."

The scene now shifts to the Presbytery of California where the drama which took place on the floor of the 1861 General Assembly was re-enacted. Instead of Anderson versus Hodge, it was now Anderson versus Scott. The basic issues under debate were the same.

Dr. Scott, as the retiring moderator, opened the fall meeting of the Presbytery of California on Wednesday evening, September 11th. Seven of the ministerial members of the presbytery were present together with several elders. Since this was the first meeting of the presbytery following Dr. Anderson's return from the General Assembly, he reported on what had taken place. He naturally referred to the Spring resolutions and told of his part in their final adoption. As is customary, someone moved that Dr. Anderson's report be received and "that his conduct be approved." This of course meant that the presbytery would endorse the stand he took in regard to the Spring resolutions. All voted for the motion except Dr. Scott who dissented and obtained leave to have the reasons for his negative vote recorded in the minutes.

Presbytery agreed to call a *pro re nata* meeting for the following Monday, September 16th, presumably for the sole purpose of examining and licensing a candidate for the ministry. Following the meeting of the 1861 Assembly, many of the presbyteries and synods of the Old School church throughout the North, in bursts of patriotic enthusiasm, endorsed the Spring resolutions. The wide extent of this practice is to be found in an article entitled "Synodical Action on the Spring Resolutions" which appeared in the November 7, 1861, issue of the *Presbyterian Herald*. Dr. Scott, no doubt, was aware of such actions and made inquiry as to whether there was any intention to introduce the resolutions into the special meeting of the presbytery. He was assured that this highly controversial subject would not be presented.

On Monday morning the presbytery met in Calvary Church. There were seven ministers and three elders present and also three ministers from other denominations who were seated as corresponding members. Among these was the Rev. J. H. Warren, editor of the *Pacific*, who had so frequently castigated Dr. Scott through the columns of his paper. Few if any were more bitter against Scott than Warren and no one more favorably situated to let that animosity be known to the public. Warren's presence at this special meeting of the presbytery must have alerted Dr. Scott to suspect that some sinister plan was afoot. The presbytery proceeded at once to the examination and licensing of the candidate for the ministry which was the announced reason for the meeting. Then came the great moment when Dr. Scott was to be put on the spot. The stage had been carefully set. The presbytery was made up exculsively of northern men with the exception of Dr. Scott. His sharpest journalistic critic was present ready to take notes on what transpired. The Rev. A. W. Loomis, who had succeeded the Rev. William Speer as missionary to the Chinese in San Francisco, introduced a series of resolutions which went far beyond the Spring resolutions in their denunciation of the southern rebellion and in their demand for full and unequivocal support of the federal government. This document as recorded in the minutes of the presbytery reads in part as follows:

> Whereas, Loyalty to one's Government is a plain Christian duty, for we are commanded to regard the properly constituted authorities as ordained of God and to pray for them, and to submit to them   .   .   .   Therefore
>
> Resolved, 1st,   That in the opinion of this Presbytery, it is the duty of ministers, at all proper times to enjoin upon their hearers their duty as citizens, explaining the difference between the powers which are ordained of God and usurpers, also the difference between a needful revolution and rebellion   .   .   .
>
> Resolved, 3rd,   That especially in a time like the present, when a long premeditated and thoroughly organized rebellion is raging in many of the States of the Union, which threatens to entirely over-

throw our Government and to destroy our liberties and prosperity, it is the duty of ministers of the gospel to warn the people of the awful crime of rebellion and earnestly to exhort them to stand by their Government and to pledge to it their full support. . .

According to the two-column report of the meeting which appeared in the September 19th issue of the *Pacific*, after Loomis had completed making his remarks,

> Dr. Scott rose and said that only one thing was lacking to the paper—only one thing—there should be a preamble resolving this ecclesiastical body into a political organization; then the resolutions would be in place. He had hoped the brethren would not meddle with politics in Presbytery, and to him this was wholly unexpected. He denounced it as being cut and dried, giving him no notice whatever of the plan thus concocted in secret. He denounced it *in toto* as a political paper, and invoked and pleaded that Presbytery should not resolve itself into a political body by passing such a set of resolutions.

According to Warren's report in the *Pacific*, Dr. Anderson then took the floor and "in a quiet and mild manner" answered some of the objections raised by Dr. Scott. Anderson denied that there had been any "cut and dried" plan for the introduction of the resolutions and insisted that this had been done "wholly and exclusively by the mover himself." He moved the adoption of the resolutions. Albert Williams and Frederick Buel spoke "supporting the resolutions and answering the objections."

Among the sources which throw light upon this incident is a rare pamphlet which Dr. Scott published under the title *My Residence in and Departure from California*. In this pamphlet he had the following comment to make about the remarks of Albert Williams. "I knew that I was alone in the Presbytery, and was well aware of the use that was to be made of my words, but when the oldest minister of the Presbytery said that 'Jesus Christ looked down [from heaven] and smiled upon the civil war' then raging in all its horrors in the country, or words of a court of his Church, and acquiesce in such blasphemous and unconstitutional proceedings and resolutions."

Deeply stirred, Dr. Scott rose a second time to speak. He was angry. Warren noted that he "spoke at length and with a great deal of vim and voice." Scott read the resolutions which had been presented, article by article. When he came to that section which called upon the members of presbytery to explain to their respective congregations the difference between "a needful revolution and rebellion," he cried out: "Where, in the word of God, did they get the authority to call it [i.e., the Southern secession] a rebellion? Would Jesus, sitting in the chair of the Moderator, give his sanction to the paper before Presbytery? Would he advise ministers to preach loyalty to the Government? Would he tell them to discriminate between rebellion and revolution? No, sir! No, sir!! I tell you NO SIR!!! Jesus would have nothing to do with such things."

One of Scott's statements was so shocking to Warren's ears that in his account of the meeting he put it in italics: *"Jefferson Davis was as much President as Abraham Lincoln was President."* When Scott came to the word "usurpers" in the resolutions, he said: "Jefferson Davis is no usurper; he is as much a President as Abraham Lincoln is." And regarding the word "rebellion:" "There is no such thing as rebellion in the country, but only rightful revolution." And he shouted out: "Jefferson Davis is no more a traitor than George Washington was a traitor." On this point, Warren remembered Scott as saying: "If George Washington had been unsuccessful, he would have been hung. If Jefferson Davis fails, you will hang him, I suppose. What history will call him depends on success or failure." The vote was called for. All responded in the affirmative except Dr. Scott. Warren not only gave a detailed report of the meeting in the September 19th issue of his *Pacific*, he also wrote an editorial on the subject in which he said:

> We hope never again to be present at another such exhibition of unquestionable hatred and disloyalty to the Government of the United States as we there heard expressed from one of its members. . . Dr. Scott in his presbytery stands alone; left alone even by his own church. "How are the mighty fallen!" God forbid that any shall stand with him, here in a loyal state, when with all his heart he acquits Jeff. Davis of treason with the same breath he acquits George Washington.

Scott's speech before the presbytery was the final act which precipitated the climactic events which took place at Calvary Church on Sunday morning, September 22, 1861. Had he been content to take his stand with Dr. Hodge in the protest submitted to the General Assembly of 1861, probably nothing more would have happened. Dr. Hodge was not hanged in effigy for his outspoken opposition to the Spring resolutions. Nor is it known that a single one of the fifty-six who signed with him were in any way embarrassed because of their stand. But Dr. Scott went beyond the language of the protest. Years later, in reviewing the stirring events of those days, Dr. Burrowes commented in his journal: "Had Dr. Scott only reefed his top-sails, he might have weathered the gale." Had he lived in some other city in California where there was a stronger Southern element, again the story might have been different. But San Francisco was a strong Union city. It was still a booming frontier community where many of its citizens remembered the vigilante days when undesirable characters were unceremoniously run out of the city and in extreme cases actually executed without benefit of a legal trial. Many still remembered how Dr. Scott himself had been hanged in effigy only five years previous. A reporter writing to the New York *Journal of Commerce* analyzed the situation by saying that there were in

San Francisco some clergymen and "pious law men" who rejoiced in seeing Dr. Scott get himself into trouble. He wrote: "To them it is enough to say that Dr. Scott is from the South, and a Democrat; and all the fire of Abolition New School-ism is and always has been like a cur dog at his heels."

In a letter of over two thousand words written while at Panama City on October 14th to the New York *Journal of Commerce,* Scott gave his version of the events that necessitated his departure from San Francisco. He characterized "the *Reverend editor of the Pacific*" as "a Congregational abolitionist and the representative of a class that . . . has always most bitterly opposed my labors on the Pacific Coast." Scott clearly blamed Warren for what happened:

> This *reverend brother* being present by courtesy [at the meeting of Presbytery] went out and reported my remarks on these resolutions for his paper in an unfair & garbled manner, and putting in italics his misrepresentations of such things as I had said, as he supposed would excite the Republican fury against me. His paper was sent in advance to the Dailies of the city. The resolutions & proceedings of Presbytery obtained without *the knowledge or consent of Presbytery* were also published by him with such comments as he thought best suited to excite the populace. Thus urged on by my ministerial brethren, several of the leading Republican papers, either suggested or began to excuse or urge the propriety of a coat of tar & feathers, lynching, exile or hanging. Such things had been said on several occasions before. Indeed for many months past, I had been informed by the police & others, & in many ways, that I was threatened with violence by way of retaliation for the death of Ellsworth & of all the cruelties alleged to have been perpetrated upon Northern men in the Southern States.

The Republican papers for Thursday, Friday, and Saturday, September 19 to 21 inclusive, whipped up such an emotional fervor for vengeance, that some of the authorities waited on Dr. Scott late Saturday night and suggested that he close Calvary Church the next day. "I was informed," he wrote, "that serious disturbances were feared . . . and that in fact my person & life were considered in danger. I could not consent to close the church. I was expected to preach & I would preach unless prevented by a power I could not resist." No one could ever accuse Dr. Scott of cowardice.

When Rev. S. T. Wells, who had served as moderator of the presbytery when the resolutions were under debate, read the September 19th issue of the *Pacific* and the parallel reports which appeared in the secular press, he was greatly troubled. So he called on Dr. Scott and asked him to write out a summary of his remarks. This Dr. Scott did on that same day when the memory of his protest was still fresh in his mind. This summary of over two thousand words Scott later included in his pamphlet *My Residence in and Departure from California.* In general there is agreement between what Warren reported and what Scott wrote, only Warren, by italicizing certain statements, probably focused more attention on them than Scott had intended. After getting this statement from Scott, Wells wrote to at least two of the city newspapers and rather mildly suggested that "an incorrect report of Dr. Scott's remarks" had been made. This letter from Wells appeared in the Saturday issues of the papers and at once prompted a reply from Warren, Williams, and Anderson who insisted that the original report was correct. Their joint statement appeared in Monday's papers.

One of the most colorful accounts of what happened on Sunday morning, September 22nd, at Calvary Church appeared in the Monday following issue of the San Francisco *Evening Bulletin.* "Soon after midnight," the reporter wrote, "there began to be something of a crowd on Bush Street, between Montgomery and Sansome. When the occasional passerby asked what was up, these early risers said—Nothing; they only came down to see what was going on; they didn't suppose anything could be done, but they came early to get good seats." In Dr. Scott's letter to the *Journal of Commerce,* a copy of which also appeared in his pamphlet, he wrote: "On the following morning, Sabbath at 2 o'c, I am informed the mob began to assemble at the church & by scaling the roof, hoisted the flag over the church building & also upon the parapets of the vestibule. And on a new building opposite an effigy of myself was hung labelled 'Dr. Scott, the reverend traitor.' " Now for the second time within five years, Dr. Scott had been hanged in effigy. No other California minister ever achieved such notoriety. According to an unidentified clipping in the Scott Collection in Bancroft Library, the chief of police cut down the effigy early Sunday morning "amid the hisses and yells of the crowd."

In Warren's account of that fateful Sunday morning, which appeared in the September 26th issue of the *Pacific,* he made special mention of the flags. Gleefully he wrote: "The edifice was adorned, outwardly as it never was before. A small American flag jutted out in front of it from the ridge of the roof, and another nailed upright to the ornamental work that crowns the building. Between the lamp posts, in front of the main entrance, a full sized regulation flag was displayed. It was beautiful." And then Warren quoted from Psalm 48:2, "Beautiful for situation, the joy of the whole earth, is mount Zion, on the sides of the North." Thus by the simple expedient of capitalizing the word "north," he twisted the verse to apply to the Northern states.

Flags were also tied to the two lamp posts on either side of the main entrance. According to the reporter of the *Bulletin,* a beautiful flag hung from the eastern lamp post "for which the rumor has it that J. F. Noyes had paid $25 for this special service." About seven o'clock in the morning, after viewing his flag with satisfaction, Noyes left the church

CALVARY CHURCH ON BUSH STREET BETWEEN SANSOME AND MONTGOMERY
From an 1869 photograph, before the building was razed. Flags were attached to the two
lamp posts, on either side of the entrance, at the time of the second hanging in effigy,
in September 1861. Courtesy of California Historical Society.

and returned to his home for breakfast. About this same time a certain
"respectable woman who lives on Bush Street, near Dupont, went down
to the butcher's on the corner to get the meat for her dinner." Her
name was Mrs. Nelson. As she looked down Bush Street she was amazed
to see a crowd of several hundred men gathered before Calvary Church.
The reporter tells what happened:

> She asked the butcher what the big crowd meant down the
> street. "Why," said he, "they're going to hang Dr. Scott and I
> have a great mind to shop up and go down and take a hand in the
> job." The woman had a large market-basket in her hand. She
> thought a moment, then said: "I'll have a hand in it, too"—at the
> same moment dashing her empty market basket, with all her force,
> in the butcher's face. She had no bonnet on, slippers were on her
> feet, and she wore a morning-gown. She made good time down the
> street—from a swift walk she soon broke into a run, and came
> down the north sidewalk to the church on a full trot. She tried
> the upper gate, but that was locked. She tried the lower, found it
> unlocked, entered, ascended the lamp-post where the $25 flag was
> waving. She rolled it up so that it would not easily tear, and in a
> trice it was hers. She wrapped it carefully around the staff, and
> had retreated with it to the basement archway before the crowd
> had waked to what she was doing. Then she came back and faced
> the people. Some of them told her they would have her arrested.
> Then her womanly pluck spoke out. "Very well," said she. "I
> honor this flag more than you. But it was put there to tantalize
> me. You may go to my house and put it up; there's a good place
> for it, but the church is no place for it. You can't put it there."
> Someone in jest cried out: "Hang her! Hang her!" And as though
> they would do just that, some person seized her by her arm. She
> jerked free and scornfully said to him: "You'd better go and get
> some more rum first." By this time, a friend in the crowd recog-
> nized her. "Let her alone," he cried. "She is an honest woman
> —a Union woman. She means no harm." Mrs. Nelson spoke up
> again for herself: "My money helped pay for this church. I am on
> my own ground. I will stay here."

She said that she had known Dr. Scott in New Orleans. She knew that
he was a good man and she didn't intend to see him insulted. But she
was only one against many hundreds. So when some of the men re-
trieved the flag from the basement and lashed it again to the lamp post,
she was powerless to prevent it.

About this time, Mr. Noyes returned from eating his breakfast. On
returning, totally unaware of what had happened, his observing eye
noticed that his flag was not hanging as he had formerly tied it. The
reporter's account continues: "So without speech or apology he went
up to the lamp-post and began to cut the lashings. The crowd would not

stand that. They thought it was a most impudent and outrageous proceeding of some Dixie man. They pitched in upon him, hustled him over the railing into the street, in short, gave him a pretty severe drubbing." The amazed Noyes cried out in anguish and protest. He was a Union man. That flag was his. He had purchased it for this occasion. All he was trying to do was to straighten it. In the meantime, Mrs. Nelson was fairly dancing with joy and crying out: "That's right. Give it to him! He's one of your sort. Give it to him!" When finally the crowd discovered their mistake, wrote the reporter, "they made ample apologies; but nobody after that thought it best to meddle with the flag."

The crowd before Calvary Church grew as the morning passed. Estimates of the number of men present vary from two to three thousand. For the most part it was made up of curious men who just wanted to be present if anything exciting happened. When the usual time came for the Sabbath School, as the Sunday School was then called, the children began arriving. Of this the reporter wrote: "The Sabbath School children and teachers came through the dense mass unharmed, and entered the basement wondering what had made their good pastor so popular all of a sudden. Dr. Burke, chief of police, and a squad of men had come too, and were quietly waiting in the basement for something to turn up."

We hear nothing about the presence of Mrs. Scott and the children, with the exception of eighteen-year-old William, Junior, at either the Sabbath School or the church service. It seems probable that in view of the repeated warnings which Dr. Scott had received, he advised them to remain at home. The article in the *Bulletin* tells of how young William, when on his way to church, was called aside by "the wife of a respectable citizen who does not herself attend Calvary" who asked him if he were armed. He answered "No." "Then," she said, "take that," and she pressed a pistol into his hand. She made him promise not to use it "except to defend your father if his life is in danger." The startled youth made the promise, slipped the pistol into his pocket, and hurried on to church. Later, when the police arrested him, the pistol was discovered to his embarrassment.

At the usual hour, Dr. Scott took the bus from his home on Rincon Hill to Bush Street. From there he walked the short distance to the church through, as he wrote to the *Journal of Commerce*, "the hissing & hooting crowd. A police officer, however, but unknown to me, kindly kept near me." Dr. Scott entered the church by a side door into the basement so that at that time he did not have to walk under the flag-draped main entrance. As soon as the doors of the sanctuary were thrown open, a great crowd of men surged into the building. Most of the male members of the congregation in alarm sent their wives home but a few courageous women elected to remain. The fifteen hundred seats in the sanctuary were quickly taken and hundreds stood in the outside aisles and in the back. Over a thousand were unable to find room inside. Among those who were able to get into the church was Mr. Noyes, the purchaser of the $25 flag, who was heard to say that this was the first time he had been inside a church for fifteen years.

"At the proper hour," wrote Scott to the New York paper, "I entered the pulpit. It happened that my subject was on 'Christian ministers, Christ's ambassadors.' I had no apprehension of personal violence and did not for one moment suppose that I was then preaching my last sermon to my dearly beloved people . . . the house was crowded to suffocation." Perhaps never before in San Francisco had a pulpit prayer been listened to with such rapt attention. On this morning Dr. Scott discreetly refrained from making any mention of "Presidents" or "Vice-Presidents." Since he had never referred to political matters in his preaching, his hearers could find nothing objectionable in the sermon. After Dr. Scott had left San Francisco, his friend, H. H. Haight wrote to him saying: "I also heard one of your 'fault finders' assert that he had been in this city since '53 and had never heard you preach until last Sunday. He expected to hear something traitorous from you but your sermon impressed him with the belief that you had been mis-represented." Haight told the man that the sermon he had heard was just as "loyal" as the sermons had been from that pulpit for the previous six months. It was just another of Dr. Scott's characteristically orthodox presentations, heavy with doctrine and liberally sprinkled with Biblical quotations. The services were conducted without any disturbance, the congregation listening with reverent attention.

When the services were concluded, Dr. Scott followed his usual custom of going to the front entrance to greet his hearers. During the previous hour, the crowd outside had increased, according to his estimate, to from two to three thousand. The police were now in evidence, but they could not prevent a chorus of boos and hisses and such shouts as "There's the traitor. Hang him! Hang him!" Mrs. Thomas Selby, wife of one of the officers of the church, offered to take Dr. Scott to his home in her carriage which drew up at that time. He accepted. As soon as Dr. Scott left the church premises and stepped upon the sidewalk, there was a menacing surge towards him. Some of the police closed around him to protect him. Some men threatened to overturn the carriage. Several, including a big burly red-haired man, grabbed the bridles of the horses. Two policemen leaped to the drivers seat and pushed the frightened driver from his perch. A policeman jumped inside the car-riage before Mrs. Selby and Dr. Scott. Dr. Burke, the chief of police, closed the carriage door, and shouted: "Put on the whip," as he too leaped to the driver's seat. The red-haired man, the last of a group who had tried to restrain the horses, relinquished his hold on the bridles when he saw the chief reaching for his gun. The horses lurched forward and the carriage rolled through the mass of men to a mingled chorus of cheers and boos.

Then came the incident involving William Scott, Junior. The reporter for the *Bulletin* tells what happened:

> As soon as the carriage had rolled out of sight, a man mounted the steps and sang out, "Three cheers for the Union—down with the traitors and seceders!" The cheers were given with a will. Among the congregation, struggling to make way through the crowd, was William Scott, son of the Doctor. . . . He was recognized by some fellow who exclaimed: "Here's the son of a ——, hang him!" Whereupon young Scott, drawing off, gave the ruffian a blow that stretched him on the pavement. A great many admired the feat, still the crowd was closing upon him, when an officer jumped into the thickest [part of the crowd], and taking young Scott by the arm, told him he must take him to the station house.

At this point, one of William's friends, a fellow by the name of Middleton, intervened and hit the officer, whereupon he too was arrested. Both were taken to the police station where it was discovered that William had a pistol. When a full explanation was made in court on the following day, both young men were released. The judge told William that he was perfectly justified in doing what he did.

Although a visiting minister had been advertised to speak in Calvary Church that evening, the trustees in a hastily called meeting voted to cancel the service and lock the building. In this they had the advice of the chief of police. Throughout the day and late into the evening, a crowd continued to loiter on Bush Street in front of the church. "They seemed to suspect," wrote the reporter, "that Secession might walk a ghost about the premises. They were Micaubers, bound to be on hand if anything turned up." Although Scott frankly confessed in his letter to the New York paper that not a finger had been laid upon him or a hair of his head touched, yet "not one who had attempted violence to me was arrested, nor any effort made to disperse the crowd."

We do not know what the chief of police told Dr. Scott as they rode in Mrs. Selby's carriage from the church to the Scott residence on Rincon Hill, but judging by later developments the chief must have warned him that he could not guarantee freedom from violence should Dr. Scott continue to preach at Calvary Church. "I was repeatedly informed," wrote Scott to the New York *Journal of Commerce*, "that the civil authorities did not consider themselves able to protect me in my right to preach, nor to guarantee to my congregation freedom to worship God with me as their pastor." It was the shocking realization of this fact that decided the issue in his mind. He had no alternative but to resign. Twice before he had tendered his resignation as pastor of Calvary Church, the first time in the fall of 1856 as a result of the first hanging in effigy, and the second time on July 1, 1861. Twice he had been induced to withdraw his resignation, but now it would be final.

The decision to leave San Francisco raised immediate problems. How was he to provide for his family and where were they to go? The two older children, Robert and Martha, were on their own, but still at home were five sons ranging in age from five to eighteen and one daughter, thirteen. There was not another church on the whole Pacific Coast to which he could turn and expect a salary sufficient to support them. All avenues of return to the South had been closed. To look for a church in the North, in Yankeeland, seemed unthinkable after what had happened in San Francisco. A number of the officers of the church, including some of Scott's closest friends, called on him that Sunday afternoon. Several advised him to take an extended leave of absence, but this he refused to consider.

In his long letter to the *Journal of Commerce*, he said: "The hardest part of my trial is to be forced away from a tenderly beloved & loving people—to be denied the privilege of preaching to an immense assembly twice every Lord's day. For it is to be remembered that my congregations were full & crowded to the very last. The galleries were always full to overflowing. Nor was there any dissatisfaction with my pulpit labors that I knew of. But I was born in a proscribed latitude. Intolerant *Abolition rule demanded that I should not remain in San Francisco."*

Quick decisions had to be made. Dr. Scott decided to leave with his family as soon as possible for Europe. They would settle for a time in England or possibly in France. On Monday, September 23rd, he wrote to the trustees of Calvary Church requesting them to act at once on the letter of resignation he had submitted the previous July 1st. A special meeting of the board was held that afternoon and the members acceded to his request and referred it to a congregational meeting. The trustees also voted to pay the balance of his salary to the end of the calendar year and to supplement it sufficiently to bring the total amount up to $5,000.

On that same Monday, Dr. Scott rented his home on Rincon Hill to one of his close friends and elders, Frank Henderson, who had also been a member of his New Orleans church. Writing from New York on September 30, 1863, Scott asked Henderson to advertise the property for sale. He wrote: "The property cost me a little over $16,000 . . . many, in fact all the Californians I see, tell me it is certainly worth $20,000. It is a choice location. . . You know there are $59\frac{1}{2}$ feet front on 2nd Street with a depth of 156 on Vernon." In their haste to leave San Francisco, the Scotts no doubt left some of their belongings, including most of his large library, in storage in their old home.

Reservations were made for the eight members of the Scott family to leave on the "Uncle Sam," which was scheduled to sail from San Francisco for the Isthmus on Tuesday, October 1st. This was the very ship which seven years before had brought them, with the exception of Benjamin, who was born in San Francisco, in through the Golden Gate. Another problem demanding solution was that of getting a passport. There was no time to write to the State Department in Washington, D.C.

Scott appealed to his friend, John G. Downey, Governor of California, who responded with an official document which requested "all whom it may concern to permit safely and freely to pass, W. A. Scott & family, a citizen of said State, going to Europe." The document, now in the Scott Collection of Bancroft Library, is dated at Sacramento, September 26, 1861, and for the following day bears the visas of the French and German consuls of San Francisco.

These were hectic days for Dr. Scott and his wife as within so short a time they had to close their San Francisco home and make preparations for a residence abroad of unknown duration. Scott requested a letter of introduction from S. T. Wells, moderator of the Presbytery of California to the "Moderator of the Presbytery of London." This Wells wrote and in his letter included the following: "He takes his companion, Mrs. Scott, a lady greatly beloved and a family of six interesting children with him." Dr. Burrowes, who as a member of the Presbytery of Stockton, was removed from the squabbles which had taken place within the Presbytery of California, consented to take over the editing of the *Pacific Expositor.*

The session of the church met on Friday evening, September 27th, with Dr. Burrowes as moderator. The main item of business was that of Dr. Scott's resignation to which the elders gave a reluctant consent. They issued a call for a congregational meeting to be held on the following Monday evening. Dr. Joshua Phelps, pastor of the Presbyterian church in Sacramento, was invited to occupy the pulpit of Calvary Church for an indefinite time. Sunday, the 29th, came with Dr. Scott staying away from his church. It is not hard to imagine the turmoil of soul he suffered that day when he realized that he had been shut out of his own pulpit.

Nearly three hundred attended the congregational meeting on Monday evening. Dr. Burrowes was in the chair. Dr. Scott's letter of resignation was read and J. B. Roberts moved that the church join with the pastor in requesting presbytery to dissolve the pastoral relation. Actually, since Dr. Scott had never been formally installed, all that presbytery could do was to recognize what had taken place rather than to authorize it. One of the pew holders present, a Mr. Nicholson, moved a substitute motion. He favored a twelve-month leave of absence. He said that there was no other living man who could take Dr. Scott's place in Calvary and that he "did not choose to be dictated to in this way by a mob." Roberts opposed any postponement. He claimed that the church could not afford to give Dr. Scott a leave of absence with pay as long as the war lasted nor "could they afford to turn the church into an arsenal every Sabbath and keep guard at the pastor's house to protect him." Nicholson's substitute motion was lost and the original motion to accept the resignation carried.

H. H. Haight then submitted a series of resolutions which in general expressed the deep appreciation of the people for the faithful services rendered by their pastor. These were unanimously adopted, although there was some question raised over the expression in one of the resolutions which read "he thus goes forth from our midst into exile." Some thought the words "into exile" should be stricken but the majority sentiment was in favor of keeping them. Dr. Burrowes gave an eloquent eulogy in which he said: "I have known all ranks and classes of ministers in the Presbyterian Church from the country village pastor to the greatest metropolitan preacher, but have not yet known one that is greater or more laborious than Dr. Scott; *and I'll say to his persecutors —to his avowed and malicious foes—that I have never heard him speak of them other than in terms of kindness and utmost magnanimity.*" The words in italics were thus marked by Dr. Scott when he included a summary of the speech of Burrowes in his pamphlet *My Residence in and Departure from California.*

San Francisco's newspapers were ablaze on Monday morning following the stirring events of Sunday, the 22nd, with such headlines as "Dr. Scott hung in effigy," "The church flagged," "His son arrested," and "Dr. Scott resigns." Judging by the extensive space given to the events of the previous day, this was one of the biggest news stories of the year. The San Francisco *Evening Bulletin* devoted two full pages of its Monday issue to the event. Although condemning the mob scene before the church, the editor wrote in criticism of Dr. Scott: "We believe that Christian humility has been strangely perverted in his breast, or altogether supplanted by pride, arrogance and a longing for the outward glitter of a martyr's crown, unbecoming in any man and especially unseemly in one of the reverend gentleman's standing and ability." And he concluded an editorial on the subject by saying: "There is, too, a general expression of hope that Dr. Scott's people will consider how much better for their pastor's health the warm air of Louisiana is than the raw winds of San Francisco." The *Pacific* likewise gave an extensive report of the events of the day and the editor concluded his remarks by saying: "God forbid that his like shall ever stand in Calvary Church again."

An undated clipping from a Santa Clara paper in the Scott Collection of Bancroft Library shows at least one editor coming to the defense of Dr. Scott. He held up to scorn the whole sorry spectacle as a "specimen of the liberty of speech and tolerance of opinion in the chief city of the Pacific Coast." He asked: "Why don't they invite Starr King . . . or some other of those reverend ruffians, who have been goading on the fanatical mob to the execrable outrage, to give them a lecture on freedom of speech and tolerance of opinion. . . What a degradation? What Californian does not hang his head in shame at such an outrage?"

The November 1861 issue of the *Pacific Expositor* contained a review of Dr. Scott's ministry in Calvary Church prepared by Dr. Burrowes. Included was the following statistical report:

Organized July, 1854, and building dedicated January, 1855

Number of members at organization	63
Received since on certificate	238
Received since by profession of faith	143
	444
Dismissed, 51; Died, 19	70
Present number of communicants	374

During Dr. Scott's ministry of less than seven years, the following sums were raised:

For the church building and lot	$ 60,000
Organ in Church	8,000
In pew rents	70,000
In Sabbath collections	21,000
For the poor	5,000
For benevolences	16,000
	$180,000

This means that the members and friends of Calvary Church contributed on the average about $25,700 each year for the seven-year period. This in itself stands as an amazing record at a time when the dollar had about four times the purchasing power that it has today.

A large crowd of friends were at the pier on Tuesday, October 1st, to bid Dr. Scott and his family farewell when they embarked on the "Uncle Sam." The Scotts took with them their six youngest children— William, age 18½; Chalmers, 16; Louisiana, 13; Ebenezer, 10; Paul, 8; and Benjamin, 5. A news item in the *Evening Bulletin* tells of his friends presenting a purse of $8,000, although Dr. Scott later denied that the sum was that large. Thoughtful members of his congregation presented each of the children with a supply of clothing, enough, according to the *Bulletin*, to last for four years. Although such outpourings of money and gifts were much appreciated, Dr. Scott could not shake off the deep concern that he felt for the future. He had to pay the travel expenses for a family of eight to Europe. In spite of his large salary, he had been unable to save any money. He had no guaranteed salary after the end of the year and no prospects for work in the immediate future. In the letter written from Panama on October 14th to the New York *Journal of Commerce*, he said: "I am going forth as an exile, I know not whither."

WILLIAM ANDERSON SCOTT IN 1862 OR 1863
A photograph taken in Birmingham, England.
From an original in the Foster family Bible owned by Miss Lou Foster.

Eight Years Exile from California

Aboard the "Uncle Sam" when she sailed from San Francisco for Panama City on October 1st were several close friends of Dr. Scott including Mrs. Thomas Selby who had escorted him to his home in her carriage following the dramatic events at Calvary Church on Sunday, September 22nd. Also aboard were some strong Unionist people who voiced objections to the captain when the proposal was made for Dr. Scott to conduct worship services on the first Sunday at sea. The ship took two weeks to make the voyage and dropped anchor at Panama City on October 14th. The Scotts found it necessary to remain at Panama City until the 23rd, when they crossed the Isthmus by railroad and boarded the English ship "Avon" which sailed the next day for St. Thomas, one of the Virgin Islands. There they transferred to the steamer "Seine" which carried them to Southampton, England.

While waiting for passage at the Isthmus, Dr. Scott wrote several letters which are extant, one being to Dr. Burrowes dated October 19, 1861. "In the agony of leaving my home, my beloved people and beloved books, and the dear old haunts of so many years of prayer and thought," he wrote, "I had not time to thank you for your fraternal sympathy and kindness from the first day even until now." Scott had the following to say about the captain's refusal to let him preach: "The same cruel narrow-mindness and bigotry and intolerance that prevailed in San Francisco at the time of my leaving, we found in force on the ship. A number of passengers wished me to preach; others opposed it; and so the officers of the ship gave me no invitation. This is the first time in my life since I have been a minister that I have not been invited to preach the word of God when on board an American ship on the seas on the Lord's day."

Dr. Burrowes published most of this letter in the December issue of the *Pacific Expositor*, but as he later explained in his journal, he deleted this reference to Scott's unhappy experience aboard ship.

With the passing of the days following Dr. Scott's resignation, more and more of his friends became indignant as they realized that Calvary Church had lost its pastor by the pressure of a mob of several thousand men who were not members of that church. In one of the resolutions presented by H. H. Haight to the congregational meeting held in Calvary on September 30th, we find this statement: "We do protest in the name of civil and religious liberty against the interference of any outside influence upon the internal management of any loyal and law-sustaining congregation of citizens . . . that in the action which has driven away their Pastor, without any show of countenance of law, this congregation have suffered an unauthorized violation of their most sacred rights as American citizens. . ." Many were asking why such an outrageous procedure should be condoned.

The Synod of the Pacific opened its annual meeting at Napa on October 1st, the very day the Scotts sailed from San Francisco. Here a postscript was written to the story of Dr. Scott's resignation and departure from the city which throws more light upon the bitterness that rankled in the hearts of some of his opponents. Dr. W. C. Anderson introduced a series of resolutions similar in tone to those which he sponsored in the General Assembly of that year and also to the ones Loomis introduced at the *pro re nata* meeting of the Presbytery of California on September 16th. The resolutions condemned the southern rebellion in the strongest terms and called upon all citizens to support the Union with all means at their disposal including, if necessary, their personal services. Dr. Joshua Phelps as moderator ruled the resolutions as being out of order and contrary to Chapter xxxi, section 4, of the Confession of Faith which stated that synods were not to intermeddle in civil affairs. Dr. Anderson appealed the decision of the moderator and was sustained by a vote of fifteen to four. The resolutions were then adopted.

On the second day of the meeting, Elder John M. Hamilton of the Presbytery of Benicia introduced the following Resolutions dealing with Dr. Scott's resignation:

> WHEREAS, circumstances have occurred by which one of the churches within the bounds of this Synod has been interfered with and deprived of the privilege of exercising its own choice in regard to its pastoral relations, and as we believe such interference is contrary to all law and order and subversive of every principle of good government; therefore,
>
> *Resolved,* 1st. That this Synod views with regret and disapproval the popular demonstration of personal violence which has deprived Calvary Church of an undoubted right to select its own pastor.
>
> *Resolved,* 2d. (a) That we recognize in Dr. W. A. Scott an able defender and advocate of the charitable Boards of the Old School Presbyterian Church, a warm advocate of the whole cause of education. (b) A faithful preacher in the pulpit of Calvary Church, and we ascribe to his instrumentality in the hands of God much of the growth, success and prosperity which our Church enjoys on this coast.
>
> *Resolved,* 3d. That while we deplore the necessity which has caused him to leave his adopted home, our love to him as a brother prompts us to extend to him our sympathies and our prayers,

that withersoever he may wander, his hands may be upheld and his heart strengthened to speak words of sober truth and earnestness, and bear the bread of life to perishing men.

As soon as the resolutions were presented, Dr. Anderson jumped to his feet and moved that the paper be laid on the table. His motion lost by a vote of seven to ten. The resolutions were then taken up *seriatim*, the second resolution being divided into two parts. The vote on each in order was as follows—1st, 13 yeas, 5 nays; 2nd (a), 16 to 3; 2nd (b), 10 to 9; and 3rd, 14 to 5. Dr. Anderson and Albert Williams were the only ones who voted in the negative for all items. John A. Anderson voted in the negative on only 2 (b). Usually he voted with his father.

In the closing moments of the meeting, J. A. Anderson introduced the following resolution which passed unanimously: "*Resolved*, That Synod has no possible sympathy with the treasonable opinions thought by some to have been entertained by Dr. Scott, and that we detest treason against the United States Government, coming under whatever name it may or by whomsoever uttered, as a heinous sin against God, and a detestable crime against the nation." Afterwards many of Dr. Scott's friends regretted that this action was taken without due deliberation. Dr. Burrowes, who was not present at this meeting of the synod, deeply resented the action taken and commented in an editorial in the November issue of the *Pacific Expositor:* "It was brought up amid the hurry and inattention of the last moments of the Synod, and thus passed without a thought on the part of many concerning its true import and bearing." Burrowes argued that the resolution actually was not intended as an expression of "Synod's abhorrence of treason" but rather to give the impression to the world that "Dr. Scott had been unanimously condemned by the highest assembly of our Church on the Pacific Coast." In this same issue of the *Expositor*, Burrowes pointed out that no Presbyterian minister on the whole Pacific Coast had such a congregation as that which went Sunday after Sunday to hear Dr. Scott. And he claimed: "All the Presbyterian congregations in California united would hardly make one as large as that which habitually gathered in Calvary Church."

On October 6th, Stephen Franklin wrote to Scott and gave him the latest news regarding Calvary Church, the actions of synod, and the reactions of the community to his departure. "Dr. Anderson manifests the same determined hostility to you as heretofore. Others I think are beginning to be a little ashamed of the part they have played in the vile conspiracy. Mr. Williams, however, is the same—a miserable impersonation of selfishness & malignity." Writing to Scott again on October 27th, Franklin said:

It is impossible to tell, however, what the malignity & arrogance of such men as Anderson & Williams may attempt under the promptings of their worthy conferees Warren & Willey. The latter, I am told, has said that he would regard what he had done to drive you away as the most righteous act of his life, or something to that effect, & the former, Anderson, in a ladies sewing circle spread himself in the exultant declaration that "now we have got Dr. Scott just where we wanted him." Alas, my dear brother, what dishonor do they bring upon our holy religion.

Two interesting comments were also included in this letter. "The trans-continental telegraph is now complete," he wrote, "& we are in daily communication with the Atlantic cities." And in a postscript dated October 30th, he noted: "Robert came in this p.m. from Los Angeles. He embarks tomorrow with his regiment for the East."

When Dr. Scott sailed out through the Golden Gate on that first day of October 1861, he left behind him for the rest of his life all controversies such as had marred his ministry in both New Orleans and San Francisco. When he returned to San Francisco late in 1869, he found an entirely different atmosphere. The emotionalism of the Civil War days was then part of history. Most of his former opponents in the presbytery and the community had left the city. John A. Anderson had joined the 2nd California Regiment as chaplain in May 1862. A news item in the *Pacific* for June 11, 1863, stated that Dr. W. C. Anderson left San Francisco on that date for the East and another item in the August 27th issue reported that he arrived on the field of Gettysburg in time for that great battle. He worked for a time with the Christian Commission. He resigned his San Francisco church on June 2, 1864. By 1869 Williams was in New Jersey; Warren was no longer editor of the *Pacific;* and Willey, whose part in the opposition movement against Dr. Scott is not clear, was then serving as acting president of the University of California. The personnel of the Presbytery of California by 1869 was almost completely changed as compared to 1861. Thus, as will be shown later, Dr. Scott returned to a different San Francisco. The days of controversy were over; years of peaceful service were at hand.

After some search, Calvary Church called the distinguished Rev. Charles Wadsworth, D.D., then pastor of the Arch Street Presbyterian Church of Philadelphia to be Dr. Scott's successor. Dr. Wadsworth accepted on April 8, 1862. Wadsworth will be remembered as the minister with whom the spinster poet, Emily Dickinson, became infatuated, all unknown to him. Inspired by this secret attachment, Miss Dickinson wrote a number of poems which reflected her feelings. Among these is the poem which scholars feel was prompted by the news of Dr. Wadsworth's departure from Philadelphia for San Francisco. This begins with the words: "I cannot live with you, It would be life, And life is over there. . ." As will be explained later, Dr. Wadsworth's resignation from Calvary Church in 1869 was the main reason why Dr. Scott returned that year to San Francisco. The spirit of attachment to Dr. Scott on the part of many members of Calvary Church was so strong that Dr. Wadsworth found it difficult to be accepted as his successor.

IN EXILE IN FRANCE

Dr. Scott and his family were in London by November 14th and left the 19th for Paris. There an apartment was rented and the children were placed in schools. The Paris correspondent for the *New York World* in a dispatch dated December 20, 1861, commented as follows on Scott's presence in the city:

> There was quite a secession demonstration on Sunday last at the little chapel in the Oratoire, usually occupied by the Scotch Presbyterian Church. The occasion was a sermon by the Rev. W. A. Scott. . . Upon his arrival here he was taken up and lionized and martyrized considerably by a lot of secessionists, and great efforts were made to recruit an audience for him on Sunday last. The attempt, however, proved a considerable failure, as there were not more than forty or fifty present, and the majority of these were rather a "hard-looking" set who evidently would have felt more at home with a pack of cards and a "brandy smash" in their hands than a Bible and prayer-book. There was nothing particularly notable in the service excepting the prayer for the "President of the Confederate States," in connection with the other great rulers of the world.

This item was picked up by the *Pacific* for February 27, 1862. In time Dr. Scott saw the printed article and in a letter addressed to R. K. N. Baynum of Boston on June 2, 1862, retorted: "It is scarcely necessary for me to say that the California correspondence from Paris about my preaching & praying for Secession in Paris are absolutely false. There is not a syllable of truth in them as to that matter."

While in Paris, Scott wrote his thirty-one page pamphlet which was published there in December 1861 under the title *My Residence in and Departure from California*. Therein Scott reviewed the events leading up to his resignation. The pamphlet contains a copy of his letter written from Panama on October 16th to the New York *Journal of Commerce;* his "Prayer for the Present Crisis;" the actions of presbytery and the resolutions passed by his congregation; his farewell letter to the congregation dated September 28th; and several letters of testimony including one from John G. Downey, governor of California dated October 1st. On a later occasion, Governor Downey informed Dr. Scott that if he had known Scott's life was in danger, he would have provided protection.

The fact that Robert Scott chose to stay with the Union army following the outbreak of hostilities caused his parents much anguish. When the unit to which Robert was attached was ordered East to join the Army of the Potomac, this concern was deepened. These feelings are reflected in some letters Dr. Scott wrote to his wife during the spring of 1861. Writing from Madrid, Spain, on March 27th, he said:

> I have felt some uneasiness about your writing Robert. Tell him how much his father loves him & his consuming anxiety about

his character & happiness. . . . But don't be too severe on him.
He may be going to a gory grave when he receives it, for I
believe there will be some very severe fighting on the Potomac.
And tho I pray God the Federals may be defeated, yet I cannot
but say with David, *Spare the young man,* yes, Merciful God,
spare him! If tears were ink, they would now suffice for writing
many pages. . . . I almost fear that anxiety will cause my death.
I have been ready a thousand times to wish, if it were not a sin,
that I too had died in my pulpit 22nd last Sept.

Again on April 11, 1862, he wrote:

As to Robert, you perhaps have never been aware of my pain
of heart at his position. He is of age, & I have felt it my duty to
let him act entirely on his own responsibility, yet he compromises
my position in the South, for they think I could have caused his
resignation & that I approve of his course. That he is on the
wrong side, you may remember that I wrote to him early in the
struggle, that as long as he remained in Oregon & as an officer of
the Army kept the Indians in order, I had no objection, but that I
could never consent to his actually engaging in arms against the
South. And yet without my knowledge he volunteered in haste
to take the oath, and is now an actual invader of Southern soil—
where he has no right from God or man to be, nor any other of
Lincoln's menacing hosts.

During Robert's four years of service at various army posts in Washington Territory, he was closely associated with Colonel Silas Casey who
took a special interest in the young man. Robert fell in love with the
colonel's daughter, Elizabeth, and the two were married in Washington,
D.C., on or before June 1, 1862, by Dr. Phineas D. Gurley, pastor of
the New York Avenue Presbyterian Church. As an Episcopalian, Elizabeth, or Bessie as she was known by her family, preferred the service
of her church but, according to a letter written by Martha Kittle to her
parents on June 6th, was "strongly urged" to have a Presbyterian
service. No doubt it was Robert who did the urging.

Shortly after his marriage, Robert rejoined his unit. The army of
General McClellan was then engaged in an attempt to capture Richmond. On June 27th the Confederates attacked a Union force at
Gaines's Mill which was the biggest engagement of the war to that time.
On the evening of that day Robert received a wound in the left arm
from a rifle ball which produced paralysis of the forearm. He was
brevetted major for gallant conduct in the engagement.

Hearing of her brother's wound, Martha, known to the family as
Mattie, made a trip to New York to see him. Writing to her parents on
July 11th, she informed them as to what had happened and said that
she "found him at the Astor House looking very well, with his left arm
in a sling. . . . He was very anxious for me to see Bessie. . . . She is

really very pretty & pleasing. . . . We all think he will entirely regain the use of his hand again." Major Scott served from June 1863 to September 1864 as senior aide-de-camp to Major General Halleck. He was brevetted lieutenant colonel in March 1865.

While passing through London in November 1861, Dr. Scott called on the Rev. James Hamilton, one of the executives of the Presbyterian Church in England. He indicated his wish to join the Presbytery of London and his hope that a church could be found for him. Writing to Dr. Scott on December 10th, Hamilton reported that the members of the Presbytery "expressed themselves as delighted at the prospect of receiving such an access to our Presb. Church in England." He explained that since Dr. Scott was coming from a foreign ecclesiastical jurisdiction, it was necessary according to their rules for the Synod of England to act upon his application for membership rather than an individual presbytery. The synod was to meet in April 1862. Dr. Hamilton also mentioned the fact that the John Street Presbyterian Church of Birmingham was without a pastor. On December 20th, Dr. Hamilton again wrote referring to the opening at Birmingham and said: "Our Presbyterian church in England is so small & the openings for its ministry are so very few. . . ." The Birmingham congregation was unable to pay more than 160 pounds which was less than $800 per annum in United States currency. Perhaps with the hope that something better would turn up, Dr. Scott did not then show interest in the Birmingham church nor did he seek membership in the synod at the April 1862 meeting.

In October 1861 the Scotts received a draft for $2,000 as the first installment on the sale of their San Francisco house. With this sum on hand and with his family comfortably located in Paris, Dr. Scott decided to devote himself to study at the theological seminary of the French Reformed (Presbyterian) Church at Montauban, located in the southwestern part of France less than one hundred miles from the Spanish border. There he spent most of the first three months of 1862. He left Montauban on March 25th for a month's tour of Spain. According to the letters written to his wife, he visited such cities as Madrid, Malaga, Cordoba, Cadiz, and Gibraltar. Although he was seeing many new cities and visiting historic sites of great interest, yet his heart was not in travel. Writing to his wife from Madrid on April 15th, he said: "I confess I have no heart for sight seeing or picture galleries. All my thoughts are with you & our poor self-destroying, maddened country. The folly, the fiendishness of the Republican party grows every day in my mind."

Two themes keep repeating themselves in this series of letters to his wife. The first reflected his reactions to the Civil War and the second showed his anxiety for their future. He devoured the war news as gleaned from newspapers "in three or four languages," and, as is characteristic of human nature everywhere, saw what he wanted to see and heard what he wanted to hear. The following extracts from these letters to his wife reveal his deep love for the South and a parallel increasing antipathy for Abraham Lincoln and the North.

March 26: I see a letter in the London Times from Pennsylvania that shows the fall of Fort Donalson not much of a· victory after all . . . that Nashville was sullen and strongly for the South. . . I have no idea the South will submit. It cannot be. But what are we to do? April 2: I see a report that a great battle had been fought at Winchester, in which the Confederates were victorious. God Almighty grant it may be so. One decided victory on the Potomac line would now bring the desired end. "You cannot, my Lords, you cannot conquer America." O that some one would repeat those memorable words of Lord Chatham in the Washington Senate & that Mr. Lincoln would arrest his horrid & bloody war. He cannot conquer the South. April 8: I infer the tide is beginning to run for the Confeds. From the light I have, McClellan is lost. Abolitionism reigns at Washington. Burnside will be defeated. . . The true South will now be more united than ever, & if they have arms, they will drive back the murdering invaders. There never was a more unholy, unjustifiable war than this since the foundation of the world. It cannot be that the South will be altogether lost. I will not believe it as long as one state holds out. Fifty days more will tell the beginning of the end. April 11: Now as to your question as to what the war is tending to? I will answer . . . it is rapidly becoming an out & out abolition war upon the South. It cannot mean anything else, if the reports we have are correct. [Regarding Lincoln] He is a most dangerous hypocrite & what is most surprising is that the people do not see it. . . There is not a more hateful tyrant on any throne in Europe this moment than Abraham Lincoln. Liberty in the Federal States, there is none. . . He means the utter & entire crushing of the Southern States, and the extinction of slavery and of course the predomination of the North in every way over the South. If I were now a citizen of the South, I would rather die & my children with me fill the grave than to submit to the Federal Government of Mr. Lincoln's platform. I would resist to the last. It has been reported here that Fort Pike is taken & even New Orleans; but I cannot think so. If so, all would seem to be lost.

New Orleans was captured by the Federal forces on April 24th, a few days after Scott wrote the above. And lastly in his letter of April 15th, he wrote: "It is impossible to restore the Union. The United States are no more. If Lincoln's armies do not succeed, the Union is lost. If they do succeed, it is more than lost. It is gone, gone forever."

A new danger suddenly arose and that was in regard to his passport. Dr. Scott and his family had gone to Europe on the basis of a document issued by the governor of California, which state was a part of the Union. "I have been told," wrote Scott to his wife on April 15th, "that orders have been given to seize all passports like mine; and that no passports are now required of Americans returning home; but that the officials have liberty at discretion to arrest any man on suspicion and compel him to take the oath [of allegiance to the Federal government]. How will all this affect us?"

Shortly before the capture of New Orleans, Dr. Benjamin Palmer fled the city leaving First Church without a pastor. Sometime in 1863 Joseph A. Maybin, one of Dr. Scott's most faithful elders in the New Orleans church, wrote to him and invited him to return to his former congregation as a temporary supply. This Dr. Scott refused to do as he would not take the loyalty oath required of all responsible citizens by General Butler, then commanding Union forces in the city.

These letters from Dr. Scott to his wife are tinged with deep discouragement as he contemplated the future. On March 28th, he wrote: "But my dear wife, what are we to do? Is it our duty to go to the South. There is no possible way now that I see to do so." He told about his several inquiries to friends in the South, to which he had had no replies. "This I do not understand," he added. "Is it part of God's way to lead me to some other part of the world?" He mentioned his hope to visit England in the near future and considered the possibility of moving the family to London.

In February 1862, R. K. N. Baynum, who was clerk of session of the First Presbyterian Church of Boston, Massachusetts, wrote to Dr. Scott asking if he would be interested in a call to that congregation. This church claimed to be one of the finest in New England where Presbyterianism was not strong. The building had been erected by the Unitarians at a cost of $75,000 about twelve years earlier. The church had about 150 members. When Dr. Scott showed some interest in the possibility of going there, a premature announcement of his acceptance was published in the *Philadelphia Presbyterian*. When news of the call of Dr. Scott to a church in the very citadel of abolitionism reached San Francisco, it aroused amazement. Commenting on the report in the April 24, 1862, issue of the *Pacific*, Editor Warren wrote: "Some of the knowing ones see in this a quiet rap at San Francisco, which virtually banished him for being a traitor, while the same man, *mirabile dictu*, is endorsed by the 'hub of the universe.' This is taken as a great triumph on the part of the Doctor's friends." Elder James B. Roberts of Calvary Church, writing to a friend on April 25th, said: "His enemies writhe under it, and should feel very much ashamed of themselves."

Dr. Scott was not satisfied with the proposed salary of $2,000 per annum which the Boston church offered. He made inquiry as to whether this could be supplemented with a grant from the Home Missions Board of the Presbyterian Church. Also, he doubted that he would be permitted to land in Boston without taking a loyalty oath and this he was determined not to do. He sent an inquiry about this to his son-in-law, Nicholas Kittle, who assured him that such an oath would not be required. Robert wrote to his father saying that he could not but laugh when he heard of the possibility of his going to Boston, but then he also assured him by adding: "But strange as it may seem it is a fact that I find a great deal more conservatism in New York than in San Francisco. The fact is that the people of San Francisco are as a community insane, and they never will forgive Father's opposition to the infernal Vigilance Committee."

Mrs. Scott expressed her willingness to go to Boston when, on August 21st, she wrote to her husband: "It seems to me we might go to Boston now with more satisfaction than at any previous time. . . The feeling sometimes steals across me that after all we may be as much at home with Yankees as with anybody here." The Boston church pressed for a definite answer. Finally on September 15th, Dr. Scott gave his decision.

> I must decline your invitation. Such is the *reign of terror* following the repulse of Gen. McClellan before Richmond that I am compelled to believe, contrary to my earnest wishes, that it would be neither safe to myself or profitable to you for me to become your pastor. . . I do not think there is any danger of a riot or mob in Boston as there was in San Francisco. The very worst that could happen to me would be imprisonment; and in comparison with the slow agony of martyrdom in idle exile, the terrors of Fort Warren [a Federal prison for rebels] are not great in my mind."

IN EXILE IN ENGLAND

Sometime after June 6, 1862, Dr. Scott left Montauban for England. After a short sightseeing trip to Geneva, Switzerland, he reached London during the latter part of the month. He was invited to serve as supply pastor of a small Presbyterian church called Albion Chapel at Moorgate and London Wall, in London, where he remained until the end of October. The site is about one-half mile northeast of St. Paul's cathedral. The church was closed in 1875. The author and his wife visited the site in the summer of 1966 and found that it had been badly bombed during World War II. The minutes of the Presbytery of London for August 5, 1862, report Dr. Scott's presence as a visitor. Mrs. Scott and the children moved to London during the summer of 1862 and in November, the family was living on Frederick Street, Gray's Inn, w.c.

Dr. Scott published two pamphlets and two books during the years he was in exile abroad. Mention has been made to the pamphlet published in Paris. The second pamphlet entitled *The Responsibility of Young Men for their influence on Society* appeared in London in 1862. This was reissued by the Presbyterian Board of Publication in Philadelphia in 1869. Dr. Scott prided himself on his ability to appeal to young men and the fact that he was so often called upon to address such audiences

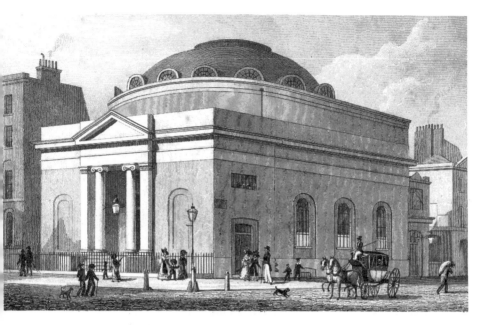

ALBION CHAPEL, MOORGATE, LONDON, ENGLAND
From an 1828 engraving. Here Dr. Scott served as pastor of the
Presbyterian congregation in the late summer of 1862.

is evidence of his success. This pamphlet contains the heart of some of
these lectures.

The first of the two books published during these years contained a
series of sermons. It appeared in New York in 1862 under the title
The Church in the Army or the Four Centurions. The preface, dated San
Francisco, July 4, 1861, states: "To the Army and Navy of the United
States, that operated together in the conquest of Mexico, as a humble
token of regard for their courage in battle, and forbearance and humanity in victory, this little volume is respectfully dedicated by the author."
This dedication to the armed forces of the United States is rather surprising from Dr. Scott at that particular time. We note, however, that
he qualified the dedication by making it refer in particular to the army
and navy of 1846 rather than 1861. A second and revised edition appeared in 1868 as *The Centurions of the Gospel*. Commenting on the
appearance of the first edition, the editor of the *Pacific* on May 22, 1862,
said that Scott's name as author would be a liability to the publishers.

In 1947, eighty-five years after the book was first published, one of the
author's students, David Jacobsen, wrote a thesis under his direction on
"William Anderson Scott as Preacher, Author, and Teacher." In the
course of gathering material for the section dealing with Scott as an
author, Jacobsen found on the bookshelf in the library of San Francisco
Theological Seminary which held Dr. Scott's volume on *The Centurions
of the Gospel* another book with a similar title. This was *The Four*

Centurions by the Rev. James M'Gill published in Glasgow, Scotland, in 1857. The M'Gill volume bore the bookplate of the Scott Collection which was pasted on the undercover of every volume of the Scott library presented to the seminary after his death. Library science had placed the two books together because of the similarity of title and content.

In comparing the two books, Jacobsen discovered a remarkable parallel of both outline and content without any acknowledgment on the part of Dr. Scott of his indebtedness to the M'Gill volume. Although there seems to be no evidence of plagiarism, there was certainly free borrowing of material which was rewritten or paraphrased by Dr. Scott. We must remember that Dr. Scott's book consisted of sermons he had preached. He turned over to his publishers the manuscripts he had used in the pulpit. As a preacher he followed the common practice of gleaning his material wherever it could be found and using it without drawing attention to sources. But when such material was published, due acknowledgment should have been made to the works used.

Dr. Scott's book on the *Centurions of the Gospel* does contain, however, much original material, including a lecture on "The Choice of a Calling or Profession" which he delivered before the San Francisco Y.M.C.A. on April 14, 1861. The chapter entitled "Christian Soldiers" contains a section about his great hero, General Andrew Jackson.

It seems strange that Dr. Scott did not take to heart the criticism he received when he was charged with plagiarism following the publication of his *Daniel* in 1853. This charge was revived by Editor Warren in his *Pacific* in December 1860. The two books have the same weaknesses. We can only imagine what Warren would have written if he had known what a student discovered some eighty-five years later. Yet this latest book by Scott received some excellent reviews. The *New York Observer* said that it "was marked by great vigor of thought, originality of illustration, and profound learning in the Scriptures." When the second edition appeared, the New York *Journal of Commerce* in its issue of March 7, 1868, commented: "Dr. Scott is one of the most able & eloquent writers of the English language, and his style is constantly attractive. The book deserves wide circulation."

Dr. Scott's second work published in exile was his *Moses and the Pentateuch: A Reply to Bishop Colenso.* This volume appeared in London in 1863. It was written to refute the conclusions set forth by the Anglican clergyman, J. W. Colenso, Bishop of Natal in South Africa after 1853, in his volume on the Pentateuch. Bishop Colenso, continuing some critical studies previously made about the authorship of the Pentateuch, is given credit for proving that the narrative portions of the priestly code of the Pentateuch are of late date and therefore unhistorical and unreliable. To Scott, who was reared in a frontier religion where textual criticism was utterly unknown, and who had had but one year in conservatively oriented Princeton Theological Seminary, such a theory was heresy. He felt moved to defend the Ark of the Lord by writing a reply.

Dr. Scott's *Moses and the Pentateuch* is the most scholarly of his eight books. He shows a wide acquaintance with the best Old Testament scholars of his day and quotes freely from many to support his views. In one respect Dr. Scott had an advantage over Bishop Colenso as he could draw upon personal experiences gained in travel through Egypt and the Holy Land to support some conclusions, whereas Bishop Colenso could not. But in general, Dr. Scott was fighting for a lost cause. Even conservative minded scholars of this generation accept much of the general thesis set forth by Bishop Colenso.

Shortly after closing his service at Albion Chapel, Dr. Scott began supplying the pulpit in the John Street Presbyterian Church of Birmingham. Dr. Hamilton had directed Scott's attention to this vacant pulpit in December 1861, but since the stipend offered was only 160 pounds per annum, he felt he could not then accept an invitation to that church. By November 1862, Scott's financial condition was becoming critical. He began as a supply pastor in Birmingham and at once won the hearts of the people. They urged him to stay and promised to provide a furnished house.

The Birmingham church was established in 1857 in a spiritually neglected section of the city where there were some 30,000 people with church accommodations of all denominations for about 4,300. Most of the people were of the artisan class with limited incomes. The original records of the church together with those of the Presbytery of Birmingham and the Synod of England are now on deposit in the rooms of the Presbyterian Historical Society of England. These the author had the privilege of examining in 1956 and from these sources most of the following material has been gleaned.

On December 16, 1862, the officers of the church met and fifteen of them signed notes guaranteeing a loan of about one hundred pounds to be used to furnish the manse. On January 1, 1863, a formal call to Dr. Scott was prepared which states that they, the officers and members of the church, "do heartily invite, call & entreat you to undertake the Office of Pastor among us and the charge of our souls." It was signed by four elders, four deacons, and about one hundred members. This call was formally presented to the Presbytery of Birmingham on February 3rd but could not then be processed as Dr. Scott had not yet been received by the Synod of England. The synod was scheduled to meet on April 22nd.

In the meantime, Dr. Scott was receiving letters from his friends in San Francisco urging him to return to California and start a new church. One of these was written by Alfred Clark in December 1862. He said: "There seems to prevail the impression that it will be our duty soon to colonize and it is the earnest hope and desire of many of us that God will direct your steps hitherward. Think of us, dear doctor, before you commit yourself elsewhere." Clark suggested that the name of the new church might be Gethsemane Presbyterian Church. Stephen Franklin, Frank Henderson, and H. C. Beals were among those who were writing.

The combination of financial insecurity, the necessity of educating his children, an ever increasing desire to return to his native land, and the entreaties of his friends in San Francisco, finally overcame the fear of what might happen to him if he should venture back to the United States. He decided to resign his work in Birmingham. It was a hard decision to make as he had been there for so short a time and already the members of his congregation had such high expectations of what he could do for their church. But it had to be. "In view of letters just received from America," he wrote in his letter of resignation dated March 24th, "I am constrained to inform you that a sense of duty will compel me to decline your call which is still in the hands of Presbytery." He told of how his friends in San Francisco "now propose to build me a new church."

A special meeting of the officers was called for the 25th and on that day they wrote a letter to Dr. Scott from which the following is taken:

> We have heard read your letter of the 24th instant with the utmost pain and concern. We have fondly permitted ourselves to look upon you as our Pastor; and indeed believed you to be so —de facto—awaiting only the legal confirmation of the Presbytery to consummate the union between Pastor and People. . . These being our views and anticipations, you will judge the surprise and shock we felt on hearing your affectionate communication read. From the depths of our hearts we sympathize with you in those feelings which must continually agitate your breast when considering the torn and distracted state of America.

There was nothing the church could do but to acquiece with regret to Dr. Scott's request.

The Synod of England met on April 22nd and even though the brethren must have known about the probability of Dr. Scott's returning to the States, yet they received him as a member of their body. At the moderator's request, Dr. Scott was invited to address the synod and in his remarks told of how he had been "hanged" twice in San Francisco. The newspaper account of the speech left out the words "in effigy." When the author visited the Presbyterian Historical Society of England in 1956, the curator showed him this newspaper report and asked in amazement: "How could a man be hanged twice and still be alive?"

The Presbytery of Birmingham met on May 5th and took up the matter of the call from the Birmingham church to Dr. Scott, perhaps with the hope that he would change his mind. He was not present but sent a letter stating "that he was undecided as to accepting the call and requesting a delay for a month." The request was granted. Within the month Dr. Scott received such favorable news from his friends in

San Francisco that he decided to return to the States. This decision was made known in a letter to the presbytery dated June 23rd. He asked for and received a letter of dismission.

The minutes of the church session show that the sudden resolve of their pastor to leave caused great sorrow but there is no criticism of his action. One record reads: "Speaking for ourselves we have to state that you have completely won our affection, confidence, and esteem." An incidental matter of business came up when the officers found themselves with manse furniture purchased with borrowed money. This was offered for sale and all but 32 pounds was realized. Another item in the minutes reads that "if in the Providence of God Dr. Scott should be again prosperously settled in America, a donation to the Funds of the Church would be gratefully accepted." It is not known if Dr. Scott was able to reimburse the church for this loss.

Scott made steamship reservations for himself and his family to leave England on Monday, June 25th. Before that date arrived, he took his family to Edinburgh so that the children could see the land of John Knox. His last Sunday at Johns Street Church was on the 24th. The Johns Street Church was closed in 1896 when the congregation moved to a new location at Handsworth, Heathfield Road. The congregation continues as Handsworth, St. George's. The membership is still about seventy-five.

The Scott family arrived in New York during the first part of July 1863, fully expecting to proceed as soon as possible to San Francisco. But discouraging news from some of his friends in Calvary Church awaited Scott. Whereas some were eager for him to return, others were of contrary opinion. Even such a strong friend as Elder J. B. Roberts, one of the most influential elders in Calvary, opposed any plan for the organization of another church. Perhaps the most decisive factor, however, was the negative attitude of Dr. Burrowes. Much to Dr. Scott's surprise, Dr. Burrowes gave his full support to Dr. Wadsworth and deplored any effort to divide Calvary and start a new church under Dr. Scott's leadership. Early in the spring of 1863, Dr. Burrowes published anonymously a twenty-four page pamphlet entitled *Impressions of Dr. Wadsworth as a Preacher.* It is quite possible that Dr. Scott received a copy of this pamphlet upon his arrival in New York. The whole purpose of the publication was to praise Dr. Wadsworth. When one reads the pamphlet in the light of known events taking place, it is apparent that the friends of Dr. Scott were claiming that he was the preacher supreme. Dr. Burrowes made no mention in his pamphlet of Dr. Scott or of any movement to start a new church. He simply majored on singing the praises of Dr. Wadsworth. Although the authorship of the pamphlet was ascribed to "a clergyman," it seems evident that all soon knew that Dr. Burrowes was the writer.

Letters and telegrams shuttled back and forth between California and New York during the summer of 1863. Among the letters was one from Elder J. B. Roberts of Calvary Church who wrote saying that the feeling of hostility against Dr. Scott "so far from being abated is more hostile than ever." There were other expressions of opposition to his return. In a letter to Mrs. Henderson dated September 28, 1863, Mrs. Scott wrote: "That Calvary Church would array herself against us and those who might come out of her. . . You can imagine how a man of husband's sensibilities would shrink from putting himself in a position of antagonism to the church which God had so blessed him in building up." So the whole subject was dropped. The Scotts decided to remain in New York.

A SIX-YEAR MINISTRY IN NEW YORK CITY

The Scotts landed in New York a few days after the battle of Gettysburg. It was now clearly apparent that the South would lose the war. Their last desperate attempt to invade the North had failed and their battle-weary troops were sent reeling back into Virginia. The new spirit of optimism which spread through the North undoubtedly worked to Dr. Scott's advantage. Nobody wanted to arrest him. He was not asked to take any oath of allegiance. As far as the authorities were concerned, he was just another American citizen returning from a residence abroad.

Within a few days after their arrival in New York, Dr. Scott received an invitation from Dr. Henry Van Dyke, pastor of the First Presbyterian Church of Brooklyn, to occupy his pulpit for the remainder of July and all of August. The honorarium was $20 a Sunday and it is possible that Dr. Van Dyke turned the manse over to the Scotts for their use during that time. Although Dr. Van Dyke occupied a pulpit in a Northern city, he is known to have entertained convictions regarding the South very similar to those held by Dr. Scott. This may have been the bond of sympathy which brought the two together. Dr. Van Dyke had a son, Henry Junior, who later became one of the most distinguished literary men of his generation. He joined the faculty of Princeton University in 1900 as professor of English Literature. He wrote twenty-five books and a number of hymns including "Joyful, Joyful, We Adore Thee." Dr. Scott's contacts were with the father, Henry Van Dyke, Senior.

Following the death of Dr. Scott in January 1885, Dr. Van Dyke wrote to Mrs. Scott on February 4th and recalled this among other things: "His habit was always to expound the chapter which he read in the service, and sometimes when in this exercise his store of Biblical knowledge was tapped, he seemed to forget himself, and make the exposition larger and deeper than the sermon." Dr. Van Dyke then referred to a certain Sunday when Dr. Scott was supplying his pulpit in Brooklyn.

An Episcopal gentleman and his wife who were in the church one Sabbath were greatly interested and absorbed in the expository reading; and when after the prayer and hymn which followed, the minister rose, and instead of pronouncing the benediction announced his text, the man turned in astonishment to his wife and said loud enough to be heard by his neighbors, "Why bless me, Mary, he's going to preach another sermon." And it was another sermon, yet not another, for it drove home and clinched the exposition of the chapter.

In this letter, Dr. Van Dyke referred to the deep friendship which developed between the two men and between their families as well. "We and our families were very intimate," he recalled. "It was our custom to spend Mondays alternately with each other. Those were blessed Mondays! They were sometimes blue without, but always warm and bright within." And he added: "But the qualities which endeared him most, and now make his memory most precious, were his big hearted loving kindness, and the sweet simplicity of his Christian character. . . He had a keen sense of humor and his shrewd simplicity was often the cause of wit in other men." Here is one of the few references to his sense of humor. Dr. Van Dyke also made mention of Dr. Scott's love for his pet cat. "I can see him now," he wrote, "swinging round in his study chair, in the midst of some profound discussion, to answer the purr and stroke the soft coat of his favorite cat, whose sleeping place was his study table."

Soon after his arrival in New York, Dr. Scott discovered that he was in no danger because of his Southern sympathies. New York was a great metropolitan city while San Francisco still had some of the characteristics of a provincial frontier community. Since it was not feasible then to return to San Francisco, he began looking for a pulpit in New York. Fortunately for him the Forty-Second Street Presbyterian Church was looking for a pastor. This church, founded in 1851, had about 350 members and a handsome new building. In her letter to Mrs. Henderson, Mrs. Scott said: "It is a plain looking house but commodious and pleasant within." A gallery surrounded three sides of the auditorium.

The church held a congregational meeting on September 15, 1863, at which time, with but one dissenting vote, a call was extended to Dr. Scott to be its pastor. Just after the vote was taken, two strangers appeared in the room where the meeting was held and begged leave to speak. They said that they carried letters from persons in San Francisco "charging Dr. Scott with being a traitor and offering to prove the charge." Commenting on this, Mrs. Scott wrote: "No attention was paid to these men as they were in no way connected with the church, but it shows that the devil is not dead." This incident reveals the depth of the animosity which some of Dr. Scott's opponents in San Francisco still harbored even after he had been away from their midst for about two years.

The original record books of the Forty-Second Street Church are now on deposit in the library of Union Theological Seminary of New York City as the church is no longer in existence. These records show that

FORTY-SECOND STREET PRESBYTERIAN CHURCH, 1863
Between 7th and 8th Avenues, New York City. From the Foster family Bible.

Dr. Scott was called at a salary of $5,000 per annum. He was formally installed by the Presbytery of New York on October 18th. The call came at a most opportune time, for his financial situation had become acute. He was so short of funds that summer that he had to borrow money to pay his insurance premiums. With some of the proceeds derived from the sale of their San Francisco property, the Scotts purchased a residence at 208 West Forty-Second Street not far from the church. A notation made in December 1866 shows that he was then paying 7% interest on a $7,000 mortgage. Within two years he was able to cancel this indebtedness. An evidence of the affection with which he was held by his people is seen in the fact that on New Year's Day, 1866, he was presented with a check for $1,050.

Dr. Scott quickly established a reputation in New York as one of the city's most attractive preachers. The January 1865 issue of *Dr. Hall's Journal of Health* claimed that his church was "the best attended Protestant church in the city of New York," and the editor elaborated:

> We have visited it in the dog days, and in mid-winter; on Sunday mornings and Sunday evenings; and whether day or night, summer or winter, it is always a well-filled church, both on the lower floors and in the galleries. We certainly do not know that the same can be said of any other church in this great city; it has grown and thrived, and spread itself like the branches of the green bay tree, because there is a man of might in the pulpit, a "devout man," whose soul is in every sentence he utters, and the people see it, and feel it, and believe! Dr. Scott is one of the very ablest Biblical expositors we have ever heard: he succeeds in interesting the whole congregation; keeps them spell-bound. . . This city needs a thousand more of just such men.

Again he became popular with young men and on several occasions delivered a series of sermons on Sunday evenings addressed especially to them. During his six-year ministry in this church, the membership increased from 350 to 457. Perhaps it is well to point out again that in those days church attendance was usually several times church membership.

Following the habit of a lifetime, Dr. Scott avoided making any references to political matters in the pulpit. With the bitter memories of his San Francisco experience always in the background of his mind, he was doubly cautious not to say or do anything in a public way that would offend. We hear of no reference to Jefferson Davis in his prayers. But in some personal letters, written to intimate friends who shared his southern sympathies, we find evidence of his continued hope that somehow the South would still win. Writing to C. L. Weller of San Francisco on June 15, 1864, he indulged in some wishful thinking: "The common belief here among the best informed & conservative men is that Sherman in Ga. is lost, & that Grant has been unsuccessful & will totally fail, & that France through Max. will acknowledge the Confeds. & be sustained by England. . . O that this horrid war was over." Actually General Sherman was not lost. He occupied Atlanta on September 2nd. General Grant pounded away at General Lee's forces during the Wilderness Campaign of May-June 1864 gradually driving them back toward Richmond and on April 9, 1865, General Lee surrendered. Neither France nor England recognized the Confederacy and Maximilian's attempt to rule Mexico ended in complete failure. Even though Scott was brokenhearted over the Civil War and its final outcome, such views, privately held, apparently caused no embarrassment.

When General W. T. Sherman was in New York in June 1865, he learned that his old friend Dr. Scott was also in the city. In the Scott Collection in Bancroft Library is a letter from Sherman to Scott dated June 4th. It reads in part as follows:

> I fear I will have to go away without seeing you and lest this should be, I take advantage of a leisure hour to write a few letters and this to you. I would like in person to assure you of my sincere respect and to talk with you of our old war at San Francisco which I still regard as one of the earliest symptoms of the Great War with *anarchy* through which our country has been struggling and still is contending. In each of these stages, I have shrunk from a prominent part and yet have been drawn in, but gladly, cheerfully, will I forego all personal fame and distinction if our people can be brought to know that there is and can be no safety to life or honor if public opinion usurps the place of *written Law*. Your task is not yet done or mine either. . .

And the General added a postscript: "I carry your volume & will read it completely." Evidently Dr. Scott had presented one of his books to the general, possibly *The Church in the Army*.

In this letter General Sherman praised Dr. Scott's stand during the vigilante crisis in San Francisco when both stood for law and order against mob rule. Dr. Scott would never agree with the parallel that General Sherman drew between the vigilante affair and the secession of the Southern states. The vigilantes, according to Dr. Scott, were in rebellion, whereas the South was conducting a revolution. To him there was a vast difference.

Scott's extreme caution to do nothing to offend is seen in an incident related in the *Life and Letters of Dr. B. M. Palmer*. In the fall of 1866, months after the Civil War was over, Dr. Palmer while in New York attended one of Dr. Scott's Sunday evening services. Even though Dr. Scott knew him at once, he carefully avoided giving any recognition either during or after the service. Later, Dr. Scott wrote an apologetic note saying that personally he would have been glad to have invited him into the pulpit but he was afraid of his people's "impatience with him [i.e. Dr. Palmer] for his course during the war." Dr. Palmer was known throughout the North as one of the "arch-rebels."

During the reconstruction days, Dr. Scott continued to be concerned for the South. In a letter dated December 4, 1867, addressed to his old friend, Dr. Thomas Smyth of Charleston, South Carolina, he wrote:

> I hope the darkness is about to break & pass away, but I am a poor blind watchman . . . with all the power of vision I can command, I cannot see thro' the darkness. I often think of Victor Hugo's image of looking through a long, dark tunnel and seeing the light, a little clear, earnest, burning thing far ahead, intimating there is an end to the dark passage. And sometimes I have thought I saw the light, but again fogs, vapor, or smoke rose around so densely, I have not been able to see it & my eyes fall down upon the impenetrable darkness. *Politically,* I see no hope for the South, but in a new Congress, which will be the next administration.

Dr. Scott never became reconciled to the fact that his son, Robert, was an officer in the Union Army throughout the war. Robert not only turned Yankee, he also married the daughter of a general of the northern troops. Moreover, she was an Episcopalian! In the Scott Collection of manuscripts is a letter written by Mrs. Scott to Robert sometime in 1870. Possibly this is the original which was never sent or it may be a copy of another which was mailed. It seems that a baby girl had been born to Robert and Elizabeth, named Anna after her grandmother, and had been baptized by an Episcopal bishop! Before reading Mrs. Scott's letter, one should remember that she was born in Northern Ireland where her ancestors had suffered for decades in various forms of religious persecutions at the hands of both Roman Catholics and the Church of England. From her earliest infancy, she had been nurtured not only in Presbyterianism but also in Ulster Presbyterianism and this meant that she had no use for the Episcopalians. In this letter addressed to "My dear son," she wrote:

> I write now to unburden my heart of a matter that has long oppressed it. I allude to your apparent repudiation of the church of all your ancestors and running after the intolerant and self-conceited Episcopalians. I can imagine two of your townsmen talking to each other—an Episcopalian and a Presbyterian. The first says, "There is Col. Scott, the son of a distinguished Presbyterian minister, has come to us." The second, looking down answers, "Yes—and we feel ashamed for him and for his father. If his father should visit us, we would treat him with every distinction. He might preach in all our pulpits. How would you treat him?" "Oh we would not let him into one of our pulpits, of course. We do not acknowledge him as a minister of the gospel at all. We would treat him as any other layman." Then answers the Presbyterian: "If Col. Scott had no more grit, and backbone, and pride of family, than to run with people who would thus insult his father, you are welcome to him. Our great historical church is not made of that kind of stuff."

Secondly, as to my little Anna—I have somehow been smelling *treason* in the air about her and had Mattie ask the question direct —if she had been baptized and by whom. Last night coming from the evening meeting, Mattie told me that Anna had been baptized by an Episcopal Bishop. I was so mortified and indignant, I could not sleep all night. After naming her for me, I consider you grossly insulted me to have her baptized thus without my consent.

Colonel Scott remained with the United States Army after the Civil War and on January 1, 1878, he was ordered to Washington, D.C., to take charge of the compilation and publication of the war records. He was indefatigable in his zeal to collect original sources, both Union and Confederate. These were skillfully collated and edited. The first number of what became a set of 128 volumes of the *Official Records of the Union and Confederate Armies* appeared in 1880. He continued working on this project until his death on March 5, 1887, about two years after the death of his father. The works which he had so carefully prepared continued to be published year after year until 1901. The exhaustive and well edited work remains to this day one of the primary sources of the Civil War. Such an authority as the late Dr. Douglas S. Freeman, author of the *Life of Robert E. Lee,* speaks in the highest terms of praise of the work done by Colonel Scott.

Dr. Scott lived to see part of these published works by his son as some of the first volumes of this set were in his library at the time of his death. No doubt the passing of the years brought some mellowing of old bitternesses and disappointments. How could Dr. Scott have helped but be proud of the literary achievements of his son? And yet one of Dr. Scott's granddaughters informed the author that "she was a girl well toward maturity before she ever heard that she had an Uncle Robert . . . that he was ostracized [by the family] because of his affiliations with the North."

There were the inevitable changes in the family circle during these years. Nicholas and Martha Kittle and their children moved to San Francisco in October 1863. William Junior accompanied them. After Chalmers had attended college for one year in New York City, he too went back to California. Colonel Robert Scott had duty in California in 1865, so by that time four of the Scott children had returned to the state they loved so much. These ties only deepened the hope of the parents that they too could return. On February 1, 1867, the Scott's youngest child, Benjamin, then in his eleventh year, died. This reduced the family circle in New York to three children, Louisiana, Ebenezer, and Paul Eli.

No controversy marred Dr. Scott's ministry in New York. He was now at the height of his power as a pulpit orator and Biblical expositor. In 1867 he brought out his eighth and last book, *The Christ of the Apostle's Creed,* with the subtitle, *The voice of the Church against Arianism, Strauss, and Renan.* Here he was striking out against recent criticism of the Bible and of Christianity. This he considered his best work.

For more than four years, Dr. Scott carried on his work without taking any vacation except "for very short intervals." He was preaching morning and evening every Sunday, two different sermons each week plus the usual midweek service. On March 2, 1868, his elders took note of this faithful service and also of his "impaired health" and voted to give him a three-month vacation with full pay. They recommended a trip to Europe and members of the congregation raised a purse of $3,000 to cover expenses. Thus for the second time Dr. Scott was sent abroad for health reasons by his congregation with salary continued and expenses paid.

Dr. and Mrs. Scott sailed for Europe on March 21, 1868. Their original passport, now in Bancroft Library, bears the visas of several foreign consulates stamped on the dates and for the cities indicated, all in 1868: April 23, Milan; May 4, 13, Rome; May 21, Berna (this was for a Russian trip valid from that date to June 2nd); May 23, entry stamp for Russia; May 27, 28, St. Petersburg; no date, Moscow; and June 2, Vienna. A trip to Russia in that day was most unusual, but then Dr. Scott was frequently going to unusual places during his travels abroad. This was Dr. Scott's fourth and last trip to Europe. They returned to New York on July 13th.

A number of invitations came to Dr. Scott during his New York ministry to move elsewhere. One of the Presbyterian churches in New Orleans wrote in 1865 to see if he would consider returning to that city, but he declined. Dr. Palmer was still pastor of First Church and Dr. Scott felt that his presence in the city would be an embarrassment. On September 28, 1868, fourteen years after Dr. Scott had left his New Orleans congregation, one of his former members wrote: "You have more warm friends in this city today than I suppose you ever had. Your hold upon the esteem and affections of the people has never been reached by any or all who have succeeded you in this field & hundreds if not thousands would hail with delight your return amongst us."

In March 1866 a call was extended by the Pine Street Presbyterian Church of St. Louis to Dr. Scott to be its pastor. Davis Scott, a brother of William, and his family were members of this church. This too he declined.

SAN FRANCISCO CALLS

Shortly after Dr. Scott had been installed as pastor of the New York church, a self-appointed "Committee" of his friends in San Francisco, which included Frank Henderson and J. O. Rountree, made another effort to persuade him to return. In a letter to Rountree written in January 1864 Dr. Scott confessed: "I have greatly preferred San F. to any other field." Ever since he left California, he nourished the hope that someday he might return. The committee forwarded another urgent request to return in February, to which Dr. Scott replied: "I am compelled to say that the way does not seem open for my return. . .

I have always since I left you said I would not return to engage in any church enterprise which was in fact or could be construed or tortured into an opposition to Calvary Church. And it is now plainer than ever, judging from all the information I can get, that my return would be construed into an opposition to my dear old church."

Several developments, however, arose in 1867 in Calvary Church which in time changed the whole picture for Dr. Scott. The shifting residential pattern of the city was westward. Calvary Church on Bush Street near Montgomery found itself too far from the majority of its members, many of whom were walking to church. In November 1867 the church bought for $35,000 a lot at the corner of Powell and Geary Streets, where the St. Francis Hotel now stands. A part of this lot was then sold for $10,000, leaving a net cost of $25,000. The new site was on the southwest corner of Union Square, about one-half mile southwest of the original location, and only one block from City College which stood at the southeast corner of the same square. The property on Bush Street was sold for $80,000. A handsome new church, large enough to seat two thousand, was erected on the new site at a cost of $180,000 including furnishings. The building was dedicated on May 16, 1869.

These changes taking place in Calvary Church gave the friends of Dr. Scott the feeling that the time was opportune for his return. The city was growing and there seemed to be room for another Presbyterian church. A subscription paper was circulated in October 1868 which promised Dr. Scott an annual salary of $6,000, travel expenses, and a suitable church building if he would return and be the pastor of the new congregation. Before the end of the month, some $4,000 had been subscribed. On November 7th, Dr. Scott wrote to Nicholas Kittle saying: "I do not wish you or any of my own family to become responsible for any movement or any part of it of the kind contemplated." He wanted to know, however, if there would be any objection to his return from Dr. Wadsworth or from the pastor of the First Presbyterian Church. "I do not wish," he explained, "to return to San F. to have war with Presby. nor with any body else."

Another development came in the spring of 1869, when Dr. Charles Wadsworth decided that he wanted to return to Philadelphia. On April 13th, a member of the Presbyterian Board of Publication wrote from Philadelphia to Dr. Scott saying: "Dr. Wadsworth has really accepted a call to the Dutch Church . . . of this city." No news of this call seems to have been known in San Francisco at that time, but it seems to have become common knowledge by the summer. Dr. Wadsworth asked for a six-months leave of absence to begin the latter part of May, after the dedication of the new church. This was granted. He and his family went east and during the following November, he notified Calvary Church of his unconditional resignation. As soon as the possibility of Dr. Wadsworth leaving Calvary Church became known to the friends of Dr. Scott, they abandoned all plans to start a new congregation in the hope that their former pastor could be called back to the church he had founded.

Another new development was taking place in the spring of 1869, when the Old School and New School branches of Presbyterianism were drawing together. The original division of 1837 arose out of differences regarding doctrine, polity, and slavery. The Civil War split each branch so that at one time there were four Presbyterian denominations branching off of the original parent body—New School, North; New School, South; Old School, North; and Old School, South. As has been stated, the two southern branches united in 1864, and in 1865 adopted the name, the Presbyterian Church in the United States. The two northern branches delayed merging until 1869, when they formed the Presbyterian Church in the United States of America. By that time, the three major reasons which had caused the first division had largely disappeared. Both the Old School and the New School then held similar views as to doctrine and polity and the Civil War had settled the slavery issue. There was, therefore, no longer any good reason why the two northern branches should remain apart and many reasons called for their union.

The year 1869 saw the completion of the transcontinental railroad. The Central Pacific, working eastward from San Francisco, and the Union Pacific westward from Omaha, met at Promontory Point, Utah, on May 10th. The promise of a new era for California and the entire Pacific Coast called for the united efforts of a united Presbyterian Church. Anticipating their coming merger, the two Presbyterian synods in California launched a new Presbyterian weekly called the *Occident* in San Francisco on January 4, 1868. The editor was the Rev. James Eells, D.D., pastor of the First Presbyterian Church. This periodical continued in publication until 1900. The only complete file is in the library of San Francisco Theological Seminary. Its columns throw a flood of light on the last fifteen years of Dr. Scott's life. Following the appearance of the *Occident*, the *Pacific* continued as the organ of Congregationalism in California and the whole Pacific Coast.

The two General Assemblies, Old School and New School, held their 1869 annual meetings in New York City at the same time during May. Both assemblies endorsed the proposed union, but by Presbyterian polity, the plan had to be submitted to all of the presbyteries for approval. Anticipating a favorable vote, plans were made by both assemblies for a joint meeting to be held in Philadelphia on November 10th, when the union would be officially consummated.

The Old School Assembly held its May, 1869, meeting in the Brick Presbyterian Church of New York City of which the venerable Dr. Gardiner Spring, then 84 years old, was still pastor. New York Presbytery elected him as their commissioner with Dr. Scott as the alternate. The Presbytery of California was represented by Rev. Albert Williams who was then without a church and who was living in nearby New Jersey. A dramatic meeting was held on May 29th when about five hundred commissioners of the two assemblies joined in a communion service. The *Occident* for June 12th reported that "an immense multitude of Christians crowded every space in the capacious Brick Church." Dr. Spring led the service of worship. Adding to the great interest was the presence of Dr. W. C. Anderson, formerly of San Francisco, who, according to the report "made the closing address, simple and exceedingly touching." Thus, the two men, Drs. Spring and Anderson, who more than any others were responsible for the division of the Old School Assembly in 1861, were working together in helping to bring about the proposed union. In all probability, Dr. Scott was present at this service. If so, we can only imagine what memories must have surged through his mind as he saw these two men together on the platform. His opposition to the policies they advocated some eight years earlier had caused him much pain and also financial loss. Now the breach was being closed. Since Dr. Anderson died on August 28th of the following year, this was no doubt the last time the two, who had fought so many battles in the small Presbytery of California, met each other.

Hearing that Dr. Wadsworth had left San Francisco on his extended vacation, Dr. Scott felt it was an opportune time for him to return on a visit to San Francisco. Friends made arrangements for him to preach in the new Calvary Church on Sunday, July 11th. He left New York by rail on June 28th. After some stops along the way, he arrived at the railroad terminal in Oakland on Tuesday, July 6th. A ferry boat ride across the bay brought him to his beloved San Francisco. His exile was over.

When Dr. Scott first visited San Francisco in 1854, he wrote to a friend back in New Orleans on June 12th prophesying: "There will probably be three great railroad trunks to the Pacific from the Mississippi valley within the next generation." He then felt that the first of these transcontinental roads would be from New Orleans, through Texas, to San Francisco. He lived to see a part of his prophecy come true and much sooner than he had believed possible. No doubt as he sped along mile after mile across the prairies and over the mountains in comfort, he remembered the gruelling stagecoach ride of twenty-one days he had taken in the spring of 1860 while en route to the General Assembly of that year. While in San Francisco, Dr. Scott was a guest in the home of the Kittles.

Everywhere Dr. Scott was given a warm welcome. The newspapers hailed his return. The San Francisco *Examiner* for July 7th stated: "This eminent divine, who was the first pastor of Calvary Church . . . returns to the scenes of his early labors to make a short visit to his children and will be cordially welcomed by a very large number of our citizens." Mention was made of the fact that he was to preach the next Sunday at Calvary Church. The *Occident* commented: "Many hearts will be delighted to learn that Rev. Dr. Scott is once more in California. . . The Dr. is looking remarkably well, in fact better than for many years. His intention is to remain but for two or three weeks in this

State as he wished to be in his own pulpit in New York by the first Sunday in August."

When the first building of Calvary Church was erected and furnished, Dr. Scott was able to secure a handsome white marble pulpit. This pulpit was moved to the new building at Geary and Powell Streets, so when Dr. Scott stood up to preach before the large congregation which gathered on that Sunday morning, July 11th, he was literally standing in his old pulpit again. The church was filled to capacity with every one of the two thousand seats taken and people standing in the aisles and in the rear. According to newspaper reports, many came from distant places. Among those present at the morning service was Governor H. G. Blasdell of Nevada and his friend of many years, Henry H. Haight, then governor of California. Among those present in the evening was ex-Senator W. M. Gwinn. The evening service was more crowded than the morning, "even to the filling of the lobby."

The San Francisco *Daily Examiner* for July 12th reported:

> This learned and able Divine, now a visitor to our city, whence he was almost driven a few years since by the violent demonstration of an intolerant spirit that then held high carnival here, preached in Calvary Church yesterday, to the largest congregation of Protestants ever before assembled in this city. Such a demonstration of sincere esteem and affection of old acquaintances for a Minister of the Gospel has never been equalled in our experience. The very spacious auditory of the church . . . was filled to overflowing; and many went off unable to obtain an entrance. When the Rev. Doctor made his appearance in the pulpit the faces of hundreds lighted up with a feeling, though unspoken welcome, and exhibited the struggle required to repress the impulses of their hearts to break forth in boisterous plaudits. . . We have never witnessed an audience listen so eagerly to a sermon as did this vast concourse on this occasion.

Dr. Scott rarely made personal references in the pulpit. His manuscript sermons examined by the author are almost completely devoid of accounts of personal experiences for illustrations. Great as the temptation must have been on this occasion to reminisce, we can believe that he refrained from doing so. Rather he seized the opportunity of exalting the Christ whom he had magnified and served throughout his ministry.

The account in the *Examiner* continues: "When the entire service was concluded, there was a rush of friends toward the altar to take the Doctor by the hand. . . Many tears were shed and the Doctor's own feelings were well-nigh overcome." In the following sentence we see an indication that the public knew there was to be a change of pastors at Calvary: "We much mistake the feeling of the Calvary Congregation if they do not make a strenuous effort to get their old Pastor back." But as long as Dr. Wadsworth had not submitted a formal resignation, any discussion of this possibility was not proper.

Never before had Dr. Scott been given such a welcome. This was a mountain top experience. There were a few present, as Stephen Franklin and his wife, who could look back in memory to the years when Dr. Scott was pastor of the First Presbyterian Church of New Orleans. Perhaps the Franklins remembered that December 1842 evening when Dr. Scott was a guest in their New Orleans home, coming as a candidate for the pulpit of their church. He was then nearly twenty-seven years old. What a growth they had seen in him during those intervening twenty-seven years.

And if Ann, his wife, could have been present on that Sunday morning in Calvary, no doubt she would have retraced the years in her mind back to the winter of 1830-31 when she first met her future husband at Huntingdon, Tennessee. He was then an eighteen-year-old stripling, clad in homespun, riding a circuit through northwestern Tennessee as a licensed Cumberland Presbyterian preacher, and carrying his Greek and Latin books along with his Bible. No one could have appreciated better than Ann the contrast between the time when her husband as a youth preached in a log schoolhouse in the backwoods of Tennessee and now as he stood before the great audience in Calvary Church. William would have been the first to say that much of his success was due to the faithful and loyal cooperation of his wife.

But only Dr. Scott himself could have gone back in memory to the time when as a ten-year-old boy he attended the log schoolhouse at Big Creek, Tennessee, where the other boys taunted him because of his lame foot and called him awkward. He alone could remember those feelings of bitter frustration when he realized that he could not compete with his playmates in physical activities. And he alone could remember that deep resolve he made as a boy to excel. There in the white marble pulpit of the new Calvary Church in San Francisco, Dr. Scott stood at the apex of his power as an eloquent and persuasive pulpit orator. If there had been any doubt in his mind before that Sunday's experience about the wisdom of returning to California, such was now removed. If the way could be honorably cleared, he would return.

Dr. Scott was back in his pulpit in New York City by the first Sunday of August. Shortly afterwards he wrote to his friend Stephen Franklin:

> I find myself greatly embarrassed on my arrival at home. This I ought to have foreseen & provided against. . . The embarrassment that I am in is that my dear people ask me at every side, Is it true as the papers say that you are going to leave us? Of course, I have to reply, I have promised to return to San F. on certain conditions. . . Until I hear further from your congregation, I am in doubt. . . The sentiment of my people here is very

decided and strong against my removal. I do not know whether I can get them to consent to a dissolution of our pastoral relationship at all.

The history of his leaving his churches in Tuscaloosa and New Orleans was beginning to repeat itself.

In the meantime Calvary Church had secured the services as a temporary supply of a young minister from North Ireland, John Hemphill. Although still a young man in his mid-twenties, he had already established a reputation for pulpit eloquence. He had been ordained by a presbytery in Ireland in July 1868 so he came without having had much practical experience. But he quickly won friends and soon came without having had much practical experience. But he quickly won friends and soon some of the members of Calvary were talking about him as the possible successor to Dr. Wadsworth. On October 19, 1869, H. C. Beals, who was one of Dr. Scott's strongest advocates for Calvary's pulpit, wrote to him saying: "It seems that Mr. Hemphill is only 24 years old—he will not do."

On November 8th, Dr. Scott left New York for Philadelphia where he served as a commissioner from New York Presbytery in the final ceremonies which brought together the Old and New Schools of the Presbyterian Church. The union was consummated on November 10th. Thus a necessary step was taken which made possible the success of one of Dr. Scott's greatest accomplishments, namely the founding in 1871 of San Francisco Theological Seminary. Such a venture demanded the support of united Presbyterianism not only in California but on the whole Pacific Coast.

Dr. Wadsworth submitted his resignation as pastor of Calvary Church on November 9th. This had been expected for some months and was accepted by the church at once. A congregational meeting was called for Tuesday evening, November 16th, for the purpose of selecting a pastor. According to an unidentified newspaper clipping in the Scott Collection, the meeting was marked with great excitement and even drama. There was loud applause when H. M. Newhall nominated W. A. Scott. We may assume that there was another outburst when the name of John Hemphill was presented. Some of the remarks made were very personal and even caustic. One speaker referred to Hemphill with contempt "as an Irishman" and "a foreigner." A General Wilson urged the election of Scott arguing that Hemphill was comparatively unknown whereas all were aware of Scott's ability. He said that the church could not afford to take a chance on one who had preached for them only four or five times. Dr. Scott's age entered into the discussion. He was then in his fifty-seventh year. Some said he was past his prime whereas Hemphill was young with a brilliant future before him. This seems to have been one of the most forceful arguments used against Scott's selection. James B. Roberts arose and after speaking highly of his former pastor as a clergyman said that "there could never be sufficient unanimity under his pastorship to make his election advisable." Even such old friends as Thomas Selby and Governor Henry H. Haight came out for Hemphill. The final vote was 93 for Scott and 124 for Hemphill. An effort was then made to make the call unanimous, but this failed. Dr. Scott's friends felt too deeply to join in this gesture of courtesy. They left the church that evening with heavy hearts.

The next day several of Dr. Scott's friends wrote to him telling what had happened. After giving the results of the voting, James Rountree in his letter said: "You will see that you are forever shut out of Calv. Church and all done by Selby, Roberts, and Coon. I feel too bad today to write a letter. I feel like I was entirely shut out from the world with a family of children to save. . . We can't go to Cal. Church any longer. . . We can't nor will we remain any longer where three men rule the whole church, nor will we listen to an *Irish Boy* only 25 years of age, without any experience." Rountree reported that there was an Episcopal church building for sale which stood on Post Street near Mason, and only about two and a half blocks from Calvary Church. The sanctuary was large enough to seat one thousand and he thought the property could be purchased for $40,000. He told Dr. Scott of the plan to organize a new church and then asked: "Now if we do so and guarantee a good salary, can we depend upon you to come? Mrs. Kittle told me you would come. We can't delay any longer."

Frank Henderson wrote on the same day: "Before this reaches you, you will have heard of our defeat, but this is no evidence that you are not the choice of the people. Every influence was used by your implacable enemies." He too referred to the plan to organize a new church and added: "I am continually being stopped on the street with offers of money to help us build a new church, not in small sums but in thousands. . . You must not refuse to come. We with many others have left the church [i.e. Calvary]." Henderson stressed the point that San Francisco was growing rapidly and that there was need for another Presbyterian congregation.

Dr. Scott, much as he wanted to return to California, was cautious about committing himself to a new venture before he was assured that there were good reasons to believe in its success. On November 17th, he wrote to his son-in-law, Nicholas Kittle: "I ask myself, what better can I do with the ten or fifteen years that God may yet grant me to labor, than to try and build up another temple to His praise on that coast. . . I wish to know who and how many are willing to be organized into a new church to be called St. John's Presbyterian Church; and will this society when organized guarantee a place of worship and a salary of at least $5,000 per annum for three years, to be paid punctually by the month, and expenses of removal including library." Dr. Scott was remarkably accurate in his estimate of the number of years he was to live, for he died fifteen years after his return to San Francisco.

Advertisements were inserted in several San Francisco newspapers announcing a public meeting of all interested in the organization of a new Presbyterian church for Monday, November 29th, in the lecture room of the Mercantile Library. About two hundred were present for the meeting which was moderated by the Rev. T. M. Cunningham, D.D., pastor of the First Presbyterian Church. Correspondence from Dr. Scott was read indicating his interest in the proposed new church if certain conditions were met. A number of actions were taken preliminary to the formal organization of the church and an invitation was extended to Dr. Scott to be the pastor at a salary of $5,000. Temporary trustees were selected and initial steps were taken to secure subscriptions. In all of this, the friends of Dr. Scott had the hearty support of the Presbyterian ministers of the city, several of whom signed a petition which was sent to Dr. Scott urging him to return.

A question of primary consideration was a building. Writing to Kittle on December 31st, Scott suggested that if the provisional trustees could raise at least $20,000 towards the purchase price of the property, then "I promise with God's help to undertake the enterprise." Negotiations with the Episcopalians moved slowly. An initial offer of $40,000 was rejected. In this same letter of December 31st, Scott wrote: "No event of my humble life has caused me half as many sleepless nights & hours of agony as this contemplated enterprise." The big question was this— should he leave a large and successful church in New York City for all of the unknown problems and difficulties connected with the establishment of a new congregation in San Francisco?

So the matter stood when 1869 came to its close.

ST. JOHN'S PRESBYTERIAN CHURCH, SAN FRANCISCO, ABOUT 1870
On Post Street near Taylor. Here Dr. Scott ministered from 1870 to 1885.

San Francisco, St. John's Church

The new year, 1870, plunged Dr. Scott into even deeper turmoil of emotions as he compared the advantages and disadvantages of beginning a new work in San Francisco with his situation in New York. The long delay in receiving some positive word from his friends in San Francisco was frustrating. They were having their difficulties, especially along financial lines. The provisional trustees discovered that the majority of the ninety three who had voted for Dr. Scott, when Calvary Church held its congregational meeting for the selection of a new pastor, were unwilling to withdraw from their church in order to unite with a new congregation. Possibly many of these felt bound to Calvary because of financial commitments made for the building. To offset this unexpected lack of support, the trustees found a number of people in other Presbyterian churches in the city who expressed a willingness to join the new enterprise. No financial assistance was available from the national headquarters of the denomination. The local people had to assume full responsibility.

Both Dr. and Mrs. Scott were eager to return to California. Four of their children were then in the West, Robert, Martha, Chalmers, and Louisiana. Lou had made the overland trip by train in the previous October and was staying with the Kittles. Only the two younger boys, Ebenezer and Paul Eli, were with their parents in New York. The family letters in the Scott Collection for this period throw much light upon the issues being discussed. On January 6, 1870, Mrs. Scott counselled Mattie: "We must never say an unkind word about any one who chooses to remain in the old church. . . Keep in mind all of you that *by a wise and kind course, Cal. church may yet fall into our hands.* This last suggestion is just between ourselves." Dr. Scott was more realistic in his appraisal of the situation. He concentrated his attention on the issues involved in getting a new church started.

When the members of Dr. Scott's New York church heard about the possibility of their pastor moving to San Francisco, they were aroused. They pleaded with him to stay. On January 6, 1870, one of the leading elders of the church, Dr. John L. Campbell, wrote to his pastor and reassured him of the love and admiration of the members of the congregation. He reminded Dr. Scott of the fact that during his pastorate there, the church had grown both in membership and attendance and had become one of the leading churches of the city. He closed his letter with the prophesy that the church would be placed "in great jeopardy" if he left. His analysis was correct, for the church was unable to find another minister of Dr. Scott's caliber. The large congregation built up by Dr. Scott's magnetic personality and strong preaching gradually declined. Within six years, the church had reached such a low state that the Presbytery of New York voted to close it.

Among those in San Francisco most eager for Dr. Scott's return to the city was Dr. Joshua Phelps who had shown himself to be such a staunch friend at the time of the second hanging in effigy, September 1861. Dr. Phelps had moved from Sacramento and was then serving one of the Presbyterian churches in San Francisco. On January 4th Dr. Phelps wrote to Scott urging him to return to California. "I do not exaggerate," he said, "when I say that there are hundreds of families now in San Francisco, having no church home, who would immediately gather together under your preaching." He stated that the total combined seating capacity of all the Presbyterian churches of the city was between 4,500 and 5,000. "What is that," he asked, "in a city of 150,000?" He stressed the fact that the attitude of the members of presbytery to Dr. Scott was entirely different from that which existed some eight or nine years earlier. He promised the "cordial sympathy and cooperation of all the Presbyterian pastors here." He passed on the information that although no formal church organization had been perfected and therefore no official call could be extended, yet the provisional trustees had "signed a guarantee for your salary which will be forwarded to you this week. The men who have signed that paper are among the first men of the city in point of wealth and integrity."

This was the news Dr. Scott had been waiting for. The sessional records of New York's Forty-Second Street Church tell us what happened next. The documents mentioned by Dr. Phelps reached Dr. Scott on Friday, January 14th. The next day he wrote a letter to his elders, which was read before a special meeting of his session called for the following evening. After referring to the fact that he had been urged to return to San Francisco, he asked for a leave of absence effective January 24th and continuing to March 1st. "It is only a sense of duty that constrains me to take the course I propose," he wrote. "I have never in my life before had so much agony of soul about any similar question."

After a frank discussion of Dr. Scott's request, the elders agreed that it would not be well for the church to grant the six weeks' leave of absence when it seemed so evident that he would remain in San Francisco. They came to the conclusion that if their pastor were determined to go to San Francisco at that time, he should resign his pulpit in their church. After coming to this unanimous agreement, they waited upon Dr. Scott at his home and informed him of their feelings. As a result, Dr. Scott submitted his resignation the next day, January 17th, to become effective February 1st. Such a decision was made with great regret and accepted by the church with sorrow. The pastoral relationship between Dr. Scott and the church was dissolved by action of the Presbytery of New York on the following February 1st. Thus a fruitful ministry of about six and one-half years came to an end.

AS PASTOR OF ST. JOHN'S CHURCH

Dr. Scott's last Sunday at the Forty-Second Street Church was January 23rd. No record has been discovered which described the leave-taking. Since he arrived in San Francisco on Monday, January 31st, we realize that he had but few days in which to pack. The main reponsibility of moving and of selling their home devolved upon Mrs. Scott. Writing to his wife from San Francisco on February 5th, he reported having "taken a clean new furnished home two or three doors from Mr. Kittle at $150 per month." This was located at 729 Geary Street, within a few blocks of the former St. James Episcopal Church. He also said that he had hired a woman cook for $30 a month. On the 8th, he wrote: "Our housekeeping is a cold, comfortless affair without you & Tom & Jim [i.e., his two pet cats]. Mary the cook is rather a nice kind of an old body." In his instructions regarding packing, he advised: "Ship your Bourbon, the voyage will make it better." A few days later he wrote requesting his son Paul "to buy $5 worth of cigars such as I use."

Dr. Scott began his second period of residence in San Francisco in an atmosphere which contrasted sharply with that which characterized his departure in the fall of 1861. The Civil War was now a thing of the past and the old animosities were largely forgotten. Albert Williams, who returned to San Francisco from his home in New Jersey sometime in the winter of 1869-70, was the only one among his Presbyterian brethren in the city who had taken an active part in the opposition. Among his old friends were Sylvester Woodbridge, Jr., and Joshua Phelps. On the whole, he was given a warm welcome on the part of all of the Protestant clergy of the city. The attitude of the press was also friendly. Now the Presbyterians had their own paper in the *Occident*. The *Pacific*, once the vociferous spokesman for those who opposed Dr. Scott, had a new editor who carried the following motto across the top of the front page: "First Pure, then Peaceable—without Partiality and without Hypocrisy." The years of controversy were gone. A new day had arrived.

Dr. Scott threw himself into the work of establishing the new church with enthusiasm. Two services, morning and evening, were announced for the first Sunday after his return, February 6, in Pacific Hall on Bush Street near Kearny. By an interesting coincidence, this hall was only two or three blocks from Musical Hall, also on Bush Street, where he had first begun his ministry in San Francisco in 1854. According to newspaper reports, "very good congregations" were in attendance at both services. A Sunday School was organized with Stephen Franklin as superintendent.

Prodded by Dr. Scott, the provisional trustees succeeded in completing negotiations for the Episcopal church on Post Street. In a letter to his wife dated February 10th, he reported that the property had been purchased for $45,000. The auditorium provided seating accommodations for about eight hundred. Some remodeling had to be done before the Presbyterians could use it, so for several weeks Dr. Scott continued to hold services in Pacific Hall.

On February 26th, he appeared before the Presbytery of California with a petition asking for authority to organize "St. John's Presbyterian Church & Congregation." Permission was granted. The formal organization of the church took place in Pacific Hall on Sunday, March 6th. Sixty-one signed the charter member roll, all of whom came by letter of transfer. Thirty-seven brought letters from Calvary Church, including Mr. and Mrs. Frank Henderson who had bought the Scott home on Rincon Hill when the Scotts left in the fall of 1861. Henderson had been an elder in Calvary during Dr. Scott's pastorate there. Fifteen came from Central Presbyterian Church including Stephen Franklin and Mr. and Mrs. H. Channing Beals. Many of this group had formerly been members of Calvary. Stephen Franklin had also served as an elder under Dr. Scott's ministry both in Calvary and in the New Orleans church. After the organization of St. John's Church, he was clerk of session for the full fifteen years that Dr. Scott served as pastor. There was no person more loyal in his friendship to Dr. Scott than Stephen Franklin. The other nine charter members came from several other churches both in and out of San Francisco, including five from First Church. Thus the organization of a new Presbyterian congregation in the city took place without any serious drain on the membership of any one church. The first two elders of the new congregation were Stephen Franklin and Edward Dillon. A salary of $5,000 was voted for Dr. Scott, beginning from January 1st. The original records make no mention of house rent. Dr. Scott was formally installed as pastor by the presbytery on May 1st.

The first services of St. John's Church in the newly purchased edifice were held on Sunday, March 27th. Large congregations were present for both the morning and evening meetings. The Sunday School began with an attendance of one hundred scholars and fourteen teachers. A newspaper account described the architecture as being semi-Gothic with a high roof, sharp angles, massive timber rafters, and beautiful woodwork, all in the "Old English style." Inscribed in quaint letters on the Gothic arch that spanned the pulpit were the following words: "Worthy is the Lamb that was slain to receive honor, glory, and blessing." A few years later, the congregation spent $20,000 adding a lecture hall large enough to seat about four hundred and installed a ten-thousand-dollar pipe organ, described as being "one of the finest in the city."

For a number of years St. John's experienced a healthy growth. The membership grew from the original sixty-one to 160 in 1871 and to 242 the following year. The peak membership during Dr. Scott's ministry was reached in 1879 when 382 were reported.

By another interesting coincidence, the Rev. John Hemphill began his ministry in Calvary Church on April 3rd, just one week after Dr. Scott began his work in St. John's on Post Street. The two churches, both located in downtown San Francisco, were less than three blocks apart. A cordial relationship always existed between the two men, one in the closing years of his ministry, the other just beginning.

Mrs. Scott succeeded in selling their New York home in the latter part of February for $20,500. There was a mortgage of about $1,000 against the property at the time of its sale. She and the boys then left for San Francisco. Striking evidence of the reputation Dr. Scott gained during his six years' residence in New York is to be seen in the fact that in 1872 the University of New York honored him with the degree Doctor of Laws. This was his second honorary doctorate. In 1844 the University of Alabama had bestowed upon him the Doctor of Divinity.

James Woods, in his *Recollections of Pioneer Work in California* published in San Francisco in 1878 when Dr. Scott was still living, had the following comment to make on the state of his health when he began his ministry at St. John's:

> When he first returned to the Coast, his bodily frame seemed feeble, his heart seemed sad, and his voice did not have the old ring of the bugle blast, which it formerly had. And his friends began to fear that the rough work of life was beginning to wear out the machinery of the physical frame. But it soon proved to have been only a temporary weariness. Soon, like a rested warrior, invigorated by repose, he came up fresh upon the battle-field of "The Sacramental Host of God's elect." Again the old fire began to burn, the old voice began to ring, the old battle-sword to flash, and sinners began to tremble and inquire what they must do to be saved.

The fifteen years that Dr. Scott spent as pastor of St. John's was the longest pastorate of the several which he held. In sharp contrast to his first period of residence in San Francisco, this was unmarred by strife or controversy. He was received back into the Presbytery of California at its March 9, 1870, meeting. Following the official merging of the Old and New School Assemblies, there was a general realignment of ecclesiastical boundaries and Presbyterian judicatories throughout the country. The New School Presbytery of San Francisco and the Old School Presbytery of California merged with the adoption of the former's name. Twice Dr. Scott served as moderator of the new presbytery, in 1870 and again in 1872.

The New School Synod of Alta California and the Old School Synod of the Pacific merged, retaining the name of the latter until 1892 when it became the Synod of California. At the time of the merger, the new synod included five presbyteries, seventy-five churches, eighty-four ministers, and 4,539 members. Among the presbyteries was the Presbytery of Oregon which covered the entire Pacific Northwest. These statistics show how weak Presbyterianism was on the Pacific Coast at that time. Dr. Scott was elected moderator of the synod in 1876.

Among the organizations in San Francisco to which Dr. Scott belonged was the St. Andrew's Society made up largely of those of Scottish or Scotch-Irish ancestry. In 1880 he was president of the society and it may be that through this connection he became acquainted with Robert Louis Stevenson who, in the fall of 1869 and through the spring of 1870, lived at Monterey, California. This was before he had written some of his best known works. A tradition current among the descendants of Dr. Scott says that Stevenson was a frequent visitor in the Scott home and that he discussed with Dr. Scott his proposed marriage to the divorcee, Fanny Osbourne, who was also living at Monterey. According to the family tradition, Dr. Scott encouraged the marriage and performed the ceremony in his home on Geary Street on May 20, 1880. The record of the marriage is found in one of Dr. Scott's notebooks now in Bancroft Library of the University of California.

J. C. Furnas, in his *Voyage to Windward, the Life of Robert Louis Stevenson*, gives the following anecdote regarding the marriage: "In addition to the conventional ten dollars, Louis presented Scott with his father's little book on the evidences of Christianity." The volume bore the inscription: "Louis from your affectionate Father, Thomas Stevenson." In turn, Dr. Scott presented Stevenson with one of the books he had written. Shortly after the marriage, the couple left for Scotland.

In 1878 Flora Haines Apponyi published in San Francisco her *The Libraries of California* in which she described Dr. Scott's library as one of the best private collections in the state:

> Dr. Scott's collection of about five thousand volumes is eminently composed of solid literature. It is a library designed for use and study rather than pleasure or recreation. To the ordinary reader the books would present a formidable array; to the owner they are a host of old friends, a little dusty, it is true, and somewhat out at elbows but old friends nevertheless. . .
>
> The collection is largely composed of historical, biographical and theological works, Greek and Latin classics and works on exegesis. It also embraces a number of works of English and American statesmen, and a goodly collection of travels, journeys, the Holy Land being made a specialty. Among the theological books are the complete works of Augustine, Calvin, and Rosenmuller [a German Orientalist]. There are dictionaries in a dozen languages, and other standard works of reference. . .
>
> Dr. Scott's library is chiefly located in a large study of St. John's Presbyterian Church, of which he is pastor; plain wooden shelves receive the mass of the books, but several wooden tables and a broad projecting shelf at the base of the shelving, are literally piled with books, papers and manuscripts. . .

The author listed some of the more scholarly titles found in Dr. Scott's library, including the following which are now in San Francisco Theological Seminary: *"Bayles Dictionary,* London, 1831; Leigh's *Critical Sacre,* Amsterdam, 1696; and Polanos *History of Council of Trent,* 1613."

Following Dr. Scott's death, Ebenezer (known within the family circle as Eb) who was the scholar of the family, was given first choice of the contents of the library. Other members then made selections and the balance, numbering some 3,300 volumes and consisting largely of books dealing with religion, was given to the seminary. All of Ebenezer's library was lost in the San Francisco earthquake and fire of 1906. Since the seminary was by then located in San Anselmo, across the bay from San Francisco, its library escaped destruction. An unknown number of books with Dr. Scott's bookplate, possibly several thousand, are now on the shelves of the seminary library. They continue to bear witness to the scholarly and literary taste of its founder, who was indeed "no ordinary man."

During these years, a number of changes in the family circle took place. Eli Davis Scott of St. Louis, Dr. Scott's younger brother by three years, died on June 5, 1872. Thus the last family connection that went back to his boyhood in Tennessee was severed. On November 19, 1874, the Scotts' fourth son, Chalmers, married Maria Antonia Couts of San Diego. She belonged to one of Southern California's oldest Spanish families and was a Roman Catholic. Although Chalmers himself did not join the Roman Catholic Church, his marriage to one of that faith brought many heartaches to his parents. In January 1875, Arthur W. Foster, a young business man in San Francisco, joined St. John's Presbyterian Church and later became an elder and one of its chief benefactors. On November 23, 1876, Foster was married to Louisiana Scott. Four of their daughters were still living in California at the time of the writing of this biography and gave much help to the author in supplying source materials. They were the late Mrs. Mary F. Kuechler of Ross, Mrs. Martha Abbot of Kentfield, Mrs. Anna Draper of San Francisco, and Lou Foster of Carmel.

CITY COLLEGE, SAN FRANCISCO

When Dr. Scott left San Francisco in the fall of 1861, the outlook for City College, which he had founded two years previously, was most promising. Two buildings stood at the corner of Geary and Stockton Streets. The college had been incorporated. Dr. George Burrowes headed a competent staff of teachers and over one hundred students were enrolled. As long as Dr. Scott remained in the city and served as president of the board of trustees, the institution was related to the Old School Synod of the Pacific. After his departure, largely because of the continued opposition of Dr. W. C. Anderson, the ties connecting the college with the synod were severed in the fall of 1862 and the college became the sole responsibility of a self-perpetuating board, most of whom, if not all, were Old School Presbyterians.

For a time the college grew even though Dr. Scott could no longer guide its affairs. By January 1863 the college boasted an enrollment of 120. A laboratory had been erected between the main building and the chapel and in 1864 an extension of sixty-four feet was added to the building on Geary Street giving it an over-all length of 128 feet. The great difficulty centered around finances. Dr. Burrowes' journal tells of the continuing struggle of those years. The board of trustees made no effort to raise an endowment. They expected Dr. Burrowes to pay all expenses, including salaries, out of tuition fees. Unable to do the impossible and suffering from ill health, Dr. Burrowes resigned in 1865 and returned East. He was succeeded by the Rev. P. V. Veeder.

Sometime in 1863, Henry H. Haight, then president of the board of trustees of City College, became interested in a real estate development at a place called University Mound on the San Bruno road about four miles southwest of Union Square in San Francisco. Title to twenty-five acres was given to City College as a campus for a boarding school. Sufficient profit was realized from the sale of lots to pay for the land and to erect a building which was not occupied until January 1870. The new school was called University Mound College. This was designed to be the boarding department of City College which was a day school. Both schools were under the same board of trustees, and both offered practically the same courses for boys. To add somewhat to the confusion of names, the two titles—University Mound and City College—were often merged into University College.

Across the Bay, the New School Presbyterian and Congregational sponsored College of California became in 1868 the University of California. The transfer was made largely because of the inability of the Congregationalists to finance the institution in view of the pending union of the New School and the Old School. This union automatically eliminated New School support. The fact that the state charged no tuition at the university complicated matters for City College where full support came from such fees. In order to meet the new competition, the board of trustees of City College added a School of Mines in 1868. At the June commencement of that year, the assets of the institution, including the value of the property at University Mound, were about $200,000 but there was a debt of $30,000. Receipts from tuition were not meeting current expenses.

In the meantime, the Old School Board of Education, mindful of the coming union of the two branches of the Presbyterian Church, felt that the time was opportune for the establishment of a theological seminary on the Pacific Coast. San Francisco was the logical location. Dr. Burrowes was approached in the early summer of 1869 by Dr. William Speer, then a secretary of the board, who urged him to return to California as its representative "in laying the foundations there of a Theological Seminary for your church." Dr. Burrowes accepted the call and left the latter part of August for the Coast. He summarizes events in the following passage of his journal: "On my arrival in the first week of Sept., as the way was not clear for a Theol. Seminary, I was urged by the Trustees of the old City College to take charge of the new building at University Mound for a boarding school. . . . The school there had not yet begun, as no suitable man had yet been found."

Dr. Burrowes opened his school in January 1870 with four boarders, which reminds us of the fact that he opened City College in the basement of Calvary Church in the fall of 1859, also with four students. In the meantime, downtown City College had not prospered under the administration of the Rev. P. V. Veeder. The deficit had increased and the enrollment had declined more than fifty percent from 1865 to 1869. Veeder was faced with the same problem which had confronted Dr. Burrowes and he too found it impossible to balance the budget on the basis of tuition returns. So when the Japanese government in 1869 offered him the attractive position of being the first American president of a college in that country, he accepted with alacrity. This left the principalship of City College vacant.

The board of trustees turned to Dr. William Alexander, who was pastor of the First Presbyterian Church at San Jose, to be Veeder's successor. Since Dr. Alexander was destined to play such an important role in the last fourteen years of Dr. Scott's life, special mention should be made of him. Dr. Alexander was born in Pennsylvania in 1831 and was, therefore, about nineteen years younger than Dr. Scott. He was graduated from Princeton Theological Seminary in 1861, and later received the Doctor of Divinity degree from Wooster College in 1876. After serving churches in both Pennsylvania and Wisconsin. and after being president of Carroll College from 1862-64, Dr. Alexander was called to the First Presbyterian Church of San Jose, California, in 1869. He had been there for only a short time before being invited to the principalship of City College. At heart he was more of an educator than a preacher. He much preferred the classroom to the pulpit. His influence in the founding of San Francisco Theological Seminary was second only to that of Dr. Scott.

This was the status of University College when Dr. Scott returned to San Francisco in January 1870. Dr. Burrowes had just begun his work at University Mound and Dr. Alexander was just beginning his service at City College. Dr. Scott was re-elected to the board of trustees, over which the Hon. Thomas H. Selby, a former mayor of San Francisco, was president, but it does not appear that Scott played a prominent part in the administrative affairs of the institution after his return to San Francisco in 1870.

As will be explained later, both Dr. Burrowes and Dr. Alexander were on the first faculty of San Francisco Theological Seminary founded by the Synod of the Pacific in October 1871. Both men found that they could not carry the double load of teaching in their respective departments of University College and in the Seminary. Dr. Burrowes was the first to resign. He closed his work at University Mound in June 1873 at which time there were thirty-five boarding students in residence. Because of his careful management, this school had been able to balance its budget. Professor John Gamble was appointed in his place and for a time University Mound prospered. The demand for accommodations was so pressing that the trustees voted to double the capacity of the building. Before such additions could be undertaken, fire completely destroyed the building on the night of April 4, 1875. There was no loss of life but practically all of the contents were burned. Months passed before rebuilding could get started. The new edifice was more pretentious than the first but the cost plunged the institution heavily into debt and this became a major factor for its eventual failure. Since the new building was not ready for occupancy until sometime in 1876, this meant a hiatus in the academic program which fact also contributed to the final closing of the school.

In the meantime Dr. Alexander became increasingly unhappy with conditions under which he was working at City College. Looking back upon his experiences, he wrote: "I found there about forty little boys. You can judge my dismay. I thought I was asked to preside over a college." With his appointment early in 1870, the outlook for City College began to improve. The board of trustees that spring issued a four-page folder which proudly announced that they had "inaugurated an entirely new order of things. The School is to be thoroughly reorganized, under a new Principal, with a view to increased vigor and efficiency." A business department was added. Evening classes were started. The trustees even began a medical school at University Mound. The peak of the effectiveness of the institution, including both departments, was probably reached in December 1872 when the December 12th issue of the *Occident* reported: "University College, formerly known as City College, is approaching the dignity of a real University, there being already in successful operation the Medical, Commercial, Theological, and Academical Departments, with their Faculties, numbering in all twenty-six Professors and over 300 students."

Dr. Alexander at City College faced the same financial problem as did his predecessors, Burrowes and Veeder. The trustees were still expecting him to pay all running costs from tuition fees. He saw that this was impossible and tried to convince the trustees of the necessity of raising an endowment, but to no avail. Looking back upon those years, he wrote: "In the three years I was there, I had a class of six young fellows ready for the freshman class in any college, and the trustees had not done a thing, and I had come to believe that they never would, and I resigned." This became effective about January 1, 1874. According to Dr. Alexander, "The failure [of the college] was not due to the ministers, but to a lot of laymen who had never been to college, and did not know what a college is, and yet were too self-important to take counsel of those who did know. And although they were men of wealth and high standing in the city, they were not liberal."

The board of trustees managed to bungle through the spring of 1874 and the academic year, 1874-75, with temporary but unsatisfactory supervision in City College. The rapidly increasing values of real estate in downtown San Francisco and the limited possibilities for future expansion at the site on Geary and Stockton Streets prompted the board to accept an offer of $90,000 for the property. This was done in 1875 and after paying off a $30,000 debt, the board took $35,000 of the balance and purchased a lot with a frontage of about 400 feet at 129 Haight Street, about two miles to the west of Union Square and within about five blocks of the new city hall.

Since the purchasers of the site at Geary and Stockton did not want the two buildings, the board of trustees decided to move them to the new location. No doubt the main structure, 128 feet long, was cut in two, but even so, the moving became a major project and cost much more than had been anticipated. Although steam power may have been used, the probabilities are that the moving was done by horses. When all bills were paid, there was not enough money remaining from the sale to pay for needed repairs on the buildings after they were re-located on Haight Street. Indeed, the whole unfortunate transaction burdened the college with another debt.

A new beginning was made in July 1876 when Dr. James Matthews was called to be principal of the Haight Street school. An announce-ment in the June 22nd issue of the *Occident* reads: "We propose to begin at the foundation. We will receive pupils in the most elementary branches, or at any stage of advancement." The ambitious title of the school being either a college or a university became a mockery. The new location proved to be inconvenient. The long intervals when both branches of the institution conducted no work had created an unfavor-able image in the mind of the public. In April 1877 the trustees of the college sold a portion of their site on Haight Street, with a frontage of about 140 feet, to the theological seminary for $12,000. Such aid, however, only postponed the final closing of the college.

Dr. Scott in March 1879 made one final effort to save the situation. He sent out a special appeal to all "friends of sound Religious Education" to meet in Calvary Church on Monday evening, the 24th. He asked all of his Presbyterian ministerial brethren to give the notice from their pulpits on the Sunday preceding and to "urge all who can to be present at this meeting as the very existence of our schools may depend on the action then taken." He wrote out the speech he would give, the manu-script of which was found among his papers. Regarding the property at University Mound, he wrote: "On this property there is a mortgage and the foreclosure was threatened tomorrow. There is a debt as already intimated on the property on Haight Street, but no mortage. The debt is, however, pressed." He mentioned the possibility of selling more of the land on Haight Street and some of the acreage at University Mound but added that it was then impossible to sell at any thing like a fair price.

Holding nothing back, he told the simple truth. "We have asked for a little longer breathing time before foreclosure, for foreclosure would throw us into bankruptcy, and as prices are now in such an event we should certainly lose all. The only possible way, as it seems to us, to escape so great a calamity is to raise $2,500 to pay interest, insurance & taxes, and by so doing get time to sell the property, all we do not need and so relieve ourselves from debt. The property at University Mound has been, I believe, advertised for sale for taxes." Dr. Scott claimed that the only money which came as an outright gift was the initial $10,000 which he was so largely instrumental in raising when the college was first started. In other words, City College had managed to exist for nearly twenty years on tuition fees and from the profits realized from the sale of the original site.

This was a speech which Dr. Scott never had the opportunity to give. Attached to the manuscript was the following pathetic note in his handwriting: "Intended for this meeting. It was a failure, only two trustees & a few persons met—adjourned without organization." This was the end for University College.

The property on Haight Street was purchased by Dr. Matthews for some undisclosed figure. For several years he tried to carry on a private school there under the old name of City College. In 1886 he changed the name to Westminster College. Dr. Matthews died in 1891 and thereafter all references to the school ceased to appear in the press.

For a time Professor Gamble carried on a school at University Mound. The May 25, 1881, issue of the *Occident* reported that he had purchased a property at Litton Springs, three or four miles north of Healdsburg, California, and that he had "transferred to that locality himself and family, together with University Mound College." He changed the name to Litton Springs College. Just how long he carried on the school at that place is not known. University Mound property passed into the hands of James Lick, one of San Francisco's financiers, who converted the building into an old people's home.

In the winter of 1958-59, the author discovered that the original City College building was still standing on Haight Street. Since the site was well outside the fire zone of the 1906 earthquake and fire, which destroyed downtown San Francisco, it escaped that holocaust. The exterior of the building had changed little from its original state. The building had been converted into an apartment house for low income people and a colored Baptist congregation was using one of the larger rooms on the main floor. This building was torn down in 1962 to make way for new construction.

Another interesting discovery was made when a sign board thirteen feet long was found bearing large hand-carved letters which read UNIVERSITY COLLEGE. Old photographs show that the sign board first hung over the Geary Street entrance of the original City College. It is conjectured that when this building was moved to Haight Street, the sign board was taken down and placed above the entrance of the building at University Mound. It so happened that one who is now prominent in Masonic circles in San Francisco, Chester Newell, got the sign when this building was being demolished in 1928. He stored it in his garage for more than thirty years and then learning of the interest taken by the seminary in the sign, gave it to the seminary's museum. This and the Bible used in the chapel are the only relics remaining which bear witness to the fact that the Presbyterians once had a college in San Francisco.

Today there is another institution in San Francisco known as City College but this has no historical connection with the earlier school of the same name.

SAN FRANCISCO THEOLOGICAL SEMINARY

San Francisco Theological Seminary was established by action of the Synod of the Pacific meeting in the First Presbyterian Church of Oakland, California, on October 4, 1871. Although there were several who took an active part in its founding, especially Dr. William Alexander, yet it can be truly said that no one worked for this objective so long and with such perseverance as did Dr. Scott. The common judgment of his contemporaries gave him primary credit for this achievement as may be seen in the following tribute paid to him by the Rev. James Woods: "Dr. Scott's great work on this Coast was the establishment of the Theological Seminary." After the seminary was started, no one did as much as he to guide the destinies of the infant institution during the first thirteen years when it was beset with many difficulties. The seminary was the crowning achievement of a long and unusually fruitful ministry and it remains today as the greatest monument to his memory.

Dr. Scott once remarked to James Curry, one of the first students to be enrolled in the seminary, that when he first sailed in through the Golden Gate in 1854 and looked upon the hills surrounding the magnificent bay, he resolved that with God's help he would see both a Presbyterian college and a theological seminary planted in that vicinity. He never lost sight of that resolve.

The first printed appeal for the establishment of a theological seminary by the Presbyterian Church in San Francisco is found in an editorial written by Dr. Scott which appeared in the August 1859 issue of his *Pacific Expositor*. The editorial was occasioned by the announcement that North-Western Theological Seminary, now called McCormick, had been established by the Presbyterian Church in Chicago. After disclaiming any criticism of the action taken, he wrote:

We are clearly of the opinion that the very next theological school established by our Church, should be at the Golden Gate of the Continent. The time may not be in our day, but it will come. Even now the foundation should be laid, and funds secured and invested. This part of the work cannot be begun too soon. As yet, we fear we have not the young men among us, whose hearts are turned to the work of the Gospel ministry; nor have we the colleges and literary institutions to prepare them for theological studies. But such institutions must soon grow up among us. An immense population will be found here at no very distant period.

Dr. Scott felt that there were too many Presbyterian seminaries, including both Old and New School, in the East and that the great West was being neglected. He closed his editorial with the following:

We write these lines with a "running pen" to throw out some hints, and especially to remind our brethren, that their whole field of labor, and *all* the sites for investing funds do not lie east of the Rocky Mountains. Though making them rich, we are ourselves poor—very poor in regard to funds for church building, and for the support of ministers, and for the establishment of schools and colleges. More on this subject at another time, if the Lord will; but we now insist upon it, that *the next theological school established by our General Assembly, shall be in the city of San Francisco.*

Other Presbyterian ministers shared Dr. Scott's convictions and were talking about the importance of having a seminary in California during the years of his absence from the state. The New School Synod of Alta California, at its October 1863 meeting, appointed a committee to study the possibility and "to report upon the establishment of a Theological Seminary on this Coast." One of the members of this committee was the Rev. William W. Brier who later became the first financial agent for the seminary after its founding in 1871. Following the Civil War, the northern branches of the Old and New Schools began discussing union. This meant that the New School gradually began to dissociate itself from the Congregationalists. As early as 1866 the Congregationalists in California began making plans for a theological seminary and on October 11th of that year founded the Pacific Theological Seminary, now known as the Pacific School of Religion. Instruction, however, did not begin until September 1869. This is now the oldest Protestant theological seminary on the Pacific Coast. The Episcopalians had a theological class in St. Augustine College, now defunct, at Benicia as early as 1868 but this effort to launch a seminary proved to be abortive.

The activities of both the Episcopalians and the Congregationalists in starting their respective programs of theological education in California spurred both the Old and New School Presbyterians to take similar steps. As plans for a national union of the two bodies began to materialize, the two synods in California drew closer together. In 1868 both synods instructed their committees on theological education to study the possibility of joint action. Dr. William Speer, of the Old School Presbyterian Board of Education, addressed the joint meeting of the two synods on October 7, 1869, shortly before Dr. Scott returned to California, on the importance of having a theological seminary in California. Dr. Speer, who had started mission work for the Chinese in California in 1852, was well acquainted with the problems faced by the Presbyterian Church on the whole Pacific Coast. After drawing attention to the fact that the two General Assemblies had approved the basis of union, he emphasized his conviction that the time had come for the establishment of a theological seminary in California. Here would be the source of future ministers for the West. It was futile, he said, to look to eastern seminaries for sufficient men as most of their graduates were staying in the East. "But California," he pointed out, "is a land of young men. Your population is a youthful population. Your church members are most of them young men and women. You have abundant material, if it can be wrought into shapes which the Master can use." The address was published in the December 18, 1869, issue of the *Occident*.

Inspired by the increased interest in the founding of a theological seminary, Dr. Burrowes announced that he would give his library of some 2,000 volumes to the institution as soon as it was started. Dr. Burrowes' library was especially rich in Greek and Latin works. Included also was the great six volume folio size Walton's *Polyglot Bible*, published in London 1755-57, which gave portions of the Biblical text in nine different languages. This was the last and greatest of a series of polyglots and remains to this day an invaluable aid in textual studies. Back in the spring of 1841, Scott had written to one of his Princeton professors, Dr. Archibald Alexander, about the possibility of buying such a work, but this he was unable to do. The Synod of the Pacific in its 1870 meeting took note of this "liberal and valuable donation," the first material gift to be received for the new seminary.

The *Occident* of August 5, 1871, then being edited by the Rev. Sylvester Woodbridge, Jr., made mention of "the munificent donation of a library" to the seminary-to-be by Dr. Burrowes and called the gift "a great encouragement to our hopes." Then Woodbridge made a nomination: "The writer ventures to add upon his own suggestion, that we have upon our coast one of the most eminent Theologians of our day, whose published writings have given him a world wide fame, whose influence in our churches is very great, and for whom as President of the Seminary and Professor of Theology a liberal endowment is believed could be obtained. His present position as pastor of one of our most promising churches need not prevent him from engaging in the work which would require but a portion of his time." Thus was Dr. Scott unofficially nominated to be president of the new seminary.

When the reorganized Presbytery of San Francisco met on September 21, 1871, Dr. Scott introduced a resolution calling upon the Synod of the Pacific to take immediate steps for the establishment of a seminary. This was unanimously adopted. In anticipation of favorable action by the synod, Dr. Alexander, in consultation with Dr. Scott, drew up a proposed "Plan of Organization" modelling it as far as possible upon that of Princeton Theological Seminary.

On Tuesday, October 3, 1871, at the meeting of the Synod of the Pacific in Oakland, Dr. Alexander presented the resolution already passed by the Presbytery of San Francisco. He stressed the fact that many felt that the time was opportune for the Presbyterians to act. He requested the synod "to appoint a committee . . . to consider and report to the Synod . . . a plan for the organization of a Theological Seminary such as the present wants and future interests of this coast demand." He presented a memorial which bore the signatures of the following ministers besides himself: T. M. Cunningham, W. A. Scott, S. Woodbridge, and George Burrowes. Several elders had also signed the memorial. The synod received the memorial and appointed a committee, designating Dr. Scott as the chairman, to bring in a plan of organization the next day. On October 4th Dr. Scott made his report, submitting the document previously prepared by Dr. Alexander. This was adopted by the synod with a few minor changes and San Francisco Theological Seminary was officially launched. It should be remembered that at this time the Synod of the Pacific embraced within its boundaries all of the area in the United States west of the Continental Divide. It should also be noted that the seminary remained under the jurisdiction of the Synod of the Pacific and, after 1892, of the Synod of California, until the time of its reorganization in 1913 when it passed under the control of the General Assembly.

On October 5th, Synod selected nine of its ministers and six elders to compose the board of directors of the new institution. Dr. Scott's name headed the list of ministers which included Sylvester Woodbridge, Jr., Daniel W. Poor, pastor of the First Presbyterian Church of Oakland, T. M. Cunningham of Tabernacle Church, San Francisco, and W. W. Brier. Among the elders were Stephen Franklin, R. J. Trumbull, and Judge H. P. Coon. The board held its first meeting in City College on November 7, 1871, and organized by electing Dr. Scott, president; Dr. poor, vice-president; R. J. Trumbull, secretary; and Stephen Franklin, treasurer. There was no president of the seminary as such, as there is now, but rather president of the board of trustees, and this position Dr. Scott occupied during the remainder of his life.

The following professors were selected at the November 7th meeting: Dr. Scott—Professor of Mental Science, Moral Philosophy, and Theology; Dr. Alexander—Professor of Biblical Literature; and Dr. Poor—Professor of Biblical and Ecclesiastical History, and Church Government. On December 4th, Dr. Burrowes was made Professor of Hebrew and Old

Testament Literature and Dr. Alexander's chair was reclassified as Professor of Biblical Greek and New Testament Literature. Nothing was said about compensation, for the seminary had no income whatever.

The first action taken at the November 7th meeting was to take up a collection in order to cover incidental expenses including the cost of a record book for the secretary. Ten of those present contributed $5 each. Four students made application for enrollment, three juniors and one middler. The first to be received was James L. Woods, the son of the pioneer minister, James Woods. The other two juniors were Andrew Lees and James L. Drum, the latter being the first to complete a three-year course. The middler was Charles W. Anthony who in 1873 was the first graduate. No degrees were granted by the seminary, only diplomas, until 1916. Two of these first four students, Drum and Alexander, came from University College.

Instruction began on November 14, 1871, in City College. For a library, the students used the books from Dr. Burrowes' collection and those on the shelves of City College. They also had free access to the libraries of Drs. Scott and Alexander. Thus some seven or eight thousand volumes were available. The four students lived in several of the Sunday School rooms of St. John's Church. James L. Woods, who published his *California Pioneer Decade* in 1922, recalls that: "The study room of the seminary was the dreary organ loft of St. John's church, then on Post Street. The place was cold and cheerless and it took consecrated young men to study in the uninviting quarters." No record has been found as to where these young men took their meals. As they walked the three blocks which separated the church from the college, they had to cross Union Square which now lies in the very heart of San Francisco.

Thus was San Francisco Theological Seminary started with four professors (each serving without compensation and each giving but a portion of his time to teaching), four students, and a modest library but with no campus, buildings, endowment, or assured income. The total strength of the Presbyterian Church, after the union of the two schools, on the whole Pacific Coast was pitifully weak with only seventy-five churches and 4,539 members. On the positive side there was the recognized need for such an institution and above all, there was the consecrated devotion of such able men as Drs. Scott, Alexander, and Burrowes. Having such, San Francisco Theological Seminary could not but survive the vicissitudes of those early difficult years.

From the very beginning, Dr. Scott and his colleagues were confronted with two major needs, students and money. The annual enrollment increased slowly, growing from the original four to nine by the fall of 1876. A total of twenty-two matriculations were recorded during the first six years when the seminary conducted its work in temporary quarters. Logically, a theological seminary comes at the apex of a narrowing series of educational institutions beginning with the grammar schools. Chronologically, San Francisco Theological Seminary was founded before there were a sufficient number of western denominational or public institutions of higher learning to provide qualified students in sufficient numbers to justify its existence. With the single exception of the weak and dying City College, there were no Presbyterian colleges on the Pacific Coast during the early years of the life of the seminary. Most of the students who enrolled came from outside the state. A surprising number came from abroad, from Germany, England, Scotland, Ireland, and one from India. In addition to the few who entered the seminary from University College, the first to enroll from a western Presbyterian college was Edwin B. Hayes who came from Occidental College in the fall of 1892 and was graduated in 1895. For a number of years, even after the seminary moved to its first building on Haight Street in 1877, the faculty found it necessary to conduct a preparatory department, for some students were not yet ready for the theological course.

Little was accomplished along financial lines during the first year. At the October 28, 1872, meeting of the board of directors, W. W. Brier was appointed financial agent for the seminary to work in the West; Dr. Cunningham was to serve in a similar capacity in the East. The directors voted to adhere strictly to a policy of no debt. They set a goal of $30,000 as the ideal endowment for a chair with the hope that this could soon be increased to $50,000. The first contribution toward the endowment of the seminary came from First Church, Oakland, in the form of the church's parsonage worth from $7,000 to $8,000 but with an incumbrance on it of more than $2,000. The first sizeable cash contribution came at this time. Thomas Breeze, a member of Dr. Scott's church, gave $2,000 in November with the specification that this was to be used as part of the endowment for the "Scott Professorship." Several other gifts of $1,000 or $500 were also made, including one of $500 from Dr. Scott. Within a short time, Brier secured $17,600 in cash and pledges but because of the financial depression of 1873, only $4,000 of this was ever paid. Dr. Cunningham reported raising $42,000 in pledges in the East but likewise because of financial conditions was able to collect only a small part of this sum. In addition to these larger gifts, there was a growing number of friends who were making contributions of from one dollar to $100 per year. In the report of the Synod's Committee on the Theological Seminary made before the 1876 meeting, we read:

> The light is beginning to dawn on the financial condition of the Seminary, insomuch that those who, for three years, had bestowed their labors as Professors, without any remuneration, except that of a good conscience, for a noble work performed, have in the last year received a small salary ranging from $300 to $400 from interest accruing on invested funds. The assets of the Seminary, including bills receiveable, real estate, deposits in savings-bank, and cash on hand are $16,632.51.

The committee also took note of "the extra labors of Dr. Scott and express the hope that in some way he may be relieved of this extra burden." The first change in the faculty came in August 1876 when Dr. Poor resigned to become secretary of the Presbyterian Board of Education in Philadelphia. He was succeeded by Dr. James Eells, who also served as pastor of First Church in Oakland.

The first large gifts came in 1876 when Messrs. Robert and Alexander Stuart of New York City gave $5,000 and Robert Bonner of the same city another $5,000. With this money, supplemented by $2,000 from other sources, the trustees of the seminary purchased a lot at 121 Haight Street with a frontage of about sixty-nine feet and a depth of $137\frac{1}{2}$ feet. This was adjoining the site owned by City College. On this lot a three-story building was erected during the summer of 1877 at a cost of $8,000. The basement contained a kitchen and dining room. Two lecture rooms and the library were on the main floor. Dormitory rooms were on the third. The building was dedicated on Sunday, September 9th with ex-Governor Henry Haight, after whom the street was named, giving the main address. Now the seminary had a home of its own adequate for current needs.

Even though the seminary had its own building, the enrollment continued small. The statistics for the classes for the six academic years, 1877-78 to 1883-84 inclusive, which cover the last years of Dr. Scott's life, are as follows:

Year	Juniors	Middlers	Seniors	New matriculations	Graduates
1877-8	3	1	4	4	4
1879-9	3	3	3	5	2
1879-80	4	3	4	6	3
1880-1	1	1	5	1	5
1881-2	3	1	1	3	1
1882-3	2	0	2	3	2
1883-4	4	1	1	6	1

During these six years, twenty-eight new students matriculated at the seminary, bringing the total to fifty for the first thirteen years. Of this number, twenty-seven were graduated. The attrition rate was almost fifty per cent. Some of those who matriculated but did not remain to be graduated, transferred to other seminaries; others abandoned their plans to study for the ministry. Even though the total enrollment for these years was small, yet it was large enough to justify the efforts made to bring the seminary into being. The first book published by a graduate of the Seminary was by Henry Gustavus Kieme of the class of 1875 whose sixty-two page *Sennacherib's Campaigns in Syria, Phoenicia and Palestine* appeared in San Francisco in 1875. The book was dedicated to Dr. Scott.

(*at left*) The first building of the San Francisco Theological Seminary, erected in 1877 at 121 Haight Street, San Francisco; now used by the First Baptist Church of the city.

(*at right*) The original City College main building, erected at the corner of Stockton and Geary Streets in 1860-61; moved to 129 Haight Street in 1876; and razed about 1962. Used in its later years by the Mount Calvary Baptist Church. Photo by Vaughn Chamness about 1959.

The financial condition of the seminary improved greatly after it occupied its first building. Dr. Scott was indefatigable in his repeated requests for funds. Reporting to the 1878 meeting of the Synod of the Pacific, he said:

> We cannot think you will be weary, brethren, with our importunity. For we are assured that you will see the vital importance of this coast to our Church in the ages to come. And now, having made so good a beginning, and our churches multiplying and growing, you will not let us perish for the want of a hundred thousand or two hundred thousand dollars, to endow fully and permanently our Seminary, so that its chairs may be filled with the ablest and best men we can get, and thoroughly devoted to the work.

The next year Stephen Franklin reported that the assets of the seminary were $54,398.00 and that the total paid for salaries had amounted to $1,906.00.

Another large gift came in the fall of 1880 when Robert Stuart of New York City gave $50,000 to endow the chair of Systematic Theology for Dr. Scott. Both Robert and his brother, Alexander Stuart, were well known in eastern Presbyterian circles for their many philanthropies and both had given previously to the seminary. During their six years' residence in New York, Dr. and Mrs. Scott had come to know the Stuart brothers and their wives. A personal friendship had been established between them. There is no doubt but that the many contacts Dr. Scott made while living in New York with prominent Presbyterian clergymen and laymen worked to the later advantage of the seminary. The designation of Dr. Scott by Robert Stuart as the first occupant of the chair he endowed is evidence of this friendship. This was the first chair in the seminary to be endowed.

Robert Stuart was as conservative in his religious convictions as was Dr. Scott. In a letter to Dr. Scott dated November 24, 1881, Stuart explained a condition attached to his gift which was that should in the future any person occupying this chair depart from the accepted doctrines of the Presbyterian Church as expressed in the Westminster Confession of Faith or as amended by the General Assembly, the funds should then "become the property of the Presbyterian Board of Church Erection."

Other important gifts came in 1881. William Thaw of Philadelphia, who also had given previously, brought the total of his contributions up to $10,000. By the will of the late Henry A. Boardman of Philadelphia, about two thousand volumes from his library went to the seminary. Shortly after Dr. Scott's death in January 1885, the library received 2,300 volumes from the estate of the late Dr. John C. Backus of Baltimore, another of Dr. Scott's eastern friends.

Although legally Dr. Scott had every right to all of the income of the endowment of his chair, this he refused to accept when his colleagues were not so favored. He was also strongly of the opinion that there should be no inauguration of professors until their respective chairs were properly endowed and he refused to be the only one thus honored. So he was never formally installed. He shared the income from the endowment of his chair with his colleagues. According to the seminary's financial report for 1881, the total amount paid for salaries to four professors the preceding year was $1,400 of which Dr. Scott received $600. In 1886 a prominent Presbyterian layman of Portland, W. S. Ladd, offered to give $50,000 as the endowment for a chair of Practical Theology if the Synod of California would raise a like amount for the chair of Church History. The Synod met the challenge and thus an endowment was secured for two additional chairs. The first inauguration of professors took place in January 1889 when Drs. William Alexander, Aaron L. Lindsley, and Thomas Fraser were inducted in the chairs of New Testament, Practical Theology, and Systematic Theology.

After the death of Dr. Scott, Dr. Fraser became president of the board of directors. In his report to the General Assembly of 1885, he stated that the "lands, buildings, library & furniture" owned by the seminary was valued at $40,000 and that endowment funds totaled $67,000. The library had 13,600 volumes. This statement as to the material resources of the seminary at the time of Dr. Scott's death reflects great credit upon his administrative ability. There was no other person in the Presbyterian Church so superbly qualified to launch and guide the destinies of the new seminary during those first crucial years as was he. No other Presbyterian minister of his stature was so well known in both East and West and so universally respected. None other could have inspired such confidence in eastern givers to contribute such large sums to so new an enterprise so far distant. The accumulation of assets of some $107,000 plus the raising of such sums needed for current expenses over a period of thirteen years, and all without a debt, was no small achievement. To Dr. Scott, therefore, above all others, goes the credit of being the primary founder of San Francisco Theological Seminary.

DECLINING YEARS AND DEATH

Old friends noted that when Dr. Scott returned to San Francisco in January 1870, he lacked his old-time zest. So far as is known, he had no outdoor hobby. There were then no golf courses in San Francisco and even if there had been, his lame leg no doubt would have precluded the game. He could not take long walks; of necessity he led a sedentary life. He continued in his declining years to be an avid reader. He and his wife spent many hours reading aloud to each other. Family letters show that they often spent their vacations in the Sierras or at the resorts in Calistoga and Clear Lake. In June 1878 they made an excursion to the Calaveras grove of redwoods, the *sequoia gigantea*, first made known in 1852. This grove is now a state park. In a letter to his daughter, Lou Foster, dated June 6th, Dr. Scott commented: "Yesterday we went to the South Grove. The road is only a horse trail through the mountains. We rode in all about 18 or 20 miles. This South Grove is the largest and grandest I have ever seen."

Dr. Scott neither wrote any more books nor edited any magazine after his return to San Francisco in 1870. Occasionally, a sermon or a commencement address would be published in the secular or religious press. His literary efforts, during these latter years, were devoted to writing lectures for his class in systematic theology. The very bulk of his lecture manuscripts, found in the large chests in the basement of Scott Hall in San Anselmo, is evidence of his conscientious work as a professor.

Sometime before the end of 1873, Arthur and Louisiana Foster and their children moved to San Rafael, in Marin County across the bay north of San Francisco. The Scotts then moved into the former Foster home at 521 Post Street which was less than a block from St. John's Church. They made frequent trips across the bay by ferry to Sausalito and then by train to San Rafael to visit their daughter Lou and her family. One of the Foster daughters, the late Mrs. Mary Kuechler, told the author of her memories of these visits by her grandparents. It is easy to imagine the Fosters taking Dr. and Mrs. Scott on buggy rides to show them the beauties of Marin County. It is altogether possible that they often took the road leading west from San Rafael to what is now San Anselmo, some two miles distant. Perhaps they saw a ranch called Sunnyside in San Anselmo, but then no one could have foreseen the day when a part of that ranch would be the present campus of San Francisco Theological Seminary. Although we have no evidence that Dr. Scott ever saw the site, yet because it was so near his daughter's home and because of the presence there of a hill commanding a broad view, it is altogether possible that he did.

On New Year's eve, 1882, a snowstorm visited San Francisco, which was an unusual event for that city. That evening while on his way to church, Dr. Scott slipped on his doorstep and suffered a severe injury. This accident marked the beginning of a physical decline. At the first meeting of the seminary's board of directors held in 1883, Dr. Scott was absent. This was the first time he had missed a meeting for over eleven years, amounting to eighty consecutive gatherings. The minutes of the board for that meeting, April 23rd, state: "For a few weeks past Dr. Scott, owing to serious illness, has been unable to attend to his accustomed duties." He was absent also from the meeting held on April 26th but was present on September 24th when the following item was included in the minutes: "Our Senior Professor was laid aside temporarily by a severe illness, and was unable to attend either the final examination or the closing exercises." Before the reorganization of the Seminary in 1913, there was both a board of directors and a board of trustees, the latter being a smaller body functioning somewhat as a committee on finances and working under the direction of the former. Dr. Scott was a member of both groups and equally faithful in his attendance upon both meetings.

The combination of two major responsibilities, the church and the seminary, plus a gradual diminution of physical strength which came with the passing of the years meant that Dr. Scott was physically unable to do as much for St. John's as some members expected. The peak of the church's membership came in 1879 when 382 were reported. The next year the number had declined to 349. In 1884 the roll was down to 338. In the meantime, the shifting population pattern was taking people away from the downtown area, making it increasingly difficult to maintain former records of attendance. This in turn meant declining receipts and the trustees of the church found it necessary to cut Dr. Scott's salary at the beginning of 1881. In a touching letter to one of the trustees dated February 12, 1881, Dr. Scott said: "Ordinarily the settlement of a Pastor according to the call which he accepts, no change can be made [in the salary] except by the Presbytery, but in this case

ONE OF THE LAST PHOTOS
TAKEN OF DR. SCOTT
Original in the Foster family Bible.

it would only add to our mortification to have anything said on the subject. It is better to keep the whole matter among ourselves." This proposed cut in salary was unique in his experience.

In the latter part of 1883, the San Francisco *Morning Call* ran a series of "pulpit sketches" of the city's ministers. The issue for September 3rd carried a half-column on Dr. Scott from which the following is taken:

Dr. William A. Scott, the venerable pastor of St. John's Presbyterian church . . . has been called . . . "the Nestor of the San Francisco pulpit." In the Protestant church at least, he is the oldest settled pastor, and his very venerable appearance, his portly form, slightly bowed as with the weight of years, his silvery hair and beard, magisterial mien, and yet kindly and paternal address, all conspire to win for him, even from comparative strangers, a large measure of deference and respect, while by his congregation and denominational friends, Dr. Scott is regarded with almost worshipful veneration. He is full seventy years of age; and yet, barring his lameness occasioned by a fall some months ago and the slight stoop already referred to, he appears hale and vigorous.

Although it is possible that the fall Dr. Scott suffered less than a year before the reporter wrote might have accentuated the lameness that went back to his boyhood, it is more likely that the reporter was a stranger and entirely unaware of the doctor's long standing disability. The account continues: "His congregation on a recent Sunday morning numbered 500, occupying some three-fourths of the sittings. . . Everything is very solemn and weighty. No jig tunes or opera airs on the organ even. 'This is the house of God and the very gate of Heaven' seems to be written everywhere in this church, and felt by all."

Dr. Scott found it increasingly difficult to carry on his work in the church and the seminary during the academic year 1883-84. The church secured the services of Andrew B. Meldrun, who was the only member of the senior class in the seminary of that year, to assist Dr. Scott. This was the first time in his long ministry that he had had an assistant. Several meetings of the board of directors during the spring and early fall of 1884 were held in Dr. Scott's home rather than in his study at the church. On May 18, 1884, Mrs. Scott, writing to her daughter in San Rafael, said: "Your father preached this morning with much power to a large congregation. Just think of what he has gone through lately— the examination of Seminary Students . . . making Seminary report for Presbytery and General Assembly. . . I marvel at his going through with so much and continuing so well." The 1884 commencement of the seminary was held in St. John's Church on April 24th.

In making his report to the annual meeting of the synod that year, the last of such he was to give, Dr. Scott pointed out the fact that "as in former years, the whole income of the Institution for salaries would barely support one professor, but by consent this has been divided among them." He felt that the seminary could easily attract more students if more scholarship aid were available. This has continued to be a problem ever since those days. When the board of directors met for its annual meeting on November 17, 1884, Dr. Scott was re-elected president for the fourteenth time.

Dr. Scott had frequently remarked that he wanted to die "with his harness on." In the early years of his ministry, while at Winchester, Tennessee, he had written in his diary that "it is better to wear out than to rust out." In similar words he wrote to his New Orleans congregation from Paris on November 25, 1850: "I have often said to you, my beloved brethren, it is one of my cherished sayings—That it is better to wear out than rust out. The motto of my pulpit memorandum book has always been (*alius inserviendo consumor*) *in serving others to consume myself*."

He never talked about retiring and taking it easy. Dr. Alexander, in his remarks spoken at the funeral, said: "Until within a few weeks before his death, he continued to occupy his pulpit and his professor's chair. And when he could no longer meet his students, and that once potent hand had lost its cunning, he still thought of them, dictating to other living hands his last message to them." He retained his mental faculties to the end. Realizing that death was near, according to further testimony of Dr. Alexander, "he arranged his affairs and gave his directions as calmly and quietly as if he had only been going on a journey."

On January 8, 1885, Paul wrote to his brother William, then in Tucson, Arizona, telling of their father's condition. "Father's mind is bright," he wrote, "& he seems to feel that the end is fast approaching." Neither William nor Robert, who was then on duty in Washington, D.C., was able to go to San Francisco at that time. The other children were there with their mother—Martha and Louisiana, and the sons, Chalmers, Ebenezer and Paul. On Wednesday evening, January 14th, he bade his children and some grandchildren who were also present an affectionate farewell. His last words were to his beloved wife who had been a faithful and loyal companion for nearly forty-nine years. The end came quietly at his home at eleven o'clock that night when the spark of life, which began in the miracle of birth in a log cabin in eastern Tennessee, departed, leaving the survivors to face the mystery of death.

Following the birth of their first child, Robert, in January 1837, Dr. Scott told some of his friends that January was his lucky month. He was born and married in that month. Several other important events in his later life also fell in January. He was called to the New Orleans church in January and he returned to take up the work of a new church in San Francisco in another January. Now the date of his death, like that of his birth, came in January. Had he lived until January 30th, he would have celebrated his seventy-second birthday.

In Mrs. Scott's brief biographical sketch of her husband, she wrote: "For some two years before his death, the Dr. suffered a great deal with nausea and pain across just below the stomach. . . The autopsy revealed hardening of the liver, a disease that had not been suspected by his physicians." No doubt this was cirrhosis of the liver for which medical science then could do little, even when a correct diagnosis was made.

Funeral services were held in St. John's Church on Saturday, January 17th, with Dr. Alexander making the principal address. Several years before Dr. Scott died, he and his old friend, James Woods, agreed that whoever passed away first, the other should conduct the funeral. But when Dr. Scott died, Woods himself was too feeble to officiate. The brief announcement of the funeral carried in the daily press requested no flowers. The pulpit and the front of the church was draped in black. The only floral tribute was a broad pillow of camellias and other white flowers, in the center of which were the words "Our Pastor" spelt out in blue and red violets and pansies. The church was crowded to its utmost capacity with many unable to gain entrance. Among those present were prominent members of the clergy of the city, including the Jewish Rabbi, the mayor of the city, officers of the army, and delegations from the St. Andrew's Society and of the Pioneer Society. Pall bearers were selected from the sessions of Calvary and St. John's churches, from the board of directors of the seminary, and from the Presbytery of San Francisco. Included was Elder Stephen Franklin who had been closely associated with Dr. Scott in three different churches and the seminary over a period of forty-three years.

The text of Dr. Alexander's funeral address was carried in the January 21, 1885, issue of the *Occident*. After reviewing the main facts of Dr. Scott's life, Dr. Alexander gave the following excellent summary of his outstanding characteristics and contributions:

> He was a great worker. With him labor was a passion. He shrank from nothing on account of the toil it took. . . He had the faculty for organization, and directed his labor with a definite aim to practical results. . .
>
> Dr. Scott was also a great student. His mind was capacious, and almost encyclopedic in its grasp. . . He had mastered several languages and spoke some of them fluently. His reading was immense. . .
>
> Dr. Scott was a prince among preachers. Endowed by nature with an agreeable and commanding presence, and a voice of uncommon compass, power, and sweetness, he poured forth . . . a stream of copious and burning eloquence. . . He was a devoted, faithful, and affectionate pastor. . .
>
> Dr. Scott was a man of immense heart-power. To this he owed his great influence, not less than to his eminent intellectual gifts. He was formed for friendship, and was singularly constant in his friendships. . . While he found new friends, he seldom lost an old one. . .
>
> Another noticeable feature . . . was the deep interest he took in the young. . . The young people of both sexes were devoted to him, and few ministers have ever been more loved by their young people than he was. . . His special delight was in young men . . . and particularly the students in the Theological Seminary. He was not only their teacher and friend, he was more; he was a father to them, and fondly called them "his boys". . .
>
> He was scarcely less interested in the whole work of the Church at large. . . He was the first, constant, and liberal friend of missions, both home and foreign. . . In later life his heart was in the Theological Seminary in this city. . . He felt its importance especially in the future, and he believed that after a few years of toil and struggle for existence . . . there would one day be found here in this City of the Golden Gate one of the greatest and

most powerful institutions for theological instruction in the land, or in the world. His faith in it never faltered. . .

Over and above all the other admirable qualities of this great man, he was a thorough gentleman. His claim to this distinction did not rest on mere attention to matters of dress, or on the external graces of motion or attitude; but on the more attractive graces of the mind and heart. . . No one ever thought of him as acting a part. He was a born gentleman. . .

The crown of all his many excellences is that he was a Christian. . . The type of his piety was just what you would expect from the character of the man; simple and unostentatious, but deep, earnest, and practical. . .

It now seems hardly necessary to speak of what he was in his home life, as a husband and father. Such a man could not have been otherwise than most affectionate and exemplary in regard to those who, of all the world, were the nearest and dearest to him. And we know that he was so. . .

In the eulogy we find ample confirmation of the judgment of the New Orleans newspaper reporter who, nearly forty years previously, had written that here was *no ordinary man*.

The body of Dr. Scott was buried in a private service in Laurel Hill Cemetery, sometimes known as Masonic Cemetery, in San Francisco. In 1913 after this land passed into private hands for residential development, the bodies there buried were moved. Those in the Scott lot were cremated on December 24, 1931, and the ashes placed in an urn in the Foster mausoleum in Tamalpais Cemetery of San Rafael.

San Francisco then had five daily newspapers in addition to some weeklies. Each ran obituary notices or editorials on the death of Dr. Scott. All were laudatory. The Presbyterian *Occident* of January 21, 1885, included a number of testimonials among which was a tribute from the alumni association of the seminary written by the Rev. Charles D. Merrill, a graduate of 1881. Merrill, writing of Dr. Scott from the viewpoint of a student, had the following insights to give:

Nearly every student in our Seminary has come from the East or the old world. Thousands of miles from their old homes and friends, the first one to receive and care for them here was Dr. Scott. He and his wife not only *bade* us welcome but *made* welcome to every young man who came to study for the ministry: "Come over to my house," would the good man say, if a new comer first called at his study. And over at the house this father and mother would without formal declaration adopt the stranger. . .

In the class-room we have heard Dr. Scott say repeatedly, "I delight to teach." One day, after question and answer and discussion of an hour and a half, he glanced at the clock and exclaimed,

"Ho, see the time—I could teach all day and not be tired of it."
None of us will ever forget the prayers before class that we heard
from his lips. They educated the mind, strengthened the faith,
renewed the courage, fortified the will, melted the heart. . .
And so in all the intercourse of Dr. Scott and his student boys, the
simple greatness of his heart and life won them to an unspeakable
affection, so that it is stronger than death and cannot be broken.

This is but typical of other outpourings of love and respect which
were spread upon the minutes of several bodies to which Dr. Scott
belonged or with which he was associated. The following comes from
the resolution adopted by the board of directors of the seminary: "To
Dr. Scott more than to any other one man, perhaps, more than to all
others, was due the establishing of the Seminary." The thousand word
tribute adopted by St. John's Church is in the handwriting of Stephen
Franklin. When news of his death reached New Orleans, Dr. B. M.
Palmer wrote a letter of condolence to Mrs. Scott and said that the session of the church had not only adopted a memorial of appreciation
but had also ordered the erection of a marble tablet in the church in
memory of Dr. Scott's services there. This memorial tablet can now be
seen in the sanctuary of the church at its present location on South
Claiborne Avenue in New Orleans.

Scores of letters of condolence were sent to Mrs. Scott. Dr. Henry
Van Dyke wrote from Brooklyn. Dr. Scott had once tried to get Dr.
Van Dyke to join the faculty of the seminary and his name hopefully
appeared as such in one of the annual reports to General Assembly.
Former students, old associates, members of his churches in New Orleans
and New York, and many others wrote. Mrs. Phebe A. Hearst, in her
letter, said: "He reached out to far more than one man's measure of
usefulness." Among these letters is one from the Rev. J. B. Warren,
then living in San Leandro, California, who as editor of the *Pacific*
back in the years 1856-61, had written so critically of Dr. Scott. He
now sent in a kindly letter of sympathy. The old bitterness had long
since disappeared. "As I always expected," he wrote, "the old warrior
fell at his post, armor on and sword in hand. He fought a good fight."

Colonel Robert Scott, who was then at work on his monumental
Official Records of the Union and Confederate Armies, was unable to
attend his father's funeral. After being notified of his father's death by
telegraph, Robert wrote on January 15th to his mother. "There is nothing that I can say to comfort you more than I wish we could be with
you. . . He leaves a proud heritage in his own unsullied name for no
one dare assert that a braver man ever lived. You know I am not a
'Christian'—but I do have the most implicit faith in the power and
goodness of God whom father has served so well." Robert's religious
views did not fit into the pattern of his parents' theology. Two of
Robert's grandsons, who were cousins, served in the navy during World

War II and retired after the war with the rank of rear-admiral. They were Robert Scott Clark and Scott Baker.

An undated clipping from a San Francisco paper states that "Dr. Scott was a prudent business man, and left to a large posterity a moderate fortune, of which a considerable part was insurance on his life." His estate including the value of the home on Post Street and his insurance was estimated to be about $50,000. Soon after her husband's death, Mrs. Scott sold the house and moved to San Rafael to live at "Fairhills" with her daughter Lou. Here she spent the last three years of her life. For several months before her death, she was confined to her bed with a spinal affection. She died on July 4, 1888, in her seventy-eighth year. Dr. Alexander conducted her funeral service in St. John's Church in the city. He paid an eloquent tribute to her many virtues and mentioned especially her faithfulness in standing by her late husband in all his "toils, trials, and triumphs." He also related "how she had been a mother to the theological students in the seminary." In recognition of the great but largely unheralded services of Ann Nicholson Scott, this book is dedicated to her memory.

THE CONTINUING STORY

Many tangible evidences remain of Dr. Scott's life and work. Eight books, many pamphlets, two periodicals which he edited, and many articles in the secular and religious press tell of his thought and of his ministry. At least two books were dedicated to him during his lifetime. In addition to the volume by Henry Gustavus Kieme, one of Dr. Scott's students, on *Sennacherib's Campaigns,* a second book was dedicated to him. This was *The Wandering Jew,* published anonymously in New York in 1881. Several children were named for him, one of whom is Scott Roundtree of Oakland, California, grandson of J. O. Roundtree who was one of the group which organized St. John's Church. Several of the third generation of the descendants of Dr. Scott have the family name as a given name. In addition to the two retired admirals of the navy previously mentioned, there is also Scott Newhall, the present editor of the San Francisco *Chronicle.* His mother, Anna Nicholson Scott, was a daughter of William Scott, and his father, Almer Newhall, was the son of H. M. Newhall, one of the officers in St. John's Church.

The two Presbyterian churches which Dr. Scott founded in San Francisco are still in existence, continuing the ministry he started. Calvary Church, now located at Filmore and Jackson Streets, is the largest Presbyterian church in the city, with over two thousand members at the end of 1963. The pastor is Dr. Carl G. Howie. This church in the fall of 1963 dedicated an addition to its physical plant which included a beautiful library room as a memorial to Dr. Scott.

Within three years after the death of Dr. Scott, the fortunes of St. John's Church had so declined that some drastic action had to be taken in 1888 to save it. The members voted to sell their downtown property and move to a new location at California and Octavia Streets. Their sanctuary was rebuilt on the new site with the same style of architecture and with much of the original interior woodwork. The original pews and church furniture were also taken to the new location. This move, however, did not stem the receding tide. By 1899 the membership had dropped to 105. A. W. Foster, who was then active in the First Presbyterian Church of San Rafael, came to the rescue. He offered to move the church to a new site at Lake and Arguello in the new and rapidly growing Richmond district provided at least fifty members would pledge to go to the new location. The condition was met and the church was torn down and rebuilt a second time. Foster paid some $75,000 to cover the costs involved. The building was re-dedicated in 1906. Dr. Haven Davis is the present pastor and the membership roll at the end of 1965 totaled 558. The interior is said to be very much as it was when the church stood on Post Street, and the original pews are still being used.

Even before Dr. Scott died, the directors of the seminary had been studying the possibility of moving to a new location. The Haight Street site, with only about a seventy-foot frontage, was always considered a temporary location. A campus of several acres was essential for future development. This was the situation when Arthur W. Foster approached the board early in September 1889 and invited the members to inspect a property he had purchased shortly before at Sunnyside in San Anselmo, Marin County. Mrs. Mary Kuechler told the author of how as a little girl of ten or eleven years she was with her father at a land auction in San Anselmo when he purchased the acreage which is now the campus of San Francisco Theological Seminary. Near the center of the nineteen acre tract is a mound which measures more than a half-mile in circumference at its base and rises to an elevation of about ninety feet. The remaining part of the site is level and was being used as a dairy ranch when Foster bought it. Two buildings, a barn and a ranch house, were standing just west of the mound.

The members of the board of directors accepted Foster's invitation to inspect the property and met with him on the site on September 16, 1889. Although some seriously doubted the wisdom of moving the institution out of San Francisco, the majority was in favor of doing so when Foster offered to donate the land. Among the conditions attached to his gift were, first, the assurance that improvements costing not less than $25,000 should be erected on the property within two years; and, secondly, that should the seminary be moved from San Anselmo, the property would revert to his estate. These conditions were accepted and the site was deeded to the seminary. In the following year's financial report, the land was valued at $5,000. Foster was elected a member of the board in 1890. A few acres of the property, which extended to the present Sir Francis Drake Boulevard, were subsequently sold and also some adjoining property was purchased. Today that campus is among the most beautiful of any theological seminary in the United States.

The question as to whether the seminary, with the name of San Francisco as a part of its legal title, could move outside the city was

Montgomery Hall and Scott Library Hall, San Anselmo
As they appeared shortly after the buildings were opened in the fall of 1892.

SCOTT LIBRARY HALL, SAN FRANCISCO THEOLOGICAL SEMINARY
After rebuilding of the tower which was destroyed by the earthquake of 1906.

submitted to some lawyers for their judgment. They gave the opinion that the move could be made provided the legal business of the institution be transacted in San Francisco. The business office of the seminary remained in the city until 1940 when the directors learned that there was no legal objection to its removal to San Anselmo.

Within a few days after Foster made his offer, a new friend of the seminary, Alexander Montgomery, a San Francisco merchant and capitalist, expressed his willingness to give $50,000, provided the seminary would match it. This offer was presented to the board of directors on September 26th. Some months earlier, the Rev. Arthur Crosby, pastor of the First Presbyterian Church of San Rafael, had been appointed financial agent for the seminary and had gone East where he had succeeded in raising about $44,000. This sum was applied to meet Montgomery's offer and the needed $6,000 balance was then raised in California. So the conditions were met. In the meantime, Montgomery's interest in the seminary increased and when the directors met on December 3, 1889, they were both amazed and delighted to learn that Montgomery had given $250,000. At that time this was the largest single gift ever made to any Presbyterian seminary in the United States. Montgomery subsequently gave considerably more. Following his death, Montgomery Memorial Chapel was erected in 1897 at the foot of the mound.

With the munificent contribution from Montgomery and other resources on hand, the directors voted to erect two cut-stone buildings on top of the mound; to endow the "Montgomery Chair of Apologetics and Missions;" and to build three dwellings for professors on Bolinas Avenue which marked the southern boundary of the property. The cornerstone of Montgomery Hall, designed to be the dormitory with dining facilities, was laid by Montgomery on April 30, 1891. The cornerstone of the library and class room building, known as Scott Library Hall, was laid by Louisiana Scott Foster on October 17th of that year. Each building cost about $50,000. They were dedicated on September 21, 1892, at which time classes began on the new campus. The enrollment was then twenty, only two of whom were students of the seminary when it was in the city.

The building at 121 Haight Street was sold to the Presbyterian Board of Foreign Missions in 1892 and was used for many years as headquarters for a Japanese mission. A private party bought the property in 1939, then sold it to the Communist Party sometime in 1941. The Communists then sold it to the nearby First Baptist Church in 1945. They used it as the main building for their San Francisco Baptist College, 1947-57. The building is now used as an educational annex of the First Baptist Church of San Francisco. Still to be seen over the main entrance is the intertwined monogram SFTS.

The earthquake of April 1906 knocked down the top of the high tower over the entrance of Scott Hall. The mass of stone crashed down through the roof, through one alcove of the library, down through the floor of the assembly hall below and on into the basement. The tower was rebuilt, but not to its former height. Scott Library Hall stands as the greatest single memorial to Dr. Scott. The seminary still conducts most of its classes in this building. When the author enrolled at the seminary in the fall of 1919, both Mr. and Mrs. Foster were still living and were frequent visitors to the grounds.

Changes were made in the plan of the seminary in 1903, and Dr. John S. MacIntosh was elected in November of that year as the first president. He died in 1906 and was succeeded in 1909 by Dr. Robert Mackenzie who remained for only one year. The third president was Dr. Warren Landon whose administration extended from 1910 to 1928. He was followed by Dr. William H. Oxtoby, 1928-36, and then by Dr. Jesse Baird, 1937-57. Great growth both in material improvements and in the enlargement of the student body came under Dr. Baird. Several buildings were erected, including a million dollar library and chapel in 1950-51, known as Geneva Hall and Stewart Memorial Chapel. This beautiful structure crowns the very top of the mound and gives an unobstructed view in all directions. A series of twenty-six stained glass windows depicting the beginnings of Presbyterianism on the whole Pacific Coast was placed in the chapel. One is dedicated to Dr. Scott. Among the other pioneer Presbyterian ministers who are also commemorated are several of the contemporaries of Dr. Scott including the three "W's" of the Old School—Albert Williams, Sylvester Woodbridge, Jr., and James Woods. The New School ministers include Timothy Dwight Hunt and Samuel H. Willey. Others remembered are William Speer, William W. Brier, Aaron L. Lindsley, and Thomas Fraser.

A second major building constructed during Dr. Baird's presidency was the commons building with dining facilities, book store, and a large social hall located on the west side of the mound and named in honor of Dr. William Alexander. Recently Montgomery Hall has been transformed into an office building with a large director's room set aside as a memorial to Mr. and Mrs. Arthur W. Foster.

Each of the two churches which Dr. Scott founded in San Francisco have memorials to him. St. John's Presbyterian Church has a large stained glass window dedicated to his memory. On December 1, 1963, Calvary Presbyterian Church dedicated its Chapel Library in its new Chapel Center "to the memory of William Anderson Scott."

In 1958 Dr. Theodore Alexander Gill was called to be Dr. Baird's successor as the fifth president of the seminary. During his seven-year administration, the seminary continued to expand. A greatly broadened program for graduate study was inaugurated which became a part of the Graduate Theological Union located in Berkeley. The library was increased to more than 100,000 volumes. At the end of 1965, the total assets of the seminary were about $7,600,000. San Francisco Theological Seminary, still the only seminary of the United Presbyterian Church west of Dubuque, Iowa, now ranks third among the United Presbyterian seminaries of the nation.

Dr. Scott's prophecy of "an immense population" on the West Coast has been amply fulfilled. His vision of the necessity and importance of such an institution has been more than justified. During the past ninety-five years since the seminary first opened its doors, more than three thousand students have been matriculated. In January 1967 the Board of Trustees unanimously elected Dr. Arnold B. Come, who had been a member of the faculty since 1952, to be the sixth president of the seminary.

Over the entrance of Scott Hall, carved in stone, is the emblem of the burning bush which was not consumed. (Exodus 3:2). Over the top of the emblem are the words in Latin, *Nec Tamen Consumebatur*, "not yet consumed." No better quotation from the Bible could have been selected to place over the entrance of the building dedicated to the memory of William Anderson Scott who had inscribed on his pulpit note-book a similar Latin phrase, *alus inserviendo consumor*, "in serving others to consume myself."

To the many memorials which have been written, carved, painted, put into stained glass, or erected to perpetuate the memory of this great and good man is now added this story of his life:

WILLIAM ANDERSON SCOTT
"No Ordinary Man"

Appendix
Bibliography
Index

Appendix

A Note by the Author

On top of the hill on the campus of San Francisco Theological Seminary in San Anselmo, California, is a cut stone castle-like building whose gray walls and round tower are covered with ivy. On a certain morning during the last week of September 1919, a new student at the seminary stood before this building. After reading the inscription over the arched entrance, he asked: "Why is this called Scott Library Hall?" He was told: "After Dr. William Anderson Scott who founded this seminary in San Francisco about fifty years ago. This building was erected as a memorial to him." I was that new student and that was the first time I had ever heard of Dr. Scott.

Since Dr. Scott had died in 1885, there were still living in 1919 a number of people who remembered him. Among them was Arthur W. Foster, a prominent Marin County business man, a trustee of the seminary, and since he had married Louisiana Scott, he was also a son-in-law of the founder. In 1889 Foster had given the seventeen-acre campus in San Anselmo to the Seminary. He was a frequent campus visitor when I was a student and I have vivid memories of his portly figure usually clad in a Prince Albert coat. His silk hat and gold-headed cane made him an impressive figure in my eyes. Mrs. Foster, who often accompanied her husband to the campus, laid the cornerstone of the library building dedicated to the memory of her father on October 17, 1891. There were others whom I came to know who also had memories of the unusual person whose biography I have undertaken to write.

After my graduation from the seminary in 1922, I served for more than fifteen years in several pastorates and then returned to my alma mater in 1938 as a member of the faculty. As Professor of Church History, it was both my duty and my pleasure to delve into the history of Christianity on the Pacific Coast. One day in the basement of Scott Hall I came across three large chests filled with Dr. Scott's manuscripts. The contents of these chests had previously been badly damaged by water as the result of a fire in the Foster home. Water poured upon the fire had settled in the basement and had innundated the chests. After the water drained away, the contents of the chests gradually dried out, but most of the papers were damaged beyond use. After the lapse of many years, the chests were sent to the seminary and stored in the basement of Scott Hall where I found them. Among the papers still readable was Scott's diary for 1836, several important addresses, some early sermons, and many lectures.

Then came World War II. After serving for five years as a chaplain in the United States Navy, I returned to the campus in 1946 and returned my attention to Dr. Scott with the hope of some day writing his biography. I began a systematic examination of the large collection of Scott papers which members of the family had given to Bancroft Library, University of California, in Berkeley. This collection contains about nine hundred letters which Scott received or wrote during the years 1832-85; diaries, journals, and record books; hundreds of newspaper clippings dealing largely with controversies in which he was involved; pictures and many other miscellaneous items. Here was a supply of primary source material exceedingly rich in detail. No one had ever made a serious study of this bonanza of biographical data.

During the years that followed, sometimes by visits and again by correspondence, I probed into historical collections and libraries scattered throughout the nation for further information about Dr. Scott's life and work. In the library of the State University of Louisiana at Baton Rouge, important material was located which dealt with the Clay controversy of 1844-47. Original Scott letters were located in the Library of Congress, the Presbyterian Historical Society in Philadelphia, in Princeton Theological Seminary, and in Huntington Library, San Marino, California. The extensive collection of original records of various Presbyterian judicatories on the Pacific Coast, on deposit at San Francisco Theological Seminary, contains a wealth of information dealing with Dr. Scott's activities in California during the years 1854-85. I also had access to the original records of the two Presbyterian churches he founded in San Francisco, Calvary and St. John's. Added to these were the original records of the seminary of which he was the chief founder.

Among the important sources of California church history owned by the seminary is the editor's file of the *Pacific* for the years under review. This was a New School Presbyterian and Congregational weekly founded in San Francisco in August 1851. The seminary also has the only complete file extant of the *Occident*, a Presbyterian weekly published in San Francisco 1868-1900. I compiled a page by page index of the *Pacific* from 1851-69 inclusive and of the complete file of the *Occident*. These indices, consisting of thousands of cards, provided the magic key which unlocked the hidden historical treasures of these important California church periodicals. The columns of the *Pacific* for the years of Dr. Scott's first residence in San Francisco, 1856-61, reveal the unpleasant story of ecclesiastical jealousies within Presbyterian and Congregational circles which contributed much to the series of unhappy events connected with Dr. Scott's ministry in Calvary Church. Much light is thrown upon the vigilante movement in San Francisco, which Dr. Scott had the courage to oppose, and also upon the conflicting emotions and prejudices which stirred California in the events leading up to the Civil War.

After Dr. Scott was forced to leave California in 1861, he and his family spent two years in France and England. In the spring of 1956, while on temporary duty with the United States Navy in England, I had opportunity to examine some original ecclesiastical records of the Presbyterian Church of England on deposit in its Historical Society in London. Some information was found therein regarding Dr. Scott's work in London and Birmingham. After returning to the United States in the summer of 1863, Dr. Scott served as pastor of a Presbyterian church in New York City for six years. The original records of this church were located in the library of Union Theological Seminary in that city.

Added to all that could be gleaned from such manuscript and published materials relating to this long neglected but important churchman, were the personal memories and family traditions. Perhaps the last individual to have personal recollections of both Dr. and Mrs. Scott, was Mrs. Mary F. Kuechler, a granddaughter, of Ross, California. She passed away on May 16, 1965. Stories about Dr. Scott are associated with a number of family heirlooms owned by several of his descendants.

In 1960, having completed some other projects which had priority, I began writing the preliminary sketches of this biography. I soon realized that a personal visit to the scenes connected with Dr. Scott's youth and to the various parishes he served before going to California was essential. In order to make such an investigation, the seminary granted me sabbatic leave beginning January 1, 1962. The American Philosophical Society of Philadelphia made a grant of $600 for expenses connected with the basic research. On February 26th my wife and I left by automobile for a tour of the South which lasted ten weeks. We visited Dr. Scott's parishes at Opelousas and New Orleans, Louisiana. He spent two years, 1834-36, in the former and twelve years, 1842-54, in the latter. In New Orleans, he came to the fulness of his powers as a pulpit orator, and from here in 1858 Dr. Scott was elected Moderator of the Presbyterian Church, U.S.A., the highest honor within the power of his church to bestow.

We then visited Tuscaloosa, Alabama, where he had a two-year ministry, 1840-42. From there we proceeded to Montreat, North Carolina, where I had opportunity of consulting Presbyterian judicatory records and periodicals for the years immediately preceding the Civil War. Also at Montreat were the original records of the First Presbyterian Church of New Orleans covering the period that Dr. Scott served as pastor.

From Montreat we drove into eastern Tennessee, first visiting Winchester where Scott, as a young newly-wedded minister, served as principal of a female academy and pastor of the Cumberland Presbyterian Church from 1836-38. From there we went to Nashville, passing within a few miles of his birthplace in Marshall County without then knowing its exact location. Scott served as principal of a female academy in Nashville from 1838-40 and also as stated supply of two small country churches. He alternated on week ends going to the Hermitage Church where General Andrew Jackson lived and to Harpeth. Each church was ten or twelve miles distant from Nashville but in different directions. In both places I found the original buildings still standing and had access to the original sessional records. The Scott Collection in Bancroft Library contains some letters from General Jackson to Scott. At Nashville I located the other half of the correspondence, the letters from Scott to Jackson.

We then drove to McKenzie, Tennessee, where the Cumberland Presbyterian Theological Seminary is located. Scott began his ministry in the Cumberland Church and did not transfer to the Presbyterian Church, U.S.A., until 1838. As a Cumberland Presbyterian circuit rider, when only eighteen years old, he spent a year on a circuit which included some thirty communities in northwestern Tennessee. McKenzie lies about in the center of that circuit. With Scott's 1830 diary before me and with the help of Dr. Thomas Campbell, president of the seminary, we were able to locate many of the communities listed.

All along the way as we followed Scott's trail, we found new material and much local color, sometimes in the most unexpected places. We met with a generous response from all to whom we turned for help, librarians, pastors, local historians, and just common folk who, when they heard of our quest, cooperated in many ways.

After returning to our home in San Rafael, California, in May 1962, I was able by correspondence to clear up many unsolved questions. By this means the place of Scott's birth in Marshall County and the grave of his mother near Raleigh were located. Bit by bit, like the pieces of a jig-saw puzzle which had been scattered through 150 years and over half of the continent, the important facts relating to the life and work of Dr. Scott were assembled. Gradually a clearer picture of the boy, the student, the itinerant backwoods preacher, the educator, the orator, the author, and the churchman emerged.

As I sat before my typewriter writing this life of "no ordinary man," I have had the feeling that Dr. Scott has been looking over my shoulder. Although the portrayal is designed to give a sympathetic interpretation of his life, yet I have not hesitated to record what appear to be personal weaknesses and errors of judgment. Dr. Scott himself would have been the first to deny any claim to perfection. The artist needs both light and shadow to sharpen the outlines of his picture. Most church members today would agree with his stand against the compulsory reading of the Protestant version of the Bible in public schools and with his opposition to the Vigilance Committee's unlawful activities in San Francisco. They would disapprove, no doubt, his attitude toward slavery and his support of the Southern rebellion against the federal government. Dr. Scott was a Southerner by birth, education, and sympathies. He lived during those critical years preceding the Civil War when the Presbyterian

Church was forging its philosophy of the relationship of the church to social issues in the hot fires of sectional controversy. Partly because of the leading role that Scott played in the national affairs of his denomination, he inevitably became a central figure in these discussions.

In order that the narrative might flow easily, I have taken the liberty to quote freely from original sources without burdening the text with footnotes. The reader may be assured that I have used my sources with scrupulous accuracy. A brief summary of the sources will be given in the bibliography. In a few instances I have used my imagination to fill in some gaps not covered by documented material in order to weave together more closely certain known facts. Such places are indicated in the text by the use of such expressions as "probably" or "it might be."

The story of William Anderson Scott is a vivid commentary on his time. His deep opposition to the Vigilance Committee, for instance, throws much light upon the lawlessness existing in San Francisco in the mid 1850's. In the events surrounding the second hanging of Dr. Scott in effigy before his church on Sunday morning, September 23, 1861, we see how deeply the issues which precipitated the Civil War stirred the citizens of San Francisco. Scott's close connection with the national leaders of the Presbyterian Church had a direct bearing upon the unfortunate division which split the Old School Assembly of 1861 into the northern and southern branches. Here is a hitherto unexplored chapter in American Presbyterian history.

To recapitulate, the great wealth of source material including nearly nine hundred letters, diaries, journals, books, pamphlets, ecclesiastical records, hundreds of articles in religious and secular periodicals, sermon and lecture notes, together with family memories and personal observations has made this book possible. Herein we can become acquainted not only with what Dr. Scott did and what he said, but also with many of his inner thoughts and feelings. As we move with him through the years, we come to appreciate his problems and share with him his sacrifices and his sufferings. We enter into his dreams and aspirations and rejoice in his accomplishments. When the full story is told, we are amazed to see how one who emerged from such an unpromising backwoods environment, handicapped by a crippled foot, and with such a limited formal education, should have been able to do so much.

No such detailed study as this is ever the product of one person's labors. I wish to acknowledge my indebtedness to many scattered over this country who have in countless ways rendered assistance. I wish especially to mention Mrs. Martha Abbot, a granddaughter of Dr. Scott, of Kentfield, California, whose encouragement and help have been constant from the beginning of my writing on this subject. In this she was joined by her late husband, Leonard. To all who have helped in any way, I wish to express my deep appreciation.

CLIFFORD M. DRURY

Pasadena, California

Bibliography

MANUSCRIPT COLLECTIONS

SCOTT COLLECTION, BANCROFT LIBRARY, Berkeley, California, contains about nine hundred letters written to or by Dr. Scott; Scott diaries for 1832, 1834, 1835, 1840, 1841, 1844-48 inclusive, and 1851; notebooks, record books, scrapbooks; hundreds of newspaper clippings; pictures, diplomas, and other items.

SCOTT COLLECTION, SAN FRANCISCO THEOLOGICAL SEMINARY, San Anselmo, California, contains some letters; diary for 1836; sermon and lecture manuscripts; pictures; complete collection of his writings; and other material.

A few Scott letters have been located in such libraries as the Library of Congress, Princeton Theological Seminary, Presbyterian Historical Society of Philadelphia, and Huntington Library, San Marino, California.

ECCLESIASTICAL RECORDS

1.   The original sessional and/or trustees records of the following churches which were once served by Dr. Scott have been examined by the author: Harpeth and Hermitage Churches, Nashville, Tennessee; First Presbyterian Church of Tuscaloosa, Alabama; St. John's and Calvary Churches, San Francisco, California. These churches still have their original records. The sessional records of the First Presbyterian Church of New Orleans were examined at the Historical Foundation, Montreat, North Carolina, where they have been deposited.

2.   The original records of the following presbyteries have been examined: Presbytery of Tuscaloosa at First Church of Tuscaloosa, Alabama; Presbyteries of New Orleans and Louisiana at the Historical Foundation, Montreat, North Carolina; Presbyteries of London and Birmingham at the Presbyterian Historical Society, London, England; Presbyteries of California and Alta California in the archives of San Francisco Theological Seminary, San Anselmo, California.

3.   The original records of the following synods have also been examined by the author: Synod of Mississippi in the Historical Foundation, Montreat, North Carolina; Synod of England, Presbyterian Historical Society, London, England; Synod of Alta California and Synod of the Pacific, San Francisco Theological Seminary, San Anselmo, California.

4. In addition the original church records of the Forty-Second Street Presbyterian Church of New York City, now on deposit in the library of Union Theological Seminary, New York, were examined by others and relevant information supplied to the author.

PUBLISHED SOURCES

1. Books. Bibliographic data about books from which quotations were taken or information gleaned have been given in the text when such works were first mentioned. Titles of these books are also given in the index. Special mention is made of the following titles:

Curry, James. *History of the San Francisco Theological Seminary.* Vacaville, 1907.

Minutes of the General Assembly of the Presbyterian Church, U.S.A. The Old School Minutes were published in Philadelphia; the New School in New York.

Williams, Albert. *A Pioneer Pastorate and Times.* San Francisco, 1882.

Woods, James. *Recollections of Pioneer Work in California* San Francisco, 1878.

Woods, James L. *California Pioneer Decade of 1849.* San Francisco, 1922.

2. Periodicals. *Danville Quarterly Review, Home and Foreign Record, Journal of Presbyterian History, New Orleans Presbyterian, Occident, Pacific, Pacific Expositor, Philadelphia Presbyterian, Presbyterian Banner, Presbyterian Herald, Presbyterian Magazine, Princeton Review, Southern Presbyterian Review.*

Index

Note: The abbreviation, "illus," indicates the pagination of an illustration. The use of "ff." refers the reader to two or three pages following the pagination given. Family relations to Dr. W.A. Scott are indicated in parentheses after the name listed. Since footnotes are not included in the text, references to books or to authors are listed in the index. Names of magazines and newspapers from which source material has been gathered are usually given under city of publication.